# *Endorseme* 

***Tim Wildmon, President of American Family Association and American Family Radio***

"My friend, Allan Parker, has been a relentless defender of unborn babies for decades now. His strategic work laid the foundation for the reversal of *Roe v. Wade* which very few thought would ever happen. I encourage you to read Allan's journey as you will be inspired to do your part to stand for the things of God."

***Janet Porter, Founder and President of Faith2Action***

"I have known Allan Parker since Operation Outcry and the effort to give women a voice was birthed. Since then, Allan Parker has persevered as a Champion for Life with groundbreaking legal work fueled by compassion. I was also with Allan when *Roe v. Wade* crumbled to the ash heap of history and the work to save lives and help women continues unhindered. Allan Parker is a general in this battle. We will win because women harmed by abortion have been given a voice."

***Sheila L. Harper, Founder and President, Save One (National Abortion Recovery Program)***

"If anyone has had their hand on the pulse of what is happening in the LIFE movement, that person is Allan Parker. Through my nearly three decades of work, Allan has always been a constant source of wisdom, a steadfast comfort, a faithful friend, and a warrior clearing the path for others to follow. I couldn't be more excited about the book you hold in your hands. The history, the personal stories, the action steps and much more are all right here in book form. Thank you Allan for once again leading the charge, and helping us all be more success-ful. We owe much of what has happened in the LIFE movement to your efforts."

*Sybil Lash, Author "Supreme Deception" © 2002*

"This book is one man's treatise in the battle against the Culture of Death that has plagued America for 50 years. Allan Parker is truly a Man of God, called to this war. Helping both Norma McCorvey (Roe v. Wade) and my friend, Sandra Cano (Doe v. Bolton) right the evil; representing them before the U.S. Supreme Court. Every American should read this book."

*Luana Stoltenberg, Iowa State Representative and Operation Outcry Advisory Council*

"What a powerful story of how Allan was called to be part of the story line to overturn *Roe v. Wade*. Allan has been an advocate and protector of all of us women who have been hurt by abortion. Thank you for this life changing book."

*Cecily Routman, MSW, President, Jewish Pro-Life Foundation*

Mr. Allan Parker's defense of life, faith, and virtue reach far beyond his memoir. He exemplifies the highest ideals for every pro-life advocate now and into the future.

*Carol Everett, Founder of The Heidi Group*

"Allan Parker is an attorney, former law professor and a man called by God to overturn the two Supreme Court decisions that unleashed abortion on demand – *Doe v. Bolton* (Georgia) *Roe v. Wade* (Texas). Allan prayed and studied using his gifts, talents and education to reverse both decisions."

"Many in the pro-life movement appreciated the fact that Allan graciously gave voice to the two women used to accomplish the *Doe v. Bolton* and *Roe v. Wade* decisions. Sandra Cano and Norma McCovey were both used, abused and wounded by pro-choice attorneys who twisted their stories to allow abortion on demand. Allan's work to overturn these infamous decisions gave the two women an opportunity to share their side of the issues, bringing a level of healing to both women."

"Beyond his legal expertise, Allan uniquely understands the pain of the post-aborted women and men, giving voice to the lifelong pain. His efforts to heal continues even today after *Roe v. Wade* is overturned. Allan understands that abortion survivors – mothers and fathers are in pain. The need to heal the other victims of abortion is ongoing."

"Allan's work to help and healing continues today."

# Reversing *Roe v. Wade*

## My Journey with *Roe*, *Doe* and God

**Allan E. Parker, Jr.**

ISBN (Paperback): 979-8-9885619-5-8
ISBN (Hardcover): 979-8-9885619-6-5
ISBN (eBook): 979-8-9885619-4-1

# Contents


Foreword ....................................................................... xi

Chapter One: Introduction: Reversing *Roe v. Wade* –
My Journey With God, Norma, Sandra,
Operation Outcry, and The Moral Outcry Petition ................. 1
- Something Amazing Has Happened ...................................1
- Who Are These People? ...................................................3
- God Speaks to the Judges ...............................................5
- Amazing and Extraordinary Acts of God............................6
- Operation Outcry: Courageous Women Speaking
  The Truth About Abortion............................................8
- The Two Great Lies of Abortion .....................................12
- Forced Abortion ...........................................................15
- Birth of The Moral Outcry Petition..................................16

Chapter Two: What are Operation Outcry and
The Justice Foundation? .....................................................17
- Helping Norma and Sandra.............................................18
- Who Are These Guys [TJF Begins] ................................20
- God's Promise to End the Covenant with Death ............22
- Anthrax Attack on Supreme Court...................................39
- Women's Health Protection Task Force ..........................43
- Birth Of The Justice Foundation......................................58

- Legal Strategy ...................................................... 60
- Strategy 1: The Donna Santa Marie Case ....................... 61
- Strategy 2: Suing the Texas Department of Health for Failure to Protect Women's Health in Abortions ........... 61
- Strategy 3: Overturning *Roe* and *Doe* ....................... 63
- The Importance of Women's Testimony ....................... 64
- Operation Outcry Saves Lives ........................................ 67
- Center Against Forced Abortions (CAFA) ..................... 70

Chapter Three: Who is Norma McCorvey? And Why Does "Jane Roe" Want to Overturn *Roe v. Wade*? .................73
- 2003 Supreme Court Affidavit of Norma McCorvey ...... 80
- Norma's Last Days .................................................... 90

Chapter Four: Who is Sandra Cano? And Why Does "Mary Doe" Want to Overturn *Doe v. Bolton*? ............95
- Early Departure ...................................................95
- Sharing Her Story .................................................98
- Getting the Records ..............................................100
- How She is Seen ...................................................101
- The Affidavit ......................................................105
- Lack of Facts ......................................................111
- Pressure on Politicians ...........................................112
- The Justices' Response ...........................................115
- The Absent Media ................................................118
- The Attendees ....................................................122
- Deliberate Deception ............................................126
- The Reason For Her Resolve ...................................128
- Connecting With The Hurting ..................................130
- A Place For Healing ..............................................133
- The Providers ....................................................136
- Update on Sandra's Death and Beyond – *Gonzales v. Carhart* ............................................142

Chapter Five: What Abortion Does to Women .......................145
- Healing Resources For Women and Men ..................... 146
- Legally Admissible Testimonies From
  Operation Outcry Women ........................................ 149
- Were You Adequately Informed of the
  Consequences of Abortion? [Lies, Deceit,
  Misrepresentation by Abortion Industry] .....................158
- Did Anyone Pressure You Into Having an
  Abortion? If So, Who? ............................................163
- How Has Abortion Affected Others in Your Life? .........168
- What Would You Tell a Woman Considering
  An Abortion? ........................................................172
- What Would You Tell a Court that Believes an
  Abortion Should be Legal? .......................................180
- Rape and Incest .....................................................187

Chapter Six: More Women's Stories – Forced Abortion, Rape,
And Incest – Why Abortion is Not The Answer ..................183
- Molly White ..........................................................184
- Nona's Story..........................................................189

Chapter Seven: 9/11 Shakes the Nation – Sheer Terror to
Understand What it Means.......................................... 191
- Critical Prayer Time At the Republican
  National Convention ...............................................197

Chapter Eight: Birth of The Moral Outcry Petition ...................201
- Denny and Mindy Thybault Share Their
  Thoughts on the Reversal of *Roe v. Wade* ..................... 204
- More Amazing and Extraordinary Things
  God Has Done! ......................................................209

- More Amazing and Extraordinary Things
  God Has Done! Here Are A Few Of The Unusual
  Prayer Events ............................................................ 213
- Unusual, Extraordinary Governmental Events ............ 218
- Unusual and Extraordinary Legal Events .................... 221
- More Amazing Things in *Dobbs* – Amazing Briefs...... 223

Chapter Nine: Final Arguments at the Supreme Court ..............225
- The Jewish Brief ....................................................225
- Excerpts From The Moral Outcry And Operation
  Outcry Supreme Court *Amicus Curiae* Brief
  In *Dobbs* ...........................................................253
- Interest Of *Amici* Melinda Thybault .........................253
- Frozen Embryo Gideon Wilberforce Thybault .............255
- Gideon Wilberforce Thybault After Birth
  With Trumpet (Shofar).........................................256
- Summary of The Argument......................................259
- *Roe, Doe* and *Casey* Are Truly A Crime Against
  Humanity Like *Dred Scott* (Slavery) And *Plessy v.
  Ferguson* (Segregation)..........................................263
- Protecting Life is a Moral Good (Gorsuch) ..................264
- Safe Haven Laws Render Abortion Obsolete.
  Mississippi's Safe Haven Laws Meet
  The Unwanted Child Needs Of Women
  Without Killing "Infant Life" (See *Gonzales*),
  Or Injuring Women With Abortion Trauma ..................265
- What Will Happen To The Safe Haven Children?
  Two Million Women Desire To Adopt
  Newborn Children Every Year....................................269
- Today Science Clearly Demonstrates That Life
  Begins At Conception Changing Prior Precedent
  Under *Stare Decisis* ...............................................269
- The Original Moral Outcry Petition............................271

- Hannah S. – The First Formerly Frozen Human Embryo to File a Brief at the Supreme Court .................273
- Hannah's Brief by Mary J. Browning ............................276
- Summary of Argument..................................................278
- How It All Began ........................................................279
- Where We Are Today ...................................................281
- History of Margaret Sanger, Planned Parenthood Founder and Eugenecist by Justice Clarence Thomas (From Prior Opinion) ......................................285
- Conclusion: "Horton Hears A Who" And Abortion.......288

Chapter Ten: How Can You Help Make Abortion Illegal in All 50 States? ......................................................... 291
- Contribute Testimonies of Abortion's Pain....................294
- Find Abortion Recovery Programs Near You .................295
- Share The Moral Outcry Petition to Make Abortion Illegal (And Unthinkable) In All 50 States.....297
- The Final Charge – Abortion Should Be Illegal And Unthinkable, Just Like Slavery And Segregation .........298
- He is Coming Soon!....................................................299

Acknowledgements..................................................301

# Foreword

*"I will bless the Lord at all times; His praise shall con-
tinually be in my mouth. My soul shall make its boast in
the Lord; the humble shall hear of it and be glad. Oh,
magnify the Lord with me, and let us exalt His name
together."* **Psalms 34:1-3 (NKJV)**

If you ever start on a journey with the Lord, reading Psalms
34:1-3 is a good way to begin. I have written this book to glorify
the Lord Jesus Christ, to praise and glorify His name. I invite you
to come on this journey with me as we magnify His name together.
This book is also intended to strengthen and encourage the saints
as we remember and meditate on the great and glorious works of
the Lord.

In 1973, the Supreme Court decision in the landmark case
called *Roe v. Wade* legalized abortion in all 50 states, which
resulted in grave consequences. Most people thought *Roe v. Wade*
would never be overturned. But the Lord called me and the incredible saints who joined me on a journey to reverse *Roe* and He has
faithfully performed His promise to end the "covenant with death".
See Isaiah 28:14-22.

# CHAPTER ONE

# Introduction
# Reversing *Roe v. Wade*: My Journey With God, Norma, Sandra, Operation Outcry, and The Moral Outcry

## Something Amazing Has Happened

A great and mighty thing has happened in the land. Something has shaken the mountain tops. It has shaken the land to its core. The enemies of God are moaning, mourning, and gnashing their teeth.[1] They cry loudly and angrily. But the people of God are rejoicing. But don't worry, no one has to be an enemy of God. "For if while we were enemies we were reconciled to God through the death of His Son, much more, having been reconciled, we shall be saved by His life."[2] This book will hopefully be full of the glory of the Lord, of His judgments, His grace, and His mercy. Abortion has been a great national sin. Perhaps the worst in our history. At last,

---

[1]  There are many Bible verses about the enemies of God. Like Satan, Matt. 16:23: human enemies of the Cross, Phil. 3:18; and friends of the world, James 4:14.

[2]  Romans 5:10.

the "covenant with death" (NAS) has been annulled. The "agreement with hell" (KJV) has been cancelled and "No longer stands."[3]

What is this mighty thing that God has done? He has cancelled the "covenant with death," the "agreement with the grave" that were entered into by the Supreme Court of the United States in two landmark cases, *Roe v. Wade* and *Doe v. Bolton.*

What many, many people said could never be done, has been done. *Roe* has been reversed! He has "risen up as at Mount Perazim", and his name is The Lord, The Master of Breakthroughs. He has done amazing, unusual, and extraordinary things. (Isaiah 28:21) He has done things which have never been done before in American history because the Lord Jesus Christ is the Prince of Life. He is the Lord of Lords and King of Kings.

I had the privilege of being part of this journey alongside so many other groups and individuals who recognized that abortion hurts women, men, families and society.

On February 11th, 2000, God gave me a mighty promise: that that the "covenant with death" created by U.S. Supreme Court's companion cases of Norma McCorvey, who was the "*Roe*" of *Roe v. Wade*, and Sandra Cano, who was the "*Doe*" of *Doe v. Bolton,* would be cancelled. How could this happen? What did He do that was "unusual and extraordinary"?

It is the purpose of this book to give glory to God for the great things He has done. I have watched the Lord fulfill His Word. I have represented Norma and Sandra, the two plaintiffs in the two landmark cases that brought abortion on demand to America, in their legal efforts to reverse *Roe v. Wade* and *Doe v. Bolton.* Now, through this book, you can go on this amazing journey with me. It also portrays an exciting future of revival, repentance, restoration, and healing for America. God is on the move as C.S. Lewis said

---

[3]  Isaiah 28:18

about Aslan the King in *The Lion, the Witch and the Wardrobe.* Jesus is on the move, the Lion of Judah. He is the Coming King!

On June 24, 2022, at 10:10am Eastern time, after 49 years of supposedly being "the law of the land," *Roe v. Wade* was overturned by the United States Supreme Court in *Dobbs v. Jackson Women's Health.*[4] As the President of the Justice Foundation and a member of the bar of the US Supreme Court, I was blessed to be Lead Counsel or Co-Counsel on five major written *Amicus Curiae* (Friend of Court) Briefs at the Supreme Court in that historic milestone case. *Dobbs* reversed *Roe v. Wade* and will go down in history as one of the Supreme Court's greatest cases. It has already affected the whole world.

Who deserves the credit for that victory? God alone. Even former President Donald J. Trump on the very day of the decision, when asked if he deserved the credit, said in unusually modest language for him: "God did it."

God did use President Donald J. Trump in "amazing, unusual, extraordinary" ways, as He also used The Justice Foundation, and others, in reversing *Roe v. Wade* and its successor case, *Planned Parenthood v. Casey. Casey* had weakened *Roe* in 1992, but not killed it completely. It allowed some safety regulations and restrictions on abortion, but still allowed the supposed U.S. Constitutional "right to abortion" to overturn every effort of every state to ban abortion. Why do I call it a supposed U.S. Constitutional "right to abortion"? Because as *Dobbs* correctly explains, a "right" to abortion never existed in the Constitution.

## Who Are These People?

Norma McCorvey is more well known as the *"Roe"* of *Roe v. Wade.* She was more visible publicly than Sandra Cano, the *"Doe"*

---

[4] *Dobbs v. Jackson Women's Health Organization,* No. 19-1392, 597 U.S. ___ (2022)

of *Doe v. Bolton*, the companion case to *Roe* which created the health exception, which allowed abortion on demand up to the moment of birth in America.

Norma lived a life of contradictions and conversion. She started out as simply a woman of the streets, a sometimes drug seller. Someone who lived a hard life. Her story is told in Chapter Three. She had three children, and the first child was raised by her mother. The second child Norma placed for adoption. The third child, who became the *Roe* baby, was also placed for adoption. Norma never had an abortion. Even though Norma became the lead Plaintiff in *Roe v. Wade*, it only takes nine months to have a baby, but it took three years to take her case from March 3rd, 1970 (the date it was filed) to January 22nd, 1973, the date the Supreme Court decided her case and that of Sandra Cano, the *"Doe"* of *Doe v. Bolton*. The Court combined them as companion cases, though Norma came from Texas and Sandra came from Georgia, to open the floodgates of abortion death into America.

On March 4, 2020, at the very beginning of the fiftieth or "jubilee" year after *Roe's* filing, the Court heard an oral argument in the *June Medical Services, LCC v. Russo*, 591 U.S. 1101 (2020), a case involving whether a state could require abortionist to have hospital admitting privileges to treat women's abortion injuries. It became the last case in which the Court struck down an abortion safety regulation on the grounds it violated *Roe*.

On March 16, 2020, shortly after they made their internal decision in that case, when only the Court and God knew what had been done, the Supreme Court announced their building would be closed to the public because of their "sheer terror" over "the overwhelming scourge" of coronavirus, which lasted over two years, until they had finally reversed Roe. They were one of the last government buildings to reopen.

Why do I call Norma and Sandra's two cases decided together on January 22, 1973 a "covenant with death," an "agreement with the grave"? It is based on Isaiah 28:14-22. I'll tell the more complete story of how the Lord gave me this amazing passage in a later chapter. But right at the beginning you need to know that on February 11th, 2000, as I was given the opportunity to represent both Norma and Sandra in their legal efforts to reverse their own cases, the Lord gave me this life changing Isaiah 28 scripture:

## God Speaks to the Judges

*"14 Therefore, hear the word of the LORD, you scoffers,*

*Who rule this people who are in Jerusalem,*
*15 Because you have said, "We have made a covenant with death,*
*And with Sheol we have made a pact (agreement).*
*The overwhelming scourge will not reach us when it passes by,*
*For we have made falsehood our refuge and we have concealed*
*ourselves with deception."*
**18 Your covenant with death will be canceled,**
**And your pact (agreement) with Sheol (the grave)**
**will not stand;**
*When the overwhelming scourge (or pestilence) passes through,*
*Then you will become its trampling ground.*
*19 As often as it passes through, it will seize you;*
*For morning after morning it will pass through,*
*anytime during the day or night,*
*And it will be sheer terror to understand what it means ....."*
*21 For the LORD will rise up as at Mount Perazim, (which means*
*The Lord, The Master of Breakthroughs (2 Sam 5:17-20)*
*He will be stirred up as in the Valley of Gibeon,*
*To do His task, His unusual task,*
*And to work His work, His extraordinary work."* (NASB 1995)

That passage marked my life from that day forward to work and pray for the reversal of *Roe* and *Doe*. God gave a promise that He would end the covenant with death that was *Roe* and *Doe*. *Doe* allowed abortion on demand and death up to the moment of birth. He also gave me the promise that He would do His work, doing unusual and extraordinary things to end that "covenant with death." Other versions call it "His alien, or incredible work." I think you will agree as you read further that He has done incredible things. This book will show you some of the "amazing, extraordinary" things that He has done, as He promised in Isaiah 28:14-22.

On June 24th, 2022, the Supreme Court of the United States released its official decision in *Dobbs v. Jackson Women's Health* which explicitly reversed *Roe* and *Casey*. *Doe* was the companion case to *Roe v. Wade*, and involves the story of Sandra Cano, told in chapter four. The *Dobbs* decision was as serious for America as doctors using a life-saving defibrillator on a dying patient – stand clear! On June 24th, the Supreme Court gave a shock to the nation. God said that *Roe* would be reversed and it has been reversed. On that day, the Supreme Court struck down one of the most evil decisions ever made by the United States Supreme Court which had stood for 49 years at that point. Other evils the court once said the Constitution supported, but no longer upholds, were slavery, segregation, and forced sterilization.

## Amazing and Extraordinary Acts of God

Here are just a few of the amazing, extraordinary things that God did to reverse *Roe v. Wade*:

1) For the first time in American history, two people (Norma and Sandra) who won landmark Supreme Court cases went back to the Court seeking reversal of their own cases.

2) In 2007, the Supreme Court cited the *Amicus* (Friend of the Court) Brief of Sandra Cano and 180 *Operation Outcry* Women Injured By Abortion to uphold the federal ban on partial birth abortion. This was only seven years after declaring unconstitutional 38 state laws banning the gruesome late-term partial birth abortion under *Roe*.

3) There was a gradual change of Supreme Court Justices over 22 years, some in very serious and unusual ways.

4) The election of a formerly pro-choice New York playboy turned President, Donald J. Trump, who became the most prolife President in American history.

5) The numerous prophetic words and their fulfillment that President Trump would have three Supreme Court vacancies in his first term and confirm three nominees in amazing ways.

6) The *Dobbs* case was considered 22 times by the Supreme Court before it was officially taken by the Court. Normally, about 99 times to 1, the Court will simply say no the first time they consider any case. *Cert.* denied – No appeal! Down comes the gavel.

7) Finally, the Court resisted slander, libel, physical, political, and verbal threats, intimidation, an actual assassination attempt against Justice Kavanaugh, and the first leak to the press of a full draft of a complete opinion, and still had the moral courage to do the right thing and reverse *Roe*.

Now, how did all that happen? Let's go back the beginning. Get ready for an amazing journey.

## *Operation Outcry*: Courageous Women Speaking The Truth About Abortion

*Operation Outcry* is a national mobilization effort of post-abortive women who have told the United States Supreme Court the truth about what abortion does to women. *Operation Outcry* overcomes the two great lies of the abortion industry with truthful testimony from those women who have personally experienced its tragedy. Those lies are: "It's not a baby" and "Abortion is good for women."

*Operation Outcry* was birthed by the Lord in 2000 to overturn the greatest injustice of the twentieth century, one of the greatest holocausts the world has ever known – the systematic destruction by a nation of approximately one third of its own children. Ironically, this women's movement was initially spearheaded by two women formerly associated with the legalization of abortion – Norma McCorvey, who was formerly "Jane Roe" of *Roe v. Wade*, and Sandra Cano, who was formerly "Mary Doe" of *Doe v. Bolton*. These two women's own infamous Supreme Court decisions together brought legalized abortion on demand to America in 1973.

*Operation Outcry* is a grassroots legal effort which *needs your help* to end this injustice to women and children by bringing about the Final Days of Abortion in America now that *Roe v. Wade* is reversed. Eventually total victory is within our grasp. You can become part of this movement to end the injustice of abortion. This book is written for those who have ears to hear and eyes to see.

*"And on that day the deaf shall hear the words of a book, and out of their gloom and darkness the eyes of the blind shall see. The afflicted also will increase their gladness in the Lord, and the needy of mankind shall rejoice in the Holy One of Israel. For the ruthless will come to an end, and the scorner will be finished, indeed all who are intent on doing*

*evil will be cut off; who cause a person to be indicted by a word, and ensnare him who adjudicates at the gate, and defraud the one in the right with meaningless arguments."*

Isaiah 29:18-21

*Operation Outcry* offers a message of hope, encouragement and forgiveness to those women who have been deceived and misled by our highest courts, and our culture.

*Operation Outcry* encourages women to seek forgiveness and healing from the Great Redeemer and Healer, Jesus Christ. Abortion is a terrible sin, but it is not the unforgivable sin. Those women who were forced, or beguiled by fear, shame or pressure of circumstances, or by spouses, boyfriends or parents into participating in the "covenant with death", namely legalized abortion, are now able to stand up and make a difference for themselves and for others. After all, let none of us forget that "all of us have sinned and fallen short of the glory of God." Romans 3:23. Their testimonies are redemptive to others who face similar difficult decisions in crisis pregnancies. They bring honor and recognition to the lives of their unborn children whose loss of life they deeply grieve.

This movement is based on a promise of God to end the "covenant with death," the "agreement with the grave", that is legalized abortion. Isaiah 28:14-22. You will learn about that promise and our need to trust in God for its fulfillment. Abortion is the silent, hidden killing of "innocent human life" and the destruction of women's consciences, futures and sometimes their lives. It is also a soul killing tragedy for many men. This book is a call for repentance and a promise of forgiveness. It points the way to healing for all women and men who have participated in abortion. It is a call to the church to offer repentance, forgiveness, healing, and reconciliation, in Jesus' name.

For the first time in American history, two women who won landmark Supreme Court decisions went back to Court to overturn their own cases. In chapter three, you will meet Norma McCorvey, the plaintiff in *Roe v. Wade*, whose identity was kept secret in her court case by using the legally fictitious name, "Jane Roe". You will learn how Norma journeyed from unsuccessfully seeking an illegal abortion, to being a pro-abortion advocate, to working in an abortion clinic, to actually facing the truth about abortion and becoming a pro-life advocate, through the hand of God.

Norma wanted the truth behind her story to be revealed. Although she believed abortion was necessary and right for many years, the gruesome reality of abortion intruded upon her conscience as time passed. You will learn how the reality of working in an abortion clinic transformed her opinions about what abortion really does to women. Her story is a proclamation to the nation about the destruction and wickedness of abortion and a call to return to God's justice, not man's. You can read the affidavit she gave to the Supreme Court in chapter three.

Next, you will meet Sandra Cano. Sandra was the real woman whose identity was hidden from the court in *Doe v. Bolton* by the legal pseudonym, "Mary Doe". You will learn about the tremendous fraud on the court that is the basis for the "*Doe* decision", which legalized abortion on demand and led ultimately to partial birth abortion. An abortion was sought in her name, by others purporting to act for her, but she herself never wanted an abortion. In fact, she fled to Oklahoma while the *Doe* case was pending to avoid being forced into an abortion by her mother and her lawyer. The real facts of her case exemplify that abortion was not about Sandra's right to choose but about the coercion of others. Abortion today in practice is often equally coercive.

You will also learn about Donna Santa Marie, (a teenager) in New Jersey. Like too many teenagers who become pregnant before they are married, Donna Santa Marie was forced by her parents to have an abortion. It was not her "choice". Though the Supreme Court in the dark years of *Roe's* reign once held even minors have the "right" to have an abortion, it was her parents and the abortionist who decided, not Donna. Although she struggled to resist the death of her child, her cries for help and her child's survival from a punch in the stomach finally ended in the abortion that took her child without her consent.

One of the most fundamental purposes for which government is established is to protect human life. That is why the Constitution says twice: "No person shall be deprived of *life*, liberty or property without due process of law." Amendments Five and Fourteen. The Constitution never mentions abortion as a right, but it expressly mentions life twice as a Constitutional right. Donna's story, while horrible, is not unlike that of many girls across this nation and is part of the silent tragedy that occurs in abortion clinics every day.

Donna Santa Marie's story is typical of many, but seldom heard. The shame and secrecy of abortion is so deep that women usually don't speak out about the pain and the hurt. Women are told by society that abortion is okay, a good thing, a "right" thing. Then why are they left alone to wonder why a "right" feels so wrong? They were told by the men they thought would love and protect them, to whom they gave their most personal physical intimacy, that it is now "their" problem. Why, if sex is so intimate, do they now feel so alone? Why, since it takes two to produce a child, is it just a "woman's right" and not a man's responsibility?

Why, if the abortion facility is there to help them, are they not told about the true nature and consequences of abortion? Why, if it is a woman's right to choose, is she never given a full range of choices? In chapter five, you will hear the truthful testimony of many of the thousands of women who have already given us legal testimonies to tell courts and legislatures about the great harm their abortion did to them and those they love.

## The Two Great Lies of Abortion

Abortion is legal in America because of two great lies. One, "It's not a baby." And two, "It's good for women." The first lie will be overcome with scientific and medical evidence. The second lie can only be overcome with the truthful testimony of women who have had abortions. Most Americans believe that abortion is legalized murder, the taking of innocent human life. Though many do not let this stop them from also wanting legal abortion to help women. And many, including some members of the United States Supreme Court, think this abortion tragedy is necessary for women to achieve full dignity and an equal place in society.

In other words, many think abortion is good for the mother. The Supreme Court once said that Americans rely on abortion. In the words of Justice Sandra Day O'Connor, in 1992, when she weakened *Roe*, but would not kill it by completely reversing it,

"But to do this [reverse *Roe*] would be simply to refuse to face the fact that for two decades of economic and social developments, people have organized intimate relationships and made choices that define their views of themselves and their places in society, in reliance on the availability of abortion in the event that contraception should fail. *The ability of women to participate equally in the economic and social life of the Nation has been facilitated by their ability to control their reproductive lives.* See, e.g., R. Petchesky, Abortion and Woman's Choice 109, 133, n. 7 (rev. ed. 1990). The Constitution serves human values, and while the effect of reliance on *Roe* cannot be exactly measured, neither can the certain cost of overruling *Roe* for people who have ordered their thinking and living around that case be dismissed."

*Planned Parenthood v. Casey*, 505 U.S. 833, 851 (1992) (emphasis added).

*Operation Outcry* (www.operationoutcry.org) seeks to mobilize post-abortive women to provide written testimony (sworn questions and answers) which are filed with the courts in specific legal challenges to abortion. Most people and judges in America have never spoken to a woman about what it is like to have an abortion. [In the *Dobbs* case that reversed *Roe*, *Operation Outcry* filed 4,728 sworn testimonies of women injured by abortion].

Most women who have an abortion never want to talk about it again. They are ashamed, secretive and hide the truth in the secret places of their heart. Many husbands do not know their wives had an abortion before they met and married. Many parents do not know their daughters had an abortion. Post-abortive women and the abortion industry go to great lengths to maintain a tremendous veil of secrecy. As a result, state laws and court cases give the highest degree of confidentiality to abortion medical records, even over most other medical records. Yet this curtain of secrecy only protects the lie that abortion is good for women. In 2000, when *Operation Outcry* began, the Supreme Court had seldom or never heard from women witnesses about what abortion actually does to women. Yet the Court has said:

"Abortion is a unique act. It is an act fraught with consequences for others: for the woman who must live with the implications of her decision; for the persons who perform and assist in the procedure; for the spouse, family, and society which must confront the knowledge that these procedures exist, procedures some deem nothing short of an act of violence against innocent human life; and, depending on one's beliefs, for the life or potential life that is aborted."

*Planned Parenthood v. Casey*, 505 U.S. 833, 856 (1992).

Even in the *Casey* decision itself, the Court admitted that abortion can cause "devastating psychological consequences" to women. *Casey, supra,* at 852-853 (1992). Later in *Gonzalez,* the Court would admit, based on an *Amicus Curiae* Brief and Testimony of 180 *Operation Outcry* Women, that "some women come to regret aborting the infant life they once created and sustained." *Gonzales v. Carhart,* 550 U.S. 124, at 159 (2007).

The media and abortion industry speak as if abortion is a good thing. Then why is it so secretive and shameful? In the absence of truthful testimony, the lie will win. If women who have had abortions, who now recognize that it was wrong, who feel its hurt and anguish, who know the truth, will come forward and tell the courts, legislatures, social media and the world the truth, then the lie can be swept away. If not, the lie will continue to win. In chapter five, there are excerpts from the sworn affidavits of some of the women who have actually had abortions. But we need more testimonies. You will know the truth and the truth will set you free.

Many people do not want to know the truth. Some say America does not want to hear, but enough women speaking out will get their attention and force the courts to look at the truth. Evil thrives in the denial of truth. For example, in the past, there were lies that Jews were not "real persons", but sub-human, or that black slaves were not "real persons", but property. The truth eventually won, and now, with women coming forward, the truth will once again prevail over the decades of lies. As Alexander Solzenitzn has said: "The most powerful weapon in the world is a word of truth."

The truth about abortion is that it is the taking of an innocent human life. No amount of denial can hide that fact from the human conscience forever. Just as "child", "toddler", and "adolescent" are all words used to describe human beings before adulthood, so too are "embryo" and "fetus". That is why every woman who participates in abortion will eventually come to know at a deep, deep level in her conscience that abortion is wrong. In 2007, in *Gonzales v Carhart,* the Supreme Court has acknowledged the child in the womb is an "infant life" at the moment the child is aborted. Thus we should use their words, – infant life. Abortion kills infants.

These affidavits reveal a variety of women's responses, in the women's own words. Some women know abortion is evil from the beginning; others may not feel it at first. A woman may not realize what she has done until she holds her next child in her arms after birth. Some women try to assuage the guilt by telling themselves the same words the abortion industry uses; that it was her "choice". She may feel better about herself if she can convince others to have abortions. How can abortion be wrong if everyone does it and it is legal?

Some women push the denial so deep that they forget at a conscious level that they even had an abortion, according to their own sworn testimony. Some hurt, but find no one will talk about it or let her grieve for the loss of her child; the child that is not only a part of herself, but a separate human being as well. The pain goes deep and becomes more and more disturbing if healing and forgiveness are not found. It becomes "complicated grief" in the words of mental health professionals like Millie Lace of Concepts of Truth. You will hear the truth from women who are not afraid to testify. You will hear the truth from women who want to prevent other women from feeling the pain of a decision they thought was the right one for them at the time, but which they now deeply regret. You will hear the truth.

## Forced Abortion

In chapter six you will read about forced abortion-which is common, but which is (Praise God) illegal now in all 50 states, and what you and others can do to stop it now through The Justice Foundation's Center Against Forced Abortion (CAFA). Courageous women share their stories about forced abortion, rape and incest and provide compelling firsthand testimony against exceptions for these things by telling America the truth that abortion hurts women, even in the hardest cases. Why add the trauma of abortion to what is already a traumatic situation for a woman?

Chapter seven explores how the 9/11 attacks shook the nation. Was it related to abortion in some way?

## Birth of The Moral Outcry Petition

Chapter eight tells about the amazing birth in prayer of The Moral Outcry Petition asking the Supreme Court to reverse *Roe*. Eventually 539,108 Signers joined an unusual brief at the Supreme Court and two of its unusual and extraordinary arguments were actually discussed by members of the court in the final oral argument and written about in final decision reversing *Roe*.

Chapter Nine allows you to put yourself in the Court. You can read some of the compelling, even shocking, written arguments that were in the five *Amicus* Briefs filed by The Justice Foundation on behalf of their amazing and unusual clients. This was the most briefs ever filed by a single lawyer or organization at the Court at least in recent times.

Finally, is this just fascinating history or is there a place for you in this journey? Read chapter ten and you decide.

# CHAPTER TWO

# What is Operation Outcry?

[This chapter was first written in 2002 – Because The Lord told us to "Record the vision and inscribe it on tablets that the one who reads it may run, for the vision is yet for the appointed time; it hastens toward the goal and it will not fail." Hab. 2:2-3 *[Material in brackets] was inserted after *Roe* was reversed to update it for the 2023 edition, and to show that God has accomplished what He said He was going to do. Now that we know *Roe* has been reversed, let's see how it all began.]

As stated in the introduction, *Operation Outcry: Silent No More* is a national grassroots and legal effort to collect evidence about what abortion does to women from the very women who have had abortions. This evidence is mostly hidden in the hearts of women who have had abortions. They have many reasons to continue to hide that evidence and not come forward, but *Operation Outcry* (www.operationoutcry.org) wants to mobilize Americans to help these women find the courage and confidence to come forward. They need to be lifted up in prayer. They need to be offered forgiveness and healing through the church. Churches need to offer counseling, embracing them with forgiveness, encouragement, and help for direction.

Why should any woman open herself up to the pain that comes from reliving her abortion memories? These women are usually painfully and actively, consciously or subconsciously, engaged in repressing these memories. They do not want to relive them. They do not want to share them with anyone. They are painful and traumatic. [They have made the unselfish decision to share intimate details of the worst thing that has happened to them, so that others might not make that same painfully devastating choice to have an abortion.]

*Operation Outcry* (www.operationoutcry.org) is a way to help women help other women avoid the pain of abortion by not choosing it, or healing from it. [It still is – we need more testimonies today because now our next big goal is to Make Abortion Illegal in All 50 States.] Not only to redeem the pain these women feel, but a way to prevent millions more women from suffering from the pain. *Operation Outcry* is a way to overcome evil with good. It is a way to redeem the pain and produce something good for women and society. It is a legal effort to bring the truth to the courtrooms [and legislatures] that brought this pain and injustice to millions of women and children in the first place.

## Helping Norma and Sandra

The Justice Foundation has [had] the honor of representing Norma McCorvey, the *"Roe"* of *Roe v. Wade*, and Sandra Cano, the *"Doe"* of *Doe v. Bolton*, in their legal efforts to overturn their two cases that brought legalized abortion on demand to America. The Justice Foundation intends to [and did and will continue to] present affidavits [and declarations under penalty of law] from thousands of post-abortive women to the courts and legislatures of this country and eventually to the Supreme Court of the United States to show legally admissible evidence that abortion should no longer be constitutionally protected.

Because Norma and Sandra were the actual parties to *Roe* and *Doe*, they are in a unique position to return to court to seek to overturn those decisions. Under the Federal Rules of Procedure, they can file motions seeking to set aside their court cases on the grounds they are no longer "just." Justice is the legal standard. They must file these motions in the original courts that rendered the decisions. In Norma's case, that is the Northern District of Texas, Dallas Division, United States District Court. For Sandra, her case was filed in federal district court in Atlanta, Georgia.

Because the State of Texas has never repealed its anti-abortion law, if *Roe v. Wade* were overturned tomorrow, [which it was on June 24, 2022], then it would immediately become a crime for a doctor to perform an abortion in Texas. No legislation would be required because the law is still on the books. [That is why Texas abortion businesses had to move to other states to kill infants very soon after *Dobbs*.] It was simply not enforced because of the decision in *Roe v. Wade* that the law was unconstitutional.

This existing Texas law is a good model for others states because it criminalizes the conduct of the doctor, not the woman. It rests on the same premise as *Operation Outcry* that women are entitled to legal protection from abortionists and others during one of the most vulnerable periods of their lives: pregnancy. The women need protection from doctors, [and those who sell chemical abortion pills today], who would prey upon them for financial gain as the abortion industry has done for many years, and as the affidavits document. The doctor can be held criminally liable because he or she is not under financial, emotional, psychological, or social pressure like the woman and should be held to a higher legal standard.

In Sandra's case *Doe*, Georgia however, had already repealed its "abortion is a crime" law and replaced it with a liberal abortion statute, even before *Roe* and *Doe*. Georgia allowed abortion, for the "health of the mother" if a panel of three doctors agreed. Even this [seemingly] modest legislative compromise to protect women from exploitative abortionists failed to satisfy the extremists on the Supreme Court. In *Doe*, the Court rejected the Georgia law and said the abortion decision would be made only by the woman under pressure and any doctor she can find to perform the abortion at any time. If you simply wanted better "healthcare", wouldn't the opinion of three doctors be better than one?

Affidavits we have already received show that many women would never have had an abortion if it had not been legal in the first place. The law is an important moral teacher for many individuals, who would never consider abortion if it were illegal. (Galatians 3:24-26) But because abortion is legal, some people participate, just as "good" Germans participated in the Holocaust and justified it on the grounds that it was legal and thus was not wrong. But the human conscience cannot be fooled forever. The still small voice that separates us from the animals and constitutes the better angel of our nature needs to be heeded. Women need to be *Silent No More*, and let the truth be known. Let a tidal wave of truth sweep over America! We need everyone who loves the truth to help us gather evidence by encouraging women to come forward now. [Still true today!]

## The Justice Foundation Begins

The Justice Foundation is a non-profit public interest litigation foundation. We represent people **at no charge** in landmark cases that affect the public interest, which means the cases are so import-ant that everyone is affected by them. We started in San Antonio, Texas as the Texas Justice Foundation. [But as we began to deal with national issues, it was later decided to drop the "Texas"] TJF is supported entirely by voluntary contributions. All contributions are tax deductible. More information about the Justice Foundation can be found at our web site, www.thejusticefoundation.org. Tax-deductible contributions can be made on the website or sent to the following address: P.O. Box 40458, San Antonio, Texas 78229.

Since our founding in 1993, we have gone to court to assist citizens at no charge in cases advancing limited government, free markets, private property, and parental rights. Prior to becoming TJF's CEO and Founder, I taught civil procedure at a school of Law in San Antonio, Texas from 1987-1993. I started my professional practice as a litigator in Corpus Christi, Texas, where I represented public school districts, as well as other business defendants for eight years.

TJF's first litigation sought a constitutional right to school choice under the Texas Constitution. The case was filed in June, 1993, and went all the way to the Texas Supreme Court. On January 30, 1995, the Texas Supreme Court opened the door for school choice, by declaring that the Texas legislature *could* adopt school choice under the Texas Constitution, though it held that whether to do so was a question for the legislature rather than the courts.

The Justice Foundation has since taken many cases in the area of education reform and is a leading advocate of parental rights. In 1995, the Texas legislature made it the number one objective of public education that "parents shall be full partners in the education of their children". This noble objective is far from achieved in practice since most schools treat the students as "their" children rather than those of the parents. Too many educators feel that they are the "professionals" and the parents are to simply drop the children off, do as they are told, and leave the real work to the professionals. I have been honored as a "Hero for Children" by the Texas State Board of Education and as a "Shining Star of Texas" by Texas Governor Rick Perry.

[Today we call our agenda "Justice For Children." We seek to welcome all children to life through birth, and then have the opportunity through school choice for an education chosen by the parents with state funding following the child to the best school for the child, whether public, private or charter.]

## God's Promise to End the Covenant with Death

What is an organization like this doing representing Norma McCorvey and Sandra Cano, *"Roe"* and *"Doe"*? TJF is not a pro-life organization, as I told Sandra Cano the first day she asked us to represent her. We are a "Justice" organization, though when we started out, we only wanted to be a "legal" organization. As a lawyer trained at the University of Texas School of Law, I did not know much about "justice", only legal matters. Another organization already had the name "Texas Legal Foundation", so my wife, Susan, suggested we call ourselves the "Texas Justice Foundation". The Board agreed, so we adopted that name. One of the board members, Fritz Steiger, particularly felt that "Justice" needed to be reclaimed from the left. God cares more about Justice than any of us can ever truly understand.

Little did I realize then how much I had to learn about "justice". I did not realize that justice and righteousness are the foundation of His throne. *"Righteousness and justice are the foundation of thy throne; lovingkindness and truth go before Thee."* (Psalm 89:14) (See also Psalm 97:2). Later the Lord began to reveal: *"The execution of justice is a joy to the righteous, but is terror to the workers of iniquity."* (Proverbs 21:15). When our first case went to the Texas Supreme Court, I saw these words were inscribed on the dais of the Texas Supreme Court, *"Sicut Patribus Sit Deus Nobis."* At the time of my oral argument, I only recognized the Latin for *Deus*, meaning "God". It gave me comfort to see His name before me. The phrase means, "As God was with our fathers, so He shall be with us." I Kings 8:57. This became the unofficial motto of the Texas Justice Foundation.

On February 11, 2000, unusual events happened that convinced me God will use *Operation Outcry* [and He did use us. The Justice Foundation still maintains the largest collection in the world of sworn testimony by women hurt by abortion] to end the covenant with death that is legalized abortion. Sometime before that date, Harold Cassidy, a lawyer from New Jersey, had called and said that Sandra Cano and Norma McCorvey would like for someone to represent them. Sandra was going to call us on Friday, February 11, 2000. We had arranged to visit Norma the following Monday, February 14th, Valentine's Day, in Dallas, Texas. At this time, I did not know where Sandra Cano lived.

All through the week, I waited eagerly for February 11th, and contemplated the journey that had led us to this day. I kept asking God, "Is this really something TJF should do?" I kept asking Him to make His will absolutely clear to us. I also realized in the back of my mind that this could be a terrible battle. It could be a life and death struggle with the forces of darkness. It was not a battle in which I eagerly wanted to participate. I kept asking God, "Are you sure? Is this really something TJF is supposed to do? How can we "break through the stronghold of abortion?" How can there be a *breakthrough*? How can anyone overturn *Roe v. Wade*?"

On the morning of February 11th, 2000, Clayton Trotter, my general counsel, and I agreed to meet at the Cornerstone Church Chapel to pray. This was Pastor John Hagee's church, of Global Evangelism Television, which was located in our neighborhood. We cried out to God and we gave our fears to Him, and asked for His anointing if this was His will. We took a brochure of the Texas Justice Foundation and threw it on the ground. We picked it up again as the staff of God. We dedicated ourselves and the Texas Justice Foundation fully and completely to accomplishing God's purpose with respect to abortion.

[On the other hand, unlike me, Clayton had dreamed of helping to reverse *Roe v. Wade* since his early days in law school when the decision had been made in 1973. He almost dropped out of law school in disgust over a profession that could not even tell when human life began and should be protected. But his family persuaded him to stay in law school so that perhaps someday he might "do something about it". That day came on June 24, 2022, but it took years to get there.]

About 2:00 o'clock in the afternoon, Sandra called me. She began to pour out a story of deception that shocked even me, and I do not shock easily. Not just the lies of abortion that, "it's not a child" and, "it's good for women," but lies about her very own case that were presented to the court by her attorney. Her incredible story is told in detail in chapter four. But for me, one of the highlights includes *the fact that during the pendency of the "Doe" case, Sandra fled to Oklahoma to avoid having an abortion forced on her* by her mother and her attorney. She came back and participated in the cased when they promised her she did not have to have an abortion.

Further, in 1988, when Sandra wanted to come forth publicly and prove to the world she was the pro-life "Mary Doe" and that abortion violated her conscience, her own lawyer fought against her to keep the records sealed. The legal pseudonym "Mary Doe," which had perhaps been originally intended to protect Sandra's identity when she did not want it disclosed, was now being used to prevent her from unsealing her own records. Her own attorney, rather than acting in Sandra's interest, worked against her to prevent the records from being opened.

Sandra is not a well-educated woman, having only completed the eighth grade. She has a heart of gold, and she knows she loves children. But she was powerless before the legal system. She went down to the courthouse many times to try to read the legal records herself. First she went to state court, then to federal court, and there the records were sealed. Then when she finally got them, it was as if they were in a foreign language to her. It was as if she were legally illiterate. Finally, she obtained the assistance of a dedicated Atlanta attorney, Wendell Bird, and Michael Farris, then President of the Home School Legal Defense Fund, who helped her unseal the records and prove to the world that she was "Mary Doe" of *Doe v. Bolton* fame.

It was also during this first conversation I told Sandra that we were not a pro-life organization. We were a "Justice" organization and if she looked at our past activities, we had not done very much pro-life work. But I told her we would be honored to represent her. I asked her where she lived and she told me she lived in Atlanta, Georgia. To my amazement, I was actually going to be in Atlanta for another meeting the following Tuesday and Wednesday and asked if I could meet with her. She was available.

Months earlier, when I had not even known I would be meeting Sandra, my secretary had asked me how many days to schedule for an Atlanta meeting. There was only one day of activity, but I told her, "Schedule two days. I just have a feeling something will come up." Now I saw that the Lord had been directing my steps to have this extra time in Atlanta to meet with Sandra. [Sandra went to be with The Lord on September 30, 2014.]

When I got home that Friday evening, my wife handed me a little booklet and said, "I think this is for you." The name of the booklet was, *"The Bed's Too Short, and Other Spiritual Essays,"* by Bob and Rose Weiner. She said, "I'm not sure why, but I think you need to read this. While I was at the home school library, I had to catalogue this book. I couldn't tell what kind of book it was from just the cover so I had to read it to determine what Dewey Decimal System numbering should go on the book." I had not told her all of my thoughts and fears, but as a kind and loving wife she knew how much we had been praying about this case.

The booklet is based on a passage in the Bible that, it seemed, I had never heard of before, nor will have many of you. It is not a common passage for preaching. Isaiah 28:20 says, *"The bed is too short on which to stretch out, and the blanket is too small to wrap oneself in."*

As I perceived the message, this essay focused on the fact that if you are receiving this message it means your ministry is going to grow. You are either going to expand your borders and accept the anointing of God, or you are going to stay where you are and feel too cramped and crowded. The essay even included the Prayer of Jabez, I Chronicles 4:10, which I did not really notice at that time, and which had not yet become very popular or so widely known in the Christian community, as it is now. This was the first time that God apparently brought the prayer of Jabez to my attention, but I actually forgot about it until many, many months later when I went back to reread the essay. [God certainly has expanded our territory as Jabez prays in that prayer.]

With the story of fraud on the Court included in chapter four that Sandra told us that day, and this little essay book, I was beginning to feel very confident that God was leading, guiding, and directing our steps. I felt excited we had agreed with the Lord to accept this expansion of our ministry to a national level and be involved in this life and death struggle. However, being the cautious lawyer that I am, and more of a Gideon than a David sometimes, I felt I should check the context of this obscure passage of Scripture to make sure that it was not being misinterpreted.

On Saturday morning, February 12, 2001, I went back to look at the verse in context. The Lord poured out a flood of revelation from His Word from Isaiah 28:14 to Isaiah 39:8. The key verses are Isaiah 28:14-22:

*"14 "Therefore, hear the Word of the Lord, oh scoffers,*
*Who rule this people who are in Jerusalem,*
*15 Because you have said, "We have made a covenant with death, and with Sheol (the grave) we have made a pact.*

*The overwhelming scourge will not reach us when it passes by,*
*For we have made falsehood our refuge and we have concealed ourselves with deception."*
*¹⁶ Therefore thus says the Lord GOD,*
*""Behold, I am laying in Zion a stone, a tested stone, A costly cornerstone for the foundation, firmly placed. He who believes in it will not be disturbed.*
**¹⁷ "I will make justice the measuring line And righteousness the level; Then hail will sweep away the refuge of lies And the waters will overflow the secret place.**
**¹⁸ Your covenant with death will be canceled (annulled), And your pact (agreement) with Sheol (the grave or hell) will not stand;**
*When the overwhelming scourge passes through, Then you become its trampling place.*
*¹⁹ As often as it passes through, it will seize you; For morning after morning it will pass through, anytime during the day or night, And it will be sheer terror to understand what it means."*
*²⁰ The bed is too short on which to stretch out,*
*And the blanket is too small to wrap oneself in.*
***²¹ For the LORD will rise up as at Mount Perazim,***
***He will be stirred up as in the valley of Gibeon,***
***To do His task,***
***His unusual task,***
***And to work His work, His extraordinary work.***
*²² And now do not carry on as scoffers,*
*Or your fetters will be made stronger;*
*For I have heard from the Lord GOD of hosts of decisive destruction on all the earth."*

Isaiah 28:14-22 (NASB)

Let me show you what the passages meant to me that day. When I read verses 14 and 15, I began to get goose bumps that God was speaking about abortion to the scoffers, who are people who do not believe in God, but who were ruling his people in Jerusalem. Some translations even call these people "judges".

*"Therefore, hear the Word of the Lord, oh scoffers,*
*Who rule this people who are in Jerusalem,*
*Because you have said, "We have made a covenant with*
*death, and with Sheol (the grave) we have made a pact.*
*The overwhelming scourge will not reach us when it*
*passes by,*
*For we have made falsehood our refuge and we have con-*
*cealed ourselves with deception."*

Isaiah 28:14-15

So, here is God speaking to judges who do not believe in Him. This is God's reaction to what they have said in their heart, *"We have made a covenant with death, and with Sheol we have made a pact."* Some translations use the word "grave" instead of "Sheol". It hit me right between the eyes that both *Roe v. Wade* and *Doe v. Bolton* were a covenant with death. They were an agreement with the grave. They were a decision by judges of the United States Supreme Court, who did not fear God, but rather either scoffed or doubted whether there was a God, and in their 7-2 agreement said in spiritual effect, "Open wide, O grave, we are about to send you millions of babies before they ever see the light of day." Some translations translate "Sheol" as "hell" so it could be said the judges have made an agreement with hell to bring death to millions. It also struck me with unusual vividness after hearing Sandra's testimony that the court had made, *"...falsehood our refuge..."* and *"...con-cealed ourselves with deception..."*. (See chapter four for a fuller description of all the fraud on the Court in *Doe*.) Later I found out the abolitionists of slavery had called the Supreme Court's pre-civil war pro-slavery *Dred Scott* decision a "covenant with death" based on the same scripture.

This is what God says to those judges next,

*"Behold, I am laying in Zion a stone, a tested stone, a costly cornerstone for the foundation, firmly placed. He who believes in it will not be disturbed (in a hurry).*

Isaiah 28:16

Of course, all Christian believers know that the stone, the tested stone, the costly cornerstone is Jesus Christ. It is only the blood of the Lamb which can atone for the blood of abortion. His sprinkled blood speaks a better word than the blood of innocent babies crying out for justice from the ground. (Genesis 4:10-16, Hebrews 12:24). It is only Jesus Christ, to whom all authority has been given in heaven and earth, who can set aside the unlawful decree of death known as *Roe* and *Doe*. It is only the Lord God who can trample out the vintage where the grapes of wrath are stored.

This was also a warning to me personally not to be too much in a hurry, which is a constant weakness of mine to push, push, and push, "Why aren't we doing this now?" "Why aren't we doing this?" Especially with so many women's and children's lives at stake, we want relief now. But God's timing is not always our timing. The Lord also states:

**"And I will make justice the measuring line, and righteousness the level; then hail shall sweep away the refuge of lies, and the waters shall overflow the secret place. And your covenant with death shall be canceled, and your pact**

> **with Sheol shall not stand;** *when the overwhelming scourge passes through, then you become its trampling place...*"
>
> Isaiah 28:14-17

I remembered vividly that just the day before I had told Sandra we were not a "pro-life" organization, but a "justice" organization. I remembered in 1993, I had not wanted to call our new organization a Justice Foundation, but the Texas Legal Foundation, and that it was my wife who said we should call it a Justice Foundation. God seemed to be saying He wanted this Justice Foundation to be involved in ending abortion directly.

More importantly, "justice" is the exact legal standard used in Rule 60 of the Federal Rules of Procedure as "the measuring line." Rule 60 of the Federal Rules of Civil Procedure states: "On motion and *upon such terms as are just*, the court may relieve a party or a party's legal representative from a final judgment, order, or proceeding for the following reasons . . . (5)(b) . . . *it is no longer equitable [just] that the judgment should have prospective application.*" (Emphasis added). Remember, *"Righteousness (which includes equity) and justice are the foundation of His throne."* (Psalm 97:2). Equity is essentially fairness or justice.

The amazing, overwhelming point for which I am thankful is the *promise of God* to the scoffing judges who rule over His people that, **"Your covenant with death shall be canceled, and your pact with Sheol shall not stand."** (Isaiah 28:18), *Roe v. Wade* and *Doe v. Bolton* will be canceled (annulled). [This promise sustained me for 22 years until it was fulfilled on June 24, 2022 in *Dobbs*.]

This was not a passage that I had sought out looking for guidance about abortion. The initial Isaiah 28:20 passage about the bed being too short was one I had never consciously heard of before. Yet here in Scripture was the written promise from the Word of God. Here was confirmation to me that we were to move forward.

In addition, the passage also tells in general terms how the covenant with death shall be canceled. It states that, *"...Then hail shall sweep away the refuge of lies, and the waters shall overflow the secret place."* (Isaiah 28:17).

Sometime between January, 2000, when I first met Norma McCorvey, and February, 2000, I had already begun to think that women's testimony would be helpful to overcome *Roe v. Wade*. [The idea had come to me in the Dallas Airport on my way home from meeting Norma at my first March for Life in D.C.] I had felt abortion could best be refuted by women who had experienced it first-hand. In legal terms, as witnesses, they could testify based on their personal knowledge.]

I had never "seen" this passage in Isaiah before, though I had read the whole Bible in a year several times at least, but how do you sweep away a refuge of lies? You sweep it away with a tidal wave of truth, an overwhelming flood. For every lie spoken there needs to be many telling the truth. A single hailstone is not very dangerous, but a storm of hailstones can destroy strongholds of lies. And the waters overflowing the secret place, I believe, are the tears of women filling out the Affidavits. No woman has yet filled out our Affidavit and told the court about her abortion without crying painful tears. Those tears allow the cleansing flood of truth to come out and be written down.

The truth that abortion hurts women is hidden in the secret place of women's hearts in America. There are millions of women who have had abortions who do not talk openly about it; but they think about it often, even decades later. It will take their tears to unlock the secret place of their heart. Tears of grief, tears of pain, tears of repentance, and finally God can turn that mourning into beauty for ashes and tears of joy. [Isaiah 61:3].

The Lord in this passage also addressed my own feelings of inadequacy to undertake such an incredibly difficult task. How could TJF succeed where so many others had failed for so many years? There are and were, certainly smarter, brilliant attorneys who have struggled against *Roe v. Wade* and those who would come forward to defend it. The Lord answered the question of who would do the decisive and important work when He said:

**"For the Lord will rise up as at Mount Perazim, He will be stirred up as in the Valley of Gibeon; to do His task, his unusual task, and to work His work, His extraordinary work."**

Isaiah 28:21

At that time, I did not know anything about Mount Perazim. Remember, I had not sought out this passage. My Bible gave two references for this unusual, Old Testament example of God's power on behalf of His people, II Samuel 5:20 and I Chronicles 14:11. Both describe Baal-perazim as a place where David fought a great battle against the Philistines. David inquired of the Lord, saying, "Shall I go up against the Philistines? Wilt thou give them into my hand?" And the Lord said to David, "Go up, for I will certainly give the Philistines into your hand." I had been constantly asking God if we should get into this battle. Could we win? How could we break through? So, David defeated his enemies at Baal-perazim, and he said, *"The Lord has broken through my enemies before me like the breakthrough of waters."* Therefore, he named that place "Baal-perazim". To my great surprise and amazement, a footnote said that Baal-perazim meant, "the master of breakthrough". Here was a direct reference to a battle where the Lord "broke through" when I had been praying, "How can anyone break through the stronghold of abortion?" Notice also that David's victory was like a breaking of waters and there is the breaking of waters in the birth of every new child and in abortion.

The Lord also goes on to point out that it will not be attorneys, but He who will do, *"His task, His unusual task, and to work His work, His extraordinary work."* Remember that this Word came to me through my wife and the little pamphlet, *The Bed's Too Short*, on February 11, 2000. Nine months later, in November, 2000, I believe this prophecy began to be partially fulfilled in the first one of the most unusual elections in America's history. [Donald Trump's election in 2016 was even more unusual and extraordinary – wow!]

The 2000 Presidential election was the most prayed about election in American history [up to that point]. It was one of the closest and most controversial, and the only one decided by the Supreme Court of the United States of America itself. I believe, in the political and spiritual realms, that the 2000 election was about abortion. George W. Bush became the President of the United States through the sovereign will of Almighty God. Like Lincoln who freed the slaves, President Bush did not receive a majority of the popular vote. [President George W. Bush did appoint Justice Samuel Alito, after conservatives rose up in an unusual fashion and demanded the withdrawal of his nomination of Harriet Myers, an unknown lawyer to most, with no judicial experience. Justice Alito went through a difficult hearing which caused his wife, Martha, to leave the hearing room early in tears. [Justice Alito eventually became the author of the *Dobb's* decision which reversed *Roe* itself.]

Vice President Al Gore; The Democratic candidate, said if George W. Bush was elected President, legal abortion would end in America. Women like Jill Ireland and Kate Michelman said if George Bush was elected President, then women will lose the right to choose. Just as Caiaphas, the high priest, was correct in predicting the death of Christ was for the good of the whole nation, though it turned out in a way he did not anticipate, these secular prophets were correct in predicting that the election of George W. Bush would end a woman's right to choose to kill her own child.

Even Sarah Weddington, Norma's pro-abortion attorney in the original *Roe* case fears and predicts that legalized abortion will soon end. [Sarah Weddington died on the day after Christmas, December 26, 2021, about a month after the *Dobbs* case was argued. The crowning achievement of her career – the Roe v. Wade case – only lasted six months after her death. Here is a photo of her huge grave marker which she is reported to have designed herself. Note the shape is that of a large woman and in the place of her uterus is the phrase – "Sarah Weddington Winning Attorney, *Roe v. Wade*, U.S. Supreme Court, 1973." According to her own testimony she aborted her only child by going to Mexico when abortion was illegal in Texas. Like many women she later divorced the man she had her abortion with, and she died childless. I actually grieved over Sarah's death when I learned of it, though it did seem to me to be a sign that *Roe v. Wade* was passing away. It appeared that she had not repented of her actions and received the salvation of The Lord that Norma – her client had. [More on this later and about Norma's death.]

[I prayed for Sarah's salvation and blessing many times over the years. I did also for Justice Ruth Bader Ginsburg and everyone involved in the abortion industry, like former Planned Parenthood Director from Texas, Cecile Richards. As I said before, "*all of us have sinned and fall short of the Glory of God.*" Romans 3:23. I never pray for the death of any human; we pray for their salvation and blessing to live as long as necessary to repent. "*It is appointed for man to die once, after this comes judgment.*" Hebrews 9:27. "*God desires that no one perish, but that all should be saved.*" II Peter 3:9. So should we.

But despite what some might hope, there is no reincarnation, and no repentance after death, only judgment. Jesus paid the penalty for our sins, but we must accept His justice, repent and surrender our lives to Him or die in our own sins and suffer eternal punishment. "*For the wages of sin is death, but the free gift of God is eternal life*". Romans 6:23. *"To as many as receive Him, He gives the right to become children of God, even those who believe in His name."* John 1:12. If you have not turned from your sinful life and received Jesus as your Savior – you can do so right now – wherever you are – whatever you have done-simply and sincerely ask Him to save you right now and promise to follow Him from this point on with the Help of His Holy Spirit. *"For everyone who calls on the Name of The Lord shall be saved."* Romans 10:13.]

Just as Abraham Lincoln was elected President of the United States without a majority vote, George Bush was elected President without a majority of the popular vote. Just as Lincoln was dragged reluctantly from his moral position that slavery was wrong, but not worth destroying the Union, to the Emancipation Proclamation; George Bush and this country may be dragged along by events beyond their control to the eventual conclusion that *Roe v. Wade* must be overturned. In another parallel to slavery, I later learned one of the most prominent abolitionists identified slavery and the *Dred Scott* Supreme Court decision as a "covenant with death."

[In 2017, when we started The Moral Outcry Petition, we called abortion a Crime Against Humanity like slavery and segregation. That argument was mentioned in Oral Argument and the final written Opinion in *Dobbs*. Wow. The Safe Haven argument was also considered by the Court. See chapters eight and nine.]

The Lord showed me many more things in that passage all the way through the end of Isaiah 39. There was a total of 48 lessons altogether the Lord showed me that weekend. There are too many to explain in this book.

If you think I am reading too much about abortion into this passage, I would also point out Isaiah 30:33, which states:

*"Topheth has long been ready, indeed it has been prepared for the king. He has made it deep and large, a pyre of fire*

> *with plenty of wood; The breath of the LORD, like a torrent of brimstone, sets it afire."*

Isaiah 30:33

This passage seemed to mean a lot in my spirit as I read it, but I did not know what "Topheth" was. I had never heard of "Topheth." A footnote in my Bible describes it as, "the place of human sacrifice to Molech". Molech was the God of human sacrifice. Women threw their babies into the belly of the idol which was heated up to kill the babies. Yet the promise of God is that, *"...the breath of the Lord, like a torrent of brimstone, sets it afire"*.

[In 2005, a group of *Operation Outcry* Women and I prayed for the end of abortion in that very Valley of Ben-Hinnom outside Jerusalem where Topheth had stood. Several women of Operation Outcry spontaneously began weeping and wailing as we prayed. The eerie sounds echoed across the valley against the walls of Jerusalem to the rocks below. It was desolate and deserted then. Since our prayers of repentance there it has become a place of life, hope and prosperity. It was one of the last places we prayed about reversing *Roe* in Jerusalem in June 2022 before *Dobbs* was released. We prayed with Rick Ridings at a 24/7 house of prayer called Succoth Hillel right over Topheth. Even though it was late evening when we arrived, a little child in a locked playground came up and smiled at me. I felt it was a sign the children would live and *Roe* would be reversed in *Dobbs*.]

There were also references to the sealed records which Sandra Cano was faced with when she first tried to prove she was Mary Doe. Isaiah 29:11 says, *"The entire vision shall be to you like the words of a sealed book, which when they give it to the one who is literate, saying, 'Please read this,' he will say, 'I cannot, for it is sealed'."* Thus her prolife lawyers in 1988 were barely able to get the books opened and were not able to reverse *Doe v. Bolton* at that time, though they considered various options. "Then the book will be given to the one who is illiterate, saying, *'Please read this,' and he will say, 'I cannot read'.*" This reminded me of Sandra who had told me just the day before that she could barely understand or comprehend the legal documents or procedures she was faced with when she got the records.

The passage below embodies the essential principle that children are the work of God's hands. This is the firmest truth for a respect for human life. And yet our Supreme Court has denied that and the Lord says to them:

*"Woe to those who deeply hide their plans from the Lord, and whose deeds are done in the dark place, and they say, 'Who sees us?' or 'Who knows us?' You turn things around! Shall the potter be considered as equal as the clay, that what is made should say to its maker, 'He did not make me'; or what is formed say to Him who formed it, 'He has no understanding?'"*

Isaiah 29:15-16

He also called for the writing of this book by saying,

*"Now go, write it on a tablet before them and inscribe it on a scroll, that it may serve in the time to come as a witness forever. For this is a rebellious people, false sons, sons who refuse to listen to the instruction of the Lord; who say to the seers, 'You must not see visions'; and to the prophets, 'You must not prophesy to us what is right, speak to us pleasant words, prophesy illusions. Get out of the way, turn aside from the path, let us hear no more about the Holy One of Israel.'"*

Isaiah 30:8-11

[This passage is why I am updating this book so that you know these things were prophesied by the Lord long before they occurred.]

I did not want to write a book like this at first. I did not understand this verse when I first read it, and some may think I still don't. A woman on our staff felt called to write a book about her experiences as a post-abortive woman so she could help other women avoid her pain. Another woman, Kathleen Cassidy, one of the founders of our Women's Health Protection Task Force, wanted to write a book. Someone who is very close to us had excellent relations with a major publisher. Yet, I resisted, feeling that a book had nothing to do with a legal effort, and that it would be too much of a burden on our resources to write a book about this project. I felt it might take time away from important legal work. I was in a hurry to get things done, as usually books take a lot of time. And I was too reluctant to go out on a limb, and publicly proclaim the coming end of abortion.

However, when I went to Wichita, Kansas, to speak to a group about *Operation Outcry*, I had committed to my staff to pray about whether to write a book and seek the Lord's guidance. While there, a woman, a faithful prayer warrior who knew nothing about our discussions about writing a book, told me she felt she had a word from the Lord for me. She told me I was supposed to write a book about this, that the Lord had told me important things people of this country needed to hear. The Lord would take the burden of writing the book upon Himself. She flecked away drops of dust from my shoulders and said, "This will be how the Lord will take the burden away from you, as if it was dust on your coat." I received her word in my spirit as confirmation and direction from the Lord. Then, as I reviewed the Isaiah Scriptures I have referenced above, I saw again that the Lord had directed the writing of His words on a tablet and in a scroll so that it might serve in a time to come as a witness forever. When *Roe* and *Doe* are canceled, it will be clear the Lord, the Master of Breakthrough, deserves the credit, not attorneys. [Amen. Hallelujah! He alone deserves the praise and glory. *Roe* was reversed on June 24, 2022.]

When I returned from Kansas, I found a totally free week on my calendar, a very rare event. I spent the week at home and the beginning of this book came forth.

Abortion is the shedding of innocent blood, which God hates, as should we all. (Proverbs 6:17) But the Good News is He sent His one and only Son to pay the legal penalty for our sins, death on a cross. Whoever believes in Him will not perish but have everlasting life. (John 3:16) Fortunately he loves us enough to die for our sins. God is doing His unusual work, which includes warning of even greater destruction to come if America does not turn back to God. If we repent, He longs to protect us again. If we persist in turning our back on Him, He will turn us over to our own lusts and the due penalty for our sins is death.

## Anthrax Attack on Supreme Court

On October 29, 2001, the United States Supreme Court, which legalized murder and "constitutionalized" injustice in *Roe* and *Doe*, was forced to meet outside the Supreme Court building for the first time since it was built. The reason: the scourge or pestilence of anthrax was detected. The Court building was contaminated and every member of the Court was placed on antibiotics to protect them from getting this first plague-like scourge to attack the Court. Yet, here is what the Lord said in the Isaiah passage:

*"Your covenant with death will be canceled, And your pact with Sheol will not stand; When the **overwhelming** scourge passes through, Then you become its trampling place. As often as it passes through, it will seize you; For morning after morning it will pass through, anytime during the day*

*or night, And it will be sheer terror to understand what it means."*

Isaiah 28:18-19

[The Supreme Court was also forced to close its doors to the public from March 16, 2020 until late 2022 because of the "overwhelming scourge" of COVID-19. One definition of a scourge is pestilence or disease. More later on this.]

I had no idea what this meant on February 12, 2000, when I first read it, but the subsequent 9/11 terrorist attacks on the World Trade Center and the Pentagon followed by numerous anthrax attacks brought "sheer terror," just as the prophet Isaiah prophesied and the scourge even reached the Court. The whole Isaiah Chapters 28-39 passage also includes the intriguing story of Hezekiah seeking the Lord's help against Sennacherib. A great king of Assyria approached Jerusalem and besieged it for the purpose of destroying it. He mocked the God of Israel telling Israel not to trust in God. Hezekiah heard it, tore his clothes, and covered himself with sackcloth and entered the House of the Lord. Then he sent one of the strangest messages in Scripture to Isaiah the prophet. Keep in mind that there is a great foreign army in front of Jerusalem. I would expect him to tell Isaiah about this great army and ask for prayer. Instead he tells his messengers to go to Isaiah and say:

*"Thus says Hezekiah, 'This day is a day of distress, rebuke, and rejection; for children have come to birth and there is no strength to deliver.'"*

Isaiah 37:3

What does a foreign army besieging Jerusalem have to do with children coming to birth and there is no strength to deliver? Children are a blessing from the Lord. They are always a blessing, and never an unmanageable burden. Yet there are millions of children who should be coming to birth every year in America, and there is no strength to deliver them. [Women who get abortions often say and feel: "I can't do this – I don't have the strength.] Instead of being delivered, babies are being killed. We need a mighty deliverance. God answered Hezekiah's prayer of repentance and faith with a mighty demonstration of His own power, forcing the foreign king to return to his own homeland where he was killed by his own sons. The covenant with death will be cancelled.

The full story of how the Texas Justice Foundation got to February 11, 2000, also shows God's leading. It begins a few years before, with TJF's General Counsel, Clayton Trotter, who was a professor of business law at Trinity University in San Antonio, Texas. We first met at our neighborhood precinct convention because we both wanted to elect pro-life candidates to office and ensure that the Republican party kept the pro-life agenda of its national and state platforms. Clayton worked as a volunteer with us on some issues, including filing our first *Amicus* Brief before the United States Supreme Court in 1994 in *U.S. v. Lopez*. Clayton and I helped prepare the San Antonio public defender for his oral argument before the United States Supreme Court in *Lopez* which struck down the Gun Free Schools Act.

In *Lopez*, for almost the first time since the New Deal era, the Supreme Court struck down a federal statute on the grounds that Congress did not have power under the commerce clause to regulate an intrastate activity such as education. This is an important principle of federalism which was reaffirmed by a majority of the Supreme Court in 1996 in *U.S. v. Morrison*. In *Morrison*, the Supreme Court struck down part of the Violence Against Women's Act which made it a federal crime to harm women. Of course, both carrying a gun at school and harming women should be and are state crimes in every jurisdiction. Policing criminals in this regard is a local responsibility of state and local governments, not a federal job under our Constitution. This "New Federalism" is an important development and could be persuasive to some members of the court in overturning *Roe v. Wade*. Some Supreme Court Justices have written they believe abortion is a matter that should be returned to the states under proper principles of federalism.

Clayton was in law school at the University of Texas in 1973 when *Roe v. Wade* and *Doe v. Bolton* were decided. He nearly left law school and refused to become a lawyer because of his disgust with *Roe*. How could he join a "profession" that could not tell when human life began? What he had thought was a noble profession trying to do good and seeking "justice", had become an instrument of injustice, mandating that every state in the union follow the Supreme Court's tyrannical, minority view of the Constitution.

A firestorm of protest among academic scholars and members of the legal profession greeted the *Roe* decision. There was, and still is, widespread agreement that *Roe v. Wade* was one of the most unsound constitutional decisions in the history of the United States as a matter of legal theory. A majority of the Supreme Court, at one time or another, have so indicated in their writings and said that *Roe* should be overturned. But in 1992 when the decision finally came back before the United States Supreme Court in a case called *Planned Parenthood v. Casey*, a majority of the Court held that even though *Roe v. Wade* may have been wrongly decided, it had become part of the fabric of society. Under the doctrine of *stare decisis*, a majority held the decision should continue to have binding effect as an interpretation of the constitution. Again, Justices Kennedy and O'Connor, the key swing Justices on the Court stated it this way:

> "To eliminate the issue of reliance that easily, however, one would need to limit cognizable reliance to specific instances of sexual activity. But to do this would be simply to refuse to face the fact that for two decades of economic

and social developments, people have organized intimate relationships and made choices that define their views of themselves and their places in society, in reliance on the availability of abortion in the event that contraception should fail. The ability of women to participate equally in the economic and social life of the Nation has been facilitated by their ability to control their reproductive lives."

*Planned Parenthood v. Casey*, 505 U.S. 833, 856 (1989).

While Clayton was working as a volunteer in the late 90's with TJF in limited government, free markets, private property, and parental rights cases, he constantly told me that TJF should do something on the pro-life issue. His constant refrain was, "If we're a justice organization, how can we not do something about abortion?" My constant reply was, "Clayton, we are not called to fight abortion. We both know it's wrong, but only God can end abortion in America and I feel God has called us to work on other issues." Clayton is a man of great faith and he continued to pray that, "*Roe v. Wade* is not the law of the land in America. There is a higher law than *Roe v. Wade* which is true justice."

## Women's Health Protection Task Force

In 1997, two recent women graduates, Kathleen Cassidy-Goodman and Anna Torres, of St. Mary's Law School in San Antonio came to me and asked if they could work on prolife activities. They began to represent women who had been injured by abortion under the umbrella of the Texas Justice Foundation. We had been contacted by Elizabeth, a young woman who had an abortion performed on her at the Alamo Women's Health Services, Inc. abortion facility in San Antonio, Texas. It turned out that her abortion was performed by abortion facility employees rather than an actual doctor. The bookkeeper and her husband thought, after watching abortions, that they could perform them as well as the doctor. [Today the abortionists claim abortion is so simple you don't have to see a doctor – nurses can do it, or you just take a pill. This gives women a lower standard of care than men, and results in death and other injuries.] They began scheduling abortions and pocketing the money themselves, instead of reporting it to the abortion doctor. Elizabeth, and numerous other women, received severe injuries during their abortions.

Elizabeth's uterus was ruptured. One of the most common risks of surgical abortion is a ruptured uterus. Since the baby is literally scraped out of the mother's womb with sharp instruments, it is very easy to puncture a woman's uterus. In fact, it is so common that when women sue for malpractice against abortionists for ruptured uteruses, the abortionist's defense is often that this an accepted, standard risk of abortion. They never tell a woman seeking an abortion the risk is so great that if they puncture the uterus it is simply considered part of the risk of having an abortion, but this is their defense after the fact and they can be successful at making that claim stick.

In addition to Elizabeth, others had also been injured in the same clinic. To our shock and dismay, as Anna Torres and Kathleen Cassidy Goodman began to work on the case, we found that the Texas Department of Health was doing nothing to protect women's health in this situation. The culture of protecting abortionists rather than women was so strong that the Department of Health was doing nothing about it. In fact, we obtained the sworn testimony of a Texas state trooper who stated the Department of Health was not cooperating with the Texas Rangers.

This was my first shocking exposure to the realities of the abortion industry. Instead of protecting women, as the *Roe* decision assumed they would, abortionists were intent primarily on exploiting women for material gain. Later in our work, in a trial in federal court in Houston, Texas, abortion doctors who performed abortions themselves in their own offices and were seeking to avoid being regulated by the state of Texas, testified that high volume abortion facilities needed regulation because they were like "cattle calls." (*Women's Med. Ctr. v. Bell*, 248 F.3d 411 (5th Cir. 2001).

I still did not feel personally called to work on abortion, but if these young women were willing to volunteer their time and work on these cases, I felt we had to go forward. Thus, we created the Women's Health Protection Task Force to try to protect women injured by abortion. We worked on strengthening abortion facility regulations in Texas, which failed to provide adequate regulations. This is sadly true in every state in the Union. The defenders of the abortion industry, represented at this time by the Center for Law and Reproductive Policy, work to protect the doctors, rather than the women.

When Texas stiffened its regulation, the abortionists sued. The abortionists won at the trial court level but were reversed by the Fifth Circuit Court of Appeals which basically upheld the provisions of Texas Abortion Facility regulations, except for two interesting exceptions. After hearing extensive testimony from abortion doctors themselves, the Fifth Circuit struck down the portion of the regulations which required abortions to be performed in a manner which enhanced a woman's "dignity," "self-worth," and "self-esteem." *The Fifth Circuit held that because abortion is nearly always a tragic decision, it cannot be objectively performed in a manner which enhances a woman's "esteem" and "dignity".* Yet, these were the very reasons given by the U.S. Supreme Court in *Casey* as to why legal abortion had to continue to be the law of the land. *Casey* claimed that abortion enhances a woman's dignity and autonomy.

"These matters, involving the most intimate and personal choices a person may make in a lifetime, choices central to personal dignity and autonomy, are central to the liberty protected by the Fourteenth Amendment. At the heart of liberty is the right to define one's own concept of existence, of meaning, of the universe, and of the mystery of human life. Beliefs about these matters could not define the attributes of personhood were they formed under compulsion of the State."

*Planned Parenthood v. Casey*, 505 U.S. 833, 851 (1992)

Yet *Casey* was not based on any evidence from women about how abortion actually affected women. The Supreme Court merely assumed abortion was good for women. To the contrary, the Fifth Circuit's decision was based on actual evidence from abortionists themselves and the real impact of abortion on real women. This shows the effect that actual evidence can have in changing the opinion of the courts about abortion.

On February 18, 1999, I had a very vivid, realistic dream of hand-to-hand combat, a knife and fist fight. I do not normally remember my dreams at all. I have never based my conduct on a dream in the past and did not significantly change my conduct based on this dream, but it is something that I have pondered in my heart ever since. In the dream I saw an evil-looking Texas "Icehouse", known in other parts of the country as a tavern or beer parlor or beer joint. There were black-jacketed thugs hanging around outside and it was a seedy-looking place. I knew it was a good place to avoid. But something was telling me that I had to go inside. I felt compelled to go inside and as I started in, I was attacked. I threw my attacker to the ground, finally, very hard. He got up with a knife and stabbed me several times, but not mortally, and I finally stabbed him to death. This was not a nightmare. I was not terrified or panic-stricken like in a bad dream. It was just a very realistic dream. I even related it to my wife, Susan, the next morning because it was so unusual.

I recorded this dream on the February 18th page of my journal at the time which was based on, *My Utmost for His Highest*, by Oswald Chambers. The passage for that day was, "Rise, let us be going" based on Matthew 26:46. Oswald Chambers stated:

"The disciples went to sleep when they should have kept awake, and when they realized what they had done it produced despair. A sense of the irreparable is apt to make us despair, and we say, "It is all up now, it is no use trying anymore." If we imagine that this kind of despair is exceptional, we are mistaken. It is a very ordinary, human experience. Whenever we realize that we have not done that which we have had a magnificent opportunity of doing, then we are apt to sink into despair; and Jesus Christ comes and says – "Sleep on now, that opportunity is lost forever. You cannot alter it, but arise and go to the next thing." Let the past sleep but let it sleep in the bosom of Christ, and go out into the irresistible future with Him."

There have been despairing times for me in my life as I looked at past failures. I know that for many of the women who have had abortions, despair can be a constant companion, or a constant threat, because they think that there is nothing that they can do to overcome this one act. But Oswald Chambers says that we can go forward and that just as the disciples sinned by sleeping when they should have been watching with Jesus, we can arise and do the next thing. He says:

"If we are inspired of God, what is the next thing? To trust Him absolutely and to pray on the ground of His

Redemption. Never let the sense of failure corrupt your new action."

Sometime later I came back to this page in my journal and wrote, "Life Litigation League – come in the Name of the Lord! Do not let past failures hinder our future action – Life Litigation League will be our greatest victory." After the second dream, which I will describe in the next paragraph, and our Monday morning meeting, we purposed to form a Life Litigation League and do pro-life work.

The next day, Saturday, February 19th, 1999, almost a year before I ever met Norma, I had another extremely vivid dream which followed the previous night's dream. This time it was about hand-to-hand combat with Roman legions. I was holding a very blunt, short sword and I had to fight very, very hard. I did not die. The battle was very vigorous, but finally I killed my opponents. It was not scary, terrifying, or panic inducing. There was a sense of great realism about the dream. Again, I felt that it was a very necessary battle, but not a pleasant one at all. Later, I learned that when Joseph interpreted Pharoah's dream, he said it came twice in different forms because the thing was certain and would come soon (Genesis 41:32).

The following Monday morning, we met with Pastor Peter Spencer and an attorney in private practice named Terry George. Terry attended Peter's church, Harvest Fellowship Church in San Antonio. Peter is an extremely brave, dedicated, artistic, talented, gifted, and passionate preacher. He has not been afraid as a preacher to speak out against abortion. In that meeting both he and Terry George encouraged Texas Justice Foundation to become more involved in the abortion issue. *Pastor Spencer felt very strongly that we needed to focus on the harm to women, not just the harm to the child.* He strongly felt the church needed to be compassionate towards women in crisis pregnancies. We must address the real harm that abortion and unplanned pregnancy does to women.

Again, I was not sure the Texas Justice Foundation should be involved in this, though it certainly was a noble, worthy purpose. By this time Kathleen Cassidy Goodman and Anna Torres were working as staff on the Women's Health Protection Task Force. As a result of the meeting, Terry George began to work with us as a volunteer on the Women's Health Protection Task Force and we began to have meetings with potential donors about whether or not Texas Justice Foundation should form a "Life Litigation League". We felt, at the time, perhaps that it was something that a separate organization should be created to do. We also considered having Kathleen Cassidy-Goodman, Clayton Trotter, and Terry George form a specialized litigation firm for the purpose of suing abortion providers for malpractice. We constantly prayed for God's guidance as to what direction He wanted us to go. The word from Oswald Chambers for that day, February 19th, was:

"We have to take the first step as though there were no God. It is no use to wait for God to help us, He will not; but immediately we arise, we find He is there. Whenever God inspires, the initiative is a moral one. We must do the thing and not lie like a log. If we will arise and shine, drudgery becomes divinely transfigured."

My Utmost for His Highest Journal:
Selections for the Year, The Golden Book of Oswald
Chambers, A Barber Book: Discovery House Publishers

We attempted to follow this advice by taking the first step, even though we didn't know where we were going. And yet, just as Oswald Chambers suggested, later events clearly demonstrated God was with us. This has happened so often now, I have begun to say to our staff, "I don't know where we're going, or how we'll get there; but He does, and He will."

On March 19th, 1999, I offered Terry George a full-time Women's Health Task Force position with TJF based entirely on faith, not on our financial condition at the time.

At this time, Clayton Trotter, was still a full-time professor at Trinity University in San Antonio, Texas. Clayton was very involved as a volunteer in our efforts at this time. The Texas Justice Foundation voted to consider starting a separate pro-life litigation foundation and offer Clayton a full-time job with the new pro-life litigation foundation. After prayer, he declined to accept the position even though he felt passionately about ending *Roe v. Wade*. It was quite miraculous that the board of the Texas Justice Foundation would vote to even consider using some of the resources of the Texas Justice Foundation for a pro-life litigation league.

TJF had been formed as an organization to fight for limited government, free markets, private property, and parental rights. Our organization had somewhat avoided social issues in the past. The decision and the calling seemed to be unanimous by the Board that we should explore our options, though there was still a desire to keep it separate from the Texas Justice Foundation by creating a separate entity.

I want to further testify to the faithfulness and provision of the Lord Jesus Christ. As a former trial lawyer and professor, I knew nothing about fund-raising. When we started the Texas Justice Foundation, we had a grant from a corporation which wishes to remain anonymous to litigate for school-choice in Texas. This $100,000 dollar grant would last us about a year.

If God had told me that I would have to raise as much money as has been given to the Texas Justice Foundation, I would probably never have taken the job. It is God who provides the resources and directs our footsteps. It is because of the Lord, working through the voluntary contributions of His people, and even secular entities, that we are able to survive. May of 1999 saw the Texas Justice Foundation in great need. I shared our great need with the staff and explained that God would be faithful if we were doing God's will. Throughout my adult life, since I became a Christian in 1981, my life verse has been, *"But seek first His kingdom and His righteousness and all these things shall be yours as well."* (Matthew 6:33 RSV). That month we received a miraculous contribution from a major corporation that had no reason whatsoever to give as greatly as it did to the Texas Justice Foundation.

I want to emphasize that I am a sinner and not a "holy" person on my own that deserves any protection, blessing, or grace from the Lord. It is His unmerited grace and favor that sustains us. Throughout this time period, there were times when I felt a lack of faith, a hesitancy, lusts of the flesh, and other sins. It is God Who is faithful, not man. Only He can make and fulfill the vision.

By July, 1999, the idea of a for-profit law firm did not seem to be going anywhere. That summer, we added "helping women who had been injured in abortion" to a list of possible projects for the Texas Justice Foundation itself and submitted it at an Executive Summit to some of our major donors, supporters, and other Texas leaders. Many people were passionately committed to supporting that type of project, though we still did not know where we were going, or how it could be accomplished.

During October and November, 1999, I received a resume from Judge Jimmy D. "Skip" Hulett, Jr., who had been appointed as a District Judge by President Bush, in Beaumont, Texas. He was planning to move to San Antonio, Texas. He had experience in family law and was a passionate Christian attorney who had spoken about the need to restore Christian justice and law in America. He seemed a perfect fit for the Texas Justice Foundation. Even though we had no money at the time, the Lord moved me to offer him employment, which he accepted, and he began work as our President in January, 2000.

Sometime in 1999, our Women's Health Protection Task Force members told me about a lawyer named Harold Cassidy and the *Donna Santa Marie* case which he had filed in New Jersey. Harold was one of the leading attorneys on the nationally famous *Baby M* case, which dealt with surrogate motherhood. He is one of the nation's leading experts on birth mothers who place their children for adoption. Donna Santa Marie was a sixteen-year-old minor who was forced by her parents to have an abortion.

They told me about Harold's very interesting theories that abortion was the termination of the mother-child relationship. Harold's analysis was very intriguing and made abortion a parents' rights case. If abortion is the termination of a parental right, then we are denying women equal protection when we treat women who go into abortion clinics differently from those who go into adoption agencies. Harold, in my opinion, is undoubtedly the best pro-life trial lawyer in America. He has sacrificed much for the pro-life cause.

Let me use a simple version of Harold's analysis here. Imagine two women in the same circumstance, facing an unwanted pregnancy that places severe pressure on them. Both are scared, alone, shocked, in emotional turmoil, and not sure what the future holds for them. They are afraid, possibly panic-stricken, and facing pressure from outside individuals or circumstances.

One woman is considering adoption. Before she can place her child, she must legally terminate her parental rights and those of the father. The law provides her extensive due process protections to protect her from being exploited at this vulnerable time in her life. For example, even if she signs a document agreeing to place the child for adoption, such a document is not legally binding in any state until at least a few days after birth. This goes against the theory of *Roe v. Wade* that what happens with her body is a woman's choice and that she can make this decision for herself. Instead, the law presumes that she cannot fully know, understand,

and appreciate the consequences of placing her child for the rest of its life until she sees that baby in her arms after birth. The law protects her from outside pressure, coercion, or financial inducement.

The fact is that many, many, many women who at first see no way to take care of their child and are willing to place them for adoption, in fact change their minds after the baby is born and do successfully care for their child. We do not allow anyone to pressure that woman into making the decision to adopt, nor do we allow others to pay her for the child, even though under the reasoning of *Roe*, it might be considered "her body", her autonomous decision.

Now in the other case, the pregnant woman decides to terminate her parental rights by going to an abortion clinic. Here she signs an immediately legally binding document which is her consent to terminate her parental rights through abortion. In most states, she receives no counseling, and certainly not from an independent, neutral, third–party agency licensed by the state to protect her like an adoption agency. This is still true even though today thousands of such independent non-profit counseling centers called pregnancy resource centers exist across America.

Instead, she is at the mercy of people who have a financial interest in pressuring her to decide quickly. In the high-volume abortion facility, which abortionists themselves have called "cattle calls", the staff is interested in processing her quickly and subtlety coercing her into making the decision. They tell her that it will be more dangerous or more expensive the longer she waits. Yet they tell women who come in later stages of pregnancy that abortion is "safe" up to the moment of birth. They do not counsel her about adoption alternatives, nor the fact that the man is legally responsible to support the child throughout the child's childhood. Nor do they give her any other advice except to get an abortion. They do not adequately inform her of the nature and consequences of abortion. This second woman is given no protection under the law.

One woman terminating her parental rights gets legal protection, the other does not. To treat women in the same or similar circumstances, a vulnerable pregnancy, differently depending on whether they go through the door of an adoption agency or an abortionist is a denial of equal protection of the law. It was the women injured by abortion who sought out Harold. These and other theories were very interesting, new, and persuasive to me. However, I doubted that anything could overturn *Roe v. Wade*.

A look at its abortion decisions shows that the Supreme Court often is not guided in this area by evidence and constitutional law, but by assumptions and a worldview that is hostile to life and does little to protect the true interest of women. I still further felt that TJF was not called to this battle, so I wished him well, but did not want to participate.

Sometime later in the fall of 1999, Harold Cassidy himself called me to discuss his theories. He was asking for our legal help and explaining his legal theories persuasively. It wasn't until quite a bit into our discussion, that Harold, a devout Catholic, let down his legal guard and informed me that he was also trying to organize a worldwide prayer campaign to support the litigation. In my mind, the possibility of success began to appear a little more likely. If there were concerted prayer efforts, perhaps something could break through the stone wall around abortion. Just having a brilliant legal theory, and excellent witnesses (Harold has some world class expert witnesses), does not guarantee success in the court room, as I had painfully learned in our school choice case.

Harold wanted me to come to his conference in Washington, D.C., in January 2000, and speak in favor of his effort. I agreed. At that time, I believed that his legal theories were correct: that they were the right thing to do. Sometimes you just have to do the right thing and let the chips fall where they may. However, I still felt that I was merely supporting Harold's efforts and that TJF was not going to be involved in a major way.

Since I would be going to the March for Life in Washington, D.C., in January for the first time, and preparing to provide some assistance to Harold in whatever way we could, I was given Norma McCorvey's book called *Won by Love*. This was the story of how Norma McCorvey, the "Roe" of *Roe v. Wade*, was transformed by the overwhelming love of God from a pro-abortion advocate to a pro-life advocate. As I read the book, I began to feel Norma should be involved some way in overturning *Roe v. Wade*. I had only read half the book by the time I met Norma in Washington, D.C., at the Rose Dinner, which is the annual banquet in conjunction with the March for Life held each year in Washington on the anniversary of *Roe v. Wade*. I was introduced to her briefly for the first time by Harold and I told her that I thought she would be very involved in overturning *Roe v. Wade*. I did not know at that time, as I hadn't even finished her book, that she had dedicated her life to overturning *Roe v. Wade*. She had even created her own non-profit ministry called "Roe No More".

The day after the Rose Dinner was the day scheduled for Harold's conference. There was a tremendous snowstorm that day that shut down the federal government and the Washington, D.C. airport and metro. Thousands of people were stranded in Washington, D.C., that day. Many people came to the conference in the March For Life hotel who would not otherwise have been able to attend. In addition, some people who were supposed to come to the conference could not.

What seemed to be a terrible disruption in Harold's plans, turned out providentially to be a blessing. We were able to discuss plans with Harold in much greater detail than we had before. Norma herself was snowed in and stayed to watch, unknown to me at the time. Norma saw me and heard me speak. TJF's President Emeritus, Judge Jimmy D. "Skip" Hulett, Jr., was with me at that time. We offered the services of TJF to file an Amicus, or Friend of the Court Brief, on behalf of Norma McCorvey and Sandra Cano in the *Donna Santa Marie* case if they were willing to have us represent them. Harold had already been in contact with the women and explained his case to them. Both of them had indicated to Harold their willingness to assist in *Donna Santa Marie*. We told Harold that he could offer our assistance to the two women who had ironically won landmark abortion cases if they so desired.

On the way home from Washington, I had to have a layover in the Dallas-Fort Worth Airport, on the way to San Antonio. I had been deeply stirred by marching in front of the Supreme Court and by meeting Norma McCorvey, the *"Roe"* of *Roe v. Wade*. I was reflecting on these things, pondering them in my heart, when it hit me for the first time that Norma McCorvey herself could file a motion to overturn *Roe v. Wade*. Such a motion would have to be filed right there in Dallas, Texas, in the original court where *Roe v. Wade* started.

It involved a little known and seldom used Rule of Civil Procedure called a Rule 60 Motion. In fact, even though I had taught civil procedure for six years, I did not know about the rule when I taught at the law school. But a few years earlier, in one of our education cases, TJF had represented a little girl who had been assaulted five times in two years in her public middle school. She was denied a transfer to a safer school on the grounds that it would violate a thirty-year-old desegregation decree. For the first time in my life, we filed a Rule 60 Motion seeking relief from the thirty-year-old decree. After a year and a half of litigation, we were successful in getting this little girl a transfer to a safer school.

I pondered the rule in the Dallas Airport. It seemed to me that it was a viable method for attacking *Roe*. There are no time limits in such a case, unlike many Rules of Civil Procedure. The Supreme Court used the same mechanism to set aside its own twelve-year-old precedent in 1995 in *Agostini v. Felton*. Agostini was a religious liberty case. Thus, I knew it was legally possible, but I kept asking God, "Is this really what You want us to do? How can anyone *break through* the stronghold of abortion?" At this point, I felt that it was a good idea, but if it was just my idea, I did not think it would have much chance of success. Then February 11th-12th, 2000, came, and after my first conversation with Sandra Cano, we received God's promise that He would cancel the "covenant with death". We became the lawyers for Norma McCorvey and Sandra Cano.

In March, 2000, we held a press conference at the Washington Press Club to announce that Norma McCorvey and Sandra Cano were filing a Friend of the Court Brief in the *Donna Santa Marie* litigation. We offered Clayton Trotter a job as General Counsel on April 29, 2000. Clayton gave up a tenured faculty position to accept as of June 1, 2000.

Around March, 2000, a woman named Susan began to meet with us at our weekly prayer sessions on Wednesdays at noon. She came to have very detailed Scriptural messages, directives, and warnings for us. These were so specific we wondered whether they came from God or Susan. However, the Lord seemed to be saying to us the same things in other areas. After a while, Susan revealed that she had suffered the pain of abortion in her life. She felt that God was leading her to help women who had been hurt by abortion. She became the Director of Women's Outreach of the Texas Justice Foundation and a leader of our efforts to reach post-abortive women.

By August, 2000, Texas Justice Foundation had the greatest number of employees that it ever had in its seven-year existence. We were doing both conservative legal cases and issues on property rights, school choice, limited government, etc. We also found that we had no money. We had dedicated our organization to the Lord as the staff of God. But in August, 2000, I wrote the death certificate of the **Texas** Justice Foundation. It was a letter of termination and release of all the employees, including myself and Clayton, who had left a tenured position two months before, because we had no funds. I wept and prayed and cried out to God. This was the 7th anniversary of **Texas** Justice Foundation. It felt like death of our vision.

## Birth of The Justice Foundation

*I believe this was the beginning of the new Justice Foundation in the eighth year of our existence.* We were forced to completely re-evaluate our priorities. We had to lay off one-third of the employees of the Texas Justice Foundation and leave only those activities which were related to our new mission. We kept only our cases which were on appeal in the area of property rights and determined that we would not take any new property rights cases. We also kept our Parental Rights Council, but very reduced. Our focus was to be overturning *Roe v. Wade*. In September, we met with a major Christian philanthropist, and talked with him about *Operation Outcry*. During that meeting, he gave us the Prayer of Jabez:

*"And Jabez called upon the God of Israel saying, "Oh that you would bless me indeed, and enlarge my territory, that Your hand would be with me, and that You would keep me from evil, that I might not cause pain."*

I Chronicles 4:10

I wrote in my journal that Jabez means, "born in pain", as the new Justice Foundation has been born in pain. It hurts to lay off employees when you have been like family. I also checked, at that time, on whether or not it would be possible to change the name to The Justice Foundation, rather than simply the Texas Justice Foundation. We later did change the name officially to The Justice Foundation. The philanthropist and his family later became one of the Pillars of the Justice Foundation, a major financial contributor.

When considering whether to fight abortion, one of the warnings I received in early 1999 from Carol Everett, the author of *The Scarlet Lady*, and a former abortionist, was we could expect our funding would decrease dramatically if we got involved. I didn't believe her, but she was right on the money. Between March, 2000, and August, 2000, we suffered a severe decrease in funding. Until *Roe* and *Doe* are canceled, [and now until abortion is made illegal in all 50 states] we will always need your help financially to continue this project. If God is speaking to your heart, please listen to Him and give generously. Tax deductible gifts can be mailed to The Justice Foundation, P.O. Box 40458, San Antonio, Texas, 78229, or made by credit card at www.thejusticefoundation.org.

In October 2000, the Lord directed me to study the faith of Abraham, because my faith was being tested severely at this time. Our financial situation was still very weak, but I wanted to be like Abraham in my faith. This is why I relate the promise that God has given to end the covenant with death when I speak about *Operation Outcry* and in this book. Even when he was old, and as good as dead, it is said of Abraham:

*"Yet with respect to the promise of God, he did not waiver in unbelief, but grew strong in faith, giving glory to God, being fully assured that what He had promised, He was able also to perform."*

Romans 4:20 (NASB)

My faith is not in legal skill, Presidents, lawyers, or judges, but in the Lord Almighty. In Genesis 18: 20, the *outcry* of Sodom and Gomorrah was so great, it reached the Lord's ears. This was the first great lesson that God gave to Abraham in righteousness and justice. Abraham was supposed to teach this justice and righteousness to his children (Genesis 18:19). The angels told Lot later they were,

> *"...about to destroy this place, because their <u>outcry</u> has become so great before the Lord that the Lord has sent us to destroy it."*
>
> Genesis 19:13

This is another sense in which the term "outcry" is an appropriate name for this legal effort. I believe that the outcry from sexual sins, abortion, and the spilling of innocent blood cries out to God. If we do not cry out for mercy, if we do not repent, then God would be unjust to Sodom and Gomorrah if He does not punish America as well for its sexual sins.

## Legal Strategy

*Operation Outcry* seeks to overturn the U.S. Supreme Court ruling of *Roe v. Wade* [and now to Make Abortion Illegal in all 50 States] by mobilizing those who have been silent about the harmful effects of abortion. This can be accomplished only through prayer and with the testimonies of women who have suffered harm from abortion.

We are engaged in a mobilization effort to gather testimonies from thousands (Norma wants millions) of post-abortive women who have suffered from the tragedy of abortion. These testimonies are collected and submitted to The Justice Foundation, who will then organize and prepare the forms to be used as evidence in litigation to preserve the life of the unborn and protect the women who are harmed, exploited, and deceived at their most vulnerable time in motherhood. These forms may be used in a series of court cases to end the systematic exploitation of women by abortion. [They have also been used in state legislatures and the U.S. Congress]

A woman has the right to be protected from exploitation during one of the most defenseless times in her life: A Vulnerable Pregnancy! In 1973 the *Roe* Court said:

"We need not resolve the difficult question of when life begins . . . the judiciary, at this point in the development of man's knowledge, is not in a position to speculate as to the answer."

TJF engaged in a Threefold Legal Strategy to Overturn *Roe v. Wade*, which proceeded in three phrases.

## Strategy 1: The *Donna Santa Marie* Case

In 2003, we filed Friend of the Court briefs on Norma and Sandra's behalf in the *Donna Santa Marie* case, in which they asked the Court to overturn their cases. This was a historic event in United States jurisprudence. This case will be appealed all the way to the United States Supreme Court.

[This was the first time the U.S. Supreme Court was legally made aware that *Roe* and *Doe* – Norma and Sandra – both wanted to reverse their own cases. But the Court declined to hear this case. Reversal had to wait for another day.]

## Strategy 2: Suing the Texas Department of Health for Failure to Protect Women's Health in Abortions

TJF filed a lawsuit January 22, 2002, on behalf of eight women hurt by abortion against the Department of Health in Texas asking for judgment that the Texas Department of Health and the Board of Medical Examiners failed to adequately protect women's health by not enforcing existing abortion facility regulations. [The case was successful, resulting in a settlement with the State of Texas that paid attorney fees, and obtained the following relief for our clients and the women of Texas:

- TDH presented to the Board of Heath ("the Board"), a recommendation it adopted, a proposed rule requiring abortion facilities to provide a pamphlet about abortion risk to all women seeking an abortion.
- TDH will send a letter to abortion facilities indicating that TDH considers the sonogram part of a woman's medical record, which she has the right to see at any time if she so requests, including a request made during the sonogram procedure.
- TDH will recommend a proposed rule to the Board that it require abortion facilities identification for all women to obtain an abortion. If the woman does not have such identification, she will be required to execute an affidavit indicating that she does not have appropriate identification and indicating her date of birth. Abortion facilities will be required to keep a copy of the identification presented or the affidavit in its files.
- TDH will send a memorandum to all abortion facilities reminding them of their statutory duties regarding parental notification and advising that surveyors will be looking for appropriate documentation that a reasonable effort was made to notify the parents in accordance with Chapter 33 of the Family Code. The surveyors will examine minors' files to ensure the reasonable effort was made. TDH will instruct its surveyors to oversample minors' files to search for evidence of parental notification.
- TDH will jointly develop a training program for abortion facility personnel concerning their individual duties to

report child abuse, how to identify and recognize abuse, and the jurisdiction of Protective and Regulatory Services and local law enforcement over child abuse.

- TDH currently conducts one unannounced yearly inspection at each of the approximately forty abortion facilities in Texas. TDH will recommend a proposed rule to the Board to change rule 139.31 (c)(1) which allows a surveyor to tell an abortion facility the exact day and time of the survey, and instead, adopt a rule that these yearly inspections be unannounced, although they will occur within a three-month period prior to the anniversary date of the facilities' licenses. In addition, TDH will conduct additional, unscheduled surveys at a minimum of ten percent (10%) of the abortion facilities in Texas each year.

- TDH will notify abortion facilities that individual counseling must be provided concerning private medical information and that a woman seeking an abortion must be given a private opportunity to ask questions.

- The Texas Medical Disclosure Panel will reevaluate the adequacy of the risk disclosure currently required for the D&C procedure on List A. The Panel also agrees to establish a separate procedure and listing of medical risks for abortion under List A.

## Strategy 3: Overturning *Roe* and *Doe*

The third strategy was to challenge *Roe v. Wade* under Federal Rule 60 as no longer just and equitable. As parties to the litigation, Norma and Sandra can reopen their cases and ask that they be reversed. We need thousands of affidavits, and we cannot file until we have enough evidence. By helping to collect affidavits, you can hasten the day we file the Motion. We will pray and seek the Lord's timing for this filing, but you must help us now.

[Norma and Sandra, though both were deceased by that time, were finally successful on June 24, 2022, when *Dobbs* reversed *Roe*. In chapter 7 and 8 we will revel in God's power and glory by showcasing the signs and wonders He performed.]

## The Importance of Women's Testimony

[Now that *Roe* is reversed, the battle begins to Make Abortion Illegal in all 50 States. Testimonies are more important than ever.]

If you are a woman who has had an abortion, we need your truth. You can fill out the declaration form online or download a form from our website at www.operationoutcry.org. The Bible says if you confess your sins, God will forgive you. *"If we confess our sins, He is faithful and just to forgive us."* I John 1:9. You may feel your sin is too great for God to forgive. But there is healing in confession.

> *"By this we shall come to know (perceive, recognize, and understand) that we are of the Truth, and can reassure (quiet, conciliate, and pacify) our hearts in His presence, whenever our hearts in [tormenting] self-accusation make us feel guilty and condemn us. [For we are in God's hands.] For He is above and greater than our consciences (our hearts), and He knows (perceives and understands) everything (nothing is hidden from Him.)"*

> 1 John 3: 19-21 Amplified Bible, Zondervan

The Bible states it another way when it says: *"He who conceals his [her] sins does not prosper, but whoever confesses and renounces them finds mercy."* (Psalm 28:13). Shame and secrecy are not from God but from Satan. Satan hides in the darkness. God lives in the light. As you cry out to God, ask Him to, *"Hide your face from my sins and blot out all my iniquity. Create in me a clean heart, O God, and renew a steadfast spirit within me.*" (Psalm 51:9-10). Finally, know this:

*"Therefore, [there is] no condemnation (no adjudging guilty of wrong) for those who are in Christ Jesus, who live [and] walk not after the dictates of the flesh, but after the dictates of the Spirit. For the law of the Spirit of life in Christ Jesus [the law of our new being] has freed me from the law of sin and death."*

Romans 8:1-2 AMP.

You are not alone. *"All have sinned and fall short of the glory of God."* (Romans 3:23). [4,728 women have already filled out an affidavit or on our declarations page which were submitted to the Supreme Court in the *Operation Outcry* Brief of 2,249 Women Injured by Abortion in the *Dobbs* case. But we need thousands more for the battle in every state.

Very soon after the *Dobbs* decision, our *Operation Outcry* representative from Indiana called us to ask for women's testimonies since the legislature was considering banning abortion. We gave them all our Indiana testimonies to put one from every county on the desks of the legislators. A few of our key *Operation Outcry* representatives testified in person. Indiana passed the law banning abortion with a few exceptions, which means we keep working. The women's testimonies show we don't need rape and incest exceptions. Incest exceptions especially only help the abuser, because the evidence of his crime is destroyed and the abuse continues. With respect to a rape exception, why add the trauma of abortion to a rape victim's life. We can do the same or more in every state where abortion is still legal.]

*Operation Outcry*: Silent No More allows post-abortive women who have suffered in silence from the harm of abortion to speak out. No longer do these women need to hide behind the fear of their shame. The abortion industry has abused, exploited, and used women, and then cast them aside, along with killing their children. This national mobilization effort provides post-abortive women the opportunity to inform America of the true nature of abortion and its consequences. The most effective people to share this message are those who have experienced abortion.

[We are asking post-abortive women today to fill out a legal form called a declaration under penalty of perjury, a one-page document consisting of nine questions about their abortion experience. A declaration form can be found online at www.thejusticefoundation.org/operationoutcry, or download the form, fill it out and mail your declaration to: The Justice Foundation, P.O. Box 40458, San Antonio, Texas 78229.] These declarations will be used as evidence to demonstrate how abortion harms women. Sharing your testimony encourages other women to choose life. Additionally, many post-abortive women are relieved when they realize that they are not alone in their suffering. Those who know their pain but have received God's forgiveness need to be Silent No More and bring America this message of hope, healing, and purpose through the testimony of God's Word and truth in your own lives. Men may fill out the declaration and describe how abortion affected them, and these will be used.

The information – but not personal contact data – from completed declarations may also be used to inform legislatures and American leaders about the risks of abortion. (The woman may tell us whether to use her first name, initials only or full name. We recommend initials or first name, unless you are publicly speaking about your abortion after healing.) The Justice Foundation is a non-profit organization and *Operation Outcry* is a legal mobilization effort. It is not political action to support *Operation Outcry,* and collecting testimonies does not jeopardize the non-profit tax status of any church or organization.

We understand that some of these women may not be in a position to allow their full names to be used. The testimonies will be kept confidential in our office. Each woman has the option of checking either full name or initials only. If the woman desires her testimony remains confidential, her initials will be used and the remainder of her personal information will be blacked out. All addresses will be blacked out when the forms are submitted to the court. TJF will make every effort to protect women's confidentiality, and courts have protected women. Most likely it will be kept confidential, but we can make no absolute guarantee in litigation.

## *Operation Outcry* Saves Lives

You might not have the faith at this point to believe *Operation Outcry* will be ultimately successful in making abortion illegal in all fifty states. I, myself, resisted involvement for many months because I did not think anything could overcome *Roe v. Wade*. Faith is a gift given by God and He gives it in different measures to different people. Yet, you might still want to participate in *Operation Outcry* simply because it is the truth. It is the right thing to do and it advances the pro-life cause. Some people feel it could be as useful as the movement to ban partial birth abortion, which was not successful in overturning *Roe v. Wade*, but certainly did increase public awareness of the gruesome nature of abortion and the fact that it was killing a human child. It also helped prepare the hearts of the Supreme Court Justices as they had to open their eyes and rule on this admittedly "gruesome procedure." (*Gonzales v. Carhart*, 2007). You might want to support *Operation Outcry* even if you do not have sufficient faith to believe in its ultimate success. It saves lives even as we are collecting the testimonies.

The first example of saving lives is a woman named Christine who heard about *Operation Outcry* on the radio. It was not even a live broadcast, but a tape delayed broadcast of a program aired at 2:00 A.M. When we came to work the next morning, we found a woman's desperate voice on our answering machine saying the women describing their abortions were just like her. Christine was also pregnant again and considering abortion again. Sharon, one of our women attorneys with abortion in her own past, called her immediately that morning. Christine was desperate, but she wanted forgiveness and repentance. She also said she was going to go to a church. While encouraging her to go to church, Sharon told her that she did not even need to wait that long and that forgiveness was available through Jesus Christ right away if she wanted it. Sharon led Christine in a prayer of salvation and encouraged her to go to a church. She also found out where she was living and put her in touch with a helping ministry right in the apartment complex where she lived. She assisted her in getting pre-natal care. Christine decided to save the life of her baby.

Another example of saving lives through *Operation Outcry* occurred in July 2001. A young girl, 14 years old, called our office and spoke to Kathleen Cassidy-Goodman, a leader on our Women's Health Protection Task Force. The teen explained she was pregnant and her mother was forcing her to have an abortion. This situation is so common, yet so infrequently discussed. The Supreme Court had given minors the right to "choose" an abortion in *Planned Parenthood v. Danforth*, but our affidavits show in too many situations it is not the child's decision, but the parents'.

The parents are often not thinking of the child, but of the shame and embarrassment that will occur to the family if this occurs, or the "harm" to their daughter's future. The harm from taking a human life and its effect on their daughter is hidden from them, but revealed in our affidavits. This young girl heard about the Texas Justice Foundation through a Crisis Pregnancy Center.

She asked Kathleen to talk with her mother on Wednesday night at 6:00 P.M. Shortly before 6:00 p.m., the young girl called Kathleen and said she wanted to talk to her mother by herself.

Kathleen said, "Fine," but asked her to call her afterwards to let her know what happened. The next morning, the young girl called again, crying that her mother was still insisting that she have an abortion. Kathleen wanted to go to court immediately to get a temporary injunction to prevent this parent from forcing her child to commit murder. However, TJF believes strongly in parental rights, though not in the right to force a child to commit murder, just as a parent could not lawfully force a child to steal or commit other crimes against humanity.

I told Kathleen we must first appeal to the mother as the one in authority before we would ever go to court. I also asked if there were any other authorities in the child's life and Kathleen explained the young girl went to church.

I asked Kathleen to contact the girl's Catholic priest since he was the family's recognized spiritual authority over the child and mother. Kathleen and the local priest went to visit the mother together. Kathleen also took affidavits already collected from women who had been forced to have abortions by their parents. The names and addresses were deleted to protect the confidentiality of the women. However, the pain of having been forced to have an abortion and the lifelong consequences of that decision were apparent to the mother. After a discussion with her priest and reviewing the evidence, the mother gave permission for the young girl to go into a home for unwed mothers. Thus, this child and this family have been spared tremendous pain. After a time of healing, the mother brought her daughter home to be with her.

In far too many instances, the sexual license of the 60's allows older men to prey on teenage girls. This is not liberation. This is exploitation of women. Yet Planned Parenthood, in San Antonio, celebrated in its newsletter the fact that it "helped" by providing birth control for a 13-year-old girl. Sex by 13-year-old girls is sexual abuse, and should be reported to the public authorities, not celebrated.

## Center Against Forced Abortions (CAFA)

As a result of collecting over 2000 testimonies of Women Injured By Abortion, TJF started a sub-ministry called the Center Against Forced Abortions. In 2009, TJF's Center Against Forced Abortion [CAFA] provides free legal resources and training for women, lawyers, police, school counselors, and pregnancy resource centers to help mothers who are being unduly pressured, forced or coerced into an unwanted abortion. We estimate the Center's training, assistance, and legal tools save between 1000-2000 mothers and babies annually. You can go to www.thejusticefoundation.org/cafa for all the free resources available to stop a forced abortion. You can also call us at (210) 614-7157.

On a final, somewhat side note, I want to say one thing about the name, *Operation Outcry*. Some don't like the name because it sounds like *Operation Rescue*. While *Operation Outcry* is not linked to *Operation Rescue* in any manner, formal or informal, I believe the historical record should show that *Operation Rescue* did produce fruit that will benefit the overturning of legalized abortion in America. In particular, *Operation Outcry*'s strategy of a Rule 60 Motion to reopen Norma's case would not be possible if Norma herself had not been converted through the efforts of an *Operation Rescue* sidewalk counselor's little girl.

As described more fully in chapter three and Norma's book, *Won By Love*, Reverend Flip Benham and *Operation Rescue* moved into the offices immediately next door to A Woman's Choice abortion clinic where Norma McCorvey was working at the time. She was a hellcat, as she describes herself. She was abusive to them, yet they overwhelmed her with Christian love and witnessing. At last, through the efforts of a little girl, the daughter of a sidewalk counselor, Norma was invited to a church where she gave her heart to Jesus Christ. It was the growing realization that working in the abortion clinic was wrong, and that she was hurting women, that lead her to give her heart to the Lord and led to her conversion first to Protestant Evangelicalism, and then to Roman Catholicism.

Second, while Sandra Cano was always convinced she would not personally kill any child, and abortion was personally wrong, she was not always actively pro-life. It was not until 1988, when *Operation Rescue* actively picketed and rescued at abortion clinics in Atlanta that Sandra was convinced she was not doing enough to stop abortion in America. Seeing the sacrifices of pro-life rescuers proved to her that she needed to do more. It was then she began the lengthy and difficult process of unsealing her records to prove she was "Mary Doe". She began to speak out against abortion because of the efforts of *Operation Rescue*. Thus, in a very real sense, if it were not for *Operation Rescue*, the two ladies who are critical may not have been part of *Operation Outcry* today.

*Operation Rescue* was a controversial effort because it involved engaging in civil disobedience in order to save the lives of women and children at abortion clinics. Many Christians are uncomfortable with the thought of civil disobedience and did not want to be linked in any way with *Operation Rescue*.

*Operation Outcry* does not involve any illegal conduct whatsoever. It does not involve sidewalk counseling or appearing in front of abortion clinics. It is merely collecting truthful testimony for use in a court proceeding. Churches should be comfortable with *Operation Outcry* because it is not political in any way. It is not lobbying. It is a justice issue, which should be of great concern to the church. It is not campaigning for any candidate or for the passage of any particular legislation. Thus, it is perfectly appropriate and legal for any church or non-profit group to participate in *Operation Outcry* in any manner since it does not violate IRS rules for 501c(3) corporations such as churches and pregnancy care centers. All the church is doing is collecting, encouraging, and sharing the truth. This is justice, not politics. TJF is also a 501c(3) organization like most churches. Churches can even contribute to TJF, and some are doing so on a regular basis.

# CHAPTER THREE

# Who is Norma McCorvey? And Why Does "Jane Roe" Want to Overturn *Roe v. Wade?*

**[This chapter was originally written in 2002, before Norma's death and *Dobbs*. Material in Brackets added after the *Dobbs* victory overturned *Roe v. Wade*]**

This is the story of Norma McCorvey, a woman who had a very hard life, who ended up pregnant and scared. She wanted an abortion as the only way to handle what she considered a "problem" pregnancy. She never set out to be the lead plaintiff in a suit to bring abortion to America. She just wanted an illegal abortion, quick and easy. She wanted a life, not a landmark lawsuit. Yet she became the "Jane Roe" of *Roe v. Wade*. She was not told, nor could she imagine what the weight of guilt would feel like for causing millions of deaths.

She felt used by the young lawyers who wanted to make abortion legal in America. One of her lawyers had had an abortion herself in Mexico and now wanted others to do it as well. How often we want others to participate in our shameful deeds to assuage our own guilt. That lawyer, Sarah Weddington, now suffers from breast cancer which evidence shows is linked to an increased risk from abortion. [She survived, and lived until Dec. 26, 2021; 25 days after the Oral Argument in *Dobbs*, but before the decision reversed what she felt was her greatest achievement.] Norma was used by the system and her attorneys to bring legalized abortion to America. Most of this part of Norma's story has been told in a made for TV movie, starring Holly Hunter as Norma, and in a book by Norma called *I am Roe*. During this period, Norma was an active pro-abortion advocate.

But Norma's story did not end there, as those favoring abortion would have liked. Now the story moves to 1995, when Norma was working in an abortion clinic in Dallas, at times with her friend. Operation Rescue pro-lifers moved into the offices next door and hell breaks loose, at least on Norma's side. Heaven seems to break loose from the other side. Even before their arrival, Norma's conscience had been bothering her greatly about the things she saw going on in abortion clinics. She saw the unsanitary conditions, the greed for money rather than concern for the women, the pain and crying of the women, and the baby parts in the clinics. She began to hear the sound of children's feet when there were none. She heard the laughter of little children when there were none.

Eventually, the love of a little girl, Emily, the daughter of an Operation Rescue sidewalk counselor, brought Norma to church and the love and forgiveness of Jesus Christ. She found forgiveness in the love of God and has dedicated herself to pro-life work, [until the illness that caused her death in 2017.] She started her own ministry, "Roe No More", and is a frequent speaker against abortion. Here is a poem she wrote about her feelings at this time.

*Empty Playgrounds*
By Norma Mc Corvey


"Dear Lord, I sit across from a playground
that I visited this eve with a small child.


I know of such places where children play
and I know I'm the cause of them not being
filled with laughter and joy.


These grounds are empty
because the innocent children were killed –
dead because of the sins that I committed.


I hope, Lord, that there is a wondrous playground
that you have in heaven,
one that is well-guarded with angels
who will protect these children
and keep them safe and happy.


Lord, please make them smile and laugh up there
so that when the glorious day comes
when I'm brought up to heaven,
the children will not hold this sin against me.


Every time I see
an empty playground, I pray
with all my heart that yours will be full.


The sun is setting low, now,
and my heart hurts for the children
who have been torn apart by abortion.

I hope that you can put them back together
and make them whole.

If you like, Lord, you can use my body parts
in order to make these children whole –
I'll give myself up gladly.

I know, Lord, that you can do this,
if not only for them,
for the love that I have for each and all.

For God, you gave your only Son
and his shed blood for us.

You offered your body so that we could be whole.
Yet all I did was give my baby away
so that other women could tear theirs apart.

For that, I'll never be able
to look you in the face without shame."

This part of the story has also been told in Norma's second book, *Won By Love*. You are encouraged to read the book *Won by Love* for the full story.

This rest of this chapter tells how Norma came to be involved in *Operation Outcry*, [and her last days on earth.] Remember from chapter two how I first met Norma briefly at the Rose Banquet in connection with the March for Life and Harold Cassidy's conference about the *Donna Santa Marie* case in January 2000. Norma watched my participation in Harold's conference, unknown to me. By February, she had asked us to represent her in Donna Santa Marie's case. We were scheduled to meet with her on Monday, February 14, Valentine's Day, 2000.

On Friday, February 11, 2000, we spoke with Sandra, and on Saturday we received the promise of God that the covenant with death would be cancelled (Isaiah 28:14-22). See Chapter Two. We were all thrilled and excited as we came to work on Monday morning for a staff meeting prior to leaving. I shared the promise of God given to me in Isaiah that weekend with my staff. Then we went to Dallas to meet Norma. The following briefly describes our first meeting on February 14, 2000, Valentine's Day.

Clayton Trotter, myself, Skip Hulett, and Kathleen Cassidy-Goodman traveled together to see Norma. She still lived in Dallas and worked with her friend, Connie Gonzales, but was now at *Roe No More Ministries*. What a change!

Kathleen told her, "We spoke with Sandra Cano on Friday."

Norma McCorvey asked, "Oh, how is she?"

Kathleen responded, "She was great. She was really willing to speak with us. Skip and Allan are going down there tomorrow. They are going to be meeting with her on Wednesday, as well."

"Oh, cool!"

Norma told us how she felt called by the Lord to speak against abortion. She said, "He likes for me to go out and speak. I wish He wouldn't sometimes. You know, it gets kind of lonely. Depressing."

Clayton introduced himself. Then I shared with Norma what the Lord had given to us that Friday and Saturday in Isaiah. As I explained in chapter two, He has given us the promise in Isaiah 28:14-22 that the covenant with death will be cancelled.

Norma asked, "It started in Isaiah 28:14?" As she read the passages, Norma gasped.

"Yeah, exactly." I said, "And He has made it very, very clear to me, if we walk in His Way and do it His Way, and we walk in the Spirit, God is going to overturn *Roe v. Wade*."

Norma responded, "I agree. I agree. Thank you, Jesus."

Clayton shared, "This morning when I was driving into San Antonio, I was playing a tape on spiritual warfare. And the first song on it is, "Some men trust in horses, and some men trust in chariots, but we will trust in the name of our Lord."

Then a very strange thing happened, I said. "That's why I probably won't be much help in this meeting because the Lord has been saying to me all weekend, that I must rely on him totally and completely, even if it seems strange or odd. When I came in, I may be the only one that got the message on your sign,

*'This is God. I will be handling all your problems today. I do not need your help.'*

(God hit me like a slap in the face that I was to just sit back and say nothing. I was not to take the lead, as I normally would, but to just let God handle the whole situation. Even though this was our first meeting, I was to say nothing.) I continued, "The Lord has been showing all of us in amazingly independent ways that *Roe v. Wade* will be cancelled. It's a confirmation that God is going to do His work through us. We have some legal ideas but it's going to be God that directs and guides our path. It has to be God who directs and guides our path. Every step of the way. If we take a big step, then we've got to seek God to be sure it's His path. But we have got to be in His Will every way and every day." From this point on, I was pretty silent.

Kathleen, our devout but very practical Catholic, [Clayton and I and most of the rest of the team are Evangelicals, or other kinds of Christians] told Norma, "We would like to tell you what happened this morning. We have an office and we have about 16 people in our office. About half of them are women, maybe a little bit more than half. We were having our Monday morning staff meeting and two or three women that were in the staff meeting walked up to me afterwards and said, 'We have to pray for you. It's a special prayer we need to pray because God has told us the women need to pray over you.' And so, there is some role for others to play and there's some role for me and I don't know what it is. I am willing to do whatever it is God is calling me to do. But I am astounded. I just get chills thinking about it now. There were two or three women, I can't remember, that said the same thing and they were all right there behind me and they said a special prayer for women, so I don't know what it is, or why it is, but I am glad to be here." (This was the first I had heard about the special women's prayer at work that morning. Unknown to me the women had anointed Kathleen's feet with oil and tears and told her she would have a special role to play that day. When she came out, I noticed Kathleen was shaken, but she wouldn't tell me what had happened. This is not her normal prayer style.)

After a long discussion with Norma about her involvement in the *Roe* case, she agreed to be part of overturning her own case. It was her heart's desire at that time, and she eagerly embraced it.

Clayton said, "Lord Jesus we need to confess that You are our Guide and You are our North Star and there's a lot of woods we're trying to go through here and as long as we look to You, we are not going to be lost. We just confess that. And Lord we thank you that you put us together as brother and sisters in the family of God and we just ask that You give us wisdom and knowledge and under-standing and forgiveness for one another and for those who do evil in the world, Lord, and just guide us by Your Spirit. We know that You will not fail because Love never fails and we praise You for that Word. Amen."

Norma added, "And Father thank You for sending these beauti-ful people to me and for making these crazy dreams come true. And You know what that dream is, Lord. I don't have to say. You know my heart. And I want You to hold these people close to you and unite them and give them the wisdom, the knowledge, the access, anything that they need, Lord God, please just let it be at their fingertips when they're praying. And we ask this in your Precious Son's Name, Jesus Christ. Amen."

This concluded our amazing first visit with Norma. She is a precious, wonderful character and a new child of God. God is shaping her and molding her into the image of His Son. She bore in her heart a heavy load of guilt for legalized killing, though she is forgiven in Jesus because she confessed her sin and asked for forgiveness. She began to speak out about *Operation Outcry* across the country. [Her personal ministry was called *Roe No More*]

[Here is the affidavit that Norma filed in the Rule 60 Motion to ask the Supreme Court to reverse her own case, *Roe v. Wade*. It presents the heart of what she wanted to tell the Court about abortion. It summarizes her life experience, her abortion clinic experience, and her pro-life experience. It is a critical piece of American history.]

## 2003 Affidavit of Norma McCorvey

### [IN THE UNITED STATES DISTRICT COURT FOR THE NORTHERN DISTRICT OF TEXAS DALLAS DIVISION

| | | |
|---|---|---|
| Norma McCorvey, formerly known as | § | |
| JANE ROE, | § | |
| | § | |
| Plaintiff, | § | |
| V. | § | CIVIL ACTION NOS. 3-3690-B |
| | § | AND 3-3691-C |
| HENRY WADE, Through His Official | § | |
| Successor in Office, William | § | |
| "Bill" Hill, Dallas County | § | |
| District Attorney, | § | |
| | § | |
| Defendant. | § | |

Norma McCorvey, being of full age deposes and says:

"My name is Norma McCorvey and I reside in Dallas, Texas. I am competent to make this affidavit. The facts stated in this affidavit are within my personal knowledge and are true and correct.

Thirty-three years ago, I came before the United States District Court, Northern District of Texas, Dallas Division as The Plaintiff 'Jane Roe', the young woman whose case legalized abortion in the United States, *Roe v. Wade*. At that time, I was an uninformed young woman. Today I am a fifty-five-year-old woman who knows the tragedy that arose from my unsuspecting acquiescence in allowing my life to be used to legalize abortion."

"In 1970, I told this Court in the form of an affidavit that I desired to obtain an abortion never really understanding the ramifications. Today, I once again appear before this Court in the form of an affidavit to present evidence never presented in my earlier case, but today I come with a complete understanding of what my participation [in]*Roe v. Wade* has brought to this country. My personal experience with this three-decade abortion-experiment has compelled me to come forward, not only for myself and the women I represented then, but for those women whom I now represent. **It is my participation in this case that began the tragedy, and it is with great hope that I now seek to end the tragedy I began.**"

"Because of my role in *Roe v. Wade* and my subsequent experience with abortion, this Court will be provided with information and a perspective unavailable from other source[s]. Previously, the courts, without looking into my true circumstances or taking the time to decide the real impact abortion would have upon women, used me, my life, and my circumstances to justify abortion. Those judges who made the earlier decisions never had the advantage of the real facts to base their decision because the entire basis for *Roe v. Wade* was built upon false assumptions. Consequently, the decision was rendered in a vacuum totally devoid of findings of facts and solely based upon what abortion advocates wanted for women. Because the courts allowed my case to proceed without my testimony, without ever explaining to me the reality of abortion, without being cross-examined on my erroneous perception of abortion, a tragic mistake was made – a mistake that this Court has the opportunity to remedy."

"The years following the *Roe v. Wade* decision have been very difficult, in a number of respects, but my life was never easy. Prior to my pregnancy with the "*Roe*" baby, I gave birth to two other children. My first, a daughter, was adopted by my mother. It was difficult to part with my child, yet I have always been comforted by the fact that my daughter is alive. My second daughter was raised by her father, a young intern at Baylor Methodist Medical School. He wanted to get married and make a home, but I wasn't ready for that kind of commitment. Later, when I became pregnant with the "*Roe*" baby, I was really in a predicament. My mother expressed her disapproval and told me how irresponsible I had been. She made it clear that she was not going to take care of another baby."

"Although I knew I was pregnant, I waited for a while before I went to the doctor. While I was waiting to be examined, I questioned some of the ladies in the waiting room about whether they knew where a woman could go to have an abortion. A lady told me where an illegal clinic was located and told me that it would cost $250.00. Following our discussion, I told the doctor that I wanted to have an abortion, but he refused stating that abortion was illegal. He didn't believe in abortion and gave me the phone number of an adoption attorney."

"When I had saved about two hundred dollars, I took a cross-town bus to the illegal clinic, which turned out to be a dentist's office that had been closed down the previous week. For some reason, I felt relieved yet angry at the same time. All my emotions were peaking; first, I was angry, then I was happy, and then I'd cry. From the abortion clinic, I took the bus to my dad's apartment and decided to speak with the adoption attorney. The attorney set up the meeting and referred me to Sarah Weddington, the attorney who represented me in *Roe v. Wade*."

"Following the adoption attorney's introduction, Weddington invited me out to dinner. Although Weddington and I were about the same age, our lives were quite different. She was a young attorney, and I was homeless and lived in a park. Unconcerned about politics, I sold flowers and an underground newspaper that described the types and availability of illegal narcotics. At the time, I simply sought to survive. During our initial meeting, I met with Sarah Weddington and her friend, Linda Coffee. Both Weddington and Coffee had recently finished law school, and they wanted to bring a class action suit against the State of Texas to legalize abortion."

"During our meeting, they questioned me, "Norma, don't you think that abortion should be legal?" Unsure, I responded that I did not know. In fact, I did not know what the term "abortion" really meant. Back in 1970, no one discussed abortion. It was taboo, and so too was the subject of abortion. The only thing I knew about the word was in the context of war movies. I had heard the word "abort" when John Wayne was flying his plane and ordered the others to "Abort the mission." I knew "abort" meant that they were "going back". "Abortion", to me, meant "going back" to the condition of not being pregnant. I never looked the word up in the dictionary until after I had already signed the affidavit. I was very naive. For their part, my lawyers lied to me about the nature of abortion. Weddington convinced me, "It's just a piece of tissue. You just missed your period." I didn't know during the *Roe v. Wade* case that the life of a human being was terminated."

"That evening, the two female lawyer[s] and I discussed the case over a few pitchers of beer and pizza at a small restaurant in Dallas. Weddington, Coffee, and I were drinking beer and trying to come up with a pseudonym for me. I had heard that whenever women were having illegal abortions, they wouldn't carry any identification with them. An unidentifiable woman was often referred to as Jane Doe. So we were trying to come up with something that would rhyme with "*Doe*". After three or four pitchers of beer, we started with the letter "a" and eventually we reached "r" and agreed on "*Roe*". Then I asked, "What about Jane for the first name?" Janie used to be my imaginary friend as a child. I told them about her and how she always wanted to do good things for people, and it was decided – I became Jane Roe, by the stroke of a pen."

"These young lawyers told me that they had spoken with two or three other women about being in the case, but they didn't fit their criteria. Although I did know what "criteria" meant, I asked them if I had what it took to be in their suit. They replied, "Yes. You're white. You're young, pregnant, and you want an abortion." At that time, I didn't know their full intent. Only that they wanted to make abortion legal, and they thought I'd be a good plaintiff. I came for the food, and they led me to believe that they could help me get an abortion."

"After our meeting, I went to my father's apartment and began to drink alcohol heavily. I was depressed with my plight in life. I tried to drown my troubles in alcohol. Shortly thereafter I even attempted suicide by slitting my wrists. When my father questioned me about what was troubling me, I responded that I was pregnant again. When he asked me what I was going to do, I responded that I was thinking about having an abortion. He inquired, "What is that?" I said, "I don't know. I haven't looked it up yet."

"Later, Weddington and Coffee presented the affidavit for my signature at Coffee's office. I told them that I trusted them and that I did not need to read the affidavit before I signed it. I never read the affidavit before signing it and do not, to this very day, know what is written in the affidavit. Both Weddington and Coffee were aware that I did not read the affidavit before I signed it. At no time did they tell me that I had to read it before they accepted my signature. I told them that I trusted them. We called ourselves 'the three musketeers.' I know now that is one place where I went wrong. I should have sat down and I should have read the affidavit. I may not have understood everything in the affidavit and I would have probably signed it anyway. I trusted the lawyers."

"My lawyers never discussed what an abortion is, other than to make the misrepresentation that "it's only tissue". I never understood that the child was already in existence. I never understood that the child was a complete separate human being. I was under the false impression that abortion somehow reversed the process and prevented the child from coming into existence. In the two to three years during the case no one, including my lawyers told me that an abortion is actually terminating the life of an actual human being. The courts never took any testimony about this, and I heard nothing which shed light on what abortion really was."

"In 1972, Sarah Weddington argued in the courts, presumptuously on my behalf, that women should be allowed to obtain a legal abortion. The courts did not ask whether I knew what I was asking for. The abortion decision that destroyed every state law protecting the rights of women and their unborn babies was based on a fundamental misrepresentation. I had never read the affidavit, and I did not know what an abortion was. Weddington and the other supporters of abortion used me and my circumstance to urge the courts to legalize abortion without any meaningful trial which addressed the humanity of the baby, and what abortion would do to women. At that time, I was a street person. I lived, worked, and panhandled out on the streets. My totally powerless circumstance made it easy for them to use me. My presence was a necessary evil. My real interests were not their concern."

"As the class action plaintiff in the most controversial U.S. Supreme Court case of the twentieth century, I only met with the attorneys twice. Once over pizza and beer, when I was told that my baby was only 'tissue' and another time at Coffee's office to sign the affidavit. I had no other personal contacts. [Ed. Norma may have had phone calls with Linda Coffee.] I was never invited into court. I never testified. I was never present before any court on any level, and I was never at any hearing on my case. The entire case was an abstraction. The facts about abortion were never heard. Totally excluded from every aspect and every issue of the case, I found out about the decision from the newspaper just like the rest of the country."

"In a way, my exclusion, and the exclusion of real meaningful findings of fact in *Roe v. Wade*, is symbolic of the way in which the women of the nation and their experiences with abortion have been ignored in a national debate by the abortion industry. The view that is presented is the view of what the abortion industry thinks is good for women. The reality of women's experiences is never presented."

"I never had an abortion and gave the baby up for adoption. It was only later in life that I was confronted with the reality of abortion. Being unskilled and uneducated, with alcohol and drug problems, finding and holding a job was always a problem for me. But with my notoriety from *Roe v. Wade*, abortion facilities, usually paying a dollar an hour more than minimum wage, were always willing to add "Jane Roe" to their ranks."

"In 1992, I began working in abortion facilities where I was always in control. I could either make a woman stay or help her leave. My duties were similar to those of a LVN or an RN, such as taking patients' blood pressure and pulse and administering oxygen, although I never took any statistics or temperatures. Basically, I would stand inside the procedure room, hold the women's hands, and say things to distract them by saying, 'What is the most exciting, or happiest period of your life?' Meanwhile, the abortionist was performing what is represented as a "painless" procedure and the women were digging their nails into me in an effort to endure the pain."

"I worked in several abortion facilities over the years. In fact, I even worked at two facilities at the same time. They were all the same with respect to the condition of the facilities and the "counseling" the women receive. One clinic where I worked in 1995 was typical: Light fixtures and plaster falling from the ceiling; rat droppings over the sinks; backed up sinks; and blood splattered on the walls. But the most distressing room in the facility was the "parts room". Aborted babies were stored here. There were dead babies and baby parts stacked like cordwood. Some of the babies made it into buckets and others did not, and because of its disgusting features, no one ever cleaned the room. The stench was horrible. Plastic bags full of baby parts that were swimming in blood were tied up, stored in the room, and picked up once a week. At another clinic, the dead babies were kept in a big white freezer full of dozens of jars, all full of baby parts, little tiny hands, feet, and faces visible through the jars, frozen in blood. The abortion clinic's personnel always referred to the dismembered babies as 'tissue.'"

"While all the facilities were much the same, the abortion doctors in the various clinics where I worked were very representative of abortionists in general. The abortionists I knew were usually of foreign descent with the perception that the lax abortion laws in the United States present a fertile money-making opportunity. One abortionist, in particular, would sometimes operate bare-chested, and sometimes shoeless with his shirt off, and earned a six-figure income. He did not have to worry about his bedside manner, learning to speak English, or building a clientele."

"While the manners of the abortionists and the uncleanliness of the facilities greatly shocked me, the lack of counseling provided the women was also a tragedy. Early in my abortion career, it became evident that the 'counselors' and the abortionists were there for only one reason – to sell abortions. The extent of the abortionists' counseling was, 'Do you want an abortion'? Ok, you sign here and we give you abortion." Then he would direct me, 'You go get me another one.' There was nothing more. There was never an explanation of the procedure. No one even explained to the mother that the child already existed and the life of a human was being terminated. No one ever explained that there were options to abortion, that financial help was available, or that the child was unique and irreplaceable. No one ever explained that there were psychological and physical risks of harm to the mother. There was never time for the mother to reflect or to consult with anyone who could offer her help or an alternative. There was no informed consent. In my opinion, the only thing the abortion doctors and clinics cared about was making money. No abortion clinic cared about the women involved. As far as I could tell, every woman had the name of Jane Roe."

"Typically, most of the women would cry as soon as the suction machine was shut off, or, at some point. Sometimes, I thought that they realized what had been done to their babies. Once, I heard a woman call her mother and say, 'I just killed my baby. I'm so glad you never killed me!'"

"The doctors always hid the truth from the mothers. I would say about 80 percent of the women would try to look down during the abortion and try to see what was happening. This is the reason the doctors would start with the scalpel: to make sure there was just blood and torn up 'tissue' for the women to see. Specifically, I remember one woman who came in for an abortion, a pretty, sweet young woman about eighteen years old, with a teddy bear. During the procedure she looked down and saw the baby's hand fall into the doctor's hand. She gasped and passed out. When she awoke and asked about what she saw, I lied to her and told her it didn't happen. But she insisted that she had seen part of her baby. A few weeks later, when she returned for her follow-up exam, she was a changed person: her sweetness had died and had been replaced with an indescribable hardness. I could not look her in the eye.

It took quite a few beers that night to make that particular day go away."

"In all of the clinics where I worked, the employees were forbidden to say anything that might talk the mother out of an abortion. While the abortionists' counseling was non-existent, my counseling technique gradually became different depending on my mood and the stage of my career. The experience of abortion began to take its toll on me. In later years, I would sometimes take all the instruments that were used in an abortion procedure and purposely leave a little of the blood on some the instruments. Laying the instruments out on the little table in front of the woman, I would tell her, 'This is the first instrument that is going to be inserted into your vaginal area.' It would have just had a little smudge of blood, and I thought it was very dramatic. In retrospect, I don't even know why I was doing these things. It was as if I was trying to talk these women out of the abortion – something we were forbidden to do."
"In other counseling sessions, I would demonstrate the position and warn her that the instruments were sharp, and that if she moved the doctor might slip, and puncture her uterus, and she would bleed to death. In other situations, when a woman asked me how much it cost, I asked her in response how much she wanted to pay to kill her baby. She replied, 'They told me it wasn't a baby.' I responded, 'What do you think it is inside you, a fish?' Other times, I would comfort them after the abortion by saying, 'It wasn't a baby. It was only a missed period.' Sometimes when I managed to make the women unsure, I would offer to refund their money except for the ultrasound."

"After I saw all the deception going on in the abortion facilities, and after all the things that my supervisors told me to tell the women, I became very angry. I saw women being lied to, openly, and I was part of it. There's no telling how many children I helped kill while their mothers dug their nails into me and listened to my warning, 'Whatever you do, don't move!' Because I was drunk or stoned much of the time, I was able to continue this work for a long time, probably much longer than most clinic workers. It is a high turnover job, because of the true nature of the business. The abortion business is an inherently dehumanizing one. A person has to let her heart and soul die or go numb to stay in practice. The clinic workers suffer, the women suffer, and the babies die. I can assure this Court that the interest of these mothers is not a concern of abortion providers. I obviously advocated legalized abortion for many years following *Roe v. Wade*. But working in the abortion clinics forced me to accept what abortion really is: It is a violent act which kills human beings and destroys the peace and the real interests of the mothers involved.

Signed and Sworn to by Norma McCorvey, the former *Roe* of *Roe v. Wade*, June 11, 2003.

[In her Rule 60 Motion to Reverse *Roe v. Wade*, eventually filed with the U.S. Supreme Court in *McCorvey v. Hill*, 385 F.3d 846 (5th Cir. 2004)(cert. denied)(2005). The Supreme Court declined to hear Norma's appeal in February 2005. They did not rule against her on the merits. They simply declined to take her case, which action has no precedential power and left her free to pursue reversal by other means. She was crushed, but grateful that her position that Roe should be reversed was officially on file at the Court. Her conscience could be clear. She continued to speak publicly against abortion for many years. Comments about her final stage of life follow later.]

## Norma's Last Days

[As Norma got older her heavy smoking years caught up with her health wise. Her final days were spent in a nursing home in Katy, Texas where she was cared for by their staff and her daughter Melissa and her family. Norma died in 2017. Before she died, I spoke with her by phone several times. We had stopped representing her by then. After the Supreme Court declined to hear her case, there was not much to do legally but wait for more opportunity and a more open-minded Court. But knowing she was ill and getting worse, I called her a time or two to reminisce and see how things were going.

Norma told me that she was happy and safe in her facility. She also said she was doing a prolife documentary on her life with a team from England and that they were paying her for her story. I was happy for her. It is customary if someone is doing a film or documentary about you that they pay you for your rights and for your time. Norma and I were glad that her conversion to the cause of Christ and the prolife side would get one more airing. In what became our final call she also thanked me for representing her at no charge all those years. She thanked me for trying and was glad that we had taken her case back to the Court, even if they did not want to listen at that time.

When she died in 2017, I was asked to speak at the funeral. The arrangements were made by Father Frank Pavone, Norma's friend, and the one who led her conversion to the Catholic faith. Later, three years after she died, and while the Louisiana Hospital admitting privileges case was before the Supreme Court that could have reversed *Roe*, a new documentary came out after Norma could no longer defend herself or tell her story. The documentary was timed for maximum political effect. It was prepared by people with a very definite pro-choice bias. Here is my press release about the documentary.

## Lawyer for Norma McCorvey (Jane Roe of *Roe v. Wade*): "Don't Trust the FX Documentary"

In the leaked excerpts of the upcoming FX Documentary "AKA Jane Roe," liberal, pro-abortion activist and film producers attempt to destroy the memory of Norma McCorvey, more commonly known as Jane Roe of *Roe v. Wade*.

Allan Parker, the founder and president of The Justice Foundation, represented Norma McCorvey from 2000 to 2005 in her legal efforts to reverse her own case. With news reports of the upcoming documentary, Mr. Parker has released the following statement:

**"In view of my many conversations with Norma and considering the sworn testimony she provided to the Supreme Court, I believe the producers of the newly-released FX documentary 'AKA Jane Roe' paid Norma, befriended her and then betrayed her. This documentary cannot be trusted and the perception it attempts to create around my friend and former client, Norma, is probably false in my opinion."**

###

Here are the most important facts:

- Norma's sworn testimony provided to the Supreme Court details her efforts to reverse *Roe v. Wade*.
- **Norma changed her mind from being pro-abortion to being pro-life after working in the abortion industry.** The actual reality of the callous disregard for women led her to change her mind on abortion.
- **Once she became pro-life, Norma fought with all of the power and effort she could muster to reverse *Roe v. Wade*, including asking the Supreme Court to hear her case again.** McCorvey's arguments in her Rule 60 Motion which she filed have still not been ruled on by the Court to this day.

- Norma McCorvey loved *Operation Outcry*, the women who had been injured by abortion and those that helped Norma collect testimonies of women injured by abortion.
- Every year on the anniversary of *Roe v. Wade*, she felt the grief, sorrow and burden of another million babies killed in America. Even though she knew she was forgiven, she still felt legally responsible for the deaths. She felt used and abused by the legal system, including her lawyers and the Supreme Court.

After viewing the video, it is still hard to know what to think or what is true without all the evidence. The documentarian's took hours and hours of film and paid Norma (the same action for which they accused others of exploiting her) and selective editing can make anyone appear to take views opposite to their true positions. I have seen such editing many times.

Even Norma's pro-abortion biographer, who was critical of Norma in many ways, wrote a book called "The Family Roe" in which he came out after her death and criticized the documentaries' claim that Norma had been paid to change sides from pro-death to pro-life by saying:

"The film would also produce one more {lie}, a big one that made national news. As a Times headline put it: '*Roe v. Wade* Plaintiff Was Paid to Switch Sides, Documentary Says:'... Norma had not, in fact, been paid to become pro-life. She'd simply been paid to give speeches after her conversion-just as she'd been paid to speak before it. Despite the headlines she's said nothing to the contrary." Prager, Joshua, "The Family Roe," WW Norton and Co., 2021, p. 469.

As to her Christianity I believe she was sincere, but not a deep Christian thinker. The film showed a sign on her nursing home bedroom wall that says: "Jesus is my boyfriend." That was kind of a picture of Norma. Not what every Christian would put on the wall, but Jesus loved her and she loved him. She had confessed her sins in public and private many times. She felt crushing guilt every year around the anniversary of *Roe* as another million babies were killed. It was enough for the thief on the cross who confessed his sins and who said to Jesus: "Remember me when you enter your kingdom." And Jesus replied: "You will be with me this day in paradise."

# CHAPTER FOUR

# Who is Sandra Cano? And Why Does "Mary Doe" Want to Overturn *Doe v. Bolton?*

Excerpted from
SUPREME DECEPTION
By Sybil Lash, Sandra's friend
Copyright © 2002 by Sybil J. Lash

## Early Departure

It's dark just before 5:00 A.M. The alarm is turned off before it has the opportunity to sound. Every time Sandra and I make another trip, I am awakened every hour by the concern of meeting our travel schedule.

Sandra and I are going to tell her story again. It's about abortion. It's about lies and being used. It means telling the personal pain of Sandra's life. But babies are dying, and women are still victims, so I feel my way through the dark house. I have left Sandra's phone number downstairs again.

Sandra Cano has become a good friend and someone that I deeply admire. She is the real "Mary Doe" of *Doe v. Bolton*, the companion case to *Roe v. Wade*, the two United States Supreme Court decisions that legalized abortion. Both decisions were announced the same day, yet most Americans don't even know about *Doe v. Bolton*.

Sandra's life is dedicated to telling the truth about the lies and deceptions involved in the *Doe v. Bolton* case, even though she supposedly "won". Her fight means Sandra must guard her privacy, living in fear for her family's safety. No phone book contains her name. Only those she trusts know her address. She was once shot at while holding her grandchild on her front porch. She has had her car vandalized because of her stand. She shuns the spotlight and lives an underground type existence.

Today she will make one more dreaded airline trip to tell a story she is convinced must be told. And as usual, she has asked for my help. That's why I stumble my way to my kitchen at 5:00 A.M. to call her.

Sandra's case changed the face of United States law. While *Roe v. Wade* left the states some authority to prohibit abortion in the last three months of pregnancy, *Doe v. Bolton* effectively removed that authority by its broad definition of "health". Partial birth abortions are based on *Doe v. Bolton*. Yet Sandra never wanted an abortion. All she wanted was legal help to get a divorce and regain custody of her two oldest children. Sandra was used and misled. She was misrepresented before the highest court in the United States. Why did this happen? Sandra believes her lawyer wanted someone to fit her own plans. Now all Sandra wants to do is set the record straight.

Many have asked, "Who is the woman named on this case? Is she a strong feminist? Is she driven to achieve abortion rights? Has she become rich and famous?" I've heard these questions and others like them so many times, and the answer is simply, "No."

Sandra is an uncomplicated person. She doesn't enjoy notoriety. She wishes that she could avoid the controversy her story stirs up. All she wants to do is get her story out, right the wrong her case has caused, and then go home and continue to raise her "special needs" grandsons.

Sandra's case helped divide this nation into two camps: "pro-life," or those against abortion; and "pro-choice," those wanting abortion to be legal. While many abortion supporters claim they only want to spare women from the burden of an unwanted pregnancy, it is a fact that eliminating the unborn has provided to be a very profitable endeavor. On the other side of this chasm rests close to forty million children in the U.S. alone who were never given the right to life. And there are so many women who underwent abortions and now struggle with feeling they were pressured and used at the most vulnerable time in their lives. These women suffer emotionally and physically, yet they have no protection or recourse under the law regarding the misinformation, physical pain, emotional suffering, and botched procedures that have left many ill and even sterile, because of *Roe v. Wade* and *Doe v. Bolton.*

Sandra suffers. She knows all too well that these procedures are allowed because of a court case that supposedly represented her. But the case was a lie. Sandra never wanted an abortion. She was used because she was too poor, too desperate to do anything but trust her lawyer. So now Sandra fights the only way she knows how, by opening the private areas of her life over and over again as she speaks to groups willing to consider the truth about her case.

I go downstairs without turning a light, shuffling sleepily through our house feeling my way into the dark kitchen. The dull light over the stove blinds me as I dial. He answers. I never know how much of what I say he understands. The only word he says is "Sandra". She is given the phone. She is already awake. She always is before one of our trips. I assure Sandra that I'll pick her up in an hour. Then I paddle off quietly to shower, dress, and pack.

The dogs have taken my spot on the bed and are all settled in. Bear, our Golden Retriever, has her head on my pillow and little Auggie is on his back with all four feet in the air sound asleep next to my husband. Bryan understands that I have to help her. When I first told him of Sandra's plight, he looked at me across the kitchen table and simply said, "Alright Sybil, we'll help her." He has been totally supportive of our commitment to Sandra. He never questions a trip and is my greatest source of encouragement when I get frustrated or discouraged by the lack of action on Sandra's behalf.

## Sharing Her Story

As the shower drags me awake, I recall the first time Sandra told me her story. She has been trying to get the world to listen to that same story for over a quarter of a century. When she first told me her story, she was nervous about the old concerns: of not being believed, being considered stupid that such events could go on without her knowledge. Because of these concerns, the facts came out in a random order. At the first meeting she brought a friend who just sat there silently, but Sandra felt more confident with this woman in the room.

The second time I heard the story was a few weeks later, Sandra just talked and again there was no timeline. The events of her life were related running from the past to present and back again. When I sat down with my notes there was one overwhelming constant, the facts never changed. No matter how disturbed the timeline was, the facts remained the same. She has written judges and telephoned anyone she thought might remotely help her. I admire her tenacity. While I dry off and dress, I can't help but wonder if other people would continue on and not give up in the face of what Sandra has encountered. I finish packing, slip from the house, get in my car and drive into the early morning fog.

The eldest of six children, Sandra grew up poor in Atlanta. Her early life began to build the desperation that caused her to become the vulnerable centerpiece in *Doe v. Bolton.* Because of financial problems, Sandra's family lived with grandparents who suffered numerous infirmities. Sandra's mother was sometimes overcome by the stress of the family's circumstances. Being the eldest child, Sandra became the focus of that frustration and stress. Her mother's experience of being overwhelmed by her circumstances and her difficulty in coming to grips with that frustration set a pattern for Sandra's life. Throughout those early years, Sandra's attempts to alleviate her mother's suffering filled her childhood.

School proved unbearable for Sandra. She was poor, overweight, and suffered from Bell's palsy, a condition that often left half her face paralyzed and drooping. To avoid the ridicule she faced each day, Sandra finally dropped out of school in the ninth grade. Her mother tried to force Sandra to return to school, once even breaking a broom handle across her daughter's back as the two argued in the front yard as the bus arrived. But Sandra's formal education had ended.

Within the next few years Sandra married the first man she ever kissed. On their third date, Joel asked Sandra to go meet his grandmother. Sandra's parents thought she was traveling a distance of fifteen miles from Atlanta. Instead, they received their daughter's call when she arrived in Oklahoma many hours later. Outraged, they ordered Sandra home with the threat of having Joel arrested. When the pair quickly returned, Sandra's parents first beat her with a belt, then drove the couple to Centre, Alabama, for a quick marriage ceremony. It was a matter of family honor. . . .

Then when her first child was only a few months old, Sandra's father died unexpectedly. To Sandra's disbelief, her mother remarried only three weeks later to a stepfather who made it quite clear he did not want Sandra and her family in his life. She was devastated in a way I can barely grasp. The only security she had ever known was gone.

How did it feel to be that vulnerable? I think about those days as I drive down Interstate 85.

## Getting the Records

The car is always a safe haven on a cold morning. It carries me to her modest home. I'm a little uneasy in this part of town and am always grateful when Sandra's new husband walks her to the car. He makes her feel a little more secure and a little less alone as he carries her suitcase out of the house.

Sandra will miss the comfort of her routine and the two "special needs" grandchildren she is raising. She has promised to bring them a gift. Preparations for a trip are so involved for her. She has to stock everything they will need during her absence because her husband doesn't drive and the children make our leaving emotionally stressful for Sandra.

We are quiet as the car travels on. I'm not sure what Sandra is thinking. As for me, I think about the role I play in Sandra's life.

I am not Sandra's manager. I am her friend. I help when she travels and assist her as she shares the truth about her involvement in the abortion controversy. Sandra and I came together from totally different directions. My life's work, after being wife and mother, developed as a public advocate for the causes my family and I believe in so deeply. I am an activist. Sandra is a victim. Our strong friendship has taken us much farther. Now when Sandra goes out to speak, I travel with her and help her present her story in a way that keeps the details chronologically correct and the focus on the main points she wants to communicate. But I have to smile at any suggestion I could ever put words in Sandra's mouth. She will not allow anyone to distort or change the facts she works so hard to tell. I may help Sandra speak, but no one speaks for Sandra.

Sandra's audiences include widely diverse groups such as legal workers, political activists, and church congregations, often combined together. For many years following the 1973 *Doe v. Bolton* decision, Sandra was ignored because she only had her word to dispute her lawyer's side of the story. Then in 1988, Sandra got her court records unsealed. She went to the courthouse where they were kept and asked the clerk how to go about finding out about her case. Only then did Sandra finally know how she was used and deceived when she was most vulnerable.

For a short time afterward, Sandra was the focus of various media. She was interviewed in newspapers and on television. She traveled to other states to tell her story. Surely, she thought, if people knew the truth about her case, they could help get this legal misrepresentation resolved. In the end, nothing changed, except that Sandra began to suffer as the threats and, later, the violence against her began.

It constantly amazes me that the popularity of an issue seems to depend more on such things as good marketing and "political correctness" rather than facts. If Sandra's situation has happened to someone with money or prestige, the wrong would have been righted over a quarter of a century ago. But at that time Sandra was naive, ignorant, and vulnerable, with neither the resources nor the outright ability to get the truth out.

## How She is Seen

We arrive at the airport ninety minutes ahead of flight time. We've learned the hard way that we need the extra time. I surprise Sandra with a new pair of comfortable shoes, a gift from a friend. It would be out of the question for Sandra to spend enough on herself for a new pair of shoes. She is raising two grandsons who have special needs, and her husband is a day laborer. The shoes fit well. She is grateful for them. Without the welcome gift on her feet, she would be walking the long way to the gate in pain, but without complaint. Eventually, I'd know by her limp that she was in pain. That is just the way she is.

Once we were late for a flight and the only parking spot I could find was quite a distance from the terminal. As we scurried along, dragging our small suitcases behind us, we spotted an abandoned wheelchair. Sitting Sandra in it, I piled both suitcases in her lap and pushed as fast as I could. One wheel rubbed against Sandra's leg, and she finally asked me to slow down. We laughed and laughed at the sight we must have presented. We made the flight but learned we must allot more time. Lessons learned.

Today, as usual, people stare at Sandra as we hurry through the airport. She is heavy and I watch as some passing people turn on her with stares, whispered comments, half-hidden laughs and looks of disgust. I hope Sandra doesn't notice. Travel is difficult enough for her. She doesn't need to be made to feel any more uncomfortable than she already is. Sandra refuses to respond to the looks, except to apologize to me. "Oh, Lord," she gasps as she gets very winded at our pace and becomes flushed. "I must embarrass you."

Reaching our gate, we show our drivers licenses for identification. This is the only reason Sandra travels under her own name. Otherwise, she fears pro-choice activists will find her again. She refused to stop speaking out when her car was vandalized with painted graffiti and, when she faced threats and name-calling. It was only after she was shot at with her grandson in her arms that she realized the danger.

Once we are seated at the gate Sandra begins to look for the pilot to arrive and board the plane. She prefers the older ones; the more experienced the better. If a younger pilot boards our plane, she'll look at me nervously. She also looks to see if the pilots appear well rested. I'm not sure how this is all judged, but I know from her countenance how her judgment goes.

It's too bad the judges in Sandra's case didn't apply the same scrutiny to the evidence and facts presented in her court hearings. Things could have turned out differently, and we probably wouldn't be sitting in this airport, waiting for our boarding call to begin.

Our seat numbers are called and we make the slow walk down the ramp to the plane's forward door. We try to stay to one side as business travelers pass us as they adhere to their busy schedules. To them air travel is part of everyday life. To us it is an endeavor packed with challenges.

Our assigned seats are halfway down the plane. As we enter, we quietly request a seat extension for Sandra. The regular seat belts are just too uncomfortable for her. As we make our way down the aisle, I watch the faces of some passengers as they see us coming, the eyes that plead, "Please don't sit in my row," and the look of total relief as we pass on by them. Sandra and I usually joke about their reactions. Sandra never judges them and is always relieved when our seating doesn't interfere with another passenger's space.

We finally arrive at our row, where we have the window and middle seats. Sandra likes the window to make it easier to sleep but she never requests it. Only after I have insisted that I have no preference does she choose her seat. After the flight attendant goes over safety features, Sandra is handed the demonstrator seat belt for her seat extension. The plane finally rolls along the runway, and after all the rush we begin to relax. We have made the flight.

Speaking will be difficult for Sandra this time, and I'm glad as she nods off for a short nap. She has been battling bronchitis for the last few days and has not slept well these past nights. She hates traveling, between being away from the grandchildren and the stress of telling her story, she's exhausted. Adding illness to her thoughts that she sounds and looks like a hillbilly means that today's trip is an especially uncomfortable one.

And then Sandra worries about her husband. He just doesn't understand her intensity about this issue. He wants her to stay home and be with the children. He resents being sole caretaker while she is away. He also becomes jealous and worries out loud that these trips may lead her to finding some other man. She and I share our disbelief at such an idea. Hurting someone else is the last possible thing on Sandra's mind. Besides, our time is always so limited on these trips even for the people we are supposed to meet. All we ever seem to do is run from one place to the next, from the car to the airport gate, to the plane, to the hotel, to the meeting, back to the hotel, to the airport, to the plane, back home.

Sandra would never purposely break a promise, yet alone a marriage vow, without justification. Sandra never accepts any speaking fees, only reimbursement for travel expenses. The only income her family has is from a small disability check and her husband's day labor wages, but a recent injury has kept him from working. Sandra's life of financial difficulty continues today.

But money is not her motivation. Sandra's worst fear is that she would hurt anyone. Though she hates to leave her family, even for short times, she does it because she knows so many women have been hurt because of her court case. Sandra was used to make abortions legal by being misrepresented before the highest court in America.

The plane levels off and the little drink cart makes its appearance. As the flight attendant works her way down the aisle dispensing drinks and peanuts, Sandra is staring at her. The flight attendant notices and Sandra is concerned that the woman will wonder why. The flight attendant gets to our row and Sandra wants the woman to know that her airplane earrings are what captured Sandra's attention. In that moment I know that Sandra notices the stares she receives and that those stares hurt. But she would never want anyone else hurt in that way, so she explains to the flight attendant why the stare. It would be a much better world, if what we are as a person on the inside, mattered more than how we look on the outside. It would be a much nobler goal to fine-tune one's character instead of one's waistline.

We get our drinks and open our worn file folder to review what we'll address at the upcoming meeting. She'll be tired this time, making the timeline of events blur in her presentation. That's where I come in, as her friend and helper. After a brief introduction Sandra and I will step to the podium. I'll ask her questions, which she will answer. This is Sandra's favorite format. Her audience will get to see Sandra's personality as well as hear her story, and hopefully they will come away admiring her as much as I do.

## The Affidavit

Even after all our time together, I am still amazed that in the American judicial system a case like Sandra's can get as far as the U.S. Supreme Court without the plaintiff being properly represented or identified. For the thousandth time I ask myself how the Supreme Court can decide a case where facts are misrepresented or not presented at all, how an individual's circumstances could be used to change standing law when that change had nothing to do with what the plaintiff originally sought.

When Sandra became pregnant with her third child, she knew clearly that she could not depend on her first husband or her family for support, financially or emotionally. Wanting her child to have a better life, she made the heart-wrenching decision to give up her child for adoption. When she became pregnant with her fourth child, her stepfather announced he had endured enough. He then gave inaccurate information to authorities to have Sandra's two oldest children placed in foster care. Sandra was frantic and desperate.

She went to Atlanta Legal Aid asking for help. She wanted to obtain a divorce from her child-molesting husband and to regain custody of her children from foster care. There she was introduced to Margie Pitts Hames, an attorney who led Sandra to believe she would work hard to achieve her divorce and regain her children. Little did Sandra know that Pitts Hames was planning a major woman's issue case, an attempt to legalize abortion.

Sandra believes Pitts Hames was looking for someone desperate enough not to ask questions, someone who probably wouldn't understand the technical legal jargon her paperwork would involve. She planned to hide her true intentions by promoting the excuse she needed to keep her plaintiff's identity a secret.

Sandra was so relieved to finally have some capable authority figure say she would help her. She trusted her attorney and signed every paper Pitts Hames put in front of her without question. She approved anything to help speed her case, get her divorce, and regain her children. To Sandra's surprise, her mother began working with the attorney, and as her family began to accept her once again Sandra grew even more trusting. She believed she would win her divorce and get her babies back soon. When someone is desperate enough, they are vulnerable to people who promise a solution to their problems, individuals who portray themselves as powerful trustworthy figures. I can't help but wonder how many others have been used as Sandra was.

Sandra insists that no one, at any time, went over the contents of the attorney's papers with her. Records show she never once testified in court. She remains amazed that no official of any court ever asked her face-to-face what the case was about. If they had, she would not have carried this burden for over a quarter of a century.

During one conversation with Pitts Hames, Sandra was surprised when she was briefly asked about her stand on abortion. Sandra was confused on why such a question would come up in a case about divorce and child custody. Sandra gave what she thought was a reasonable answer that would pass over what she saw as an unrelated topic. Sandra said that she did not believe in abortion for herself, but she couldn't say for anyone else. To Sandra's relief, the matter was apparently passed over. In fact, Sandra's sister has stated that at that particular time Sandra didn't even know what an abortion actually was. Today, Sandra believes that the lawyer was trying to get her to volunteer words that could be used to benefit the arguments for abortion.

In the legal hearings that followed, Sandra appeared in a courtroom only one time, as part of a group of pregnant women who remained seated and silent. She was never identified or singled out in any way. In fact, the only evidence filed in the case that supposedly came from Sandra was an affidavit signed May 5, 1970. That affidavit will be addressed during Sandra's presentation when she speaks tonight. This is how that affidavit describes Sandra:

"I am presently pregnant with my fourth child and am very disturbed at the thought of carrying another child, as I feel I cannot care for the child properly. I am very nervous and upset at the thought of raising another baby. I cannot cope with the responsibility of caring for another child. It drives me almost crazy to think about it."

"I have two children in a foster home because I was unable to care for them. I adopted out a third child last year. I feel I cannot love another baby and I am depressed all the time thinking about my pregnancy. I do not want another baby."

"I have been a patient at Central State Hospital in Milledgeville (Georgia) and I am afraid I will end up there again because I am so nervous over being pregnant. My health is poor and the thought of carrying another child for nine months and having to give it up again makes me feel like crying all the time. I know if I had to give another baby away I would end up in Milledgeville for sure. I understand an abortion is a dangerous thing and that there are risks involved in performing an abortion, even under the best of circumstances. Knowing all these risks and problems, I still desire an abortion."

"I feel that after this abortion is performed that I do not want any more children. I desire to be sterilized, in any manner the Doctor sees fit, at the same time as the abortion is performed."

Sandra refutes this affidavit point-for-point in nine specific parts:

(1) Sandra was not, "nervous and upset at the thought of raising another baby." That statement is simply a lie. Sandra was nervous and upset at having to live with a convicted child molester. She was nervous and upset about not knowing how her babies in foster care were doing or who was watching them. She even worried about simple things like whether or not the foster caregiver remembered how her children liked to be put to bed. The affidavit begins with a lie and simply continues.

(2) The affidavit states that she, "cannot cope with the responsibility of caring for another child. It drives me almost crazy to think about it." As Sandra says, this is an outright lie. Sandra always asks me to consider why she sought out a lawyer to get her children out of foster care and returned to her if she could not cope with the responsibility of caring for her own children. When the time came to place her next children up for adoption, she didn't go crazy. She made a difficult decision based on what she believed was best for her children.

(3) The affidavit continues by stating, "I have two children in a foster home because I was unable to care for them." The

only reason Sandra's children were in foster care was due to information furnished to authorities by Sandra's stepfather, who had made it well known he did not want either Sandra or her children around. The affidavit gives the impression that Sandra willingly put her children in foster care, which is compounding the lie.

(4) The same statement stresses that Sandra, "was unable to care for" her children. Again, this is simply not true. These words have hurt Sandra the most. At the time her children were taken from her Sandra was gainfully employed. She has never been on drugs or abused alcohol. She has always tried to be the best example she could be to her children, regardless of the circumstances. Her life has been one long sacrifice for others.

(5) Another affidavit statement says, "I have been a patient in Central State Hospital in Milledgeville." This is factually true but very misleading. Central State is a mental hospital. Sandra was there for a few days to be observed. She has never been readmitted. The misinformation given to the hospital, which led to Sandra's observation, came from her stepfather, the same person who had her children placed in foster care.

(6) The affidavit supposedly quotes Sandra as saying, "I know if I had to give another baby away, I would end up in Milledgeville for sure." Sandra did place this baby for adoption. It was heart-wrenching and difficult, but Sandra wanted to do what was best for her child. And for the record she did not wind up in a mental institution.

(7) The affidavit states that, "I know an abortion is a danger- ous thing and that there are risks involved in performing an abortion, even under the best of circumstances." It is an absolute lie to say Sandra knew such things at that time. Sandra was never told about the effects of an abortion at

any time throughout the legal process, yet alone that her case was about abortion. In fact, it seems ironic that such a statement was ever included in the argument for abortion, since the mental and physical risks of abortion are not told to women. They are not even told of the medical or physiological risk, e.g., breast cancer or post abortion syndrome. Special laws have had to be passed so that a woman can know the identity of the abortionist.

(8) The affidavit continues, "I desire to be sterilized." Again, the affidavit includes a lie. Sandra's attorney and her mother forced this decision, and it did happen. Sandra found herself alone in a hospital room after giving birth to her fourth child who was given up for adoption. Her husband was not around, being in trouble with the law again. At this most vulnerable time she was again pressured by people who wanted to control her life and use her circumstances for their own gain and was sterilized.

(9) Finally, the affidavit highlights the statement, "Knowing all these risks and problems, I still desire an abortion." This is the height of all the lies contained in the affidavit. Sandra's lawyers did try to arrange an abortion for her before the case was heard in an Atlanta federal court. Horrified at such a plan, Sandra fled to her husband's family in Oklahoma to avoid being forced to have an abortion. She only returned to the Atlanta area once she received assurances that she would not have to undergo an abortion.


Lies, lies and more lies! And Sandra pays the price of those lies each and every day.

Sandra never had an abortion. On November 7, 1970, Sandra gave birth to a baby girl and gave her up for adoption. As for Joel, he remained in trouble with the law as he kidnaped and molested children three times in six weeks towards the end of 1970. Joel was apprehended and pleaded guilty. On January 21, 1971, he was sent to prison and subsequently served ten years.

On May 17, 1971, Sandra's divorce was granted. She had been married for six years and the union produced four children. Joel died in November of 1988 at the age of 46.

## Lack of Facts

Our plane arrives and our host is waiting for us. We check into our hotel room and Sandra immediately heads for a long, hot, uninterrupted bath. I know of no one who enjoys this little ritual more than Sandra does, for this brief time she will be alone with no demands on her.

While she enjoys her private time, I think back to when I first read the transcript of the case's arguments presented before the U.S. Supreme Court. How can it be possible that someone wanting a divorce and the rescue of her children from foster care could be so misrepresented by a lawyer? Was the deception so easy that all that was needed was an affidavit included in a stack of papers Sandra signed in simple trust?

In oral arguments before the Supreme Court, Dorothy T. Beasley, representing the State of Georgia, made several statements that leap out from the transcript to even a non-lawyer like myself. They include:

"We know of no facts. There are no facts in this case. No established facts."

"It is not a complete divulgence of the facts surrounding her (plaintiff's) circumstances."

"We know of no facts about her at all."

And finally, "No interrogatories were answered, no proof was submitted."

Twice the justices asked if "Mary Doe" was a real person. Pitts Hames, responded, "Yes, your honor," and referred to the affidavit that Sandra points out was so full of lies. Dorothy T. Beasley, arguing on behalf of the baby, was asked the same question and her response was, "I don't know, we know no facts." And yet in spite of these statements, the court continued with the case.

## Pressure on Politicians

The only parallel that I can personally draw out is from my experience in the political arena. I have witnessed some politicians ignoring facts when it comes to legislation. Allow me to explain.

In my background I have some appreciation and understanding of the pressure put on those in the political arena. I have lobbied for five years and I served as a legislative aide for six years in my home state of Georgia. I was an aide to Representative Mitchell Kaye of the 37th House district. I got to watch closely how laws are introduced, debated and either passed or rejected. I was very fortunate to work for an intelligent and honest man. Representative Kaye always wanted facts to back up every opinion. He would listen to opposing views but, in the end, relied on the facts and the desires of his constituents to make a final decision. There are others I have encountered who are unwavering in their stand to defend and protect the Constitution of the United States. I do think that we need more men and women to run for political office who will carry out the intention of the Constitution to secure freedom and rights for the Sandras of this world, the vulnerable in our society.

They must be unyielding in their stand because great pressure is put upon them. Individuals and groups enter this arena with the sole objective of furthering their own causes and agendas. In a lot of instances, the omission of some facts or reporting one side of the issue is concerned fair game. Allow me to share this example:

Sandra and I are both residents and taxpayers of the State of Georgia. I am sorry to say that at the time of this writing, the political party that favors the death of children through abortion currently holds power. [As of 2002.]

For more than a decade a simple bill known as, "A Woman's Right to Know" has been introduced and reintroduced in the Georgia legislature. I have watched this bill closely for over ten years while pro-life individuals tried to get it out of committee. And even now, the bill continues to be reintroduced. It has never made it out of committee, has never been given the opportunity to be voted on by the General Assembly.

This simple bill that keeps being reintroduced in the Georgia legislature would require a woman's referring physician or the doctor scheduled to perform an abortion procedure on her to provide her with six basic items of information at least twenty-four hours before the abortion procedure took place. These items include:

(1) The name of the doctor performing the abortion.

(2) The medical risks associated with the particular abortion procedure the doctor plans to use.

(3) The probable gestational age of the unborn child.

(4) The medical risks associated with carrying the child to term instead of proceeding with the abortion procedure.

(5) The medical assistance benefits that may be available for prenatal care of the unborn child.

(6) The fact that the father is liable to assist in the support of the child.

Supporters cannot get this simple and basic law passed in Georgia even though seventeen other states have enacted this legislation.

The forces that work against such laws are truly amazing to watch. Opposition to such a law is openly led by paid lobbyists. They know when any such bill is going to be heard in committee before any "pro-life" supporters are informed.

When hearing meetings are scheduled, these opposition lobbyists are seated front and center in the hearing room. Their associates, those friendly to their cause, fill the rest of the room. At one such meeting there were only three "pro-lifers" able to make it into the hearing room. I know because I was one of them.

I don't know what the influence is that creates and supports such a system, but it has worked effectively for more than a decade. You have to acknowledge their ability to manipulate the political process, and "John Q. Public" back home never suspects a thing.

One-year post-abortive women came and lobbied the Georgia State Legislature in favor of "A Woman's Right to Know" legislation. They roamed the hallways of the state capitol and called on any senator or representative who they thought might listed to them. It was emotionally and physically draining for these women, but they didn't give up.

They begged for "A Woman's Right to Know". They explained the pain of living with making such a monumental decision with the little information given to women at abortion clinics now. They didn't want other women to suffer as they have suffered. But even with all their efforts, the bill was never brought out of committee to be voted upon.

You see, in a Georgia State legislature committee there is no mandatory-recorded vote on any issue considered. Legislators can go back to their home districts and lead people to believe anything they want, because there is no proof either for or against then.

The fact is the actions of some Georgia state legislators are really nothing more than dirty little secrets that stay behind the closed doors of committee rooms during final wrangling and decisions. Such a system allows a legislator to remain in good standing with abortion supporting forces in the capital city of Atlanta, (where the abortion industry is strong and active) yet return to their home districts throughout the state appearing as if they are a true "pro-family" elected official. They can run the roads back home presenting a "pro-family" image, then come to Atlanta and vote however the head of their political party tells them to vote so they can keep their prestige and power and take their share of "pork" back home.

Why would anyone be opposed to a bill that simply gives a woman about to undergo a serious medical procedure all the reasonable information she needs in order to make a complete and thorough decision? Make no mistake. If the governor or the lieutenant governor or the speaker of the house wanted such a bill to come out of committee, it would have years ago.

## The Justices' Response

As we dress for dinner, Sandra is nervous about her appearance. She gets "butterflies" about speaking and feels the anxiety of getting her message across. There isn't one element of speaking in public that she enjoys.

She looks in the mirror a final time, combs her hair again and gives it a final touch of hair spray.

We go to meet our host for dinner. Sandra and I are introduced to those sponsoring this event. They are kind, gentle and dedicated. They too are frustrated with the response to their efforts to get the truth out about abortion. The simple fact is that it is wrong to lie, to deceive and to manipulate women at any time, but especially when they are vulnerable. They are unwavering in their desire of "justice for all". Yet, they are ridiculed and mislabeled and their motives generalized to fit the stereotype of extremists and hate mongers. Hopefully our presence will encourage them to continue with their efforts to educate the general public that abortion scars women.

Sandra and I take our seat at the head table. Sandra carefully watches to see which fork to use. She is accustomed to simple fare and the place setting with its multiple forks and the 1000 people seated in front of us are intimidating. She endures the discomfort as she bares the undeserved guilt over her involvement in the court case, with a little shrug and a look in her eye that indicates, "I don't want to disappoint anybody."

After all, the decision of whether or not to allow the elimination of a woman's unborn child would be a huge load for anyone to carry. The court's decision determined whether Sandra would end up getting shot at or not. The justice's decision determined whether she would live in fear for the rest of her life. Their response would influence how people would judge Sandra sight unseen. Passions from both sides of the abortion issue would be focused on Sandra once they discovered who she really was.

But how did the courts consider Sandra personally? In the *Doe v. Bolton* case, the United States Supreme Court issued a ruling that I still have trouble comprehending. The court plainly said,

> "If the (original federal) court says the proffer of proof was unnecessary, then why do we need to be concerned about whether she (the plaintiff, "Mary Doe") is fictitious or a real person?"

In other words, the justices of the U.S. Supreme Court didn't care who Sandra was. She didn't matter in their rule of law. The truth about her case didn't matter to them. Her circumstances didn't matter. Desires didn't matter. Everything in the *Doe v. Bolton* decision was based on the lower court's record, throughout the process judges were continually told lies and then based their decisions on the lies they were fed.

It would be justice if they could experience what Sandra's life has become. It would be justice if they received the same treatment that she has endured all these years. *Doe v. Bolton* was supposed to be a class action suit about pregnant women, but Sandra was the only pregnant woman named in the suit (hidden as "Mary Doe"). The rest were health professionals, physicians, nurses, and counselors. All of them wanted abortion to be legal. All needed a desperate woman who would sign whatever papers were placed in front of her.

It didn't matter who she was or what she really wanted. It didn't matter to the U.S. Supreme Court if she was real or not. Sandra didn't matter. It didn't matter that she was just a poor woman asking for help in obtaining a divorce and regaining custody of her children.

When the Supreme Court ruling was announced Sandra was with her mother watching television. Her mother was ecstatic and told Sandra that she had changed the law. At that moment Sandra felt a great doom and weight come upon her shoulders. She still bears that guilt today.

I have seen how that weight has permeated every area of Sandra's life. I have seen her pain up close. As long as she is physically able, she'll continue to speak out until her name is no longer associated with the killing of the unborn.

It is time for us to speak. We are given a warm introduction. We make our way to the podium and adjust our two microphones. I encourage her under my breath and look her in the eye to make sure she is ready.

As we stand before the crowded banquet audience, I remind myself that I can never fully comprehend the pain or frustration Sandra has experienced. Although we have gone over and over exactly how this happened to her, a part of her will never understand. Sandra is afraid of the courts and believes the worst will happen if anything goes before a judge. She steadfastly believes the justice system works only for those with the most influence and money.

Sandra believes that others have found "Lady Justice" not only blind but also tone deaf and mute as far as their circumstances were concerned. Those vulnerable in our society too often watch from the sidelines while the rich and politically connected get the speedy trials and "special justice". Too often the winners are those who can hire the attorney that can best spin the truth and plant doubt. In Sandra's eyes, American Justice has become a debate club where justice and truth are not the primary goals, only winning the argument. The person with the most money hires the best defender and wins.

Even though she voices these thoughts she still believes with her whole heart that, eventually, the truth will stand, especially concerning her case. Otherwise, she wouldn't put herself through the ordeal of speaking tonight.

Sandra has an abiding faith in the power of Jesus Christ. The assurance of His love overshadows all other knowledge in her life. This great love sustains her and gives her strength. Her belief is basic but unshakable. She believes with her whole being that someday the right person will listen to her story and come forward to right this great wrong. She doesn't know when or where, but she knows this in all certainly. Until that time, we'll continue to accept speaking engagements and endure the discomfort of travel.

## The Absent Media

Everyone at this evening's banquet knows that no T.V. footage about this event will be seen on the nightly broadcast. Stories like ours are never considered important news. I have sadly learned from experience that in order to be promoted in today's media, an item has to be "politically correct," and those in control define what is and isn't politically correct. They do not believe our side of this controversial issue is worth hearing. Those who hold the power to "keep the public informed" will ignore Sandra's appearance.

I often watch news shows and read newspapers and news magazines that supposedly feature "investigative reporting". Isn't it funny how the percentage of blacks on death row is front-page news but the percentage of black children aborted is not considered "newsworthy"? Blacks in America number roughly 12 percent of the population but account for more that 35 percent of the abortions. In my home state of Georgia 54 percent of the abortions performed last year were on blacks by mostly white doctors. The vast majority of black political leaders in the state of Georgia and black voters belong to a political party that is committing genocide to their race. No one sees any contradiction and no one thinks that that is newsworthy.

Where are the experiences of post-abortive women reported? I've never seen that as a topic on a talk show, a television news magazine, or the headline of a supposedly "unbiased" investigative series. Both former workers from the abortion industry and women who have undergone abortions are more than willing to testify, to tell what they know. I have seen post-abortive women plead for someone, anyone who would listen to the truth of what happened to them. Some of the medical professionals who clean up the carnage are willing to speak. Why is this side of the abortion issue never covered by the media?

Only once have I experienced the frustration that Sandra lives with every day. I'll never forget that day, the day I learned that there is bias in the media. I realized there is a force that decides what is newsworthy and what is ignored depending on what is "politically correct".

The date was Thursday, January 22, 1998. Sandra and I were in Washington, D.C., to attend the annual March for Life, the massive "pro-life" rally held every year on the anniversary of the *Roe v. Wade* and *Doe v. Bolton* decisions. Nellie Gray and her volunteers have been staging this pro-life event every year since these decisions became law. She would not let the anniversary of this murderous decision pass without being remembered. Nellie and her volunteers work all year to plan, organize and orchestrate the dinner and the march.

While many American cities hold their own March for Life events, the central one in Washington, D.C. is a huge celebration for life. Families from all over the U.S. come every year, no matter what the weather or inconvenience. The children literally grow up with this event as part of their family history.

The 1998 program was very special, as it commemorated the 25th anniversary of the court decisions. Surely this time the media will listen, I kept telling myself. This time they will have to cover the story fairly. March for Life's 25th anniversary of *Roe v. Wade* and *Doe v. Bolton* was just too well planned, too big of a story for the media to ignore. There were hundreds of people at the Rose Dinner and thousands at the March for Life. This landmark event featured the three main people who have had more to do with abortion that anyone in the United States. Dr. Bernard Nathanson was there. Norma McCorvey was there. And Sandra was there. All scheduled to speak. All ready to say they were "pro-life".

You can't ignore someone like Dr. Nathanson who for years ran the largest abortion clinic in the nation, in New York City. It was open for business 364 days a year, only closing its door for one day every twelve months. Dr. Nathanson coined the phrase "pro-choice" and "a woman's right to choose". He was there when the statistics of how many women died from illegal abortions were falsified. They were deliberately embellished and presented before the United States Supreme Court as the truth. These made-up facts are part of the record of *Roe v. Wade*. But Dr. Nathanson could not live with the facts he came to know so well, the truth he could no longer deny. Not only did he stop performing abortions, Dr. Nathanson produced a powerful video entitled, "The Silent Scream" to show the world what a baby does as the abortion instruments approach the child in the womb. This video indisputably shows the baby realizes something is wrong and tries to get away from the invading object. It is not the peaceful end of the baby's life that woman have been led to believe. Dr. Nathanson was convinced that when Americans saw the video, they would realize what abortion really was. He has converted to Catholicism and was there that day to share his story.

Norma McCorvey, better known by her court case name, "Jane Roe" of *Roe v. Wade*, was present. Norma has also experienced a religious conversion and is now actively "pro-life", telling the world at every opportunity that she is convinced abortion is the termination of a unique and irreplaceable life. She too was not given complete information regarding her court case. She has started the ministry "Roe No More" and works tirelessly to get her story out. She was ready to share her experience, who better than the woman whose name is most associated with abortion.

The third person, of course, was Sandra Cano. "Mary Doe" of *Doe v. Bolton* would once again tell the world that she never believed in abortion and never had an abortion. She would explain that her attorney did not carry out Sandra's desires in the courtroom, and that her case was based on lies and deceit.

So, the 1998 March for Life has the three most publicly associated people concerning abortion there to firmly state their "pro-life" positions at the Rose Dinner the evening of the 25th anniversary of these monumental court decisions. Could there be a more perfect opportunity or better setting for the media to inform America about an important event filled with truth everyone needs to know so they can decide about such a divisive issue as abortion for themselves?

We believed this 25th anniversary event was so important that Sandra and I spent two nights away from home instead of our usual one. She worried about her grandchildren terribly, but Sandra was determined to support this special event in every way she could. And with our high expectations, we made sure we were in our room to watch the news, to judge the quantity of the coverage for ourselves.

But the lead stories on the major networks were not about the March for Life. None of their reporters covered the Rose Dinner speakers. As Sandra and I sat in our hotel room and switched to every channel, we did find two stories, over and over again. One dominated the news, and the other was the only coverage we could find related to the 25th anniversary of *Roe v. Wade* and *Doe v. Bolton*.

The main story was about Monica Lewinsky. The day we arrived for the March for Life event was the day the story broke about the White House intern sexually involved with the President of the United States. Well, you say, of course such a huge news story would overshadow an event that has taken place annually over the past twenty-five years. The only problem with such reasoning is that the media had not just found out about the problems with the presidential intern. The story had been ignored for months; some say for more than a year. Why was the decision made to broadcast the story on the 25th anniversary of the *Roe v. Wade* and *Doe v. Bolton* decisions? By doing so, the media was able to pigeonhole the March for Life event by claiming to have something bigger to cover instead.

As for the second story, the media showed Vice-President Al Gore across town attending the "pro-choice" dinner celebrating the 25th anniversary of legalized abortions. The "pro-choice" dinner was featured. The "pro-life" dinner, with its three highly visible speakers, was ignored. So much for objectivity by the media.

## The Attendees

Someday there should be a special place in our history books for the individuals who work so hard to produce events like the March for Life. You have to admire these people for going forward year after year and not giving up, especially when you consider the odds that are against them. These people continue in their fight to remind the world that "we are endowed by our Creator with certain inalienable rights," and that the first of these rights is the right of life.

After all, if the people influencing the politicians and the news controllers can make the world think that a life is of no value, then what is the next step? Is it too hard to carry that thought forward to where someone can argue that others may also not hold value to society? Those too sick, those too old, those in the wrong ethnic group, those too religious, or those not holding to the "right" religion? Who can determine when someone does not contribute enough to society, and should be denied to their right to life? It happens every day, in abortion clinics across America. "Pro-life" people are really fighting for all of us. Someday the world will see, but for now it is truly an uphill battle for these defenders of the unborn. After all some of their biggest opponents hold power in the media.

I look out over the crowd before us and wonder just who is listening to Sandra this time. Have they always been "pro-life" or are some seared by a personal abortion experience?

Abortion providers supply trained individuals who know just how to apply the proper pressure to get their desired result; another confused mentally manipulated woman; another aborted baby. The providers spread such lies as, "It's just like having your tonsils removed," or "It's no more than the cartilage in your ear," or "The fetus doesn't feel pain." Are those who have lived through this deception here for this meeting?

Some present claim to be pro-life Christians who vocally oppose abortion and speak against anyone involved in abortion procedures. But I know of some who didn't keep to their spoken convictions when their daughter became the victim of an unwanted pregnancy. They quickly and quietly had their daughters take advantage of the abortion procedures they speak against now. Hypocrisy can abound when an issue hits too close to home.

Will such a family live the rest of their lives holding onto the lie that, "If the neighbors don't find out, then it's as if the pregnancy never happened. Our family is pro-life, don't you dare tell anyone we took you to a clinic."? Betrayed by her own family, the woman is left to bear the loneliness, the guilt, and the regret. The child is never to be mentioned again and the woman has no one with whom to share her thoughts. Are such people here to listen to Sandra's story?

I see many men in the audience. Are any of them recalling a time when they forced a wife, a sister, a daughter, or a lover to have an abortion? This so-called "great feminist victory" has reduced the responsibility of fathers to a few hundred dollars and ride to a clinic. Some men actually claim to believe that such an offer somehow absolves them of their responsibility to both the woman and the child. His life goes on unaffected; the abortion is a quick fix to any pending financial or social responsibility. Sandra is about to start telling her story. Are those men listening?

Many women are present. How will Sandra's story affect them? Throughout America, especially inside abortion clinics, women are not told the risks of an abortion procedure, such as the increased chances of later miscarriages, breast cancer or sterility. Women are never told of the sensation they will experience when the tiny life they carry is removed. Later in life they describe the experience as an actual loss of part of themselves physically, mentally, and emotionally. They are never the same.

Are there women present who have had an abortion? If so, will Sandra's story dig up memories they have tried so hard to put behind them? What mind games must these women play in order to bear the consequences of their abortion?

So many women who have undergone abortions now routinely state that they are left with feelings of guilt, condemnation, and self-loathing. These women are haunted by thoughts like, "How could I not know it was a baby?" or "He didn't love me enough to want his child and stand by me." And then there is the mystery of what the child would have looked like and what he or she could have become. The ache of wanting to let the child know, "I loved you, and I still love you. I'm so sorry. Please forgive me."

Of course, not all women who have undergone an abortion experience these emotions. Some are in very deep denial. I believe, some would even destroy their "unwanted" born children if it were legal. They could strap them in a car and watch it roll in a lake or systematically drown them in their own bathroom or throw them in the trash once they are born. After all, isn't that what legalized abortion does, just before birth instead of after? Isn't it supposed to be a quick fix, a solution to a problem pregnancy, an unwanted life?

Abortion supporters claim their position provides the answer for such chilling statements as, "A pregnancy at this time would ruin your life." Or, "What about your career, your college degree? These are more important at this time." Or what about, "It would destroy your parents if they knew you'd gotten pregnant." And then there's, "This pregnancy can be taken care of quickly and quietly and no one will ever know. You can spare everyone if you just go forward with this procedure." As a result of following this logic, millions of women are carrying a pain so horrific and so penetrating that they dare not speak about abortion, lest the memories, fears and emotions overwhelm them. The secret remains a closed door in their mind and soul, and few want to open it.

Sandra shares the burden of these women. She blames herself for being used in the court proceedings that have allowed abortion to be declared legal. Sandra believes that her case made women fair game for the mental manipulation these women have endured. That's why she is here, to let them know she was used as they were. She never wanted her case to be a landmark anything, just a routine divorce.

## Deliberate Deception

Sandra and I begin by explaining why there are two of us behind the podium. The fact that Sandra is much more comfortable with a question-and-answer format. She doesn't worry about her thoughts rambling or about having to think too far ahead. We will be reviewing what we went over on the plane. If something is omitted or not covered with the proper detail we can go back over it. They will experience her personality more if she is relaxed. Our goal to have them appreciate Sandra for who she is and what she has been through.

We cover her humble childhood, her marriage, and the circumstances that caused her to go to Atlanta Legal Aid. We get to the Supreme Court case and I am deeply concerned that the audience will not grasp this information. Here is the proof that Sandra's facts never changed but her lawyer, Pitts Hames, told completely different versions of Sandra's actions. In the Supreme Court transcript Pitts Hames stated that:

> "She applied to the public hospital for an abortion, where she was eligible for free medical care. Her application there was denied. She later applied, through a private physician, to a private hospital abortion committee, where her abortion application was approved.

She stated that:

> "She did not obtain the abortion, however, because she did not have the cash to deposit and pay her hospital bill in advance."

The truth is far different. Quite simply, these events never occurred. Sandra never applied to the public hospital for an abortion. Her application was never denied because her application never existed. She never requested for a private physician to submit an abortion application on her behalf. These statements are a complete fabrication on Pitts Hames part to make her desire for abortion on demand legal. How do we know this?

Pitts Hames was betrayed by her own words. After Sandra got her records unsealed in 1988, interest in the story was directed not only to Sandra but to her attorney, Margie Pitts Hames, as well. Pitts Hames was interviewed and her version of events appeared in the Fulton Daily Report, a legal newspaper in Atlanta. There she revealed that an abortion had been scheduled for Sandra at a private hospital, Georgia Baptist. The cost of the procedure was taken care of for Sandra. "As for the hospital bill, Sandra's lawyers raised money to cover it." Also, according to the article, Dr. Donald Block volunteered to perform the abortion for free. This is the same doctor who delivered Sandra's first three children. He would eliminate the fourth at no charge.

The revealing thing about this recollection is that it contradicts the argument Pitts Hames made to the United States Supreme Court. Remember she stated before the justices that Sandra applied to a private hospital for an abortion and that the application for abortion was approved but she did not obtain the abortion, however, because she didn't have the cash to deposit and pay her hospital bill in advance. The truth of why Sandra didn't go ahead with the abortion is quite different than what the court was led to believe.

So, what did happen? Yes, an abortion was scheduled for Sandra. Without Sandra's will or consent, the lawyer and Sandra's mother had planned to eliminate the child. Sandra found out about the plan the night before she was to enter the hospital. She fled to Oklahoma by bus to save the life of her child.

Sandra believes that the Supreme Court was deliberately deceived. Things that Sandra had no knowledge of, and never consented to, were presented as actual events. There were two miscarriages of justice. The first was Dorothy T. Beasley's statements concerning the lack of evidence.

"We know of no facts about her at all."

"There are no facts in this case."

"It is not a complete divulgence of the facts surrounding her circumstances."

"We know no facts about her at all."

"No interrogatories were answered, no proof was submitted."

The second were the lies that were presented to the justices as truth. Once again, what Sandra wanted didn't matter. The true facts didn't matter. Sandra believes Pitts Hames had a goal and nothing would stand in her way. The tools used to accomplish this goal were lies and deception brought before the highest court in America.

## The Reason For Her Resolve

Near the end of Sandra's presentation is where she has the most difficulty emotionally. Sometimes she is unable to go on and I have to finish for her. When she first related her life's story to me, it was the only time she wept.

After her records were unsealed in 1988 there was much publicity that caused Sandra to be reunited with the daughter she had placed for adoption, the child who was the center of the Supreme Court action. Sandra took her daughter and grandchildren into her life and home.

Shortly afterwards, while standing on her front porch holding a grandchild in her arms, Sandra was shot at, the bullet coming close to striking both Sandra and the baby. Fearing for her life and the lives of her family, Sandra decided to give up public life and "go underground". She might have remained that way living in fear of being discovered again, and her story might have ended there. But Cory changed everything.

Sandra's newly found daughter gave birth to Cory on April 26, 1992, twenty-two years to the day after the filing of the *Doe v. Bolton* case. Cory was premature. According to his birth certificate, he was only 28 weeks old and 9 inches in length, weighing 9.4 ounces. Although he was a perfectly formed baby boy, his lungs were not developed enough to sustain life. Sandra and her daughter watched as Cory fought for every breath, he only lived a few hours.

Through those hours, the nurse on duty never referred to Cory as anything more than a "fetus". Cory was given no medical aid. He was simply allowed to die.

Sandra realized something that afternoon. Cory was considered nothing more than a "fetus" because of her Supreme Court case. And babies bigger than Cory were dying every day because of her case. Some are full term. In the procedure known as "partial birth abortion" the baby is delivered feet first and stabbed in the back of the head with scissors, the child's brain is suctioned out before the head leaves the mother. All this has happened because of Sandra's case, all because she was used and the facts were not important.

Has she become angry and bitter? No, she is Sandra. She tries to do the right thing and tries to please. At one point, she lived in an apartment where the residents were mostly Spanish speaking. Some were in this country legally and some illegally. Their children didn't know about Easter baskets, so she used $200 of her $900 disability check to buy them all Easter baskets. She is raising two grandchildren with this money and the funds were not discretionary by any means. She needed the money for her basic living expenses but wanted the apartment children to experience the joy of Easter. These children were not all planned. They weren't from two-parent households. Some don't even know their fathers. There isn't enough money for all these children's basic needs. None of these things mattered to Sandra. The only thing that mattered to Sandra was that they were children whom she wanted to show love and kindness. To have this unselfish, loving grandmother carry the responsibility of the killing of children is so unjust.

At this point in our presentation, Sandra sometimes becomes so overcome with emotion that I have to finish for her. But Cory set Sandra's resolve. His life, though brief, changed Sandra forever. No matter what, she will continue in her effort to have America know the truth.

## Connecting With The Hurting

We work together to complete Sandra's presentation. After we close and the master of ceremonies makes the usual remarks and comments, people come to speak with Sandra. Some clasp her hand and offer support. I once saw a woman remove her religious medal from her own neck to give to Sandra for comfort. Sandra was deeply moved. On the trip home she held the medal and marveled at the woman's thoughtfulness. Some come with tears in their eyes to offer sympathy that she was treated so unjustly by the courts. Some come to have their photo taken with her.

And then there are those at the edge of the crowd. I thought some of them might be with us this evening. And they are. It seems they always are. They come forward when the others have left. They are the women scarred by abortion. [See *Operation Outcry* Chapter.]

These women live with the fact that some people will never understand how they could have undergone such a procedure. They always expect to hear condemning comments such as, "How could you not know it was a baby?" or "Surely you must have known what you were going to do was wrong." They expect to be rejected by people who cannot comprehend the pressure that led to their vulnerability, so they wait for the others to leave first. Their actions that fateful day, when they were so desperate, remain unknown to others for fear of ridicule, and to keep their own self-loathing hidden.

They come forward quietly. They share what women aren't told before an abortion procedure. Once again, I hear them say things we've heard before in different cities.

"They never told me my baby would feel pain."

"They told me it was no more than the cartilage in my ear."

"They didn't tell me that my baby girl had brainwaves and fingerprints."

"They never told me of the sensation that I would feel when the life was removed from my body, or that the same feeling would engulf me with the same intensity every time the procedure was remembered."

"They never told me about the nightmares."

"They never told me of the depression that I would experience every year on the anniversary of that event."

"They never told me how hard the secret would be to carry."

"I cannot pretend that it never happened."

I hear those comments so often, as I stand beside Sandra. I hear their voices and hope in some way that we've made them feel less alone and given them the hope that in the future other women will not be treated as they were. Just as they judicial process manipulated Sandra; clinic personnel manipulated these women.

These women share so many of the same things. There's always the burden of the secret. Some anxiety of,

"The friend who took me to the clinic knows, but will she keep the secret?"

"They never told me how to tell my current husband. When you first meet a man, you don't tell him. Later, as you get to know him and realize you want to share your life, how do you tell him?"

"How do I tell my children? If they knew, would they ever see me in the same way again?"

"Will this one event that influences every other area of my life remain a secret?"

"They never told me at the clinic how complicated the "simple procedure" makes your life."

Some of these women tell us they have even asked women to go with them while they tell their husband that they are post-abortive, because they just couldn't face him alone. I've yet to hear a "happy" story about abortion. I have yet to hear the clinics give a response that has satisfied these women's tortured souls.

On average it takes two years of counseling for a post-abortive woman to come out of such a tormented life. That's two years of struggling and dealing with the results of an abortion procedure after years of denial. [Some women are getting healed more quickly today with more healing resources available. Each woman is different.]

Post-abortive women regularly deny the connection between eating disorders and abortion, between a promiscuous lifestyle and abortion, between attempted suicide and abortion, between the fear of intimate relationships and abortion. Some are left facing how abortion left them physically as well as emotionally.

## A Place For Healing

There is one place where the secret is revealed. The naked truth of the abortion experience is faced head on. I've witnessed women come out of the denial with a sorrowful dignity. They can finally mourn the little person they've tried to ignore for so many years. This place of restoration and healing is called the "National Memorial for the Unborn".

It is in Chattanooga, Tennessee. My husband, Bryan and I first learned of the Memorial when we were asked to help Sandra with her role in their dedication ceremony. The "National Memorial for the Unborn" is the site of a former abortion clinic purchased by "pro-life" supporters.

The abortion clinic opened in 1975. One-half of the building housed the actual abortion chambers. In its years of operation, 35,000 lives were lost in those rooms. Ten years after the abortion clinic opened, a small group of Christians rented an office in the building just across the street from the abortion clinic. There they established AAA Women's Services, a crisis pregnancy center. They were joined and supported over the following years by those desiring to assist women in a crisis pregnancy and help save children. Together with individuals from various church denominations and pro-life activists, they formed the Pro-Life Majority Coalition of Chattanooga (ProMaCC) in 1999.

Within the span of two years, the co-owners of the abortion clinic, both women in their fifties, were diagnosed with cancer and died. The commercial landlord who had leased out the building to the abortion clinic was forced to file for bankruptcy. Word of the impending sale of the building containing the abortion clinic was passed along to the ProMaCC coalition members with only four day remaining to enter a bid.

Before the deadline the coalition put together $300,000 to bid towards the purchase of the property containing the abortion clinic. The main opponent to the coalition in the bidding was the abortion doctor, but the abortionist dropped out of the bankruptcy auction when the coalition bid reached $294,000.

As the new owners, ProMaCC was able to evict the abortionist, since the clinic's lease had expired two days before the sale papers were signed. Half of the building was remodeled to provide a center of support for women dealing with a crisis pregnancy.

The other half of the building, which had contained the abortion chambers, was demolished with a bulldozer. In the ruins the next morning a neatly placed little teddy bear was found. Someone had come in the night and left it. A memorial was built on this site to remember those valuable lost lives, and to recognize the grief carried by the millions of living victims of abortion.

The "National Memorial for the Unborn" is a fifty-foot-long granite wall, which holds memorial plaques ordered from forty-seven states throughout America. These plaques bear names, dates and messages expressing in adequate words the outpouring of grieving hearts.

This memorial site provides a tangible and accessible place for people to express grief and remembrance. And people come, all sorts of people come. Grandparents come to acknowledge the grandchild they will never hold. Fathers come, some who wanted the baby, but their desires were determined "immaterial" to the wishes of the mother and/or those putting pressure on her to eliminate the baby. Other fathers come to try and get over the guilt of giving a woman in their life the unfair ultimatum of, "Kill it or I'll leave". Family members come who wished they had intervened to save the life of a child they now will never know.

Most moving of all are the mothers of the aborted children that come to this place. Over and over, on the brass plaques that are composed by individuals and placed on the wall, and in letters to the aborted children left on the ledge, one reads, "Please forgive me. I'm so sorry. I'll hold you in heaven."

I have taken post-abortive women to the Memorial. When they first experience the Memorial site, they are engulfed in regret and sorrow. But as we stand there and they read the letters and the plaques from other post-abortive women, they are fortified with the realization that they are no longer alone. The emotional toll and energy that was extracted feeling shame is replaced with a quest for truth and justice. They are renewed to fight against the manipulation of women and to end legalized abortion on demand, to no longer live a lie or have the truth of what living with the secret of an abortion is like hidden and denied in their mind.

[Abortion Recovery Healing Resources are available nationwide now. Call or text Option Line at 800-712-4357 or go to OptionLine.org to chat.]

On some days the guilt these women suffer seems bigger than life. But on other days the factors that worked against them help relieve the guilt they carry. Days like when they visit this memorial.

When these post-abortive women unite, and they will, when their truth is known, and it will be, the legislative, executive, and judicial systems will have to act. The simple question of, "Is this a separate human being?" will be addressed. The basic DNA evidence used by agents of many courts today will have to be applied.

During the argument in *Doe v. Bolton* heard before the Supreme Court Wednesday, October 11, 1972, one of the justices actually compared an abortion to a tonsillectomy. And I quote, "But you wouldn't contend, would you, that the State would have authority to enact a statute or sustain a statute that would forbid tonsillectomies, for example?"

No longer will that argument be a substitution for scientific evidence. Once basic DNA evidence, the type regularly used in other court cases, is applied to abortion cases judges will have to face the truth. Science, logic, and common sense will someday enter this arena of lies, deception and manipulation. I firmly believe that with all my heart.

[Sadly that day has not yet come, but The Moral Outcry Petition, Chapter 8, continues to make the DNA and other new science argument.]

## The Providers

Shouldn't it be wrong to manipulate a woman at the most vulnerable time in her life? Shouldn't women have the same legal protection and rights during this medical procedure as during adoption, when full medical disclosure and a complete review of all the rights and options available must be given and understood before final action can occur?

Even if a woman abuses her child, the parent-child relationship has legal protection and legal recourse before the relationship can be terminated. Shouldn't it be wrong to permit a woman to make an irreversible decision with insufficient information.

Some abortion providers have left the industry. Some were the owners of clinics, some were the doctors who performed the abortions, some were the counselors who talked to the girls, and some were the medical assistants whose job was to make sure all of the baby was removed from the womb. They are willing to speak about their experiences, what they saw, and what they did. I have heard their stories on more than one occasion.

It is not easy for these individuals to relive their roles in the "pro-choice" movement. But their desire for the world to know the truth is greater than the pain of facing the damage they caused.

At a convention in Chicago, former abortion providers shared their experiences as the video "Meet the Abortion Providers" was made. It is available through the Pro-Life Action League offices in Chicago, IL and on YouTube. This video along with other videos and written testimonies are a window into the abortion industry that presents a picture they certainly don't volunteer.

Abby Johnson's life as a former Planned Parenthood Employee of the Year, who comes to the truth and deeply regrets her "choice" is told in the movie "Unplanned". Abby's ministry can be contacted at "And Then There Were None".

For starters, I was shocked to learn from these people, that they and their former co-workers used to laugh behind closed doors at the term "pro-choice". There was no "choice" given by the "counselors" at their abortion clinics. The only "choice" concerned which clinic a woman would use for their abortion procedure.

I am told that in such "counseling sessions" all focus is taken off the baby and put instead on some trivial expectation. For example, a teenage girl may be told, "If you have a baby, you won't be able to be a cheerleader. You won't be able to enter a beauty pageant." What kind of logic is that, on one side cheerleading, on the other the destiny of a unique, irreplaceable human being?

What happens with that "logic" after the young woman undergoes an abortion procedure? These women have come forward with notarized affidavits [*Operation Outcry*] stating they have redefined themselves and their self-image. Motivated by self-loathing, they become promiscuous, sometimes ending up having multiple abortions. They never become a beauty queen or cheerleader because of the emotional pain caused by their abortion.

Former abortion providers have admitted that their clinics intentionally prescribed the lowest dose birth control pill. Without informing the patient, the pill would have a 30 percent failure rate. The result was repeat business.

Some former providers say their clinics treated women for venereal disease without informing their patients that the antibiotics prescribed would negate the effects of their birth control medication. The outcome? Another 10 to 15 percent repeat business rate from the women who had supposedly been "helped" by the clinic they trusted.

If abortion is so right, why do post-abortive women and former abortion providers feel so bad? Why are these former clinic workers now so horrified about the work they did?

I have learned abortion clinic workers are taught to deny the experience of "post-abortion syndrome". If a woman who underwent an abortion procedure calls the clinic back asking about her nightmares or depression, she is told that she must have had such problems before the abortion took place.

One former clinic director came to the sad realization that abortion is not about helping women but about greed. She regularly encountered providers who didn't care about the woman and didn't care about the baby or the undeniable fact that "so many women are dying" following legal abortion procedures. This director found her conscience would no longer permit her participation and she quit.

In 1997 in the United States, there were 1,186,039 legal abortions reported to the Federal Center for Disease Control. Using an average cost per abortion of $450 that means the abortion industry generated $1,462,050 each day in 1997 alone. That is $533,648,250 a year. Eliminating the unborn is a very profitable endeavor.

[The Abortion Industry is a big 2-billion-dollar business with total assets of 2.165 Billion:

Total Income ......................................... $1,665.1 million
Government ............................................ $ 563.8 million
Donations .............................................. $ 630.8 million
Non-Government clinic income .............. $ 365.7 million
Other ..................................................... $ 104.8 million
Profits ................................................... $ 244.8 million
Abortions ......................................................... 332,757

National Office & Affiliate Financial Data
Combined Balance Sheet: National Office and Affiliates

June 30, 2018
Total Assets 2,165.6
Total Liabilities 283.9
Net Assets 1,881.7

Source – Summary from – https://www.plannedparent-hood.org/about-us/facts-figures/annual-report People who perform abortion procedures consistently deny any damage to post-abortive women, physically, or emotionally. These women are left alone with their fears. I know. I have listened to them tell Sandra and me their stories.

Pro-choice supporters are right about one thing. Abortion is about women. Only the supporters and advocates promoting abortion focus on their cause. What is in the woman's best interest, complete information, is never considered.

How sad that these women are alone with the fear that their husbands will leave them if they learn about the abortion. So, they keep the knowledge to themselves, even if the abortion took place before their marriage. These women fear their children may end up hating them if they learn about their mother's abortion experience. They even fear the judgment of their friends if they confide in them about an abortion and seek comfort for the struggles they now silently battle.

Most sad to me are the post-abortive women who fear the condemnation of their churches if anyone learns they underwent an abortion procedure, regardless of how long ago it happened. I have seen how a relationship with Christ has brought comfort and healing to Dr. Nathanson, Norma McCorvey, and Sandra Cano. The simple fact that God loves me brings peace. Because of Christ's sacrifice, God, in His great love, has forgiven me. God is giving me strength to face each day. I pray they will all experience that comfort someday.

For now, these women are isolated, guilty, and abandoned. They think their experience is safely locked away. But the truth keeps surfacing again and again, with great remorse. They feel pressure from (family, lover, counselor, etc.) to keep quiet. As long as they remain quiet there is no threat to the powers that put them in this cauldron. The women are left to bear these scars alone for the rest of their lives.

But the truth will always stand, and a legal effort is underway to overturn *Roe v. Wade* and *Doe v. Bolton*. Allan Parker, CEO and Founder of the Justice Foundation (www.txjf.org) is representing Sandra Cano and Norma McCorvey. There is now a legal opportunity for all post-abortive women and people who stand with them to be able to have their truth known in court. See www.operationoutcry.org.

Would there be a need for such questions if the procedure were anything but abortion? A television commercial for a prescription medicine contains more information and warning than these women received in their entire abortion process.

Finally, a chance to be heard. I believe that these organizations will persevere. In the end the courts will decide the abortion issue based on fact and testimony. I believe the U.S. Supreme Court will rectify the way *Doe v. Bolton* was heard. This time it will matter that the people represented in the cases are real.

For more information on this court proceeding or to learn how anyone can stand with these women, please contact: The Justice Foundation, P.O. Box 40458, San Antonio, Texas 78229, (210) 614-7151 or log on to www.operationoutcry.org.

Sandra and I return to our room emotionally spent, moved by the women's pain, and deeply humbled that Sandra's story brought them comfort.

We will catch a few hours' sleep before returning to our homes. It is both an honor and responsibility when someone like Sandra has given you her trust. Bryan and I don't want to do anything that would let her down.

Sandra has been hurt and used so many times. And until more Americans know the facts behind Sandra's case, I will again set my alarm for 5:00 A.M. We always need extra time at the airport.

As I am finishing this manuscript the United States is still reeling from the events of September 11, 2001, and its wanton destruction. Nearly 3,000 precious lives were lost at the World Trade Center alone. President Bush has rightly declared war on terrorism and more than 85 percent of Americans support him in this decision. Yet every day more than 3,000 innocent, helpless babies die from legalized abortion in the United States. When will the war against them end? Speak up, you can help put an end to these acts of terrorism.

**Sybil J. Lash, permission granted to include this material in this book.© 2002**

## Update on Sandra's Death and Beyond – *Gonzales v. Carhart*

[Sandra died on September 30, 2014, before she could live to see Roe reversed in *Dobbs* on June 24, 2022. But she would be rejoicing in Heaven if she could see it.]

The Supreme Court declined to take her Rule 60 Motion case in 2006. They did not rule against her, they just refused to hear the case. The Supreme Court gets around 8,000 to 9,000 requests to take an appeal (known as *cert.* petitions), but only accepts 80-90 or less per year. Thus, every appeal has a 99% chance they will not take your case, known as denying *cert.* So, the Court was not ready to hear her case. Then, their decision had no binding effect as a precedent. The legal battle continued, but in another way.

Finally in an amazing, extraordinary way in 2007, Sandra's name was cleared at the Supreme Court on April 18, 2007, in *Gonzales v. Carhart.* The Court actually cited her *Amicus* Brief (primarily prepared and authored by Lead Counsel Linda Schlueter) at the Supreme Court filed by The Justice Foundation attorneys on behalf of Sandra Cano and 180 Women Injured by Abortion. Sandra was finally able to explain how she and the Court were deceived in her case.

In addition, based on the testimony of the 180 Women of *Operation Outcry* Injured By Abortion on the Brief, for the first time ever the Court called the child an "infant life" at the moment of abortion. Why? The Court explained why in writing in its decision by citing to the actual pages of Sandra and the Women's Brief saying:

"While we find no reliable data to measure the phenomenon, it seems unexceptionable to conclude some women come to regret their choice to abort the infant life they once created and sustained. See Brief for Sandra Cano, *et al.,*

[180 Women Hurt by Abortion] as *Amici Curiae* in No. 05-380, pp.22-24. Severe depression and loss of esteem can follow." *Gonzales v. Carhart*, 550 U.S. 124, at 159 (2007) (emphasis added).

In addition, the Court upheld the federal partial birth abortion ban, after declaring 38 partial birth abortion bans at the state level unconstitutional in 2000 in *Stenberg v. Carhart* (2000).

Consider this! In 2000, the year we were called to collect the testimonies of women and take Norma and Sandra back to the Court, they had just said *Roe* was so strong that governments could not even ban a procedure in which the child was almost born alive, but the head remained in the body with the legs sticking out, while a suction devise crushed the baby's skull and suctioned out the child's brain. Unimaginable horror!

In fact, a senior leader of the pro-life movement whom I had gone to in 2000 to tell about *Operation Outcry*'s call to reverse *Roe* told me: "Al, they just looked into the pit of hell and didn't blink. They will never overturn *Roe v. Wade*."

He was crushed in 2000 right after Stenberg. But in 2007, only seven years later, a remarkably short legal time, Sandra and 180 Women's voices were heard in the Court through their Brief. This time the Court upheld the ban on partial birth abortion and in effect reversed its 2000 decision and actually cited the women's testimonies as one of the reasons. Pages 22-24 of The Brief, cited by The Court contains quote after quote of women's testimonies of the devastation caused by abortion. Actual quotes you will read in the next chapter. How do we overcome Satan? By the Blood of the Lamb and the word of their testimony. Revelation 12:11 And by hearing the Word of the Lord and obeying Him. Obedience is a neglected doctrine in much of Christianity today, but blessing comes when we hear and obey.]

# CHAPTER FIVE

# What Abortion Does to Women

By 2002, hundreds of women had already come forward with written testimonies to let the truth be known about abortion. By 2003, when we filed the Rule 60 Motions for Norma and Sandra about 1000 testimonies were provided to the Court. Far more than the one affidavit of Norma and Sandra in their original cases. But for hail to "sweep away the refuge of lies," (Isaiah 28:17), we need a flood of hailstones. A few hail stones are not a threat, though you might scurry for shelter, but thousands pelting the ground can destroy a building. By the time of the *Dobbs* decision, we filed 4728 legally admissible written *Operation Outcry* testimonies, with the Supreme Court, because the Lord told us to do so.

Prior to *Dobbs*, the Supreme Court viewed motherhood as suffering saying:

"The mother who carries a child to full term is subject to anxieties, to physical constraints, to pain that only she must bear. That these sacrifices have from the beginning of the human race been endured by woman with a pride that ennobles her in the eyes of others and gives to the infant a bond of love cannot alone be grounds for the State to insist she make the sacrifice. Her suffering is too intimate and personal for the State to insist, without more, upon its own vision of the woman's role, however dominant that vision has been in the course of our history and our culture."

*Planned Parenthood v. Casey*, 505 U.S. 833, 856 (1989).

This view ignores the suffering that abortion brings to women. Abortion was viewed by the Court in *Casey* as an end to women's suffering from pregnancy. We need women to tell the court the truth about the suffering of abortion.

In this chapter, answers to the questions we have asked women about their abortion will be shared in their own words. I always felt the women are far more eloquent and knowledgeable about the lies of abortion than I am. You will read excerpts from the women's sworn answers, with first names if they have signed their testimonies in such manner, or initials if the women prefer.

I am inspired by the courageous women who have allowed us to use their names. This is the sworn truth, admissible in a court of law. They join us in calling on other women to share their testimony in courts and legislatures across the country.

But first, if you have had an abortion, you are not alone. If you need healing, as these women did, there is help all across the nation at no cost to you. Here are the toll-free numbers:

## Healing Resources For Women and Men

### 1. International Helpline for Abortion Recovery (based in the US):

The International Helpline for Abortion Recovery trained phone consultants have experienced the pain of abortion and are ready to help you with your abortion recovery healing process.

- *They provide 24/7 confidential help and care.*
- *They listen to you and help you find the abortion recovery program nearest you.*
- *They mail resources and follow up to make sure you get the help you need.*

If you have questions or need help after abortion, please call 1-866-482-LIFE (5433).

For more information go to www.internationalhelpline.org.

CALL NOW! The first step in the journey of healing can begin with your call.

## 2. Option Line:

It doesn't matter if your abortion was yesterday or 20 years ago. Option Line provides emotional support after abortion through a hotline where you can speak to someone about the way you feel right away or connect you with a group in your area that meets in person.

For help with your unplanned pregnancy visit:
- OptionLine.org to chat
- Or call/text 800-712-4357.

Option Line also provides weekend retreats ready to help women sort through any difficult emotions from a past abortion. Option Line is here to help.

## 3. Support After Abortion

In an atmosphere of acceptance and flexibility, Support After Abortion provides an options-based approach to emotional and spiritual healing. You can choose a program that best suits your needs. Over 800 agencies are available to help you.

- ***Call Support After Abortion: 844-289-HOPE***
- ***Visit Website: www.supportafterabortion.com***

Their mission is "To end the demand for abortion through healing people impacted by abortion."

## 4. H3 Helpline – Help, Hope, Healing

H3 Helpline is a national after abortion helpline. They offer after abortion support and help, hope, healing for the pain of abortion.

- ***Call 1-866-721-7881***
- ***Visit Website: www.h3helpline.org***

Call H3Helpline and one of their Phone Coaches will provide you with healing information.

According to a peer reviewed article in the prestigious British Journal of Psychiatry,

"Women who had undergone an abortion experienced an 81% increased risk of mental health problems, and 10% of the incidence of mental health problems was shown to be attributable to abortion."[5]

If only ten percent of one million women a year who have abortions suffer these symptoms, then 100,000 women a year are suffering. I believe it is far more. In fact, the evidence of the link between abortion and suicide is so strong that in my legal opinion

---

[5] Coleman, Priscilla, "Abortion and Mental Health; Quantitative Synthesis and Analysis of Research Published 1995-2009," (2011) 199, 180-186, DOI: 10.1192/bjp.bp.110.077230 (a meta-analysis of 22 studies).

every suicide hotline and every therapist or counselor who deals with depression and anxiety has a legal duty to screen for abortion in a woman's past and refer her to those who are competent by training to deal with post abortion trauma.

The women tell us what this psychological trauma is really like.

## Legally Admissible Testimonies From Operation Outcry Women

### How has abortion affected you?

"The truth was that two months following the abortion I would lose my womb causing a gradual reduction in my estrogen production, leading to estrogen deprivation resulting in delayed depression during an early and hard menopause. An abortion, not pregnancy, caused serious consequences. The truth was that the night before my abortion I asked aloud, God, is there anything wrong in what I am going to do? Man says it isn't even life. What do you say? I didn't hear an audible response and assumed it was OK. However, in the morning, a clerk from the clinic called to let me know that the doctor had to cancel his appointments for that morning and asked me what I wanted to do? I did not remember the night before; I did not make the connection. I was not listening. I informed my husband and he asked about the next Saturday. So I made another appointment and I became responsible for my child's death.

Myra, Texas

"No one forewarned me of the repercussions of an abortion. It was a simple procedure of removing "tissue," so why the pain, the sudden emptiness? I awoke night after night to the sound of screams, they were mine! There are no words to express the deep dark hole I found myself in, no phrase to describe the depth of my despair."

Kay, Idaho

"I fell into deep depression and battled nervous tension that even affected my bodily functions. I developed stomach ulcers and was put on sedatives to which I became addicted. By age nineteen, I could take no more of the heartache and torment resulting from my abortion and decided one day to end my life. I know the Lord had other plans for me, as I was found unconscious and rushed to the emergency room where my stomach was pumped. My life continued, but I lived in hidden shame and guilt, with the pain and knowledge that I was responsible for ending my baby's life. I don't know if there is any greater agony on this earth."

Daria, Alabama

"A part of me died that day as I realized I would never hold or see that child. I became angry and depressed. I started drinking heavily, doing drugs, and became very promiscuous. I didn't think anyone would love me unless I gave them sex in return. I got pregnant two more times and choose abortion each time. With each abortion my addictions got worse. I even attempted suicide 3 times. Because of the choices I had made my life was a mess and was spiraling out of control."

Luana, Iowa

"There was an increase of self-destructive behavior regarding sexual activity, drugs, and alcohol. I was irrational and full of fears. I would become overwhelmed and fall apart emotionally but not knowing why. Ten years passed before I was able to admit to myself that I had killed my child and was able to grieve for him. After thirteen years, I have given up hope of conceiving another child."

Mayela, Texas

"Immediate depression – long term guilt and unforgiveness – I have no other children."

Barbara, Texas

"Many ways. Emotionally, physically. Started doing drugs after abortion. Relating to my children. Loving my children. Depression, rages. Guilt, shame, bad relationships."

Mary Frances, California

"Great sorrow and shock when I realized what I had done out of sheer ignorance. I miss deeply the child that I lost by spontaneous abortion and the two children whom I murdered. I love my living three children with all my heart and wish I knew the other three that I don't have. I have so much time for them all now."

Cheryl, California

"The women's center told me "It is just a glob of pregnancy tissue"... "it will be a short outpatient procedure"... "problem solved." Instead, **the abortion ushered me down a staircase, as I found myself spiraling into deep depression. The abortion became my prison cell of postabortion grief, substance abuse, shame, and heartbreak**. No one at that women's center told me the truth of the development of my baby, my option for adoption, or the devastating fallout from post-abortion grief and regret. The abortion tore through my life like a hurricane...I changed from a young woman entering nursing school, hard-working, eager to help people... to a broken, promiscuous, alcohol indulging, partying girl, looking for any way to numb the emotional pain from the gnawing reality of the loss of my child and what I had done."

Sue, Ohio

"I am always feeling unwanted and empty. I have a hard time feeling close or attached to the two children I do have."

F.A., Wisconsin

"Depression, angry. Pain, hopeless."

G.I.C., Texas

"My abortion has affected me in numerous ways. I felt tremendous guilt and confusion in the recovery room. I felt I had done something terribly wrong but didn't understand why I felt that way. I was very depressed and withdrawn afterward and could not talk about what I was feeling. I was unable to discuss the abortion for many years, despite my husband trying to discuss it with me. I never revealed my abortion as part of my medical history. It affected my relationship with my husband for over 20 years. I worried about being punished for killing my baby and feared I would lose my children after they were born. I have had many medical problems that I attribute to having the abortion including pre-term pregnancies, abnormal paps, and abnormal periods."

S., Texas

"Ashamed and saddened."

Joanne, Georgia

"If I imagine what hell is then I say that is how my life was before I found counseling and healing. I became an alcoholic, lost my will to live, hated life in general."

Lisa, Oregon

"Years of mood swings, eating disorders, promiscuity, low self-esteem and relationship with my other children."

Reatha, Maryland

"A lot of guilt. I was a Christian at the time and I chose my husband over God. It also allowed the spirit of death to enter my soul."

Jeanne, California

"I spent years going from relationship to relationship and I became more sexually active. Alienated from family, problems in school, old friends became distant." (3 abortions)

Maureen, Pennsylvania

"After my abortion, my life was very emotionally unstable. I had severe episodes of depression and found myself crying uncontrollably for no reasons. Thank God a few years ago I accepted that God had forgiven me for killing my baby or allowing doctors to kill my baby, and God has healed me of depression."

Tina, Georgia

"Emotionally – physically. I was 25 when I had my abortion. I'm 42 now and there is not a day goes by I don't think about how I murdered my baby."

M.A.C., Texas

"It's BEEN HELL!!! Grief, anger, low self-esteem, condemnation, feelings of immense regret – wondering how my life would have been different with my child. If I had allowed my child to live, I would have felt so much better about myself."

Mary Jane, New York

"Severe depression, especially in January, knowing my child would be another year older."

Wendy, New Jersey

"It affected me in so many ways I can't list them all. I lost trust in people – in love – in God. I looked into reincarnation in hopes that my child would return in another pregnancy. I felt hopeless inside and used "cocktail hour" to get through my life."

Dianne, New York

"Ten years after the abortion I almost had a nervous break-down. Have suffered emotionally for twenty-five years."

D.E., Georgia

"Made me feel ashamed and guilty."

Beverly, Texas

"Severe guilt knowing I killed my baby. Depression, lack of self-respect. Most of all, the empty arms and not having known and experienced my baby."

Sandra, Georgia

"Emotionally, I feel now like I killed those babies and just because it was legal didn't make it right."

Florence Anne, Texas

"I dealt with years of shame, guilt, and loss. It was not until I began speaking of the abortion, did I start healing."

Jennifer, Colorado

"I struggle with intimacy. I also feel like I have to keep it a secret – almost as if I would not be accepted in society."

Karyn, Texas

"Very negatively! I have had depression, guilt, sleeplessness, counseling, etc. Not a day goes by that I don't think about killing my baby."

D.K., Arkansas

"I was an emotional wreck for several years because I thought God was punishing me by not allowing me to carry a pregnancy to term."

K.E.K., Maryland

"It's robbed me of peace, joy in the blessings of my life, my self-esteem has been shot to pieces."

Victoria, North Carolina

"I went from being on the Dean's List in college to getting F's, incompletes, and withdraws. I attempted suicide. I was depressed. The guilt was overwhelming."

H.A.K., Tennessee

"It caused me to have emotional problems and a lot of nervous problems. I regret what I have done. I did have nightmares in the very beginning after my abortions. I was in complete denial. I have serious problems with men. It is hard for me to trust them."

J.L.K., New York

"It has affected me in the following ways: One, it changed my life dramatically. I was in denial for the first two years. Trying to ignore it had happened and trying to suppress. I didn't think anyone would understand. I certainly felt like I could not go to God because how could He forgive me. It hurt me because I had killed my child. It hurt me because I would not know that child. I went through anger, severe depression, insomnia, and fear. I had no peace whatsoever. I was miserable."

Cori, North Carolina

"Emotionally/mentally: Guilt, shame, isolation, depression, despair, regret, remorse, self-hatred, self-destructive, suicidal (hospitalized), inability to forget baby, baby's death date and baby's due date, in ability to forgive myself, loss of sexual interest, outbursts of rage and anger, helplessness and troubled relationships. Physically: Precancer of cervix two years after abortion. Stillbirth four years after abortion."

Paula, Wisconsin

[We could go on, and on, and on with the agony of abortion. When the 2002 *Operation Outcry* book was written, there were ten more pages like these. Eventually, our 4,728 legally admissible testimonies were given to the Court in the *Dobbs* case. I, along with Clayton Trotter, Mary J. Browning, Kathleen Cassidy-Goodman, and Mary Ann Randolph also filed a brief on behalf of 375 Women Injured By Second and Third Late Term Abortions and Melinda Thybault, acting on behalf of 336,214 Signers of The Moral Outcry Petition described in chapter eight. This was one of only eight pro-life briefs filed at the *Cert.* Petition phase of *Dobbs.* That's when you ask the Supreme Court to take a case, but they turn you down 99% of the time.

In a truly unusual, extraordinary way, the *Dobbs* case was reset and reconsidered by the Supreme Court 22 times before it was accepted. The decision to accept it was announced on May 17, 2021. That day was Shavuot, or the Day of Pentecost on the Jewish calendar that year.

After the Court agreed to hear the case, 80 pro-life briefs were filed of which four more were written by The Justice Foundation. See chapter nine.]

**Were you adequately informed of the
consequences of abortion?
[Lies, Deceit, Misrepresentation By The Abortion Industry]**

"I was told that at this stage that the baby had not taken form yet and it was just a mass of tissue and the procedure would be like a D & C."

Barbara, Texas

"No. I had a second trimester miscarriage less than a year after my abortion, never knew this was a risk."

Mary Frances, California

"No. Not at all. I was encouraged by the abortion clinic doctors that it was painless and without consequences."

Cheryl, California

"Not at all. I was not told that there would be any consequences."

G.B., Wisconsin

"No. I had no idea how much it would affect me emotionally."

Sylina, Georgia

"No – the emotional consequences for me were devastating!!"

Tamela, Maryland

"No, not the mental or emotional ones only the physical ones, like cramping and possibility of punctured uterus. Not breast or cervical cancer increase."

Lisa, Oregon

"No one talked to me about anything. I was put in a room with other girls to wait until they called me."

L.M.C., Tennessee

"I was told it was only tissue not a baby."

M.C., California

"No, I was told it was a procedure, relatively painless – no side effects."

Wendy, New Jersey

"No – I was not told of the depression that followed."

Mary Anne, Georgia

"Not the emotional consequences."

Cecilia, Florida

"No. The only problem they mentioned was infection if you went swimming in a lake, or excessive bleeding under very rare circumstances, according to the clinic."

Shawn, Texas

"No – I didn't know there were any consequences. Everyone acted like it was nothing – no big deal."

Christina, Delaware

"No. I didn't know that the hurt would never go away. Any future physical problems were not discussed."

Dianne Marie, New York

"No. I did not ask. My doctor did not offer any information."

Lisa, Virginia

"No. I was told it was a quick fix for everything and there were no consequences to 99.9% of the women."

Candice, California

"Absolutely not – it was only described as a quick fix – "no one has to know."

Debbie, Nebraska

"Looking back, I remember being told it was the right thing to do. I was told the difficulties of being a mother and rais-ing a child. I was so young and had my whole life ahead of me. There were so many girls there that day."

P.C.O., Louisiana

"I do not recall being told of any serious consequences, physically, emotionally, or psychologically. The Santa Ana Health Department where I had the pregnancy test advised me that I couldn't afford to have the baby."

Rashelle, California

"None were explained to me. I was asked if I felt I could live with myself after abortion – no information was given to me so how could I honestly answer this question, so I lied and said, "yes"."

Donna, California

"No. I was told there were no side effects."

Amy Marie, Colorado

"No – not at all; no consequences were discussed, physical, emotional, mental, etc. They told me, "You know it's just a bunch of cells, don't you?" I didn't believe it in my heart."

Kimberly, Ohio

"No!!! Not one person informed me of anything, it was just an "option"!"

Erika, Oklahoma

"No one discussed with me any moral issues whatsoever. I was told there was nothing to be embarrassed or ashamed about."

Scherrie, Kansas

"I was not informed of any consequences of the abortion. I was not told of the emotional or physical consequences. While I was still under the effects of the sedation, but after the procedure was completed, I began loud, uncontrollable sobbing. I remember coming out from under the anesthetic hearing the nurse telling my mother that I had been crying uncontrollably. I don't know when I started sobbing, but I can say that even though my body had been numbed to the pain, my mind had not. I can honestly say this was and is the lowest day of my life."

Debera, Texas

"No. No one told me that I would hear cries in the middle of the night."

Brandy, Georgia

[We could go one and on. The original 2002 *Operation Outcry* book included another 20 pages of this. We have thousands of similar testimonies. The abortion industry lies to and damages women. Billions of dollars in civil damages are due to abortion industry victims. May these lawsuits come soon!]

**Did anyone pressure you into having an abortion? If so, who?**

[The pressure comes from different sources, but huge numbers of women feel pressured. [About one-half of the 4,728 women's testimonies we submitted in *Dobbs* say they were pressured.] Is this a woman's choice? These answers give the lie to the phrase – "It's a woman's choice."]

"Yes. My gynecologist because I had been "spotting"."

Cheryl, California

"Yes. Psychiatrists, social worker, my mother, boyfriend, "friends", even a minister. In the first instance the money was borrowed. In the second it was "decided" for me."

Nancy, Iowa

"Yes. Parents."

I.S.A., Texas

"Yes. The man who I was pregnant by."

Paula, Ohio

"Yes. My husband."

Grace, North Carolina

"Not my first one but my second one was due to the pressure of the father."

Lisa, Oregon

"Yes – the babies' fathers. Two abortions per father."

Kimberly, California

"Yes. My husband at the time."

Lillian, California

"Friends and father of the baby."

Reatha, Maryland

"Yes. My fiancé at the time and supported by my father and stepmother. My ex-husband said I couldn't marry him if I was pregnant. My parents said I could get pregnant again."

Jeanne, California

"Boyfriends – fear of telling parents, no support." (3 Abortions)
    "Yes. Parents."

Lisa, Arizona

"(1) My father and brother. (2) My husband."

Mary Ann, Florida

"Yes. My boyfriend – the father. Planned Parenthood recommended it."

Pamela, California

"Family Planning Clinic in Victoria, Texas – gave me money for abortion."

Joy, Texas

"Yes, the counselor, when I told her I was afraid of being a parent she used my fears to make the decision easier and faster."

R.A.C., Texas

"Yes, my boyfriend and my co-workers."

Mary Anne, Georgia

"Yes, my husband the first time. The Department of Family Children Services."

Cecilie, Florida

"Yes, the father and his friend – an older attorney who assured me that I would ruin everyone's life if I carried the baby and that my husband could take my kids – I would be an unfit mother. Like killing my baby would make me a fit mother?"

Dianne, New York

"Yes. Mother – she was too embarrassed. We were in a Lutheran Church that was/is pretty much a "social club".

Ra Shelle', Kansas

"Yes. Mostly my parents but also my then boyfriend."

Janet, Wisconsin

"Yes, someone did pressure me. It was my husband at that time."

Betty, California

"I felt pressured because I was asked a question and not given the option to think about it and get back to Planned Parenthood with my decision."

Charlene, Pennsylvania

"Yes, the father of the child, my husband. That I had to or else."

Michele, Texas

"Boyfriend was insistent that abortion was the only acceptable solution. I was so afraid of losing the relationship, I went ahead and aborted. The abusive relationship ended four months later." [Very common with abortions.]

P.B.M., Illinois

"Yes. The nurse practitioner that I saw at Kaiser Permanente. She made many comments about needing to get rid of a problem I had, which at that time, I didn't think I had one."

Tara

"My mother and the doctors and nurses."

C.M., Texas

"Yes. The father of the baby and friends." [Very common.]

P.C.O., Louisiana

## How has abortion affected others in your life?

"I regret very much not telling my father the truth when I was pregnant. I couldn't live with myself and when I finally did tell him, he just wept because he would have helped me."

L.A., New York

"My parents were grieved and I believe the people performing abortions are searing their own consciences."

Tamela, Maryland

"When my daughter had her abortion, she said, "You did it."

Kathleen, New York

"Yes, my first born."

Grace, North Carolina

"Yes, it definitely has, especially my other children. I took out my frustration on them and then didn't understand it at the time. When I explained it later they were hurt and shocked by my decision to have an abortion."

Reatha, Maryland

"I drew others in, e.g., roommate gave me the money against her better judgment. We spent years not talking to one another."

Maureen, Pennsylvania

"My husband told me I was going crazy and it caused problems between us."

L.M.C., TN.

"Both sisters who took me and my parents carried guilt. It also made for bitterness. My husband has to deal with my anxiety and crying spells at times. I don't trust men. I fear having to have a hysterectomy."

Christina, Delaware

"They feel that part of me died. They have watched me die slowly over the years. Time did not heal. My family worries constantly because of my self-destructive nature."

Sheila, Florida

"My abortion put up walls between me and my children and I became verbally abusive to them."

Kathy, Oklahoma

"My husband and family suffered emotionally from my depression."

Diane, Tennessee

"I was feeling guilty for the last 19 years, that made me incapable of letting myself receive abundance and the blessings they have to give. My children and my husband didn't get the best of me."

Brenda, Texas

"They've had to deal with me and my emotional problems and depression."

S.M. J., Michigan

"The father was torn up from it. We went our separate ways. No one else seemed to mind."

Jeanne, Oklahoma

"My husband, who wants a child of his own – will never have that blessing because of my abortion experiences."

Joy, New York

"My sister-in-law and I have cried over the death of my child, her niece/nephew. We both look forward to holding/hugging "Baby Christian" in heaven, though our loss on earth is great."

P.B.M., Illinois

"It caused a lot of problems in my marriage. My husband was with me when I had the abortion. It has affected me as a mother. I had two children before and it has affected the way I treat them. I could not get close to them because of the guilt and remorse of what I did with the child I aborted I did not deserve to enjoy them."

Melanie, Illinois

"I had a hard time bonding with my daughter. I was also angry at my husband, who was my boyfriend at the time of the abortion, and I would treat him very rudely. Forgiveness has made our relationship grow."

Tara

"Because of the fact that I still struggle with anxiety and depression at times as well as a slight stutter, it has affected my whole family financially, socially, and emotionally."

Lori, Ohio

## Based on your own experiences, what would you tell a woman considering an abortion?

"Never, never have or consider an abortion – it will stay with you the rest of your life. The pain never really goes away."

Barbara, Texas

"You do not want to go down the road I have been down. It will affect you the rest of your life. Having an abortion does not make you not a mom. Your nightmare just begins."

Mary Frances, California

"Never to destroy the precious miracle of life that God has blessed her womb with. Someday in the future she will long to hold that child and love that child and it would be too late if she killed him or her."

L.A., New York

"Not to have one. Listen to your gut instinct, which tells you this is a baby and as a mother you naturally want to take care of it, not kill it. That if I could do it over again, I would not let it happen again."

I.S.A., Texas

"Please don't. You will truly regret it. In this critical time there are people who want to help you. People who will love you not just your baby. I wish I had known about the Care Pregnancy Center in my area. Go to them. They will support you."

K.H.A., Georgia

"There will be consequences to future pregnancies, depression after; premature births, non-healthy pregnancy; regular hospital stays during the pregnancy. Fear of not having healthy children and sex life to follow."

G.B, Wisconsin

"I would tell her to reconsider and to not have an abortion. I would tell her of the many long-term effects of the abortion. I would tell her of the physical, emotional, and spiritual consequences of having an abortion. I have shared my personal experience many times with women considering an abortion and the pain associated with having the abortion, as well as the effects of those that have trusted me with their abortion experience. I would tell her that I think it is murder."

Susan, Texas

"Don't do it – EVER for any reason! The emotional consequences alone are not worth the quick fix – you'll spend the rest of your life regretting it."

Shirley, California

"Please don't have an abortion. You'll regret having one for the rest of your life. The child deserves a chance, even if you're not ready for a baby. You can always give it up for adoption."

Dennie, New Hampshire.

"It is a self-destructing decision that pulls you into a downward spiral. Every aspect of your life is affected. You eventually feel tremendous guilt which you try to cover and compensate for and never can."

Maureen, Pennsylvania

"That it is something you never forget. It is not the easy way out because there are consequences you have to live with the rest of your life."

Lisa, Arizona

"The scars are on your heart forever – you'll remember the child's predicted birthday for years. The hole in your heart doesn't fill even if you have other beautiful children."

Mary Ann, D.C.

"DON'T DO IT!! It hurts more than you can imagine. It's murder!"

Charlene, Michigan

"Please, please get all the information available to you, check with family members for their input, talk with the father's family (if possible), and find out if there is the possibility of adoption as a solution rather than abortion."

Pamela, California

"I would tell her the hell I have been through and that they people who represent the clinics either lie or withhold the truth to complete the abortion and they don't care about her or the baby."

Rhonda, Texas

"It may seem right at the time or the only thing you can do, or it is okay or you're right but the emotional pain you will feel later will be unbearable."

L.M.C., Tennessee

"Not to abort because sooner or later you will deal with the guilt and shame of the choice to murder your baby."

M.C., California

"It never goes away and you will always think of what could have been and the anger of how the government allows this hideous procedure."

Nora, Georgia

"There is a lot of pain, and blood. Unbelievable pain. Depression, grief! Lots of grief."

M.A.C., Texas

"Please pray. There are so many other options. You can never forget you have murdered your own baby."

Cecilia, Georgia

"Don't do it. It will be the worst mistake of your life. As difficult and painful as your situation may be, nothing compares to the agony of killing your child. Don't ignore the subtle voice from within that tells you it's wrong. That is the voice of God pleading with you to keep your child alive."

Shawn, Texas

"I have talked to friends who have thought of having an abortion – told of my terrible experience and told them that it was the worse choice I ever made."

Linda, Texas

"Don't do it. You cut off your own soul when you take the life of your child. You will deeply regret not experiencing the life of your child. The mental and emotional damage is beyond description. It's torture."

Sandra, Georgia

"Don't do it! Life is such a precious gift. If you feel you can't take care of a child then adoption is the only answer."

K.E.K., Maryland

"It's a permanent solution for a temporary problem – too permanent. The pain of giving a child for adoption doesn't come close to the pain of realizing what you've done."

Victoria, North Carolina

"I would tell them of the overwhelming suffering that I went through. I would tell them that the guilt is too much to bear, and that it stays with you forever. It changes you and destroys you."

H.A.K., Tennessee

"I would share with them that they do not have to know the torture and torment that I dealt with. That there are far more consequences in having an abortion than in having a child. It is a decision that they cannot erase. It will impact them for the rest of their lives. It is total destruction both physically and emotionally."

Cori, North Carolina

"Don't do it. I will happily take her baby if she's not willing or able to be a good mom. Something spiritual, emotional, and physical will happen. It's a painful experience in all these areas."

Jeanne, Oklahoma

"It's not worth it!!! Give the child a chance to live! Killing the child may cure your pregnancy, but there is NO CURE for the years of pain and agony that will follow. Only God can and will restore you after the aftermath of abortion."

Melissa, Kansas

"Don't do it – it will change your life in a way you can't imagine – it's NOT a quick fix – it's the worst thing I've ever done – It's absolutely unnatural for a woman to kill her child."

Debbie, Nebraska

"I [would] try to explain the hell it creates. I counsel at a pregnancy center now. We give the women all the information they need to make their decision."

Sheila, Florida

"I would tell her that abortion is a short-term solution with long term consequences. The emotional and possibly physical consequences outweigh the temporary relief felt when the pregnancy is "taken care of." An abortion once performed, can never be reversed and is very difficult to handle emotionally. It is very possible that an abortion would hinder future pregnancies."

Elizabeth, Minneapolis

"Be prepared to face a lifetime of guilt, shame, disappointment, anger and the possibility of never being able to have children again because of the scar tissue that an abortion leaves behind."

Yvonne, Illinois

"Your emotions, fears, and increased hormones have made you vulnerable and the quick and easy "out" of abortion looks like the only solution. It is not. It is a trap that once sprung will leave you with a lifetime of regret. You will never stop counting the birthdays that should have been."

Linda, Texas

## Based on your own experience, what would you tell a court that believes an abortion should be legal?

"Think of a mother's heart. It should not be legal to kill human babies. Do you wipe away the tears? Iowa is experiencing a shortage of workers. The children are innocent and have the potential to contribute to society. Adoption would be better. Abortion destroys faith and family. It will make you feel dead."

Nancy, Nebraska

"That abortion is murder. A mother knows by instinct – that abortion is killing her baby – that is why there is emotional turmoil in making the decision to have the abortion."

I.S.A., Texas

"They are wrong. It destroys more than just a child's life. It also destroys the mother's. Life is precious, please uphold it."

Karen, Georgia

"I would first say I believe it is murder to kill an unborn child. I would say that if women knew what they later learned from their mistake, they would understand that it was murder. I would tell them of the hidden statistics of the many long-term effects women suffer in relation to having an abortion such as miscarriage, reproductive problems, and the mental anguish of taking a life. I would say to the courts that if a woman saw pictures of what a fetus was like developmentally, how brutal the abortion procedure is, how a baby suffers during the procedure, and the possible long-term effects, they would never choose to end their babies life. I would tell the courts of the many women I have met who are still suffering because of their abortions and they don't know why. I would say I have not met anyone who has had an abortion who has not expressed regret in having it. I would tell the courts they should be protecting women from this harmful procedure and to not be influenced by those profiting from abortions. I would tell them to listen to the experiences of those who have gone through an abortion and to not listen to those who have something to gain from performing them."

S., Texas

"That they are allowing mothers, out of ignorance and lack of information, to destroy their relationships with their children and that abortion being good for women is a lie!"

Jennifer, Georgia

"Just because a "fetus" doesn't have a name doesn't mean it's not a person. At 28 days it has heartbeats; does that constitute life? It is the most unnatural act of the "civilized" world for a mother to kill her own baby."

Paula, Ohio

"Listen to those voices of those who have experienced the physical and emotional consequences. A whole segment of society – men and women – are suffering because they did what was wrong even though it was legal."

Shirley, California

"It seems like an answer to a difficult situation. As with most quick fixes, though, it creates tremendous psychological and emotional difficulties that overflow and stay hidden for years. In most cases continues into the following generations if not addressed. God is the only answer at that point."

Maureen, Pennsylvania

"I would ask them since murder is illegal and they know it is, then why are they allowing millions of babies to be murdered each year. ABORTION IS MURDER!!! I would also ask them do they care about all the emotionally and physically scarred women and men left over after an abortion."

Tina, Georgia

# More Women's Stories – Forced Abortion, Rape, And Incest – Why Abortion is Not The Answer

As you can see from the previous chapter, the women's own words are very powerful. The Bible tells us our testimony and Jesus can overcome Satan, the Father of Lies.

*"And they overcame him because of the blood of the Lamb and because of the word of their testimony, and they did not love their life even when faced with death."*

Revelations 12:11

One of the ways that Abortion Hurts Women is that once it is legal it allows other people to force women to have abortions to solve their problem, not because the woman wants an abortion. As you read in chapter four, Sandra Cano herself, the *"Doe"* of *Doe v. Bolton*, had to flee to Oklahoma to avoid having an abortion performed on her against her will. As you saw in the previous chapter, many people unduly pressure women into having abortions. As a result of what we learned from collecting women's testimonies, we created the Center Against Forced Abortion in 2009. Fortunately, forced abortion is **illegal** in every state. Even in pro-abortion states like New York or California, only a voluntary abortion is legal. It is illegal to unduly pressure, coerce or force a woman to have an abortion in every state.

The three most common types of forced abortion are:

1. Adult parents or guardians forcing a minor female to abort.
2. An adult male forcing a woman to abort his child.
3. Human trafficking or prostitution with forced abortion by the trafficker.

All forced abortions in every state are illegal. You can find free legal tools and training to help anyone stop forced abortion on our website: www.thejusticefoundation.org under Center Against Forced Abortion (CAFA).

**Here is Molly White's statement about parental pressure. Molly White was our Texas *Operation Outcry* Leader for many years.**

"How could you get pregnant again? How do you think you are going to be able to take care of another baby? What are our friends going to think? You are going to have an abortion and if you don't your father and I will not help you anymore. You will be on your own!" Those are some of the things my parents yelled at me when I told them I was pregnant."

"On February 13, 1985 after buckling under intense pressure from my parents, I was taken to an OB/Gyn clinic in Temple, Texas for a scheduled abortion. My mother drove me and did all the talking to the doctor who was going to perform the abortion. I did not say a word. I was emotionally numb and withdrawn. I can't remember the conversation, but I do remember my mother coming up with all the excuses as to why I needed to have the abortion. The doctor did not ask me any questions. If he did, I don't remember. I don't even remember what he looks like or what his name is.

All I do remember is that we were in the same clinic where the doctor who delivered my triplets just a couple of years earlier practiced. This doctor and the nurses had to know me well. Not too many women delivering triplets were patients at their center. They had to remember the trauma that I experienced when two of my triplets were stillborn. I have no doubt the whole clinic staff knew very well the details of that delivery."

"After the consultation with the doctor I was taken to an examining room where he would begin the two-day procedure that he and my mother agreed upon. Looking back, I was just in the early stages of a first trimester pregnancy. Nine maybe ten weeks is all. Why a second trimester procedure? I believe now it was for more money. Second trimester abortions are more expensive than first trimester abortions. They are also more emotionally traumatizing for the patient."

"After the doctor finished inserting laminaria to dilate my cervix he left the room. I crawled off the table and began getting dressed. The more I thought about what was about to happen to me and my baby, the angrier I got. All of the pent-up frustration, hurt and anger that I felt because my parents were pressuring me to have an unwanted abortion exploded. I began to yell and cry very loudly. The nurse rushed back in the room and asked me what was going on? I told her to get the doctor and explained that I did not want to have this abortion, I never wanted to have the abortion. I wanted the doctor to remove the laminaria."

"The nurse retrieved the doctor. I told him, "I don't want to have an abortion. I never wanted to have the abortion. My parents want me to have it. I have already had an abortion, I just buried two babies and I have a little boy at home. I DO NOT WANT TO DO THIS", I told him."

"'It's too late now', the doctor replied. "If I remove the laminaria it could damage your cervix". Feeling like a trapped animal and believing what the doctor said, I slumped in despair and left."

"I had a miserable night from the pain of my cervix being dilated and the emotional anguish I was feeling. I told myself that I was NOT GOING TO GO THROUGH WITH IT. I will simply tell the doctor that I do not want the abortion. Surely he will listen and help me, I thought."

"I was taken back to the clinic the next day with the resolve of not having the abortion. I spoke with the doctor and told him, again, that I did not want to go through with the abortion and all the reasons why I didn't want the abortion."

"Again, he said, 'It's too late. Now you have dilated and you will miscarry if I don't complete the procedure.'"

"That did it, being vulnerable, ignorant, emotionally traumatized and feeling like I had nowhere to go, no help and no support, I went through with the rest of the procedure the whole while crying and telling the doctor repeatedly that I did not want to have an abortion, I did not want to have an abortion."

"I left the clinic that day a walking dead woman. I was dead to myself. I was dead to my feelings and I was dead to my emotions. I locked them deep within the recesses of my heart just so that I could go through the motions of living."

"That pressured, unwanted abortion caused me to have deep emotional problems and deep seeded anger and hatred towards my parents, doctors, nurses, and men. It also caused damage to my cervix, endometriosis and a tumor which grew within my womb. But, most of all, that abortion caused bonding and nurturing issues with my adorable son who had to live with an emotionally and psychologically traumatized mother for many years."

"Legal abortion has opened the door to violence and exploitation of pregnant women. I am angry with the medical establishment, the legal system, and our lawmakers for allowing pregnant women to be victimized everyday by abortion providers and family members. According to research, 64% of women who have had an abortion report being forced, pressured, or coerced into an unwanted abortion decision. (Rue VM, Coleman PK, Rue JJ, Reardon DC. "Induced abortion and traumatic stress: A preliminary comparison of American and Russian women." Medical Science Monitor. 10(10):SR5-16 (2004).) Lawmakers should make sure this does not continue to happen in the United States or anywhere else in the world for that matter. I hope my testimony brings light into this shameful consequence of a so called "woman's right to choose" and leads to the end of legal abortion across America and more pregnancy support and care centers to help pregnant women have healthy and happy pregnancies and babies."

## Rape and Incest

Incest is actually the easiest "exception" argument to refute. Incest is rape by a family member against a minor child. If the abuser can take the child to get an abortion without anyone knowing, and claiming someone else is the father, then the abuse simply continues, sometimes for years. That is what happens in many cases, and abortion facilities notoriously do not follow child abuse laws and report minor abortions. An under-age girl is prima facie evidence of a rape or sexual assault because such a minor cannot legally consent to sex.

Soon after *Dobbs* reversed *Roe v. Wade*, a classic example of this made national news. The case of a ten-year-old girl who was raped made national news when her abortionist, with the abortion industry publicists and sympathetic national media, released the story of the tragedy of a girl who had been raped, and had to travel to another state to get an abortion.

Of course, the rape is a tragedy and a crime. Did the abortionist notify the authorities about the rape as required by law? Not according to authorities. Did anyone ask the girl what she wanted? Or did everyone just assume she wanted an abortion.

The abortionist was investigated and potentially charged with failure to report this child abuse. Thankfully, because of the publicity the authorities investigated and charged the mother's boyfriend with the crime. In the normal case, the abortionist would have just killed the child, destroyed the evidence, and allowed the abuse to continue.

Why add abortion trauma to the trauma of rape? Why do we assume that abortion is the answer. My experience with the testimonies of women who have been raped show two kind of responses. In one, the woman chooses to keep the child and finds that healing actually comes from giving life. Whereas she was a victim of a heinous crime. Now she was a heroine who gave life. Some kept the children and found that the child gave her life new meaning.

Others chose to abort. They can report feeling after abortion as if they were the criminal now. Someone who had killed a child, instead of a victim of crime.

We cannot imagine the bond and life-giving healing that can occur even after the horrible tragedy of rape. As strange as it may seem, in Nigeria, the Nigerian army has been accused of forced abortions. https://www.reuters.com/investigates/special-report/nigeria-military-abortions/. The women were captured by Islamic terrorists and forcibly impregnated. Then they were returned to their homes, and the Nigerian soldiers felt the children were going to be terrorists who must be eliminated. The women were traumatized even further by forced abortion and had become deeply attached to their babies in the womb. The babies are innocent human beings who deserve life.

Of course, no woman has to parent the child if she does not want do so. She should receive free counseling and support from society and use The Safe Haven laws if she so desires.

## Nona's Story

Nona was date raped when she was 15 years old. Everyone thought abortion was the answer to her problem. Here is her testimony when she was testifying against a rape exception in an abortion ban law, except to save the life of the mother, before the Arkansas legislature. After hearing her testimony, and reading the testimony of Arkansas *Operation Outcry* women, Arkansas passed a law in 2021 to ban abortion except to save the life of the mother, with no rape exception. Arkansas and all 50 states allow a woman to use Safe Haven laws to relinquish the child at birth. All pro-life laws allow abortion to save the life of the mother. The lead sponsors were State Senator Jason Rapert and State Representative Mary Bentley.

Here is Nona Ellington's testimony before the Arkansas Senate:

"My name is Nona Ellington. Thank you, Madame Chair. It is an honor to be here today. I am in support of SB6, the Unborn Child Protection Act. I represent thousands, and probably millions, of women that have been hurt by abortion.

**I was 15 years old. I was a victim of date rape and as horrible as that date rape experience was,** when I went to Planned Parenthood realizing I was pregnant, they told me "the best thing you can do is since it is just a blob of tissue, is to go ahead and have an abortion since you are so young and still in high school."

"Well, my mother and my sister took me to have an abortion as I wasn't given any other options at all. As a result of that one abortion at age 15, I was never able to have children – ever. Instead I had five miscarriages. Three of them were tubal pregnancies that required emergency surgery and very near-death experiences. I also in 2014 went through breast cancer as a result of that abortion.

Studies have proven the link between abortion and breast cancer. I had the genetic testing done proving that I am not a carrier of the breast cancer gene. Thank you for considering this bill for all of the women of Arkansas".

# CHAPTER SEVEN

# 9/11 Shakes the Nation – Sheer Terror to Understand What it Means

One of the most horrific and devastating events in American history was the terrorist attack of 9/11 against the World Trade Center. Could this have been related to the issue of abortion? I believe with all my heart that it was. Let me explain.

We began to collect the testimonies of women hurt by abortion in the year 2000. In 2001, Molly White of *Operation Outcry* and I attended our first National Press Conference at the National Press Club in Washington, D.C. We were with a group of major national pro-life leaders in a combined effort called "Shake the Nation". It was organized by incredible pro-life activist, Janet Folger Porter.

Janet had also been the one who gave us the name Operation Outcry: Silent No More in Fort Lauderdale, Florida, shortly after we had begun to collect women's testimonies by appearing on national Christian radio and television programs with women with abortion in their past. The women would tell their stories and then we would ask other women to call or write us and tell us their stories.

One of the first national ministries to have us on the air was the D. James Kennedy Center for Reclaiming America. Janet was their Executive Director at the time. After hearing our story of why we were collecting testimonies and the promise of God that *Roe v. Wade* would be reversed, Janet asked if we had a name. I said no, she said, "Let's pray." We held hands, we bowed our heads and she prayed. At the end, she said, "How about *Operation Outcry*: Silent No More?" I said, 'That's amazing." We all felt it was the perfect name. We continued to pray into it.

Later I contacted Bill Gothard of The Institute in Basic Life Principles and asked him if he would pray for our ministry and help us. He said, "Al, you don't just need prayer, you need outcry." He knew nothing about the name that that Janet had proposed, but that we were not quite using yet. Instead he said, "I'm just now writing a book on the power of outcry. For something like this you don't just need regular prayer, you need the power of crying out to God." This was a real confirmation to me. His book *The Power of Crying Out* can be found at Barnes and Nobles, https://www.barnesandno-ble.com/w/the-power-of-crying-out-bill-gothard/1103165279.

Back to Washington, D.C., The Shake the Nation Campaign was going to send rattles to Congress asking them to pass a national pro-life law banning abortion. It also had a television ad associated with this campaign that would be shown across the nation. The ad showed millions of babies on the National Mall. which disappeared one at a time, as the headline "*Roe v. Wade* is Decided" displayed on a newspaper above the babies. The disappearing babies continued until one-third of the babies were eliminated, the number of aborted children because of abortion in each generation.

This was the first time for the women of *Operation Outcry* to appear in public, and perhaps the first time post-abortive women had appeared at a national pro-life press conference. The other pro-life leaders spoke first and towards the end, Molly White was allowed to give her testimony. In my opinion, it shut the mouth of the lions. The hostile media which felt perfectly free to attack pro-life leaders were silenced by the powerful testimony of Molly White.

At the end of the press conference, some of the female reporters came to Molly and asked questions, almost sympathetically. One asked: "I'm sorry you had a bad experience, but wouldn't you want other women to be able to have abortion, if it doesn't hurt them?" Molly answered, "It always hurts women. You can't kill a child without it wounding you." I remember that then one of the reporters' friends said to her, "You know my daughter just aborted my grandchild." She said it with deep sadness. The other reporter turned and said to her, "I didn't know that." She said, "I know, I haven't told anyone." And they turned and left. Abortion wounds everyone.

At the end of the press conference, as we were finishing up and preparing to leave, I said, "Janet, I have a feeling that God's going "Shake the Nation" somehow." That was September 4th, 2001. One week later, God shook the nation when the planes of terrorists crashed into the symbol of America's financial and economic power, the World Trade Center. America was so shocked that we had to pull our national ad campaign "Shake the Nation" because the nation had been shaken to the core.

Now, how is that attack related to abortion? Remember that on February 12th, 2000, the Lord had given me the passages from Isaiah all the way from Chapters 28 to 36, especially focusing on Isaiah 28:14-22. One of those key passages said that it "shall be sheer terror to understand what this message means." It also said that the overwhelming scourge would be coming day after day.

So I guess you could say that one week before 9/11, after our Shake the Nation press conference, I had a premonition, a feeling, that something bad was going to happen. Was the Holy Spirit trying to tell me something? But I had no idea what the words God had told me really meant in Isaiah 28:19 which said, "And it will be sheer terror to understand what it means." In the footnotes, it said to understand the report or the message. So all I had was a feeling and I talked about it with Janet, but I didn't tell anyone else that something was coming. Then on September 11th, America was shaken and shattered. With what kind of a problem? "Terror attack." I went back to the passage and I found this also, that the Lord had told me would happen in Isaiah 29:2-4,

> "I will bring distress to Ariel, and she will be a city of grieving and mourning; And she will be like an Ariel to me (Ariel is another name for Jerusalem, the capital). I will camp against you encircling you, and I will set up siegeworks against you and I will raise up battle towers against you. Then you will be brought low; from the earth you will speak, and from the dust where you are prostrate Your words will come. Your voice will also be like that of a spirit from the ground, and your speech will whisper from the dust."

Verses 5-8 continues:

> "But the multitude of your enemies will become like fine dust, and the multitude of the ruthless ones like the chaff which blows away;and it will happen instantly, suddenly. From the Lord of armies you will be <u>punished with thunder and earthquake and loud noise, with whirlwind and tempest and the flame of a consuming fire</u>. And the multitude of all the nations who wage war against Ariel, even all who wage war against her and her stronghold, and who distress her, <u>will be like a dream, a vision of the night</u>. It will be as when a hungry person dreams—And behold, he is eating; But when he awakens, his hunger is not satisfied, or as when a thirsty person dreams—And behold, he is drinking, but

when he awakens, behold, he is faint and his thirst is not quenched."

Note that there were a multitude of nations represented by the Islamic terror groups that joined forces to bring that attack on America. It was a terror attack. Remember that it was like a dream to everyone, one of the most common things that I said to other people and that I heard on the television was "I cannot believe it." "It is like a dream" or "it is like a nightmare". I cannot believe this is happening." What brought down the two towers? It was not the initial explosion which was like a thunderous earthquake, like a loud noise with whirlwind and tempests and the flame of a consuming fire. It was the consuming fire which melted the steel girders which brought the towers down. Doesn't that describe the attack?

Then the next year after the attack, I watched the Memorial at Ground Zero and I was shocked that a small dust devil came down and began to swirl. It lifted up dust as the names of the dead were read the first year. It seemed to me as if verse four was fulfilled.

"Then you will be brought low from the Earth. You will speak, and from the dust where you are prostrated. Your words will come. Your voice will also be like that of a spirit, from the ground, and your speech will whisper from the dust."

It seemed as if the cries of the dead to be remembered as their names were read came up from the dust. I have to confess that I feel I failed the Lord in not bringing this message to America at that time, but perhaps America and the Church were not ready to hear it, or even I to say it. I believe 9/11 was a judgment of God for the sin of abortion, one of America's four great sins.

I believe that America has committed the four great sins that can bring national destruction as prophesied, foretold and explained in the Bible. God punished his own chosen people, the nation of Israel, with national destruction when they committed these four great sins. Are we any better than Israel? No. Is God a fair and equal and just judge judging all the same? Yes.

What are the four great sins? Number one: Forsaking God. This is the greatest and original sin. I believe that we committed that sin in 1962 in the school prayer case when the Supreme Court removed God from our public schools and our public life in *Engel v. Vitale*. You can chart the history of America and it is an increasingly downward spiral after 1962. A perversion, degradation and loss of national prestige has occurred from that day forth. Slow enough that there's time to repent, and unstoppable without repentance.

Number Two: Shedding Innocent Blood. The second sin that man committed after eating fruit from the tree of knowledge of good and evil and forsaking God in the garden was the sin of shedding innocent blood. Cain killed his brother Abel because he wanted his own way and he was angry.

Number Three: Sexual Immorality on a vast scale.

Number Four: Greed.

You can find references to all these things in the Bible as the reason for the national destruction of Israel. It is time for America to repent. We need national days of repentance and even a year of repentance before the final judgments of God come upon the Earth and America.

How do you escape the judgment of God? How do you escape the wrath of God which is justifiable wrath because of the killing of so many children and the rank perversion that we are experiencing in our culture today? You have to ask for forgiveness and turn to God. Psalms 147:3 (NASB) "He heals the brokenhearted And binds up their wounds." God is saying to America right now: "America, return to me and I will return to you."

I first heard that message from the Lord as I cried out under the Cross of the First Great Awakening on Saint Simons Island. As I cried out in a language of unknown tongues, I didn't even understand it as I cried out to God. But George Pond, a fellow employee then and now a TJF Board member, who was with me at the time then said, "I know what it means. God is saying America return to me and I will return to you." God has said that many, many times to Israel and other countries throughout the history of man. He longs for us to repent rather than to suffer judgment.

If you have not turned from your sins and accepted the salvation and healing of Jesus Christ, please, for your own sake and His, do it now.

## Critical Prayer Time At the Republican National Convention

The importance of prayer to the success of this effort was further highlighted to me at the 2000 Republican National Convention in Philadelphia where our Declaration of Independence and our Constitution were drafted. On August 1, 2000, I was in the guest section. I walked down from the top section to the floor and I went out to the hospitality suite. I thought I'd go through there and get a little something on my way home. I had never been in the hospitality suite. As I was wandering around, I noticed an interfaith chapel. "Oh, that would be great. I'll just say a prayer before I go home." I went in and introduced myself. Some very, very sweet people said, "Oh, would you like us to pray for you?" And I said, "I would love that!" I started to tell them we represented Norma McCorvey and Sandra Cano, that we were working to overturn *Roe v. Wade*. They immediately pulled a man over named Richard J. Simmons, who I did not recognize.

I began to tell him a little bit about our work and before he even heard much, he said, "Oh, we need to pray for strength to those who turn back the battle at the gate. That's what we need to pray for you, for strength to those who turn back the battle at the gate."

I asked him, "What do you mean?"

He said, "That's what you are in. You're in a battle. You need strength to turn back the battle."

I said, "Where's that come from?"

"Isaiah 28:6." This was before I had told him about the Isaiah passages 28:14-22.

I said, "I believe we have been promised by God that He is going to end *Roe v. Wade* soon and TJF is to be part of it." He was very aware of the passage: "*...your covenant with death will be annulled...,*" (Isaiah 28:18). I shared with him our vision and how it came to us. He said it was amazing how God had shared the same passages with him. He was familiar with Topheth being a place of human sacrifice and he had been praying against abortion for many years.

Richard, better known as Dick, also had an apartment right behind the United States Supreme Court. He was there to pray for the Supreme Court and Congress. He has had as many as 30 men sleeping and praying there. Before that, when Clayton and I were walking in the Supreme Court area, Clayton said, "Allan, we've got to have an apartment here. We've got to have an apartment or office right near here. We're going to be working here. We need to be here." I said, "Oh, yeah. Well, Clayton, when and if we need it, the Lord will provide it." And sure enough, the Lord provided a place to stay or work whenever we are in D.C. at Dick's place. Dick is now with The Lord and his place is now called the American Center for Prayer and Revival. Thousands of prayers for the end of abortion have filled that place over the years.

Dick was also the leader of *Men for Nations*, a pre-dawn national prayer offensive for men. Richard believed men particularly need to be involved in offensive prayer, before dawn as in war. Men often ask, "Is there a role for men in *Operation Outcry*? We've been hurt, too." We need men to lead in prayer. Praying for those in authority like the Supreme Court, the President, and Senators, is particularly spiritual warfare. 1 Timothy 2:1-8. Richard believes it's pre-dawn attacks that are the most successful in the military. Jesus arose before dawn. David arose before dawn. Richard called for a men's pre-dawn national prayer offensive. He agreed to lift us up and be one of our prayer warriors for *Operation Outcry*.

Dick told me, "We have to pray so that God can do *His* work. If we pray, then God will do *His* work, but if we don't pray, then God will watch *us* try to do *His* work." He told me this even before I had shared the Isaiah 28:14-22 passages, but it reconfirmed for me again what God said in Isaiah 28:21.

> *"For the Lord will rise up as at Mount Perazim* (Master of Breakthrough), *He will be stirred up as in the valley of Gibeon* (when the sun stood still), *To do His task, His unusual task, and to work His work, His extraordinary work."*
>
> Isaiah 28:21

This confirmed again for me that I should not be a mocker or a scorner or despise the things of God or not believe that God will do His unusual work or work in unusual ways in *Operation Outcry*. After hearing His promise to cancel the covenant with death, the Lord warns us as believers:

> *"And now do not carry on as scoffers, or your fetters will be made stronger; For I have heard from the Lord God of Hosts of decisive destruction on all the earth (land in RSV)."*
>
> Isaiah 28:22 NASB

God is the one who does the work. Our job is to believe and obey. He has guided and directed us on this journey so far.

Also, read Isaiah 29:5-8 below and see if it does not chillingly describe the collapse of the World Trade Center by a consuming fire.

*"But the multitude of your enemies will become like fine dust, And the multitude of the ruthless ones like the chaff which blows away; And it will happen instantly, suddenly. From the LORD of hosts you will be punished with thunder and earthquake and loud noise, With whirlwind and tempest and the flame of a consuming fire. And the multitude of all the nations who wage war against Ariel, Even all who wage war against her and her stronghold, and who distress her, will be like a dream, a vision of the night. It will be as when a hungry man dreams, And behold, he is eating; But when he awakens, his hunger is not satisfied, Or as when a thirsty man dreams, And behold, he is drinking, But when he awakens, behold, he is faint And his thirst is not quenched. Thus the multitude of all the nations will be who wage war against Mount Zion."*

Isaiah 29:5-8

A *consuming* fire destroyed the World Trade Center, and the Pentagon driven by the jet fuel of the planes hitting them directly. How many times did you hear people say, "It seems like a dream. It can't be real."

# CHAPTER EIGHT

# Birth of The Moral Outcry Petition

We started out in 2000 with *Operation Outcry* and then, in 2017, we began to represent Melinda Thybault (pronounced "Té-bo"), the Founder of The Moral Outcry Petition. On Jan 15, 2017, I was watching Glory of Zion's Sunday morning program on TV at my home. As I listened, I bolted right out of my chair because one of the prophetic intercessors there was saying something like "What was tried 17 years ago, but was not ready, is now ready. The roads are completed." I felt immediately that the word was for me because it was 17 years after the time from 2000 when we first began to try to overturn *Roe*. I felt the Lord was telling me the roads were complete to go back to the Supreme Court. My wife felt the word also meant that networks were complete that were needed for the work. I was excited, but what did it mean? What could I do? I just waited in expectation to see what the Lord would do next.

In March 2017, a few months after receiving that word, Melinda Thybault contacted me and said "Has anybody ever filed a petition to reverse *Roe* at the Supreme Court?" She had had a vision in prayer or a picture in her mind of people rolling out a petition before the Supreme Court. So she contacted me. She was one of the Pro-Life Prayer Directors with her husband, Denny, at the International House of Prayer in Kansas City. (IHOPKC).

She had seen a vision while praying one day of a scroll being rolled out before the Supreme Court as was rolled out in Parliament by Willian Wilberforce in the movie "Amazing Grace" to end slavery in England. She said, "I think we ought to do this. Has it ever been done before?" I said, "I don't think its ever been done before". Then she said, "Can it be done?" I thought a bit, then said, "Yes. I think it can be done. There's no rule against it, so why not?" And we prayed, prayed, prayed, and that was the birth of The Moral Outcry Petition.

Along the way on this God journey since 2000, I had visited IHOP-KC several times with great prophetic significance. The very first time I visited, a prophetic intercessor group there prayed for us. One of the groups who knew nothing about us said, "I feel Isaiah 28 is a very important scripture for you." As you know by now, Is. 28 was an incredibly important passage to me. It had changed the direction of my life. This encouraged me to believe that it really was the Lord Himself who gave us the promises in Isaiah 28, and that the "covenant with death would be annulled; that the agreement with the grave would not stand"; that He would "breakthrough" with amazing, extraordinary events; and that it would be sheer terror to understand this message. See Isaiah 28:14-22. I had the promise, but little did I know how it would unfold.

Later I learned that IHOPKC had gone into 24/7 prayer in September 1999. One of the things they were praying for was an end to abortion. Just four months later in January and February 2000, we got the call to start *Operation Outcry* and go back to the Supreme Court with Norma and Sandra. I believe that Operation Outcry was birthed in part by IHOP-KC's prayers. In addition, in 2000, Lou Engle and "The Call" got the call from The Lord to start The Call to End Abortion. Through action and through prayer he gathered 400,000 young people in 2000 to pray on the National

Mall for the end of abortion, Lou crafted a 22-word prayer that has been prayed millions of times: "Jesus, I plead your Blood over my sins and the sins of my nation. God, end abortion and send revival to America." Now *Roe* has been reversed and revival is coming next!

In 2017, The Moral Outcry Petition was created to ask the U.S. Supreme Court to reverse *Roe v. Wade*, *Planned Parenthood v. Casey* and *Doe v. Bolton*, the Court's abortion decisions.

We called it The Moral Outcry because of a phrase used by Justice Scalia before his death. He sent out a friend to thank intercessors who wore red tape on their lips with the word "LIFE" emblazoned on it as they prayed in a Silent Siege in front of the Supreme Court. (See bound4life.com) He thanked them, but said Justice Scalia had asked, "Where is the moral outcry against abortion?"

On December 1, 2021, in oral argument the Supreme Court Justices discussed two of the reasons for reversing *Roe* given in The Moral Outcry Petition. On June 24, 2022, the Supreme Court reversed *Roe* and *Casey* and actually wrote in the decision about two of the reasons for reversing *Roe* given in The Moral Outcry Petition for doing so.

The Moral Outcry Petition achieved justice by seeking the reversal of *Roe* and will now further galvanize that Moral Outcry to Make Abortion Illegal in all 50 States. It will continue to wake up the nation and galvanize the national conscience to end the scourge of abortion in America. It will declare that as a people, we do not accept the compromise that leads to the unnecessary death of millions of innocent babies.

The Moral Outcry Petition, through its Founder, Melinda Thybault, operates under the non-profit umbrella of, and is represented legally by The Justice Foundation. As a signer of the petition, your name (but no other data) may be shared with various courts and legislatures across the nation, as they consider to restrict or ban abortion in their states. Our ultimate goal is to make the Crime Against Humanity, which is abortion, illegal in all 50 States.

Here are the reasons why abortion will be illegal and unthinkable in all 50 states.

1.  Abortion is a Crime Against Humanity
2.  Abortion Hurts Women
3.  Safe Haven laws in all fifty states eliminate all burden of parenting without killing the child if the mother wishes to relinquish her child at a safe place at no cost, unlike abortion
4.  Millions of women are waiting to adopt newborns
5.  New science shows life begins at fertilization

See www.themoraloutcry.com.

## Denny and Mindy Thybault Share Their Thoughts on the Reversal of *Roe v. Wade*

These are some thoughts shared by the Thybaults at our Celebration of the Reversal of *Roe v. Wade* on Sept. 24, 2022.

"Hi, everyone, Mindy (Melinda) Thybault here. We just want to say hi to everyone and I'm glad we could join you briefly to celebrate The Lord's greatness in overturning *Roe v. Wade*. After our original children left home, and we were empty nesters, the Lord led us to adopt three beautiful biological children we love dearly. Through prayer, the Lord told us to adopt four frozen human embryos. The Lord eventually placed two of their frozen embryo baby pictures before the U.S. Supreme Court, thanks to Allan Parker and The Justice Foundation. They provided years of representation for us, numerous briefs, advice, and assistance, all at no charge, and countless prayers. We just want to thank the Lord for this. This was His idea. He was the one that orchestrated this whole Moral Outcry Petition. So, we give Him all the glory, all the honor unto Him. We're just really honored to be a part of it with Allan Parker."

"So we wanted to mention a few little bullet points of how this even happened, how just a mom and a dad with way too many kids at our age came up with this idea via The Lord."

"We were contending in the Global Prayer Room here in Kansas City International House of Prayer for the overturning of *Roe v. Wade*. We were given a scripture by somebody up in Michigan who gave Denny the scripture, Ezekiel 21:27. "I will overturn, overturn, overturn. It will be no more." Mindy and I (Denny – Mindy's husband) grabbed a hold of it with our prayer team. We shared that and said, "Let's go after it. Let's spend some energy in this." We asked, "God, what do you mean? You're going to overturn *Roe v. Wade*? What does that look like?" "So then shortly after that we had a prophetic word given to us." Somebody came to Mindy and said, "I think you're supposed to be a part of challenging *Roe v. Wade*." And the woman followed it up with, "I wasn't sure if you're going to be pregnant." I thought, "What on earth?"

On another early occasion, Mindy had received a prophetic word about a pregnant woman finding favor with the Supreme Court which we actually were planning on doing because The Lord had asked us to loan Him my womb. He wanted us to adopt frozen embryos and place them into my womb, even after menopause and give birth. Wow. We really had to pray into that one, but He convinced us it was Him, and we obeyed. Prior to that we had adopted, through traditional adoption, three precious newborn girls who were in danger of abortion."

"So we really went after this because Denny had gotten that Scripture and we said, 'Okay, Lord. This has got to be your idea and you've got to Do it.' Our three traditionally adopted girls were still young and with us as a major part all the way on this journey. So we decided to adopt four frozen human embryos who would otherwise die if they were not adopted by someone." "And one morning

I (Mindy) woke up a few weeks later and we were both in prayer and I kept seeing William Wilberforce roll out his petition before Parliament to overturn the slave trade. So we contacted Allan and said, 'Has anybody ever petitioned the Supreme Court to reverse Roe?' and the rest is history. In the *Dobbs* case that reversed *Roe*, we included over half a million signatures on The Moral Outcry Brief and we just can't believe that it happened."

"The Lord told us to adopt four frozen embryos at the start of this process. They were another couple's children who would otherwise be discarded or destroyed. Their precious human life would be ended. They are just as precious to God as any other human life. While we believe in vitro fertilization in some highly regulated practices may be ok, it is very often abused and ends with the death of human beings. But we believe saving human life is always morally good."

"So we knew Gideon (our first frozen embryo child) was the start of the petition because he was born first. His picture and story were in the very early Moral Outcry briefs. We knew Pearl was the end piece to this journey. The two boys in the middle were miscarried naturally. And so while Mindy and I (Denny) were in the hospital, she was giving birth to Pearl. We're in labor, she's pushing hard. Day Two: We had a conversation in the room and I just said, 'You know, I really want the Lord to give us a scripture and I want Him to just really point out Daniel 7:22, which states that God made a judgment in favor of the saints. You can go back to read it, but Daniel 7:22 is a critical prophetic passage to us and this time we are living in. And so I really wanted him to give us some kind of sign during this delivery with Pearl – that this is truly the end of *Roe v. Wade*.'"

"Long story short, Day Two of the delivery goes by, Day Three goes by, Day Four of pretty hard labor since Mindy is over 50 years old at this time, I completely lost track of that thought of asking for a sign until we had to have a C-section right away. So the doctors threw us in a room and they get Mindy all prepped and everything. Then all of a sudden, when Pearl is now finally on a table after birth, I'm like 'Oh, Daniel 7:22, where's that?' So I asked how much did she weigh? And how long is she and all those things, but they did not mention 7:22. Then I said, 'Okay, no sign I guess. Okay wait, wait. What time was she born?' And the nurse flips through her paper. She was born at exactly 7:22."

"It was amazing and the Lord kept giving us hugs like this. The whole journey along the way. So we just knew at that point that was a hug from the Lord, saying I am going to do this – this will be the one that reverses *Roe*. Here's your sign: Daniel 7-22. A judgment in favor of the Saints, so she was born Christmas Eve, December 24, 2021, just a few weeks after the Oral Argument in *Dobbs*. But six months to the day later on her six-month birthday, June 24, 2022, *Roe* was overturned.

"We love you guys. Have a great time and join us as we and The Justice Foundation have now turned The Moral Outcry Petition asking the Supreme Court to reverse *Roe v. Wade* into **The Moral Outcry Petition to Make Abortion Illegal in all 50 States.** Praise the Lord. Thank you all for signing The Moral Outcry Petition. (See www.themoraloutcry.com) Be blessed in the Lord and in the power of His strength." From Denny and Melinda Thybault.

In the Book of Exodus, the Lord asked his people to make a contribution for the work of the Lord and the Sanctuary. He said:

*"Tell the sons of Israel to raise a contribution for Me; from every man whose heart moves him you shall raise the contribution. And this is the contribution which you are to raise from them: gold, silver, and bronze, blue, purple and scarlet material, fine linen, goat hair, rams skins dyed red, porpoise skins, acacia wood, oil for lighting, spices for the anointing oil and for the fragrant incense, onyx stones and setting stones, for the ephod and breast piece. And let them*

*construct a sanctuary for Me, that I may dwell among them. According to all that I am going to show you, as the pattern of the tabernacle and the pattern of all its furniture, just so you shall construct it."*

Exodus 25:1-9

The continued work of *Operation Outcry* and *The Moral Outcry Petition to Make Abortion Illegal In All 50 States* will not be easy. It takes more than just money. It cannot be done by one person, or one group alone. It is a massive work that will require the contributions of many people in many ways whose heart is moved to be part of ending legalized abortion in America. The Lord's pattern is for each to give as they have been blessed. To freely and cheerfully give. I want to lay out all the ways anyone can be involved and ask you to prayerfully consider your role.

First, cry out to God. Everyone reading this book can and should pray that God will help us. Then sign The Moral Outcry Petition to Make Abortion Illegal in all 50 States at <u>www.themoraloutcry.com</u>. (See Chapter 8) I would ask you to stop right now and pray for the success of this effort as the Holy Spirit leads you. Do it now so that you can be a part of this effort even if this is all you are ever moved to do. Organize prayer in your area. *The Moral Outcry* is a crying out to God first. Then it is a powerful truthful witness and legal strategy. There is power in crying out, which is more than just prayer. There is a special reason why this project is called *Operation Outcry*.

*The Moral Outcry* continues to emphasize the key role of women who have had abortions. If the women remain silent, if they refuse to tell the truth, then the lies of abortion will continue to deceive millions. *The Moral Outcry* and *Operation Outcry* recognize that too much of the truth has remained locked up in the secret place inside women's' hearts until now. This is the opportunity for women who have had abortions to overcome evil with good, to confess their sins and receive healing and bring healing to a nation.

Outcry is also a key phrase because it involves the deepest level of communication with God. It is not just a casual prayer. It is not just once a week on Sunday. It is not a prayer someone else prays for you. It is a deep cry from the heart. It conveys pain, grief, shame, hurt, longing, struggle, and the need for God's help in the face of our human helplessness.

## More Amazing and Extraordinary Things God Has Done!

In the *Dobbs* case, we filed 4,728 women's testimonies *Operation Outcry* collected over the years. If you've been a financial supporter, you have kept us alive in order to do that work. I want to thank you. Thank you. Thank you. We cannot exist without financial contributions from people like you.

Now, what are just a few of those unusual and extraordinary events in American history relating to reversing *Roe*? See Isaiah 28:14-22.

1. First of all, in 2000, that two landmark litigation winners would ever go back to the Supreme Court to say, "Please reverse our cases." That has never happened before that they would even ask for reversal, and it's even more amazing that they would eventually succeed. At first, they were denied, but on June 24, 2021 their desire was granted.
2. Then in 2007, the Supreme Court upheld the federal ban on partial birth abortion in *Gonzales v. Carhart*, 550 U.S. 124 (2007). "Abortion Foes See Validation for New Tactic." Here's the New York Times:

# Victory at the Supreme Court!
### Citing The Justice Foundation's brief,
### Court acknowledges abortion hurts women

Thirty-five years after the Supreme Court legalized abortion-on-demand up to the day of birth, the tide has turned. It's the beginning of the end of *Roe v. Wade.*

Declaring the horrific and gruesome "partial-birth abortion" procedure illegal, the Supreme Court cited The Justice Foundation's Amicus Brief (also known as a friend of the court brief) in its ruling on the case. The brief – the only one cited by the Court – was filed on behalf of Sandra Cano, who was "Mary Doe" of *Doe v. Bolton* (the companion case to *Roe v. Wade*), and 180 women hurt by abortion.

Citing evidence The Justice Foundation presented, and accepting our argument that "abortion hurts women," the Court acknowledged that "some women come to regret" having an abortion. "Whether to have an abortion requires a difficult and painful moral decision" and is "fraught with emotional consequence," the Court said.

## The New York Times

*May 22, 2007*

### Abortion Foes See Validation for New Tactic

**Excerpts from**
*The New York Times*
Article by Robin Toner

*Allan Parker, President of The Justice Foundation*

**Read**

*The Justice Foundation's brief and the Supreme Court ruling at* **www.operationoutcry.org**

... [The] **Supreme Court decision** upholding the Partial-Birth Abortion Ban Act **marked a milestone** for a different argument advanced by anti-abortion leaders ... . They say that **abortion, as a rule, is not in the best interest of the woman**; that women are often misled or ill-informed about its risks to their own physical or emotional health; and that the interests of the pregnant woman and the fetus are, in fact, the same.

The **majority opinion** in the court's 5-to-4 decision **explicitly acknowledged this argument**, galvanizing anti-abortion forces and setting the stage for an intensifying battle over new abortion restrictions in the states.

The anti-abortion movement's focus on women has been building for a decade or more, advanced by groups like the conservative **Justice Foundation** ... .

It is also at the heart of an effort — expected to escalate in next year's state legislative sessions — to enact new "informed consent" and mandatory counseling laws that critics assert often amount to a not-so-subtle pitch against abortion.

... **Allan E. Parker Jr., president of the Justice Foundation**, a conservative group based in Texas, compares the campaign intended for women to the long struggle to inform Americans about the risks of smoking.

## ~ Excerpts ~

**From affidavits in
The Justice Foundation
Amicus Brief cited by the
U.S. Supreme Court**

**"For 23 years, I went into
crying spells, depression,
suicidal thoughts. Emotionally
it devastated me."**
*Cynthia, Oklahoma*

---

**"Depression, nightmares,
hospitalizations, suicidal
thoughts and actions, guilt,
anger at myself and those
who forced the abortion."**
*Teresa, North Carolina*

---

**"Devalued, dehumanized
me. Took away my dignity
and self-worth. Suffered
shame and guilt."**
*Janice, Florida*

---

**"My abortion immediately led
to hopelessness, promiscuity,
and drinking binges. I could
not escape the pain and guilt.**
*C.L.R., Arizona*

"We're kind of in the early stages of tobacco litigation," Mr. Parker said.

---

All sides agree that the debate reached a new level of significance when Justice **Anthony M. Kennedy,** writing the majority opinion in the **Supreme Court** case last month, **approvingly cited a friend-of-the court brief filed by the Justice Foundation.**

---

The **foundation**, a nonprofit public interest litigation firm that has handled an array of conservative causes, has increasingly focused on abortion through its project called **Operation Outcry**. Mr. Parker said the group began hearing from women in the late 1990s who considered themselves victims of legalized abortion — physically and emotionally — and wanted to tell their stories. **Operation Outcry**, which grew to include a Web site, a national hot line and chapters around the country, eventually collected statements from more than 2,000 women, officials said.

---

In its friend-of-the-court brief, the group submitted statements from 180 of those women who said that abortion had left them depressed, distraught, in emotional turmoil. "Thirty-three years of real life experiences," the **foundation said**, "attests that abortion hurts women and endangers their physical, emotional and psychological health."

---

The case before the Supreme Court involved a specific type of abortion, occasionally used after the first trimester, that involves removing a fetus intact after collapsing its skull. Justice Kennedy upheld that ban on narrower, legal grounds, but he used the **Justice Foundation** brief to write more broadly about the emotional impact of abortion on women.

---

"[I]t seems unexceptionable to conclude some women come to regret their choice to abort the infant life they once created and sustained," **Justice Kennedy wrote, alluding to the [Justice Foundation] brief.** "Severe depression and loss of esteem can follow."

---

The abortion-rights side was caught off guard, in part because its strategists believe the scientific debate has been so decisively settled against the Justice Foundation's argument over the years. "We thought that brief was so extraneous that we didn't even bother coming up with a response to it," said Mr. Evans of Planned Parenthood.

---

This focus on women by the anti-abortion movement has real power, many experts said.

Mr. Parker said his organization planned to make its legal argument, and the accompanying testimonials from women, available to more state legislatures. Every time he speaks on the issue, he said, he receives more phone calls from women who have had abortions.

Source: "Abortion Foes See Validation for New Tactic" by Robin Toner, *New York Times*, May 22, 2007

What is the new tactic? Bringing women's voices and testimony to the Court and the New York Times declares it a victory for this new tactic of abortion foes. This was a big national news story. Just seven years earlier in 2000, in *Stenberg v. Carhart*, 530 U.S. 914, the Supreme Court declared unconstitutional 37 state laws that banned partial birth abortion. In the same year, the Lord told us to begin to collect women's testimonies and take Norma and Sandra back to the Supreme Court. The New York Times says "Abortion Foes See Validation For New Tactic."

Based on the new tactic – collecting the women's testimonies and giving it to the Court, here is what the Court said because God told us to help the women come forward. God told the women to be courageous. We took their voices to the Court and here's what the Court said for the first time in American history: **"Some women come to regret their choice to abort the infant life they once created and sustained."**

Breakthrough! Before that, the Court had always called the child at the time of abortion a "fetus" or "potential life", thus dehumanizing the infant in the womb. And the Court also said **"see pages 22 to 24 of the Brief of Sandra Cano and 180 Women Injured By Abortion, "… Severe depression and loss of esteem can follow."** That brief was primarily authored by Linda Schlueter, also a former professor of law who was a Justice Foundation employee at that time.

What was on pages 22-24? Line after line of women's testimonies. What God had told us in Isaiah 28:14-22 had finally come true. How do we overcome Satan? By the word of their testimony and the Blood of the Lamb. Rev. 12:11. So the Court admitted the child at the moment of the abortion was an infant life, and thus in effect that "Abortion is a crime against humanity" because you're killing humans and you're hurting women. A crime against humanity occurs when the government withdraws legal protection from a class of human beings. If that's true, abortion simply couldn't last forever, could it?

## More Amazing and Extraordinary Things God Has Done! Here Are A Few Of The Unusual Prayer Events

Now, here are just a few of the unusual prayer events along the journey. Millions of prayers have been offered for the end of *Roe v. Wade*. I thank God for every one of you who prayed over the years. How many of you have attended prayer events to pray for the end of *Roe v. Wade*? Thank you, thank you. Thank you to everyone who prayed and took action in some way for the reversal of *Roe*. It was all important and it was all necessary in the fullness of God's time.

It took millions of prayers to accomplish this. I believe God hears the cries of His people. The Bible says He allows evil to flourish for a while, so that men have time to repent, and that the wicked may be punished. He doesn't want to bring anyone to death and eternal judgment. Jesus came that we might have life and have it abundantly. He wants everyone to repent and have eternal life in Jesus Christ. John 3:16.

But in 2000, we began to really pray in earnest. I knew God had promised to end the covenant with death, but I knew it could not end without prayer. I am grateful to the Catholic Church which was faithful even in the original *Roe* case to file a brief telling the Court abortion was unjust and not in the Constitution. I am grateful to the millions of Catholics who prayed over the years. Sadly, at the time of Roe, mainline apostate Protestant women's groups filed briefs urging the Court to find a right to abortion to help women. However eventually, I am grateful to say, millions of people like myself in other Christian churches were awakened and also began to pray and act for an end to abortion. When His people pray together in unity with Him, it pleases God.

I have now lived through two tremendous historical events which surprised most people at the time. I believe both were the result of God's grace and the prayers of His people. The first was the fall of the U.S.S.R. and Russian Communism and the tearing down of the Berlin Wall. The second was the reversal of *Roe*. Millions were praying for both. I persisted in the battle for so long, ultimately 22 years, because of God's promise; I knew His people were praying and I had lived through the fall of the Berlin Wall.

I prayed with many, many prayer movements. For example, on February 2, 2016, The Justice Foundation joined with many national prayer groups coordinated by Dai Sup Han of Prayer Surge Now, and began 10 days of 24/7 prayer for the Supreme Court. It moved into a daily prayer for the Supreme Court from 2016 to today. Every day we pray for the Supreme Court. But on the 11th day, right after we ended the 10th day of 24/7 prayer and switched to one hour a day; Justice Scalia died under unusual circumstances.

Was that an unusual thing in American history concerning a Supreme Court Justice? Justices have died before, they've retired before, but his vacancy by death under unusual circumstances at that time galvanized the eyes of our nation on the Supreme Court! And wasn't it miraculous that Senator McConnell grew a steel spine and held that seat open for a year in an election year? That's unusual.

On April 16th, 2016, an unusual event called "United Cry" was organized on the National Mall. I went with the women of *Operation Outcry* and we prayed. It was hosted by United Cry, founded by Rachel and Lewis Hogan, to stir pastors to pray for the end of abortion and revival in America. See www.unitedcry.org.

The Justice Foundation and myself began a friendship at that event with Johnathan Cahn, the bestselling author of "The Harbinger" and many other amazing books like his most recent book "The Return of the Gods". His books deeply impacted me along the journey, as well as my relationship with Lou Engle and the Call, and Matt Lockett of Bound4Life in D.C., as well as Jason Hershey and the amazing story of David's Tent in our nation's Capitol along with Sara Ballenger and Capitol Hill Prayer Partners, Pierre Bynum of Family Research Council, and so many others.

In June 2016, Donald Trump met with 1000 evangelical leaders in New York City. I was blessed to be there, wondering why me? And if I should support this man? Who would dream that a former playboy, pro-abortion, reality TV star, New Yorker who never held public office before would become the most pro-life president in American history. In fact, on the day *Roe v. Wade* was overturned, Fox News reporters even asked Donald Trump, "Do you take credit for this? Some might think he would say yes, but he said, "No, God did this." Donald Trump said that. See Fox News, June 24, 2022. (https://www.foxnews.com/politics/trump-praises-supreme-court-decision-overturning-roe-v-wade) CNN reported to the contrary and the New York Magazine, ran an article the same day called "No, Trump, God didn't overturn *Roe v. Wade*". I suppose opinions will always differ, but after what I have seen and heard and experienced, I believe God did it. To God be all the glory.

Along the journey of The Moral Outcry, we eventually unrolled The Moral Outcry scrolls as Melinda had envisioned in prayer and as you can see from the following photos at several places.

The first scroll had a quarter million names. It was five feet wide and 125 feet long. I never would have dreamed of creating such a thing, but a worship leader, artist and musician at IHOP-KC named Jonathan Baldwin created the scroll based on Mindy Thybault's dream. We unrolled it at the beginning of the Supreme Court 2019-2020 term after marching the scroll on a pole carried between two men from the Spirit of Justice Park in D.C. a few blocks away to the Court itself.

We later unrolled that scroll in various other places. We unrolled two of them, which were necessary to include all half a million names, at the Lincoln Memorial, the man who defeated slavery, and the Martin Luther King Memorial, the man who defeated segregation. That same night, we prayed in front the Supreme Court on Nov. 30, the day before the *Dobbs* Oral Argument which was held on December 1, 2021.

The Scroll was also rolled out in the Rotunda of the Arkansas Legislature shortly before they adopted a law outlawing abortion in Arkansas except to save the life of the mother. They made the five reasons in The Moral Outcry Petition the legislative finding of fact in the law. (You can see pictures on pages 217 & 218.)

The Moral Outcry Petition Scroll with 250,000 Signatures in the
Arkansas Capitol Rotunda

## Unusual, Extraordinary Governmental Events

Before The Moral Outcry Petition was born, a book came out called "The Law of Judicial Precedent" which gave me the idea for The Petition and the argument that it was a legitimate legal strategy to severely criticize a wrong Supreme Court decision as a way to reverse the Supreme Court. That was in 2016, one year before Melinda called me and said, "Could someone do a petition?" An unusual book called "The Law of Judicial Precedent" was co-authored by eight judges, including then Judges Kavanaugh and Gorsuch as appellate judges, saying that "severe criticism" was a valid reason for a court to overturn a prior wrong decision.

Few even saw the book when it came out. Who reads books like these? But for some reason I saw it and when Melinda called me in 2017, one of the reasons I said "Yes, you can do a petition" was because we need to tell the court abortion is a crime against humanity. That is "severe criticism" indeed since the Nazis were given the death sentence after their crimes against humanity. Abortion hurts women and the Safe Haven laws in all 50 states are a better alternative than killing children and injuring their mothers.

Here's another unusual and extraordinary event. Do you remember the Trump/Clinton debate when he said: "yes, I will appoint two to three judges who will reverse *Roe v. Wade*." That was a prophetic statement, one that no other Republican candidate would have said. The standard Republican line was they would appoint "strict constructionists." But a status quo Republican judge would preserve the status quo of *Roe v. Wade*, as they had for years. On the other hand, a strict Constitutionalist would honor the Constitution and the meaning the people who ratified it gave it.

The legitimacy of our form of government in a secular sense comes from the consent of the governed. For the first time in American history, a President got to nominate and confirm three justices in their first term. Who gets credit for that? Donald Trump didn't do that. God bless him. I thank God for Donald Trump and all of us who acted over the years to reverse Roe, but God did it, as President Trump credited Him with it. I often said during these years that Donald Trump was not our Savior, but his meteoric rise from nowhere to President was evidence that there is a Savior.

Then we had the nomination of Neil Gorsuch to the U.S. Supreme Court. It took the "nuclear option" to get him on the court; the elimination of the filibuster rule in the Senate, just for judicial nominations. There is still a filibuster for legislation, but it was eliminated for judges, so Neil Gorsuch could be confirmed to the Court. His name means Champion and he was one of the five justices to overturn *Roe v. Wade*.

Then came the Brett Kavanaugh nomination. He had to go through the Hearing from Hell, didn't he? And then, once the preliminary decision in *Dobbs* was released, he had to face an assassination attempt. A man was arrested outside his home with instruments of death and burglary in his hands. And yet, Justice Brett Kavanaugh was one of the five judges who held firm and reversed *Roe v. Wade*.

Then there was the death of Justice Ginsburg on Rosh Hashanah 2020. Why is that date significant? Because Rosh Hashanah is the beginning of the Ten Days of Repentance on the Jewish calendar. She was Jewish and she died on the first day of the ten days of repentance. We don't pray for anyone's death, but her death led to the nomination of Amy Coney Barrett in the middle of the Ten Days of Awe (Repentance) on a day called the "Sabbath of Repentance", Sept. 26, 2020, leading to Yom Kippur – The Day of Atonement for our sins. Only God could arrange that timing.

In the middle of the Ten Days of Awe on Sept. 26, 2020, we, The Justice Foundation and *Operation Outcry*, were on the National Mall playing The Moral Outcry video where the words of the Supreme Court's 1973 Oral Argument in *Roe* were heard. You can see the video at The Moral Outcry Petition website. See <u>www. themoraloutcry.com.</u> We prayed that day with millions of people around the world for the end of *Roe v. Wade*. It was called The Return with co-leaders Kevin Jessip, Jonathan Cahn, and many other groups, including our group co-sponsoring it.

Franklin Graham held the March in Washington the same day as the Return in 2020 from the Lincoln Memorial to the White House, to the Congress and the Supreme Court. Catholics, Evangelicals, Charismatics, Christians of all flavors were united in praying for the end of *Roe v. Wade*, and eventually the end of legal abortion, just as slavery and desegregation were ended. And we don't have any exceptions today for slavery and segregation, do we?

At 5:04 in the afternoon, The Return ended with shofars blowing the trumpet, the ram's horn which is what the Jewish people do on Rosh Hashanah. Who blew the first Ram's horn? The Bible says when the law was given to the Jewish people on Mount Sinai, a shofar blew, and it was God himself or an angel of the Lord blowing that shofar. At the same exact time the shofars were blowing at 5:04 p.m. on the National Mall, Donald Trump came out of the White House into the Rose Garden. You could hear the shofars blowing as he said, "I nominate Amy Coney Barrett to be the next Associate Justice of the Supreme Court."

## Unusual and Extraordinary Legal Events

Now what are some amazing and unusual legal events in the *Dobbs* case? It will be as famous in American history someday as *Brown v. Board of Education*, the case that ended segregation in America. *Dobbs* is now the case that ended the supposed Constitutional protection for abortion.

This is amazing. When did the *Dobbs* case arrive at the Supreme Court? Almost all cases at the Court come on a petition for certiorari. Mississippi said in effect: "please take our case because the lower court struck down our law, which was only a minor restriction on abortion." The law banned abortion after 15 weeks gestation, and still would have allowed 90 percent of abortions at earlier stages to continue. Every petition to the Court concludes with a prayer. So they prayed legally. That's in the document.

Mississippi prayed-please take the *Dobbs* case from the Fifth Circuit and reverse it and uphold our law. That Petition arrived on March 16th, 2020. That was the exact same day that the U.S. Supreme Court shut its doors because of the coronavirus. Coronavirus was a scourge, a pestilence, the "overwhelming scourge" (see Isaiah 28) that came in waves, day by day.

The Court was shut down for over two years because of the overwhelming scourge of coronavirus, a plague of worldwide Biblical proportions. And because of the sheer terror it caused them. Fear of death. Because the Court locked down and began to put their Oral Arguments on their website live, more people could listen and pray for the Supreme Court in the *Dobbs* case than I believe in any other case in American history.

March 16, 2020, was shortly after the March 4, 2020 Oral Argument when The Supreme Court upheld *Roe* again in the *June Medical Case*. But then the "overwhelming scourge" of coronavirus hit. See Isaiah 28:14-22.

So *Dobbs*, the case that would reverse *Roe*, arrived on March 16, 2020, the same day the Court shut down because of the pandemic. 99 times out of 100, the Supreme Court rejects these petitions. In order to help the Court decide to take the *Dobbs* case, The Moral Outcry and *Operation Outcry* filed a joint brief asking them to do so with over 336,000 signatures. **We were one of only eight pro-life groups, who said, please take the *Dobbs* case.**

Then, after ours and other briefs were filed, the case was "considered" by the Court. Should we take the case? But the Court normally says no, no, no. Around 99 times out of 100 they refuse. The first time it was set for consideration, they said we're going to reconsider this again. They reset it another time. Then they said we're going to reconsider this another time. They reset it, reset it, reset it. The case was reset 22 times and considered just on the decision whether to take the case and hear it. That number alone is amazing. But they finally released their decision to hear it on May 17th, 2021, which was the day of Shavuot on the Jewish calendar, which we know as Pentecost. On the day of Pentecost, when the Holy Spirit came down, and the Law was given to the Jewish people, the Court said: "*Cert.* granted: we're going to take *Dobbs*."

It caused a firestorm just that *Roe* would be reconsidered. But on the day of Oral Argument, as I was standing in front of the Court, I was shocked to hear a new slogan from the pro-death crowd. They were shouting **"Abortion Forever. Abortion Forever. Abortion Forever,"** just as the segregationists like Gov. George Wallace of Alabama said "Segregation Forever" as he blocked the schoolhouse door. But just like segregation (which the Supreme

Court had upheld in *Plessy v. Ferguson* for 58 years) was eventually reversed, so the issue of *Plessy* and segregation came up in the *Dobbs* Oral Argument and The Moral Outcry Petition. The Solicitor General of the United States had to admit that *Plessy* and segregation were wrong. This was one of the two arguments made in the Moral Outcry Petition that was brought up in Oral Argument and written about in the final decision.

Eventually *Dobbs* was even the first Supreme Court decision ever to be leaked in full to the American public through Politico. But instead of intimidating the Court as intended, the leak mobilized more millions of people to begin praying for the Supreme Court, didn't they? How many of you prayed after that?

## More Amazing Things in *Dobbs* – Amazing Briefs

First of all, the whole pro-life movement filed 80 *Amicus Curiae* Briefs at the Court on the merits, compared to 40 for the pro-abortion side. This overwhelming predominance occurred for the first time in History. In a similar way, the pro-life side outnumbered the abortion side in front of the Court for the first time in history. In fact, at one point 20 buses from Liberty University arrived and groups of 50 students at a time kept coming like companies of soldiers to stand guard before the Court, while the oral argument thundered inside. Unusual and extraordinary and thrilling as I saw it unfolding. The Young People have arrived!!

Let's get to the amazing things that even more directly impacted us at The Justice Foundation and our new, unusual, and extraordinary clients. We filed written arguments called *Amicus Curiae* Briefs for *Operation Outcry* and The Moral Outcry at the Court in *Dobbs*. But some new clients arrived on the scene as well. The Justice Foundation ended up filing four more briefs in the *Dobbs* case at this merits phase, when the ruling on the merits of the arguments is made, for a total of five in *Dobbs*, including the earlier brief at the cert petition phase asking the Court to take this case. We had been working on reversing *Roe* for 22 years. God had given us a lot of good evidence and arguments. So we were prepared to file, hopefully with God's help, excellent briefs. We thought we would file two. No other group filed so many directly.

But He had more amazing things up His sleeve. One of the amazing new briefs we filed was for the Jewish Pro-life Foundation, The Coalition for Jewish Values, Rabbi Yakov David Cohen, Rabbi Chananya Weissman, and Bonnie Chernin (President, Jewish Life League). The Jewish Pro-Life Foundation called our liaison to Israel, Allison Ngo Griffin, when the Court announced it would take *Dobbs*. Allison had built a great relationship with the Jewish Pro-life Foundation. Cecily said, do you think you could ask your boss if he would file a brief for us in the *Dobbs* case? We rejoiced to represent them at no charge, as we do all our clients. This was so unusual that an article came out later in a secular Jewish magazine asking in effect, "Why are Christian lawyers representing Jews?" It was a great article because it explained that we love the Jewish people and we are both pro-life.

But what else about this Brief was unusual? Beside a Christian group representing a Jewish group? As far as we know, it may have been the first time a Jewish voice at the Court was pro-life. Think about Justice Ginsburg, a vocal, prominent pro-abortion Jewish woman. Think about secular Jews. Many Jewish briefs even in *Dobbs* said, in effect, women need abortion for women to be successful. But the new Jewish voices in this brief were the first ones that quoted the scripture saying the Torah (Old Testament) says that child sacrifice is an abomination to God. Judaism was the first religion which eliminated child sacrifice according to the Rabbi's. And very powerfully, they acknowledged that as victims of the Holocaust themselves, we Jewish people know a crime against humanity when we see one and abortion is a crime against humanity.

# CHAPTER NINE

# Final Arguments at the Supreme Court

## The Jewish Brief

### INTEREST OF *AMICI*

The Jewish Pro-Life Foundation promotes life-saving solutions to unplanned pregnancy by providing the Jewish community with much needed pro-life education, Jewish-friendly pregnancy care and adoption referrals, and healing after the terrible trauma of abortion.

The Coalition for Jewish Values ("CJV") is a charity incorporated in the State of Maryland and operating pursuant to 26 U.S.C. §501(c)(3). CJV represents over 1,500 traditional, Orthodox rabbis and advocates for classical Jewish ideas and standards in matters of American public policy.

Rabbi Yakov David Cohen is the founder and director of the Institute of Noahide Code (www.Noahide.org). He received his Bachelor's Degree at the Rabbinical College of America and was ordained Dayan at the United Lubavitcher Yeshiva NY. He is a Renowned Talmudic scholar and Dayan-Jewish Judge.

Rabbi Chananya Weissman received his rabbinic ordination from Rabbi Isaac Elchanan Theological Seminary (RIETS) and received an M.A. in Jewish Education from Azrieli Graduate School of Jewish Education & Administration. He is the author of hundreds of articles and seven books on a wide range of subjects, including *Tovim Hashnayim: A Study of the Role and Nature of Man and Woman*, a scholarly work based on primary Torah sources.

Bonnie Chernin is Founder and President of the Jewish Life League and serves on the Board of Directors of the Jewish Pro-Life Foundation. The Jewish Life League maintains that human life, both before and after birth, is sacred and that the pro-choice position of mainstream Jewish organizations is antithetical to the Jewish faith. She is a Grief Recovery Method Specialist and a Certified Professional Coach assisting women in achieving their life and career goals.

<u>*Amici* are Jewish religious leaders and organizations who agree that legal abortion in America is an egregious wrong that must be rectified.</u> Jewish law prohibits abortion and Judaism obligates us to protect innocent life in the womb. The views of other religious groups have been repeatedly presented to the Court. This pleading to the Court is *Amici's* attempt to rescue innocent children in the womb from execution, as commanded in our Bible, Proverbs 24:11-12: *"Rescue those being led away to death; hold back those staggering toward slaughter. If you say, 'But we knew nothing about this', does not He who weighs the heart perceive it? Does not He who guards your life know it? Will He not repay everyone for what they have done?"*

# SUMMARY OF ARGUMENT

Judaism has a strong legal tradition of protecting human life and prohibiting the murder of "infant life"[6] in the womb. Pregnancy and childbearing are considered religious and social responsibilities, making it incumbent upon Jews to protect the safety and health of both mother and child. Jewish doctrine also recognizes that in very rare cases the infant life in the womb may pose a serious threat to the mother's life, and in this rare instance a termination is permissible.[7]

This very narrow exception to the prohibition of abortion in Judaism was biblically justified for a breech birth. Life threatening situations now occur in less than 1% of all pregnancies, making this exception almost inapplicable.

Abortion is antithetical to Torah principles. The act of abortion, and the industry that promotes and benefits financially from it, violates all Jewish ethics and morals.

The history of Judaism includes many existential threats to Jewish life in the form of state sponsored mass murder. This makes us especially sensitive to the plight of the child in the womb, whose protection under the law was completely abrogated by *Roe v. Wade, Doe v. Bolton and Planned Parenthood v. Casey.*

This tragic human rights violation must be remedied. The Mississippi law in this case seeks to protect the God-given right to life for babies of 15 weeks gestation and beyond. Yet, most significant developmental milestones occur during the first eight weeks following conception. A baby's heart beats at 22 days, and her brainwaves can be measured at 6 weeks.

---

6 *Gonzales v. Carhart*, 550 U.S. 124, at 159 (2007) hereafter *Gonzales*.

7 Rotzeach uShmirat Nefesh – Chapter One. No 9. https://www.chabad.org/library/article_cdo/aid/1088917/jewish/Rotzeach-uShmirat-Nefesh-Chapter-One.htm

At 9 weeks all internal organs are present and the baby is sensitive to touch.[8]

As early as 8 weeks, the "infant"[9] feels real physical pain during an abortion.[10] This is much sooner than the 15-week issue before the Court, a gestational age when the pain felt by the baby must surely be considered. Jeremiah 22:3 admonishes us to avoid causing pain and death to the powerless: *"Do what is right and just; rescue the wronged from their oppressors; do nothing wrong or violent to the stranger, orphan or widow; don't shed innocent blood in this place."*

Science has advanced a great deal since 1973 when *Roe v. Wade* and *Doe v. Bolton* were decided. A new human being is formed at the moment of conception, a human being that never existed and will never exist again. This Court has a providential opportunity to correct its misguided error of 1973. The Jewish concept of Teshuvah allows for Heavenly forgiveness of sins against the most vulnerable among us. *Amici* implore the Court to study our arguments in this filing and thereby find the moral authority and conviction to overturn *Roe, Doe* and *Casey*. Indeed, to apply the protective elements of the 14th Amendment of the Constitution to all children.

---

[8] Endowment for Human Development. Prenatal Summary. https://www.ehd.org/prenatal-summary.php

[9] *Gonzales* 159, 160.

[10] Expert Tells Congress Unborn Babies Can Feel Pain Starting at 8 Weeks. Ertelt, Steven. May 23, 2013. Life News. https://www.lifenews.com/2013/05/23/expert-tells-congress-unborn-babies-can-feel-pain-starting-at-8-weeks/

## ARGUMENT

### I. Judaism Is The Original Pro-Life Religion. It Was The First Religion In Human History To Sanctify Human Life From Conception To Natural Death And To Prohibit Child Sacrifice.

Judaism has a strong legal tradition of protecting human life and prohibiting the murder of innocents. Jewish law and tradition emphasize and support the moral right to life for all human beings at every stage of development based on the understanding that all people are created in the image of God; therefore, each of us has intrinsic value and worth with a destiny to fulfill God's vision for humanity on Earth. Psalm 139:13-16 reveals this: *"For you created my inmost being: you knit me together in my mother's womb. I praise you because I am fearfully and wonderfully made... My frame was not hidden from you when I was made in the secret place. When I was woven together in the depths of the earth, your eyes saw my unformed body. All the days ordained for me were written in your book before one of them came to me."*

Rights in the Jewish tradition are entitlements given by God through the Torah. A right entails a duty not to interfere with the rights-holder's exercise of her or his right, or a duty to actively save anyone from having their right violated. Duties are commanded (*mitzvot*) to enforce legitimate rights. Hence a baby, from the moment of conception, has the right not to be prevented from continuing to live and grow in utero, and to be nurtured there.[11] All of us who are able to do so have the duty to enforce this right of the child in the womb: Leviticus 19:16: *"Do not stand idly by when your neighbor's life is at stake."* Pro-abortion groups "support every

---

[11] Jewish Pro-Life Foundation Response to National Council of Jewish Women. Jewish Pro-Life Foundation. July 27, 2020. https:// jewishprolifefoundation.org/pro-life-blog/f/jplf-response-to-ncjw

woman's legal right to make decisions about and have control over her own body." While this is true about a number of decisions, nobody has the moral right to kill another human person. In fact, the child in the womb is a separate individual from the mother with a different genetic code, often a different blood type or gender. The child in the womb may not even have any of the eventual receiving mother's DNA or race in cases of in vitro fertilization (IVF). According to the International Covenant on Civil and Political Rights: Article 6.5 – a pregnant woman cannot be executed.[12]

The Almighty gives clear instructions on the life issue in Deuteronomy 30:19: *"This day I call the heavens and the earth as witnesses against you that I have set before you life and death, blessings and curses. Now choose life, so that you and your children may live."*

Judaism considers abortion to be murder. One of the most prolific and influential Torah scholars in the history of Judaism, rabbi, legal authority, physician and philosopher Moses ben Maimon, referred to as Maimonides, declared in his compilation of Jewish law, the Mishneh Torah: *"The definition of murder according to the Noahide[13]-Laws includes a person 'who kills even one unborn in the womb of its mother,' and adds that such a person is liable for the death penalty."*[14]

The Talmud[15] (Sanhedrin 57b) says that an unborn child is included in the Noahide prohibition of bloodshed that is learned

---

[12] Sentenced to death when pregnant. https://law.stackexchange.com/questions/3495/sentenced-to-death-when-pregnant. See also Cornell Center on the Death Penalty Worldwide. In almost every country in the world, it is illegal to execute a pregnant woman. Of the 92 countries that retain the death penalty, 83 have passed laws prohibiting the execution of pregnant women.

[13] Pertaining to Seven Laws of the Noahide Code. http://noahide.org/sevenlaws/ These laws apply to all humans, not just Jews.

[14] Abortion and Judaism. The Noachide prohibition on abortion. https://en.wikipedia.org/wiki/Judaism_and_abortion

[15] What Is the Talmud? Definition and Comprehensive Guide. Chabad.org.

from Genesis 9:6-7: (from a direct translation of the original text), "*He who spills the blood of man within man shall have his blood spilt for in the image of God made He man. And you, be fruitful, and multiply; swarm in the earth, and multiply therein.*"[16] The Talmud interprets "the blood of man in man" to include a fetus, which is the blood of man in man. Things that are prohibited under the Noahide laws are also prohibited to Jews.[17]

<u>Clearly, the Jewish religion prohibits child sacrifice, the modern-day version being abortion, as stated in the Torah:</u>

Leviticus 18:21: "*Do not give any of your children to be sacrificed to Molek, for you must not profane the name of your God. I am the Lord.*"

Psalm 106:35-38: "*They mingled with the nations and adopted their customs. They worshipped their idols, which became a snare to them. They sacrificed their sons and their daughters to false gods. They shed innocent blood, the blood of their sons and daughters, whom they sacrificed to the idols of Canaan, and the land was desecrated by their blood.*"

Rabbinical opinion on the issue of abortion in Judaism includes that of the supreme halakhic[18] authority in modern times, **Rav**

---

https://www.chabad.org/library/article_cdo/aid/3347866/jewish/What-Is-the-Talmud-Definition-and-Comprehensive-Guide.htm

[16] Abortion in Halakhic Literature. J. David Bleich. Contemporary Halakhic Problems Vol.1 KTAV Publishing House. 1977. pp. 330-331. https://drive.google.com/file/d/1RgE1RnuQvB4hiCa-v7123LqOK3MuA9--/view?usp=sharing

[17] Ibid.

[18] Refers to Jewish legal code. What Is Halakhah (Halachah)? Jewish Law. Posner, Menachem. https://www.chabad.org/library/article_cdo/aid/4165687/jewish/What-Is-Halakhah-Halachah-Jewish-Law.htm

**Moshe Feinstein**, who stated, "Not only are Jews prohibited from having an abortion, but they are prohibited from assisting non-Jews from having an abortion, too. According to halacha, abortion is prohibited for non-Jews; it's actually a capital crime. A Jewish doctor may not perform an abortion even if it would result in antipathy towards Jews." (Igros Moshe, Choshen Mishpat 2:73:8). In responsum 69, Rav Moshe not only categorizes abortion as bloodshed; he unequivocally warns against relying on an erroneous *heter* (decision)[19] for aborting babies with physical abnormalities.[20]

Additional rabbinical authority declaring protections for children in the womb follows:

### Rav Joseph B. Soloveitchik

"I consider the society of today as insane...I read from the press that in Eretz Yisrael [Land of Israel] they permit abortions now! Sapir [Pinchas Sapir, Israeli Minister of Finance] comes to the U.S. and asks that 60,000 boys and girls should leave the U.S. and settle in Eretz Yisrael. When a child is born, it's also immigration to Eretz Yisrael, and yet you murder the children."…. "And if you kill the fetus, a time will come when even infants will be killed... The mother will get frightened after the baby will be born...and the doctor will say her life depends upon the murder of the baby. And you have a word, mental hygiene, whatever you want you can subsume under mental hygiene...And there is now a tendency for rabbis in the U.S. to march along with society, otherwise they'll be looked upon as reactionaries." In 1975, Rabbi Joseph Soloveitchik

---

[19] Loophole in the law. How does "getting a heter" work. https://judaism.stackexchange.com/questions/56224/how-does-getting-a-heter-work

[20] The Halakhic Debate on Abortion Between Moshe Feinstein and Eliezer Waldenberg. p.7. https://drive.google.com/file/d/1kwN0eLWj8VS2ropFLEjKD32voGuxdpXB/view?usp=sharing

said: "to me it is something vulgar, this clamor of the liberals that abortion be permitted."[21]

## Rabbi J. David Bleich

"A Jew is governed by such reverence for life that he trembles lest he tamper unmindfully with the greatest of all divine gifts, the bestowal or withholding of which is the prerogative of God alone. Although he be master over all within the world, there remain areas where man must fear to tread, acknowledging the limits of his sovereignty and the limitations of his understanding. In the unborn child lies the mystery and enigma of existence. Confronted by the miracle of life itself, man can only drawback in silence before the wonder of the Lord."[22]

## Rabbi David Novak

"At this point I would ask my fellow Jewish ethicists, especially the traditionalist ones: Does our reverence for human life as the image of God not require that we treat every human life, even the miniscule human life of the newly conceived embryo, with what the Jewish tradition calls 'human dignity' (*kvod ha-beriyot*)? Surely we are not obligated or even permitted to kill a human life, however prehuman it looks, for the sake of someone else's therapeutic needs – that is for the sake of somebody to whose life the embryo is not a direct threat. We certainly are not obligated or even permitted to kill an embryo for the more indirect benefit of the advancement of possible helpful scientific information. I believe that we are neither obligated nor permitted to do so. I believe that

---

[21] "You Murder the Children": Rav Soloveitchik on Abortion. Menachem Ben-Mordechai. The Jewish Press/ https://www.jewishpress.com/blogs/a-banner-raised-high/you-murder-the-children-rav-soloveitchik-on-abortion/2013/09/23/

[22] Abortion in Halakhic Literature. J. David Bleich. Contemporary Halakhic Problems Vol.1 KTAV Publishing House. 1977. p. 370. https://drive.google.com/file/d/1OncqrDEfIxlmYkgwnWKOz18VhKhlzVJj/view?usp=sharing

we are prohibited from doing so. We can discover that prohibition (*issur*) in philosophy and thus argue it to anyone, anywhere, at any time. The argument need not be confined to persons who are required to live according to our own moral theology, although our moral theology certainly can confirm it."[23]

## Rabbi Chananya Weissman

"It should not need to be debated that unborn children have the right to be born, and the lives of the elderly and infirm are no less precious than the lives of society's most fortunate. The rich and powerful do not have the right to decide the value of anyone's life, nor when someone has 'already lived their life' and it's time for them to go. That is strictly the purview of God, who forbids us to make such distinctions or calculations, even for the alleged 'greater good.' It is always for the greater evil. It is always to displace God. The Torah teaches that every life is a unique world, and every moment of every life is infused with the potential to achieve great spiritual heights."[24]

## Rabbi Norman Lamm, Retired Chancellor of Yeshiva University.

"The freedom of parents to crush prenatal life, which now seems to be in vogue, will eventually lead to utter destruction," Rabbi Norman Lamm stated in 1970, "because it is only a small leap of logic from feticide to infanticide, to getting rid of infants who may not fulfill our ideals of mental and physical health, or eventually, ethnic and genetic respectability." Rabbi Lamm reiterated those themes in a sermon from 1976: "Never, never, must we allow this desacralization of life — whether in the form of benevolent euthanasia or free and easy abortions ... or any of the other

---

[23] The Sanctity of Human Life. Novak, Rabbi David. Georgetown University Press; 1st edition (May 1, 2009). P. 68. https://drive.google.com/file/d/1DQ1 TLuVdxsCi0jxEX7DdtYFSDEzTgCCB/view?usp=sharing

[24] A War on God and Creation. Weissman, Rabbi Chananya. https://www. chananyaweissman.com/article.php?id=288

manifestations of this fundamental antagonism to life — to influence us."[25]

## Rabbi Shimon Cowen

"The opposition of Noahide law to the abortion of an unborn life, except in very special circumstances, embodies one of the deepest norms of human society, the protection of life. In other words, Torah forbids abortion on demand, whether by a Jew or non-Jew."[26]

## Rabbi Pinchas Teitz

"Shedding innocent blood in Jewish life is so reprehensible that at times even those not responsible for the act of murder who hear of such an incident must dissociate themselves from it. This is expressed by the recitation of the elders of the city in whose proximity a dead man is found.

In the *eglo arufo*[27] ceremony that the Torah mandates, they must wash their hands, saying: 'Our hands did not shed this blood,' even though there is no reason to assume that they were directly involved in the death. How, then, are we to respond with less than shock to the killing of 100,000 fetuses through abortion in Israel, year after year? This is certainly a sin against Torah ... It is a crime against Jewry, against mankind, and even against the Land itself – for the Torah clearly warns that the Land, in its sensitivity to corruption, can tolerate no bloodshed."[28]

---

[25] Ben Shapiro, Judaism And The Unborn: Which Stance Is The Right Stance?. Kantor, Miles. The Daily Caller. https://dailycaller.com/2018/07/18/judaism-unborn-ben-shapiro/

[26] Should We Care If Non-Jews Abort Their Babies? Kantor, Myles. August 10, 2018. https://www.jewishpress.com/indepth/opinions/should-we-care-if-non-jews-abort-their-babies/2018/08/10/

[27] Refers to the hand washing commandment. Deuteronomy 21:7. https://www.chabad.org/library/bible_cdo/aid/9985

[28] Rabbi Teitz' Opinion on Abortion Law in The Jewish

## Rabbi Menachem Mendel Schneerson

Advising an expectant mother in 1971, Rabbi Schneerson (the Lubavitcher Rebbe) wrote, "Should there be those who desire to persuade [you] that — God forbid — you perform an abortion: Tell them that this constitutes deliberate murder of a creature who is as yet unable to protect himself from those who seek to murder him."[29]

Jews were active in the early pro-life movement in America. The following rabbis stood in the public square defending life.

## Rabbi Joshua Sperka

"We have experienced the impact of a society which, step by step, has betrayed humanity's essential reverence for the sacredness of human existence," he said during a Senate Judiciary committee meeting in 1967. "These words disguised the mass murder of a people. We are dealing with human life and the consequences of this proposal no man can foresee."[30]

**Rabbi Joseph Karasick,** Past President of the Union of Orthodox Jewish Congregations of America.

"To destroy a human embryo is sacrilegious interference with life itself and akin to murder. Only when there is actual and acute danger to the life of the mother does Jewish religious law permit termination of pregnancy," he said. According to Rabbi Karasick, the

---

Observer May 1976. P.10. https://drive.google.com/file/d/1_kXEfSrCXi6koc6-kyZZCjWW9ZtU-17n/view?usp=sharing

[29] Ben Shapiro, Judaism And The Unborn: Which Stance Is The Right Stance? Kantor, Miles. The Daily Caller. https://dailycaller.com/2018/07/18/judaism-unborn-ben-shapiro/

[30] We should be terrified': What Michigan women should know if abortion becomes illegal. Gray, Kathleen. Detroit Free Press. Aug. 8, 2019. https://www.freep.com/in-depth/news/politics/2019/08/08/abortion-illegal-michigan-roe-wade-overturned/1790907001/

Talmud asserts that 'whoso sheds the blood of man within man his blood shall be shed.' This has been traditionally interpreted as constituting a commandment against the killing of unborn children."[31]

**Rabbi Bernard L. Berzon,** Past President of the Rabbinical Council of America.

"In Judaism, the life of an unborn child is sacred and only when It (sic) is a threat to the mother can the moral issue of abortion be resolved. For each person to decide arbitrarily, on the basis of economics or convenience, whether a fetus is to survive is literally for man to play God and is religiously blasphemous and socially destructive."[32]

## Victor Rosenblum

Mr. Rosenblum was a Jewish attorney who helped defend the Hyde Amendment case before the Supreme Court.[33] In March 1973, Mr. Rosenblum expressed his disagreement with the *Roe v. Wade* decision before the McLellan Committee of the U.S. Senate, stating that, "The real test of our humanity is not formal viability. It is not our ability to survive outside the womb. The test of our humanity, rather, is our concern with facilitating human survival and human achievement through developing science's capacity to nurture and enhance human life in all its manifestations."[34]

---

[31] 2 Top Orthodox Rabbis Score 'Blanket 'Abortion Permission. Dugan, George. July 11, 1970. https://www.nytimes.com/1970/07/11/archives/2-top-orthodox-rabbis-score-blanket-abortion-permission.html

[32] Ibid.

[33] Harris v. McCrea, 448 U.S. 297 (1980), https://aul.org/wp-content/uploads/2018/10/1980-Harris-v.-McRae.compressed.pdf

[34] Statement of Professor Victor Rosenblum, Vice Chairman of Americans United for Life, before the McLellan Committee of the US Senate. March 7. 1973. https://aul.org/wp-content/uploads/2020/08/1973-03-07-AUL-U.S.-Senate-McLellan-Committee-Statement.pdf

Even when New York passed the Reproductive Health Act in 2019, the Rabbinical Council of America (RCA) released a public statement. "Jewish law opposes abortion, except in cases of danger to the mother. Most authorities consider feticide an act of murder; others deem it an act akin to the murder of potential life." The RCA maintains that "abortion on demand, even before twenty-four weeks from the commencement of pregnancy, is forbidden," the statement continued. "There is no sanction to permit the abortion of a healthy fetus when the mother's life is not endangered."[35]

## II. The Prohibition Of Abortion In Judaism Has One Narrow Exception, To Save The Life Of The Mother In Extremely Rare Circumstances. This Exception Is Reflected In Every Pro-Life Law And Should Not Be Used To Justify Unlimited Legal Abortion.

If the life of the baby is being mortally threatened, then it is mandated to save that baby's life by whatever means are appropriate. On the other hand, Judaism provides a permission to abort a child only to save the life of the mother if the infant in the womb mortally threatens her life. In biblical times, this exception to the prohibition of abortion was intended to be used only in the case of imminent death of the mother because of breech birth, when the baby would act as a danger "*rodef*" to the mother.[36]

Currently, less than 1% of the abortions performed in the United States are done in order to save the life of the mother, and

---

[35] Jewish women express anger after Orthodox rabbis compare abortion to murder. By Sales, Ben. Feb, 3, 2019.
The Times of Israel. https://www.timesofisrael.com/jewish-women-express-anger-after-orthodox-rabbis-compare-abortion-to-murder/

[36] One who is "pursuing" another to murder him or her. According to Jewish law, such a person must be killed by any bystander after being warned to stop and refusing. https://drive.google.com/file/d/11uEtR7DLESaDKg8Q6_aLqiToxYQmFRCF/view?usp=sharing

all legislation drafted to protect "infant life"[37] includes this exception. Justifiable abortions are very much the rare exceptions to the prohibition of "shedding innocent blood" (*shefikkhut damim*), which the Jewish tradition recognizes to be a universal prohibition. When the mother experiences a life-threatening medical crisis during pregnancy, it is now often possible to remove the growing child from the womb and place him/her in a neonatal intensive care unit to grow to term. Therefore, ectopic pregnancy is now primarily the only case where the pregnancy must be terminated to save the mother's life.[38]

A note about Exodus 21:22-25, the mistranslation of which has led many to conclude that Judaism condones the mass slaughter of infant life.

This conclusion is entirely false. The verse describes a case in which fighting men in close proximity to a pregnant woman inadvertently cause a miscarriage. The Torah specifies that the guilty party would be prosecuted for involuntary manslaughter only if the pregnant woman herself dies. If the infant in the womb dies, they must pay only a monetary fine.

Long used by abortion advocates to reframe abortion as legal in Judaism, this text is not a license to abort infant life; rather, it is a reference to involuntary manslaughter requiring an adjudicated fine. It is not a capital crime. Rabbi Ahron Soloveitchik warns against using biblical text to justify unholy attitudes and actions. He stated, "the Torah is compared to the *sneh*, the Burning Bush, because "fire gives heat, light and devours fuel, but the light of Torah must only give warmth and light, love and hope; it must

---

[37] Per *Gonzales* 159, 160

[38] What is AAPLOG's Position on "Abortion to Save the Life of the Mother? https://aaplog.org/what-is-aaplogs-position-on-abortion-to-save-the-life-of-the-mother/

never be used to destroy or kill. This is not Torah; it is a perversion of Torah."[39]

Jewish Pro-Life Foundation board member, Rabbi Shlomo Nachman, corrects the mistaken translation and bias that permeates much of pro-abortion arguments stemming from this religious text. He clarifies, "This verse must be carefully understood. Many translations read 'and a miscarriage occurs' rather than 'a premature birth results' as I have it here. The passage, in my opinion, is to 'a premature birth' when the context is considered. The text actually says that if the child 'departs' ["*yasa*"] the womb and no other damage ensues from the event. In other words, if because of the struggle the baby is born early but is otherwise fine, then the men may be required to pay damages for their carelessness but no more. 'But if other damage ensues,' i.e. the baby is born with some deformity or born dead, then the standard penalties will apply, 'an eye for eye, tooth for tooth'. If the child dies as a result, the men are guilty of the murder, a life for a life. The text makes no sense any other way. The Hebrew term *shachol* references an abortion or miscarriage. That word is not used here. There is conclusive evidence that both Torah and Rabbinic halacha regarding the pre-birth child as fully human and subject to the same protections and respect as all other people."[40]

## III. Abortion Is Antithetical To Torah Principles, All Of Which Provide Sensible, Effective, And Wholesome Guidelines For Human Thriving And Human Interaction, Both Personally And Professionally. The Act Of Abortion, And The Industry

---

[39] Rabbi Ahron Soloveichik and NCSY—An Appreciation. Jewish Action. Luchins, David. Jewish Action. Winter 2011. https://jewishaction.com/tribute/rabbi_ahron_soloveichik_and_ncsyan_appreciation/

[40] Abortion and Related Issues. Nachman, Rabbi Shlomo. April 17, 2018. http://learnemunah.com/being/abortion.html

**That Promotes And Benefits Financially From It, Violate All Jewish Ethics And Morals.**

Judaism leads the way in providing support to women, children and families. Discussion about abortion must include acknowledgment that an innocent child dies in each abortion, and that abortion poses great dangers to vulnerable mothers, fathers, families, and communities. Our tradition teaches us to advocate for vulnerable and victimized targets of abuse and murder. Proverbs 31:8 demands, *"Speak up for those who cannot speak for themselves."* We acknowledge the harms done by abortion and speak out to prevent them.

Women suffer horribly after abortion with devastating physical, emotional, psychological, and spiritual problems.[41] Many regret the abortion decision and suffer in silence. Mothers and fathers endure a chronic sense of desolation and alienation from God. Abortion has become an accepted means of birth control, encouraging irresponsible, dangerous sexual activity leading to an explosion of sexually transmitted disease. Women die from legal abortion.[42]

The devastating effects of abortion on men go unspoken in pro-abortion circles. It is now confirmed that men grieve lost fatherhood, resulting in broken relationships and dysfunctional family life.[43] We heed Jeremiah 29:6, emphasizing the importance of the family even in difficult times: *"Marry and have sons and*

---

[41] See *Cert.* Petition *Amicus Curiae* Brief of 375 Women Hurt By Late Term Second And Third Trimester Abortion previously filed in this case for actual testimonies.

[42] Abortion Side Effects | Abortion Dangers – After Abortion. The Elliot Institute. https://afteraborton.org/abortion-risks-abortion-complications-abortion-dangers-abortion-side-effects

[43] Men's Pain and Need for Healing After Abortion Is Real. Feb. 2, 2018. The Elliot Institute.
https://afteraborton.org/mens-pain-and-need-for-healing-after-abortion-is-real/

*daughters; find wives for your sons and give your daughters in marriage, so that they too may have sons and daughters. Increase in number there; do not decrease."*

Judaism demands a high level of compassion and mercy for the vulnerable and defenseless. No other demographic is as vulnerable as the defenseless child in the womb. Abortion allows no compassion for infants in the womb who are given no pain medication before being starved, poisoned, burned, dismembered, and whose skull is punctured and crushed after partial delivery or who are delivered perfect and alive for organ harvesting.[44]

Judaism's biblical tradition identifies the child in the womb as precious, valuable, and unique. Isaiah 49:1: *"Before I was born the Lord called me; from my mother's womb he has spoken my name."* And Jeremiah 1:5: *"Before I formed you in the womb I knew you, before you were born I set you apart, I appointed you as a prophet of nations."*

The weekly Sabbath is considered the most holy event of the Jewish calendar. Jewish law forbids many daily activities on the Sabbath in order to concentrate on God's presence and spiritual pursuits. Nevertheless, when human life is endangered, a Jew is required to violate any Sabbath law that stands in the way of saving that person. The concept of life being in danger is interpreted broadly; for example, it is mandated that one violate the Sabbath to take a woman in active labor to a hospital. Jewish law also not merely permits, but demands, that the Sabbath be violated in order to save infant life in the womb. As lifesaving activity is the only situation in which a Sabbath violation is permitted, were the infant child not deemed alive by the Torah, this behavior would be entirely prohibited.[45]

---

[44] Live Action Simulated Abortion Procedure Videos. https://www. abortionprocedures.com

[45] Pikuach nefesh, https://en.wikipedia.org/wiki/Pikuach_nefesh

Jews have a keen sense of injustice and speak out against it without reservation, as in the case of a death row inmate who may be wrongly accused. Yet, innocent infants in the womb have no comparable advocate; instead, American law under *Roe* allows killing them for any reason with no second opinion or legal defense required. The United States Legal Code[46] considers the murder of innocent people a capital crime, therefore, killing innocent infant life should be a crime, not a right, as abortion advocates claim. The American priority of assigning a severe penalty for taking innocent life corresponds to the moral foundations of our Republic based on the Judeo principle that life is of paramount concern. Because children in the womb are innocent persons, the law must provide them with equal protection.

This also pertains to the challenging cases of children conceived in rape or incest. According to traditional Jewish law, people conceived through these unfortunate circumstances are not given the death penalty. Rather, they are not allowed to marry a Jew or have a Jewish lifestyle.[47]

The emotional health of the mother and the reputation of the family can be better served through the life-saving option of adoption rather than termination, allowing the child to live a productive life and the parents to live without guilt after abortion.[48]

Abortion industry practices dramatically contrast with Jewish ethics and moral guidelines in business, cleanliness, sexual propriety, responsibility to protect friends and neighbors from harm, honesty, and women's safety. Exodus 23:7 admonishes us: *"Keep*

---

[46] 18 U.S. Code § 1111

[47] Negative Commandments. Chabad.org. https://www.chabad.org/library/article_cdo/aid/901723/jewish/Negative-Commandments.htm

[48] Sexual Assault Pregnancy and Abortion: What the Research Says. After Abortion. The Elliot Institute. https://afterabortion.org/sexual-assault-and-abortion-survey/

*away from fraud, and do not cause the death of the innocent and righteous; for I will not justify the wicked."*

Abortion providers have long been exempted from standard medical practices and regulatory oversight. They perpetuate sex crimes by routinely failing to report evidence of sexual assault and sex trafficking. They fail to provide informed consent to patients and fail to counsel patients on alternatives to the abortion procedure or possible immediate and long-term negative consequences of the procedure.[49]

Jewish ethical standards run contrary to the profiteering within the abortion industry, activities that media outlets suppress to maintain public support for a sanitized perception of the industry. The illegal sale of body parts and the extreme violation of basic moral standards regarding dismemberment of born alive babies runs contrary to Jewish ethics. Judaism prohibits desecrating the human body, but abortion destroys a human body, and the harvesting of baby parts for profit defies Jewish respect for the dead.[50]

When *Roe v. Wade* and *Doe v. Bolton* were decided, abortion industry leaders, lawyers, and abortionists used the limited evidence of life in the womb to argue successfully for unlimited abortion legalization. Dr. Bernard Nathanson, was a Jew, a founding member of NARAL, and the owner of the largest abortion clinic in Manhattan where over 60,000 human beings were aborted. Eventually, scientific evidence in the form of new ultrasound guided abortion technology convinced him that he had denied these children their humanity and presided over their deaths. He spent the remainder of his life defending the rights of infant life.[51]

---

[49] Behind Closed Doors. LiveAction.org. https://www.liveaction.org/what-we-do/investigations/

[50] In the Market for Fetal Body Parts, a Baby's Brain Sells for $3,340. The Daily Signal. April 20, 2016. https://www.dailysignal.com/2016/04/20/in-the-market-for-fetal-body-parts-a-babys-brain-sells-for-3340/

[51] Bernard Nathanson's Conversion. Catholicism. https://www.ewtn.com/

Today, the Justices have all the information needed to fully understand and acknowledge the status of the infant life, and have done so in *Gonzales*, at 159, 160. From conception onward, children in their mother's womb manifest humanity to such an extent that only a decision that protects their lives and futures is humane and just.

## IV. Jewish Experiences Throughout History As State Sponsored Targets Of Genocide And Eugenics Gives Us A Unique Opportunity To Recognize The Injustices Wrought On Our Innocent Unborn Brothers And Sisters By Abortion.

### Genocide

Jewish victims of genocide throughout history have been redefined as subhuman, legally stripped of personhood and civil liberties, tortured, and murdered. Similarly, infant life in the womb is redefined as subhuman, legally stripped of personhood and civil liberties, tortured, and murdered.

Pro-abortion advocates deliberately employ propaganda successfully utilized by Adolf Hitler to reconstruct compassion and concern for women facing unplanned or unwanted pregnancy into lethal tools that facilitate elimination of "infant life," per *Gonzales* at 159. Evidence of this technique is exposed in a memo dispatched to Nazi indoctrination outlets. "We must use every means to install in the population the idea that it is harmful to have several children, the expenses that they cause and the dangerous effect on women's health…It will be necessary to open special institutions for abortions, and doctors must be able to help out there in case there is any

---

catholicism/library/bernard-nathansons-%20%20%20conversion-12002 See NY Times article also.

question of this being a breach of their professional ethics."(Adolf Hitler 1942)[52]

Commonplace descriptions of babies in the womb declare that the presence of arms and legs isn't an indication of human life and that the baby is nothing more than a parasite. These lies rob infants in the womb of their humanity, dignity, and divinely created existence. The lies originated with Nazi propaganda, when the sub-humans and parasites in question were Jews in their shops, homes, synagogues, and yes, in their mothers' wombs. Consider the following illustrations found in the brochure, Abortion: The Hidden Holocaust:[53]

**THEN**

**"In 1936, The German Supreme Court refused to recognize Jews living in Germany as legal 'persons.'** From that point on they had no rights or protection under the German Constitution. Shortly thereafter the Nazis began their "Final Solution"[54] – putting over 6,000,000 Jews to death."

**NOW**

**"In 1973, The U.S. Supreme Court in its *Roe v. Wade* decision ruled that unborn babies are not legal 'persons.'** From that point on they had no rights or protection under the U.S.

---

[52] Doctors, Pregnancy, Childbirth and Abortion during the Third Reich. Chelouche, M.D., Tessa. Medicine and the Holocaust. Vol 9 March 2007. https://pubmed.ncbi.nlm.nih.gov/17402341/

[53] Abortion: The Hidden Holocaust. AbortionFacts.org. https://www.abortionfacts.com/literature/abortion-the-hidden-holocaust

[54] The Final Solution. Holocaust Encyclopedia. https://encyclopedia.ushmm.org/content/en/article/the-final-solution

Constitution. Since that decision, over [60,000,000] babies have been put to death by abortion in this country."

**THEN**

**"Jews are 'sub-human.'** The sub-human, that biologically seemingly complete creation of nature with hands, feet, and a kind of brain, with eyes and mouth, is nevertheless a completely different, dreadful creature. He is only a rough copy of a human being, with human-like facial traits but nonetheless morally and mentally lower than an animal... For all that bare a human face are not equal." (Pamphlet published by the Race Settlement Main Office, Germany, 1942)

**NOW**

**"Unborn babies are 'sub-human.'** Fetuses, especially those as old as five or six months, elicit our sympathy... because they look disconcertingly like people... But, this sympathy is misplaced... While [it] may, perhaps, possess some flickering of sensation, or some capacity to feel pain, this is equally true... of creatures like fish or insects... a proper respect for the right to life requires that it not be respected where it does not exist." (Commentary on "Can The Fetus Be An Organ Farm?[55])

**THEN**

**"Jews are 'parasites.'** The Jew was always only a parasite in the body of other peoples." (Adolph Hitler, Mein Kampf, p. 419.)

---

[55] Mary Ann Warren, Case Studies in Bioethics, October 1978, p. 23-24. https://onlinelibrary.wiley.com/doi/abs/10.2307/3561446?sid=nlm%3Apubmed

## NOW

**"Unborn babies are 'parasites.'** A woman would have the right to abortion just as she has a right to remove any parasitic growth from her body." (Gloria Steinem, author and feminist leader, on CNN, Sept. 9, 1981.)

Another propaganda tactic used by abortion industry lobbyists justifies child murder for research purposes. Billions of taxpayer funded research dollars support gruesome experiments on aborted babies, the immoral and unimaginable procedures hidden in scientific language and dubious claims of benefits to society. Jewish torture and murder by Nazi doctors such as Josef Mengele at Auschwitz were designated as medical research, too, and declared good for society.

## THEN

**"Torture is 'medical research.'** To explain the concentration camp experiments, Dr. August Hirt[56] supplied this rationale, "These condemned men will at least make themselves useful," he said. "Wouldn't it be ridiculous to execute them and send their bodies to the crematory oven without giving them an opportunity to contribute to the progress of society." (Aziz, Doctor of Death, 3, 305)

## NOW

**"Human fetal tissue research is the gold standard,"** Professor Irving Weissman, head of Regenerative Medicine at Stanford University, August 2020.[57]

---

[56] Auschwitz-Birkenau: Nazi Medical Experimentation. Jewish Virtual Library. https://www.jewishvirtuallibrary.org/nazi-medical-experimentation-at-auschwitz-birkenau

[57] Members of NIH human fetal tissue research ethics advisory board

Many abortion influencers and judges apply competency tests to infant life the womb, denying their personhood based on limitations in intelligence, consciousness, development and independence. *Amici* recognize the audacity and short-sightedness of denying anyone personhood based on arbitrary measures, knowing that this leads to unbridled crimes against humanity as in the Final Solution[58] and the abortion holocaust.

Elie Wiesel, Romanian-born American, Jewish writer, professor, political activist, Nobel Laureate, and Holocaust survivor personally experienced the irrational racism that leads to dehumanization and mass murder. In 2005, he gave a speech at the opening ceremony of the new building of Yad Vashem, the Israeli Holocaust History Museum: ***"Jews were not killed because they were human beings. In the eyes of the killers they were not human beings! They were Jews!"***[59]

In a 1999 speech in Washington, D.C., Mr. Wiesel stressed our obligation to defend the defenseless. "We must always take sides. Neutrality helps the oppressor, never the victim. Silence encourages the tormentor, never the tormented."[60]

The dehumanization of children in the womb has allowed millions and millions and millions of abortion crimes in the name of justice, rights, healthcare, biomedical research, improving the gene pool, convenience, and even religious liberty. Millions and millions and millions of human beings brutally killed for profit, to avoid criminal prosecution or social embarrassment, to keep a job, or regrettably due to fear, uncertainty, coercion, manipulation, and threatening ultimatums.

---

revealed. LifeSiteNews. Aug 4, 2020. https://www.lifesitenews.com/news/members-of-nih-human-fetal-tissue-research-ethics-advisory-board-revealed

[58] The Final Solution. https://encyclopedia.ushmm.org/content/en/article/the-final-solution

[59] Elie Wiesel. Wikipedia. https://en.wikipedia.org/wiki/Elie_Wiesel

[60] Elie Wiesel The Perils of Indifference. April 12, 1999. American Rhetoric. https://americanrhetoric.com/speeches/ewieselperilsofindifference.html

## Eugenics

Eugenics abortion of imperfect babies has increased in scope with improvements in genetic testing. Jewish resistance to this modern genocide is based on our respect for life and our experience as targets of eugenics-based mass murder.

The rise of eugenics ideology and science started in America with the Racial Hygiene movement. Eugenics science provided the foundations for Hitler's war against the disabled and eventually the Jews to create a pure Aryan race.[61] Margaret Sanger and her American Birth Control League became primary sponsors of eugenics during her lifetime. She associated herself with Adolph Hitler, praising him for his racial politics of eugenics. She changed the name of her organization to Planned Parenthood during WWII in order to disguise her affiliation with the Nazis.[62] This year the President of Planned Parenthood has finally admitted publicly the founder's racist and tragically eugenicist past.[63]

Frederick Osborn, who signed Margaret Sanger's "Citizens Committee for Planned Parenthood,[64] became president of the Population Council in 1957. The Population Council brought the abortion pill to the United States in 1994. Originally called Zyklon

---

[61] Eugenics in the United States. Cultural Anthropology; https://courses.lumenlearning.com/culturalanthropology/chapter/eugenics-in-the-united-states/

[62] Uncovering the Racist and Anti-Semitic Roots of Abortion. Margaret Sanger's Search for the Pure Race. Scholar's Corner. https://www.scholarscorner.com/uncovering-the-racist-and-anti-semitic-roots-of-abortion/

[63] Planned Parenthood CEO Admits Its Founder Margaret Sanger Was a White Supremacist, But Still Embraces Her. Bilger, Micaiah. LifeNews Apr 18, 2921. https://www.lifenews.com/2021/04/19/planned-parenthood-ceo-admits-its-founder-margaret-sanger-was-a-white-supremacist-but-still-embraces-her/

[64] The Population Council, which brought the abortion pill to the U.S., has a shocking history that's nothing to celebrate. Novielli, Carole No 14, 2017. Life Action. https://www.liveaction.org/news/population-council-founded-eugenicists-promoting-abortion-turns-65/

B, Nazi scientists developed it in gaseous form to kill Jews in concentration camp 'showers.'[65] RU-486 is now used in 40% of all abortions due to inflated pricing and low overhead costs.[66]

Nat Hentoff, a Jewish champion of "inconvenient life," opposed eugenics abortion of imperfect babies after discovering reports of experiments in what doctors at Yale-New Haven Hospital called "early death as a management option" for infants considered to have little or no hope of achieving meaningful "humanhood." Nat then interviewed happy handicapped adults whose parents could have killed them but didn't. In 1984, Mr. Hentoff investigated the post-birth murders of Down Syndrome Infant Doe and a spina bifida Baby Jane Doe. He realized that eugenics abortion was the beginning of a slippery slope that would one day justify the slaughter of innocent human beings based on cost, inconvenience, and imperfection. He became a vocal advocate for life among his pro-abortion peers.[67] In 1991, Mr. Hentoff spoke out against the abortion industry's campaign to exploit parental fears of disability to increase business.[68]

Seen for what it really is, the abortion holocaust parallels and rises beyond crimes against humanity from which Jews have suffered dearly. After WWII, international consensus coalesced

---

[65] Company That Made Zyklon B for Nazi Holocaust Made RU 486 for Abortions. Novielli, Carole. Feb 23, 2014. LifeNews.com. https://www.lifenews.com/2014/02/23/company-that-made-zyklon-b-for-nazi-holocaust-made-ru-486-for-abortions/

[66] Some GOP-led states taking closer look at abortions done through medication. Crary, David. The North State Journal. Apr. 15, 2921. https://nsjonline.com/article/2021/04/some-gop-led-states-taking-closer-look-at-abortions-done-through-medication/

[67] To be liberal and pro-life. Nat Hentoff, Champion of 'Inconvenient Life'. Donohoe, Cathryn The Washington Times. Nov. 8, 1989. http://groups.csail.mit.edu/mac/users/rauch/nvp/consistent/hentoff.html

[68] The Specter Of Pro-Choice Eugenics. Hentoff, Nat. The Washington Post, May 25, 1991. http://groups.csail.mit.edu/mac/users/rauch/nvp/consistent/hentoff_eugenics.html

around the need to hold to account those responsible for genocidal activities. The Nuremberg Trials identified major players involved in implementing the Final Solution, as well as those engaged in gruesome medical research on prisoners condemned to death. Abortion experiments on Jewish women and their unborn children was a specialty of Dr. Josef Mengele, who in his time was a respected medical authority and doctor. The knowledge and skill he acquired from his research transferred into an illegal abortion practice during his exile in Argentina.[69]

## CONCLUSION

We must end abortion, an appalling crime against humanity. To begin the process of reconciliation with our Creator, to restore the dignity of those who have perished, and to return our country to a life affirming nation. *Amici* ask the Court to rise above political concerns and to contemplate the Divine promise bestowed upon every human being as pledged in Jeremiah 9:11: "*For I know the plans I have for you, declares the LORD, plans to prosper you and not to harm you, plans to give you hope and a future.*"

## PRAYER

*Amici* respectfully pray this Court to reverse the decision below.

We owe a great debt of gratitude to Cecily Routeman, the Executive Director of the Jewish Pro-Life Foundation, for the collation, collaboration, and the writing of the Jewish Brief. She was the major author, and since our clients were the real experts in this

---

[69] Auschwitz Concentration Camp. Josef Mengele. Auschwitz – Stories. https://www.fold3.com/memorial/285875898/holocaust-survivors-their-stories-page4/stories

area, we acted as their servants getting their viewpoint before the Court.

After the Jewish Brief, we then filed The Moral Outcry Brief that now had over 500,000 signatures. The names of The Signers were in The Brief in a Dropbox link. So in just in the extra year it had taken from the filing of the Mississippi Appeal, the number of Moral Outcry signers grew massively. We also represented 2,249 *Operation Outcry* women as *Amicus Curiae*. This was a beautiful combination of the original *Operation Outcry* women and the new Moral Outcry Signers. These women were saying to the Court in effect: "Please don't hurt other women as we've been hurt and Safe Haven is a better alternative". Here is their brief we filed:

## EXCERPTS FROM THE MORAL OUTCRY & OPERATION OUTCRY SUPREME COURT *AMICUS CURIAE* BRIEF IN *DOBBS*
**(filed by Attorneys Allan E. Parker, Jr., R. Clayton Trotter, and Mary J. Browning)**

### Interest of *Amici*

Melinda Thybault (pronounced Té-bo), the founder of The Moral Outcry Petition, who has collected over 539,108 signatures as of July 4, and the Signers, are convinced that this Court's abortion cases are a crime against humanity. "Severe criticism" like this, as well as significant major changes in factual and legal circumstances, constitute a compelling new mandate for the Court to do justice by reversing *Roe v. Wade* (hereafter *Roe*), *Doe v. Bolton* (hereafter *Doe*) and *Planned Parenthood v. Casey* (hereafter *Casey*). Melinda Thybault is filing this Amicus Curiae Brief, individually, while acting on behalf of all The Moral Outcry Petition Signers. She is joined by over 2,249 Women Injured By Abortion, The National Institute of Family and Life Advocates (NIFLA), and

Florida Voice for the Unborn. *Amici* seek a more humane society with justice for the children, with mercy and compassion for the mothers, and with love for the new families that will be created by Safe Haven laws, if women so choose. Melinda Thybault and The Signers, as do all citizens, have the right to petition the United States government for redress of grievances. U.S. Constitution Amendment I. With all due respect, *Amici* believe the Supreme Court is the specific branch of their government which has committed this crime against humanity by forcing all states to legalize abortion.

Many states, if not most, would make abortion a crime if they could do so in order to perform one of government's most "self-evident" and important purposes, to protect and defend the fundamental and unalienable right to human life. The Declaration of Independence states: "We hold these truths to be self-evident, that all men are created equal, and endowed by their Creator with certain unalienable Rights, among these are Life, Liberty, and the Pursuit of Happiness –

That to secure these rights, Governments are instituted among Men, deriving their just powers from consent of the governed, . . ." (emphasis added) Therefore, it is the duty of this Court to redress and correct this grave injustice which the Court itself created. A crime against humanity occurs when the government withdraws legal protection from a class of human beings resulting in severe deprivation of rights, up to and including death.

Melinda Thybault and her husband Denny are also passionate practitioners and advocates for children's lives and adoption. After raising three of their own biological children, they felt the call to adopt three additional children through domestic newborn adoption. With these three little adopted ones still in the home, and after reaching menopause, Melinda and Denny "adopted" human beings at the frozen embryo stage. These "unwanted" children were conceived through another couple's in vitro fertilization process.

These frozen embryos were viable outside their mother's womb and thus "potentially able to [and actually did] live outside the mother's womb, albeit with artificial aid." *Roe v. Wade*, 410 (1973) U.S. at 160. (The Court's definition of viability).

These "unwanted" children's biological sex (male or female) at the early embryo stage can actually be determined in the lab six days after fertilization, as Melinda's doctor's notes show:

"EMBYROS GRADE PGS RESULTS
TVBE #4 4AA 46, XX Normal Female
#6 4AA 46, XY Normal Male"

Their first human embryo child was placed in Melinda's womb after being viable, but frozen outside his mother's womb for seven months. See his human embryo photo below:

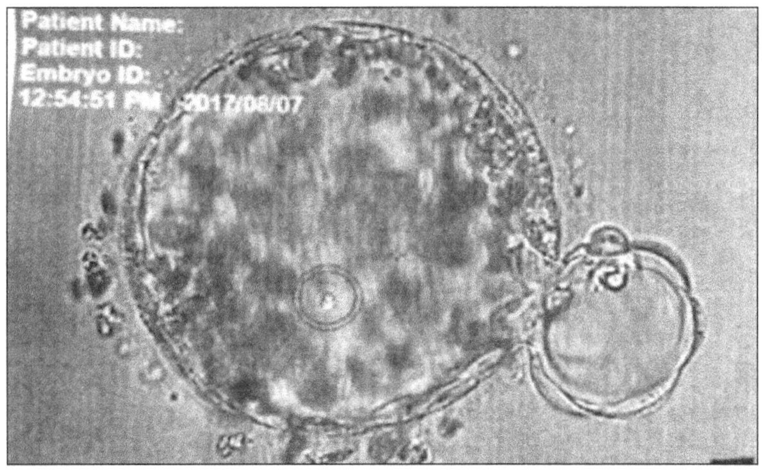


**Gideon – Outside His Biological Mother's Womb,
"albeit with artificial aid." Roe at 160.**

That human child, named Gideon Wilberforce Thybault, was later born alive because he was viable and alive outside and inside her womb. Here he is after his birth.

**Gideon**

This loving act of adoption of frozen human embryos outside the womb at fertilization is the opposite of abortion. Gideon's journey from his viable frozen embryo stage (while outside his biological mother's womb) to his birth through his adoptive mother Melinda as a beautiful child provides living evidence that, with today's science, viability begins at fertilization. Melinda is now [July 22, 2021] carrying Pearl, Gideon's biological sister, in her womb, another human embryo child that has been frozen outside the womb. Melinda is very much "with child" at this time.

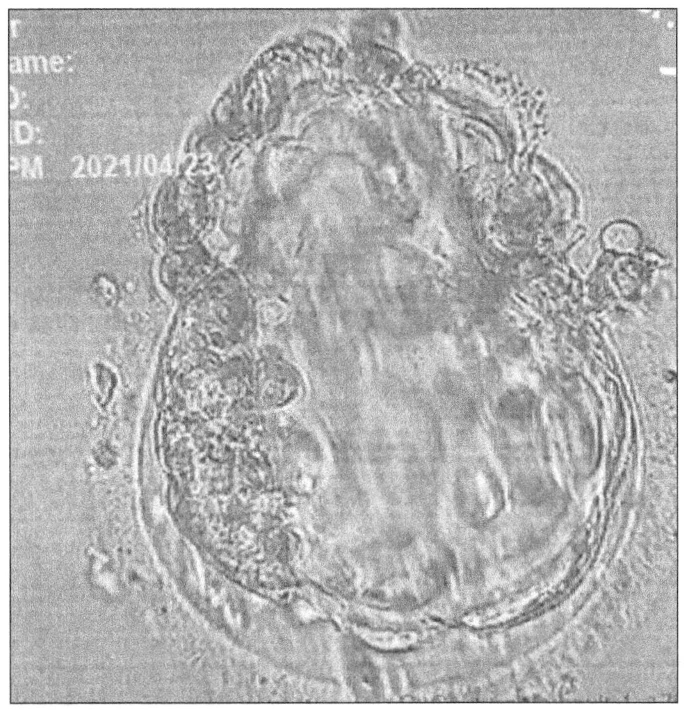

**Pearl-Viable Outside Her Biological Mother's Womb**

## 2,249 WOMEN HURT BY ABORTION

*Operation Outcry* Women Injured by Abortion are women who were injured by their own abortions and their abortionists. Most of the Women Injured by Abortion suffered grievous psychological injuries, but many suffered severe physical complications as well. All were exposed to the risk of serious physical injury, as well as serious psychological injuries, and thus have a profound interest in protecting other women from such injuries. All of the *Operation Outcry* Women have personally experienced abortion in actual practice, not just theory.

*Operation Outcry* Women have experienced first-hand, some multiple times, the callous reality of the abortion industry. They and the vast majority of women who go to high volume abortion facilities like Respondent's, are treated as a business asset or customer, not as a patient. Therefore, the word "patient" will not be used in this Brief because there is no real doctor/patient relationship in most abortion facilities, only the technical or legal fiction of a doctor/patient relationship. It is standard practice for a woman to not even see her doctor until she has paid her money and is prepped for the abortion. A normal doctor-patient relationship does not exist, despite the fundamental expectation espoused in *Roe v. Wade*, 410 U.S. 113 (1973) (hereafter "*Roe*"), that the decision should be left to the woman and her doctor alone.

## NIFLA

The National Institute of Family and Life Advocates (NIFLA) is a national legal network for pro-life pregnancy resource centers and medical clinics. Its purpose is to provide legal training, consultation, and education to its membership of pro-life centers, which number 1,600. Of these members, over 1,300 operate as medical clinics providing medical services, such as ultrasound confirmation of pregnancy to mothers contemplating abortion, and STI testing and treatment.

## FLORIDA VOICE FOR THE UNBORN

Florida Voice for the Unborn is a pro-life grassroots lobbying group based in Florida's capital city, Tallahassee. It exists to positively influence laws and regulations that affect, directly and indirectly, all infant lives – from the moment of conception onward. The work of Florida Voice for the Unborn is guided by faith in God's only Son, Jesus Christ. The group seeks to attract the support of all Christians as well as other persons of good will, while operating entirely independently from any church or other organization.

**SUMMARY OF THE ARGUMENT**

*Roe, Doe,* and *Casey* should be reversed at this time under stare decisis and *The Law of Judicial Precedent* in the interest of Justice. Five sound and necessary reasons to reverse *Roe, Doe,* and *Casey* exist independently, under *The Law Of Judicial Precedent,* on grounds that would warrant such a course, even if the makeup of the Court had remained unchanged, see *The Law of Judicial Precedent,* §50, p. 415. These reasons are based on "severe criticism," new science, women's actual abortion experience, and major changes in factual circumstances and law.

## A. First, Abortion Is A Crime Against Humanity.

The first sound and necessary reason for overturning a Supreme Court decision [and making abortion illegal in all 50 states now] is as follows:

> §47[D] "The decision has been met with general dissatisfaction, protest or severe criticism."

"The Law of Judicial Precedent", at p. 399 (emphasis added). Through The Moral Outcry Petition, over 500,000 Americans have correctly identified legalized abortion as "a crime against humanity" which is very, very "severe criticism." With due respect to the Court, every single signature on the Moral Outcry Petition is, by itself, evidence under The Law of Judicial Precedent because each person calling abortion a crime against humanity is "severely" criticizing this Court's abortion jurisprudence.

*Operation Outcry* respects the Court and its desire to do justice, and believes the Court will eventually find the wisdom, courage, and fortitude to change the law in light of these remarkable, new, changed circumstances and continued "severe criticism" for 48 years. Most reasonable observers would agree that *Roe* has been met with general dissatisfaction and major protest since its inception. The Court has an ethical and moral duty to never forget past crimes against humanity, to never stand by silently while one is occurring today, and to rescue the perishing. "Yes, rescue those being dragged off to death – Won't you save those about to be killed? If you say, 'We know nothing about it', won't He who weighs hearts discern it? Yes, He who guards you will know it and repay each one as his deeds deserve." Proverbs 24:11.

*Roe*, *Doe*, and *Casey* are truly a Crime Against Humanity like *Dred Scott* and *Plessy v. Ferguson*.

## B. Second, Abortion Hurts Women.

The second reason or "new circumstance" is that substantial new evidence now shows that abortion hurts women, as does the *Operation Outcry* Women experience expressed in this Brief. See 4,728 Testimonies of Women Injured By Abortion, https://www.dropbox.com/sh/p2fi4taxmrbivyz/AAAP_aenldXwXb34K-tcq_X8la?dl=0. These testimonies were collected by *Operation Outcry*, a project of The Justice Foundation, beginning in 2000 on behalf of Norma McCorvey (the former *Roe* of *Roe v. Wade*) and Sandra Cano (the former *Doe* of *Doe v. Bolton*) as they filed Rule 60 Motions in their efforts to reverse their own cases.

## C. Third, Safe Haven Laws in All 50 States.

This case presents an excellent opportunity to reverse *Roe*, *Doe*, and *Casey*, while still preserving for women the freedom of

"*Roe*" from the burden of parenting an unwanted child – a freedom which *Casey* felt constrained to continue, since there was "nothing more" for women at that time. *Casey* stated:

> "Abortion is a unique act. It is an act fraught with consequences for others: for the woman who must live with the implications of her decision; for the persons who perform and assist in the procedure; for the spouse, family, and society which must confront the knowledge that these procedures exist, procedures some deem nothing short of an act of violence against innocent human life; and, depending on one's beliefs, for the life or potential life that is aborted. . . . Her suffering is too intimate and personal for the State to insist, without more, upon its own vision of the woman's role, . . . "
>
> *Planned Parenthood of Southeastern Pa. v. Casey*,
> 505 U.S. 833 (1992)
> page 853. (emphasis added)

Yet today there is "much more." As a matter of law, there are no more "unwanted" children in America because of the major change in circumstances known as Safe Haven laws. Because of Safe Haven laws in all fifty states, women can now have the freedom" of *Roe*, and make their own decision about the ultimate direction of their life, without the crime against humanity of killing the child and injuring themselves.

Today, in all fifty states, a better alternative to abortion exists through the Safe Haven laws. This is a major evolution of society and the law of criminal neglect or abandonment which started in 1999.

Freedom from the "unwanted" child can now be obtained without killing the "infant life" (per *Gonzales*, at 159) that this Court has already recognized exists in the womb when it is aborted. Even if states ban or restrict abortion completely, or if only one clinic exists in a state, no woman would have to parent for a baby if she does not have the desire or ability to do so.

Safe Haven laws in all fifty states allow every woman to relinquish her child at a designated safe place within a designated time after birth and eliminate all burden of parenting and providing for the unwanted child. She can transfer responsibility to the state with no questions asked, no legal procedure, and unlike abortion, at no cost.

## D. Fourth, Millions Of Women Desire to Adopt Newborn Infants. Instead Of Being Killed, Children Will Be Loved By These Waiting Families. Safe Haven Children Will Be Adopted, Not Indefinitely Placed In Foster Care.

There are millions of Americans who desire to adopt newborn infants. Safe Haven will allow these children to go to loving homes instead of a painful, early death. The result would be a more just, humane, and healthy society, even for women who might choose abortion today. Thus, it is time to advance to a society in which we provide justice for the "infant," mercy to the mother, and love to the families that are longing for children.

## E. Fifth, New Evidence Proves Life Begins At Conception.

Fifth, new science, including but not limited to DNA testing, in vitro fertilization (IVF) and sonograms, which were not available to this Court in 1973, now show what the *Roe* Court did not know, or even the *Casey* Court, that life begins at conception. But the Court has now correctly found in *Gonzales* that abortion terminates an "infant life," at 159 at the moment of the abortion.

## *Roe, Doe,* And *Casey* Are Truly A Crime Against Humanity Like *Dred Scott* And *Plessy v. Ferguson*

Abortion is a crime against humanity. Like *Dred Scott v. Sanford*, 60 U.S. 393 (1857), which purported to enshrine slavery in the Constitution forever. It is unjust. *Dred Scott* also decided unjustly that African Americans "had no rights which the white man was bound to respect", at 400. The *Dred Scott* decision prevented national compromise from occurring and many commentators feel it eventually led to the Civil War. A crime against humanity occurs when the government withdraws legal protection from a class of human beings, as this Court did in *Scott*.

*Roe, Doe,* and *Casey* also constitute a crime against humanity like *Plessy v. Ferguson*, 163 U.S. 537 (1896) (hereinafter *Plessy*). *Plessy* denied legal protection to a class of human beings, African-Americans, as *Dred Scott* did. *Plessy* ignored the plain language of the Fourteenth Amendment, as *Roe* does. *Plessy* accepted the gloss that "separate but equal" was "equal;" while *Roe* ignores the right to "life" explicitly mentioned, but not yet guaranteed in full, in the Fifth and Fourteenth Amendments ("nor shall any state deprive any person of life, . . . without due process of law,").

The preferred dehumanizing euphemism for abortion is "termination of pregnancy." But what is a human mother pregnant with? A human infant life. *Gonzales, supra.* Unlike the abortion industry, which only mentions "liberty" (but not "life," both of which are guaranteed in the same sentence), the Fourteenth Amendment actually protects the explicitly mentioned right to life. When the government withdraws legal protection from a class of human beings, it is the classic definition of a crime against humanity.

*Amici* remind this Court of its universally respected decision in *Brown v. Board of Education of Topeka*, 347 U.S. 483 (1954) (hereinafter "*Brown*") for two major reasons. First, the Supreme Court reversed its own 58-year-old decision which had approved segregation in *Plessy v. Ferguson*. Reversal did not require a constitutional amendment or civil war, but it was controversial. *Roe* is only 48 years old, not 58. Second, *Plessy's* Court-approved segregation as the "law of the land" was well settled, and unjustly relied upon by millions. Yet the Court courageously, justly, and wisely overturned its own 58-year-old precedent, its own "crime against humanity" to use the modern expression. *Brown* was ultimately vindicated by widespread acceptance. *Roe* is still not uniformly accepted even after 48 years.

## Protecting Life is a Moral Good (Gorsuch)

In addition, there is the persuasive moral and legal argument that "the intentional taking of human life by private persons is always wrong." "The Right to Assisted Suicide," Harvard Journal of Law and Public Policy, Gorsuch, 2000, Summer; 23(3), 599-710, at 697. The Court in Gonzales has acknowledged that abortion involves a "painful and difficult moral decision," and the American common law has always been based on the basic proposition that protecting human life is a moral good. "Human life qualifies as such a basic value." Gorsuch, id. at 699.

> "The fundamental and irreducible value of human life is further evidenced by the fact that it is essential to well-being. To have a good and fulfilled life, one must have life. Human beings are not merely rational beings, but corporeal bodies. Their fulfillment depends on their having physical lives, life is intrinsic to human fulfillment." *Id*. . .

Justice Gorsuch goes on to state:

"The alternative to an absolute rule against private, intentional killing, moreover is troubling territory." *Id.* at 701.

Justice Gorsuch makes a compelling "argument for respecting life as a sacrosanct good" in the article. *Id.* at pages 696-702. *Amici* agree wholeheartedly, as does the common law and American tradition. Most doctors have a conscience that is bothered by the taking of "infant life" per *Gonzales*. Human life in the womb is an undeniable fact, and killing that life can produce depression and trauma in anyone, including doctors, who take that life. Only one abortion facility exists in Mississippi despite an abundance of qualified doctors, because most doctors do not want to kill "infant life."

Abortion Hurts Women, see *Amicus Curiae* Brief of 375 Women Injured By Second and Third Trimester Late Term Abortion filed in this case. *Amici* 2,249 Women Injured By Abortion's written affidavits and declarations under penalty of perjury describe for this Court the women's gruesome experience of abortion's "devastating psychological consequences" *Casey* at 882 from abortion at all stages of pregnancy. Many, many women are morally conflicted as this Court has recognized. Many women feel they have murdered their own child, with devastating consequences.

**Safe Haven Laws**
**Render Abortion Obsolete And Constitute A Major
"Change In Circumstances." Therefore, They Are A Sound
And Necessary Reason To Reverse *Roe*, *Doe* And *Casey* Under
The Law Of Judicial Precedent. Mississippi's Safe Haven Law
Meets The Unwanted Child Needs Of Women Without Killing
"Infant Life" (See *Gonzales*), or Injuring Women
With Abortion Trauma**

Today, there is a better way to give women the freedom and liberty envisioned by *Roe* and *Doe* without killing the "infant" in the womb, *Gonzales*, at 160, and injuring the child's mother. That better way is the dramatic social evolution in the law of criminal child abandonment called Safe Haven laws. Beginning seven years after *Casey*, in 1999, today all fifty states have now adopted Safe Haven laws which allow women to be free from the burden of an unwanted child without killing the child. These laws remove all risk of injury to herself from post-abortion trauma as a matter of law.

Under the Court's current legal abortion regime, women have the "liberty" to kill "infant life," but when they do so, many suffer the associated trauma, grief, and "devastating psychological consequences" as stated in *Casey* at 882, and "severe depression and loss of self-esteem" as stated in *Gonzales* at 159, that comes from killing an innocent human being. Under Safe Haven laws, any woman can now relinquish her baby at a hospital, fire station or other designated safe place in each state, within a set period of time, which is 3 days in Mississippi. She will suffer zero abortion related trauma, which *Operation Outcry* Women attest can last for decades, if there is no abortion.

The Safe Haven law is totally free to women, unlike abortion, making this liberty equally available to the rich and poor. Freedom or "liberty" from the unwanted child described in *Roe* and *Casey* is now absolutely and totally guaranteed in all states, with much wider availability than abortion, at no cost to the woman, unlike abortion. Even small communities usually have a fire station, police station or emergency room of some kind. Some type of "medical facility" is far more abundant than abortion facilities. There are about 128 hospital Safe Havens in Mississippi, plus adoption agencies.

Using Safe Haven laws, women don't have to suffer the grief and trauma that many, many women have experienced after their abortion. Safe Haven laws often give women far longer than the abortion industry does to decide which option they will choose – to personally care for the child or Safe Haven relinquishment or traditional adoption. Abortionists constantly pressure women to make quick decisions about abortion, claiming it is riskier the longer one waits, while also telling women it is "safe" no matter how late into the second or third trimester one has the abortion. Safe Haven Laws give the full length of pregnancy, plus additional time after birth to decide. State laws vary with 3, 30, 60, 90 days, commonly, or up to 1 year after birth in North Dakota. If she is low-income, a woman can have Mississippi Medicaid pay for her pre-natal care and delivery of the baby at no cost, with no legal obligation to care for the child whatsoever. The Safe Haven law eliminates the need for any woman of any color, income, or sexual orientation, to bear the burden of an unwanted child.

Low-income women are much better protected by the Mississippi Safe Haven law than they are by the abortion industry because baby relinquishment is free to all women as opposed to an often-expensive abortion, especially late term abortions. The abortion industry and its supporting *Amici* express concern for low-income women and are willing to disproportionately abort low-income women's children, especially Black children, as Planned Parenthood has admitted. But Mississippi has decided this concern can be better served by providing free Safe Haven relinquishment and 18 years of freedom from parenting and providing for the child through adoptions by the millions of waiting families. With the Safe Haven laws, no abortion-related guilt or trauma from taking the life of one's own child will fall on the pregnant mother.

America is deeply divided on the issue of abortion. Yet everyone wants to help women in difficult pregnancies. Many view abortion as a "necessary evil." Many people view it as simply "evil." With Safe Haven, abortion is now absolutely an "unnecessary evil." Since, as *Gonzales* admits, abortion is the taking of "infant life," it is in fact a crime against humanity. That is why even *Casey's* attempted "compromise" designed to end the controversy has been met with intense, "severe criticism," including being called "The Worst Constitutional Decision of All Time."

Indeed, Safe Haven laws did not exist in the past when many women of older generations had their abortions. *Casey* (1992) did not consider Safe Haven laws since the first came into existence seven years later in Texas in 1999. The abortion industry does not inform women of these Safe Haven laws, nor of the "devastating psychological consequences" (*Casey*) or "severe depression and loss of esteem" (*Gonzales*) suffered after abortion. See testimonies of Women Injured By Abortion.

The burden of an "unwanted" child was a large factor in the Court's analysis in *Roe* itself and *Casey.*

> *"Maternity or additional offspring, may force upon the woman a distressful life and future. Psychological harm may be imminent. Mental and physical health may be taxed by child care. There is also the distress, for all concerned, associated with the unwanted child, and there is the problem of bringing a child into a family already unable, psychologically and otherwise, to care for it."*

> *Roe*, 410 U.S. 113 at 153. (emphasis added)

**But today, with Safe Haven as a far better alternative, as a matter of law, there are no unwanted children in America and legal transfer of responsibility is free to every woman for any or no reason, if she so chooses.**

The Safe Haven laws completely eliminate the "reliance" interest which so concerned the Court in *Casey*. Now, in exchange for relatively short months of pregnancy, society (either the state or adopting parents) will provide 18 years of freedom from the once "unwanted child" burden. This is a major, substantial change in circumstances that has never existed before in American history. Today in every state, every woman has a deeply controversial right to 1) abort her child in the womb – the "infant life" which used to be treated as murder in most states, or to 2) the uniformly accepted transfer of responsibility for the child, (which used to be treated as criminal neglect or abandonment). The Signers believe the right to abort should be eliminated in favor of Safe Haven transfer of responsibility, if she chooses.

## Two Million Women Desire To Adopt Newborn Children Every Year Which is a "Major Change in Circumstances" Under The Law of Judicial Precedent

At least two million Americans every year are now waiting to adopt newborn children. Far more people are waiting to adopt newborns than the number of aborted children per year. American Adoptions https://www.americanadoptions.com/pregnant/waiting_adoptive_families

This development satisfies *Casey's* stare decisis reliance test because there is no longer a need for abortion to give freedom from unwanted children to women. Women do not seek abortion for its own sake, they seek to be free of the child.

So it is time to say as a country, "Don't kill the children. Don't hurt yourself. Give us your baby and we will transfer those children to the vetted families who are waiting to give them a loving home. We will love them all: love the mother, love the baby, love the adoptive families."

## Today Science Clearly Demonstrates That Life Begins At Conception. New Scientific Advances Justify Changing Prior Precedent Under *Stare Decisis*

Children like Gideon are undeniably and obviously viable at the frozen embryo stage, outside their biological mother's womb. A complete, separate, unique, living human being exists from the moment of fertilization. A human being is created when the sperm and the egg are fused in fertilization. Today, with in vitro fertilization, that process can and does occur outside the mother's womb in many cases. Pearl was frozen for over 4 years. Pearl was alive and viable, though frozen and maintained artificially outside her biological mother's womb, until ready to be received into Melinda's womb.

If one believes in human rights today, the most important question should be, "When do 'human rights' begin?" The answer is when we become human – at conception. Melinda Thybault's "adopted" son, Gideon, was alive and viable outside the womb. Human fathers and human mothers produce humans.

The Law of Judicial Precedent further notes in Section 50, p. 415,

> "A change in the court's organization or in judicial personnel should not throw former decisions open to reconsideration or justify their reversal except on grounds that would have warranted such a course if the makeup of the court had remained the same."

The majority of lower court federal judges, who are the only ones to have considered, based on factual evidence presented, these five reasons to reverse *Roe*, *Doe* and *Casey*, have been persuaded by them that it is time to re-evaluate *Roe*, *Doe*, and *Casey*. For example, in a unanimous decision, the Eighth Circuit recently urged this Court to consider re-evaluating abortion based on these five reasons stating: " . . . good reasons exist for the [Supreme] Court to reevaluate its jurisprudence." *MKB Management Corp., et al. v. Wayne Stenehjem, et al.*, 795 F.3d 768, at 733 (2015) (*cert.* denied). The Court further stated:

> "To begin, the Court's viability standard has proven unsatisfactory because it gives too little consideration to

the 'substantial state interest in potential life throughout pregnancy.'"

*Casey*, 505 U.S. at 876, 112 S. Ct. 2791

(plurality opinion)

## PRAYER

The cry of Melinda's heart, and the voice of her plea and that of the other *Amici*, echoes the ancient cry of Esther who dared, with trembling, prayer, and fasting to humbly appeal as follows:

*"If it please the Court, and if I have found favor, let there be a decree that reverses the orders of this Supreme Court who ordered that infants in the womb throughout all of America should be destroyed. For how can I endure to see my people and my family slaughtered and destroyed." Adapted from Esther (Est) 8:5-6.*

## Appendix 1:

## THE MORAL OUTCRY PETITION

**A Petition to the Supreme Court of the United States from the People of the United States**

**To the Honorable Justices of the United States Supreme Court:**

We, The People of the United States, humbly petition you to redress and correct the grave injustice and the crime against humanity which is being perpetuated by your decisions in *Roe v. Wade*, *Doe v. Bolton*, and *Planned Parenthood v. Casey* (the abortion cases).

WHEREAS: The United States Supreme Court committed a grave injustice and a crime against humanity in the *Dred Scott* (slavery) decision by denying personhood to a class of human beings, African Americans; and

WHEREAS: The Supreme Court committed a grave injustice and a crime against humanity by upholding the "separate but equal" doctrine in *Plessy v. Ferguson* which withdrew legal protection from a class of human beings who were persons under the Constitution, African Americans; and

WHEREAS: A crime against humanity occurs when a government withdraws legal protection from a class of human beings resulting in severe deprivation of their rights, up to and including death; and

WHEREAS: In *Brown v. Board of Education*, the Supreme Court corrected its own grave injustice and crime against humanity created in *Plessy v. Ferguson* by reversing and abolishing the 58-year-old "separate but equal" doctrine, thus giving equal legal rights to African Americans; and

WHEREAS: Under the doctrine of *stare decisis* the three abortion cases mentioned above meet the test for when a case should be overturned by the Supreme Court because of significant changes in facts or laws, including but not limited to the following:

a)  The cases have not been accepted by scholars, judges and the American people, as witnessed to by the fact that these cases are still the most intensely controversial cases in American history and at the present time.

b)  New scientific advances have demonstrated since 1973 that life begins at the moment of conception and the child in a woman's womb is a human being.

c) Scientific evidence and personal testimonies document the massive harm that abortion causes to women (see <u>www.operationoutcry.org</u> and <u>www.afterabortion.org</u>).

d) The laws in all 50 states have now changed through Safe Haven laws to eliminate all burden of child care from women who do not want to care for a child. See <u>www.nationalsafehavenalliance.org</u>.

e) Public attitudes favoring adoption have created a culture of adoption in the United States with many families waiting long periods of time to adopt newborn infants.

BE IT RESOLVED: We urgently plead with you and pray to the Lord Jesus Christ for the United States Supreme Court to do the right thing, as you did in one of your greatest cases, *Brown v. Board of Education*, which overturned a 58-year-old precedent of the United States, and reverse, cancel, overturn and annul *Roe v. Wade*, *Doe v. Bolton*, and *Planned Parenthood v. Casey*.

*"We hold these truths to be self-evident, that all men are created equal, that they are endowed by their Creator with certain unalienable rights, that among these are Life…"*

Agreed to and signed by 539, 108 Signers whose names are in a Dropbox in footnote 2.

## Hannah S. – The First Formerly Frozen Human Embryo to File a Brief at the Supreme Court

And then the last brief came along. I did not think we would have time or resources to file something, but God….

I'll just tell you the story. A wonderful woman I had never met named Marlene called me and said, "I have read a story about what you're doing from a pro-life website. I think I have an interesting story that might help you." Marlene and John stated: We completed all of the requirements for the State of California for adoption; we were chosen by Hannah's placing family and we chose them and their frozen embryos. We have an open adoption. You don't get that with a donor embryo program as this is through a physician and due to HIPPA, the doctor cannot tell you who the donor family is. We did a home study and all that entails (FBI background check, adoption education classes, social worker visits before and after Hannah's birth, financial records, health records showing John and I were healthy and had the means to raise a child) an adoption contract between us and the placing family. We were fully vetted. Hannah does not have to wonder about where she came from or any medical concerns. We do not have an adoption decree because Hannah and her siblings that we adopted were legally property and not boys and girls protected by the Constitution under the law.

In an embryo donation, you pick from a list of frozen embryos that the doctor has the couples have donated to him. You choose based on the egg donor and sperm donor's physical characteristics (hair color, eye color, skin color, etc.) and their GPA as many times these are college students looking to earn money for tuition for their sperm/egg."

After she told me her story, and more prayer, we agreed to represent her and her husband John, and her daughter, Hannah S, **who is the first known formerly frozen human embryo to ever file a brief before the U.S. Supreme Court**. That's amazing folks. We didn't plan it.

Clayton Trotter was one of the lawyers on the brief. He is the General Counsel of The Justice Foundation, Mary J. Browning, from Missouri was our lead counsel on this case. We were all three lawyers on it, but I called Mary and said, "I don't know if we can do this one, unless you're really willing to take the lead." Which she did.

All of us are former embryos but most of you weren't frozen.

## Clayton Trotter Discussing Hannah's Case

I was a first-year law student when *Roe v. Wade* was decided. I had black hair and a black beard and I could play handball 2 hours a day. I was sitting in the Student Union at the University of Texas School of Law reading the daily Texan. The headline said that Lyndon Baines Johnson had died and *Roe v. Wade* had been decided allowing the abortion of babies in the womb as a constitutional right. This has been a 50-year journey for me.

I wanted to quit law school. I mean, I had this extensive conversation with my mom, my dad, and my wife, Susan. How can they not know a baby is a human being? Any farm boy knows that. And they said, "Why don't you stay in law school? You worked very hard to get there. Go ahead and finish Law School, maybe one day you'll be able to do something about it."

Well, June 24, 2022 is the day that something was done about it, praise God. But God! God is faithful. God is faithful. So first thing I want to do is thank you. Thank you, and thank you some more. We also want to thank our supporters and prayer warriors. You have been an integral part of creating a new culture of life in America. I believe we are going to see pro-life California. We're going to see pro-life New York. We are going to see pro-life Alaska without abortion on demand.

And now let's talk a little bit about Hannah and Marlene. I love telling Hannah's story. I tell Hannah's story every chance I get. It's an amazing story. She never lived in her genetic mother's womb. Hannah was conceived in a Petri dish. And then Marlene says, "Like a lot of birth moms who want their child but are unable to parent that child; Hannah's genetic parents were unable to parent any more children. So, they lovingly, courageously and heroically chose an adoption plan for Hannah and her siblings while they were all frozen embryos." Hannah was frozen for two years.

But Marlene is a hero. She came in and said, I will adopt that embryo and placed it in my own womb. Nine months later Hannah was born in the natural way and she's now a graduate student at Baylor University in Texas. She proves that Life begins at fertilization. With a little technical assistance, an embryo can survive and thrive outside the womb.

I like to think of Hannah as standing in the Supreme Court. I wish we could have had her there during the Oral Argument, standing in kind of in the back waving, "Hi, I'm viable. I'm here." But COVID and court protocol would not allow that, but her brief includes her baby embryo and later pictures. We asked for an extraordinary five extra minutes of Oral Argument as an *Amicus* so that she could speak which we felt was very justified. But the Supreme Court didn't grant it. Now here you can see her photos and read her story as the Court actually read it in her Brief.

## Hannah S. – The First Known Formerly Frozen Human Embryo To Ever File a Brief at the U.S. Supreme Court – By Mary J. Browning

### INTEREST OF *AMICI CURIAE*

Hannah S., hereafter *Amicus* Hannah, began her life through in vitro fertilization. She was formed outside her mother's womb and was sustained there, in a frozen state, for two years. Hannah was a human being from the time of fertilization. She is now an adult and a graduate student pursuing a Master's degree in Social Work. Hannah plans to help others, orphans, adoptive children, and families seeking options regarding adoption. To the best of our knowledge, Hannah is the first formerly frozen embryo person known to file an *Amicus Curiae* Brief at the United States Supreme Court. Normally, today frozen embryos are treated as property, as slaves were once treated. They are donated to others but not legally adopted.

### *John and Marlene S.*

Hannah's parents are John and Marlene S. They were the first couple to "adopt" a human frozen embryo as their child, that is, Marlene was the first woman to have an "adopted" embryo, frozen shortly after fertilization, placed in her womb. As the "adoptive" mother, allowing Hannah to be placed in her womb, Marlene supplied oxygen, nutrients, a warm place to grow, and love. Isn't that what every human needs? Up to that point, the vetting and selection criteria such as a home study required to adopt a child had not been applied to obtaining a frozen embryo, but it was voluntarily chosen by Marlene S. and John S. before "adopting" Hannah in the frozen embryo form of life.

## <u>SUMMARY OF ARGUMENT</u>

The story of this adoption and this *Amici Curiae* Brief will reveal that *Roe's*[70] measuring line for viability has now been moved all the way back to fertilization by the modern scientific advancement called in vitro fertilization. *Roe*, at 160, has this viability definition: " *'viable,'. . . potentially able to live outside the mother's womb, albeit with artificial aid."*

Advances in science have eliminated the distinction between previability and viability. Previability prohibitions on elective abortions should be constitutional because viability occurs at fertilization, as proven through in vitro fertilization techniques.

---

[70] *Roe v. Wade,* 410 U.S. 113, 93 S. Ct. 705, 35 L.Ed.2d 147 (1973).

# <u>ARGUMENT</u>

Since *Roe,* viability has been identified as the pivotal point for balancing of interests between the mother's rights to privacy and the state's interest in "potential" life. In 1973, the *Roe* court stated:

"With respect to the State's important and legitimate interest in potential life, the 'compelling' point is at viability. This is so because the fetus then presumably has the capability of **meaningful life outside the mother's womb**. State regulation protective of fetal life after viability thus has both logical and biological justifications. If the State is interested in protecting fetal life after viability, it may go so far as to proscribe abortion during that period, except when it is necessary to preserve the life or health of the mother."

*Id,* at 163-164, (emphasis added).

The *Roe* court declined to 'speculate" as to when life begins, stating:

"We need not resolve the difficult question of when life begins. When those trained in the respective disciplines of medicine, philosophy, and theology are unable to arrive at any consensus, the judiciary, **at this point in the development of man's knowledge,** is not in a position to speculate as to the answer."

*Id,* at 159 (emphasis added).

In vitro fertilization, non-existent at the time of the *Roe* decision, is defined by Webster as: "fertilization of an egg in a laboratory dish or test tube; specifically: fertilization by mixing sperm with eggs surgically removed from an ovary followed by uterine implantation of one or more of the resulting fertilized eggs – abbreviation IVF." The baby is created in a laboratory and transferred to a uterus. The baby contains all the components of a separate life to become fully developed, **at the time of fertilization**. The frozen embryo lives outside his or her mother's womb, "albeit with artificial aid," *Roe* at 160, which is part of the scientific advancement of "man's knowledge." *Roe* at 159. Hannah's life is proof-positive of this fact.

## How It All Began

In December of 1997, John and Marlene invited Ron Stoddart, the executive director of Nightlight Christian Adoptions, and his wife, to join them for a dinner play. The play was "An American Christmas" and was set around 1900, with actors in full Victorian regalia. John and Marlene were longtime family friends with Ron and had broached the idea of "adopting" frozen embryos with him. He was in favor of the idea. During the dinner program, an actress playing the role of a relative from Germany was lamenting that San Diego, unlike her native country, had no snow at Christmas. Touching the cheek of a little girl, she began a soliloquy about a snowflake:

*In the intricate design of each flake of snow, we find the Creator reflecting the individual human heart.*[71]

The name of the embryo adoption program was settled: The Snowflakes Embryo Adoption Program.

**Backing up.** John and Marlene were married in 1985. When it was time to start a family, they were unable to become pregnant, like

---

[71] Author Unknown.

so many others. After several years, they sought answers from a fertility doctor and went through treatments. Still no pregnancy. Finally, in January of 1997, Marlene was diagnosed with premature ovarian failure. She posed a question that would change their family's history, and maybe history itself: "Are there any embryos we could adopt?"

This is when John and Marlene began working with Ron Stoddart and the Snowflakes Embryo Adoption Program was born. Babies born through the Program are now known as Snowflake babies, a term that has become ubiquitous in embryo adoption. Wikipedia even has a "Snowflake Children" page. Hannah was the first snowflake "adopted" and born alive. (She was not the first embryo viable outside her mother's womb, that was Louise Joy Brown born on July 25, 1978, five years after *Roe*.)[72] And the rest, as they say, is history.

While going through the in vitro fertilization process, Marlene's doctor suggested **donor embryos**, where couples anonymously donate embryos to a doctor, who decides what is done with them. John and Marlene learned they might be able to choose the genetic hair and eye color. That seemed more like buying a car, than growing a family.

John and Marlene also learned the "donation" process was nothing like adoption – there were no screenings of the couples who received the donated embryos, no home studies and no background checks. John and Marlene thought, "Things are donated – money, food, clothing, time. You don't donate **life**." A frozen embryo is a life, created at fertilization, but is currently treated as property. For example in *McQueen v. Gadberry*, 507 S.W. 3d 127, at 149 (Mo. App. 2016) the Court treated frozen embryos as property "with special characteristics."

---

[72] www.history.com This Day In History, July 25, 1978.

## **WHERE WE ARE TODAY**

On June 24, 2017, a picnic at Fairgrounds Park in Loveland, Colorado, was like so many other picnics, yet unlike any other. There were families and friends, food and fun. But what set this picnic apart was that all the children there had been "adopted" as frozen embryos. The occasion was the celebration of the 20th anniversary of the Snowflakes Embryo Adoption Program at Nightlight Christian Adoptions. As indicated, *infra*, John and Marlene had a role in the founding of the program as their daughter, Hannah, was the first "adopted" frozen embryo.

It was not a small undertaking to launch an entirely new category of adoptions. There were legal issues, as well as finding couples interested in placing their unwanted embryos for adoption, along with couples desiring to adopt them. But the success of the program is proof of both – the willingness to acknowledge that frozen embryos are lives and couples desiring to adopt them.

Science, and the life of Hannah, and the other "snowflake children" or "IVF babies", prove that viability outside the womb actually occurs at fertilization. Hannah was one of the frozen embryos "adopted" from a couple that already had five children. With their family complete, the couple was concerned and selfless enough that they wished to give the remaining embryos a chance to be born.

Doctors can take photographs of the embryos, substantially magnified, as embryos are too small to be seen by the naked eye. See the first pictures for Hannah's baby book. *See* below:

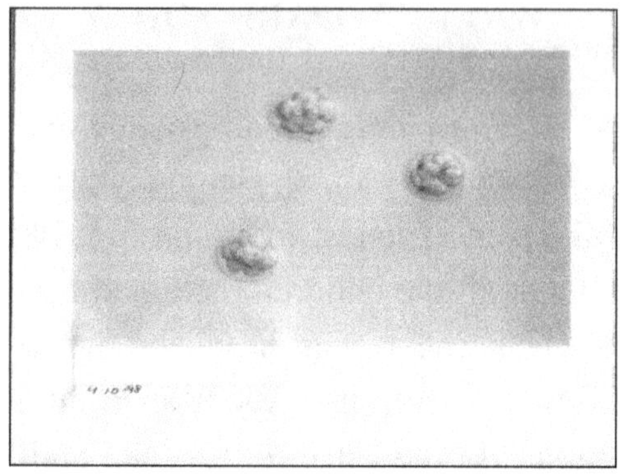

**Hannah and Two Siblings Viable Outside the Womb
Day of Thaw**

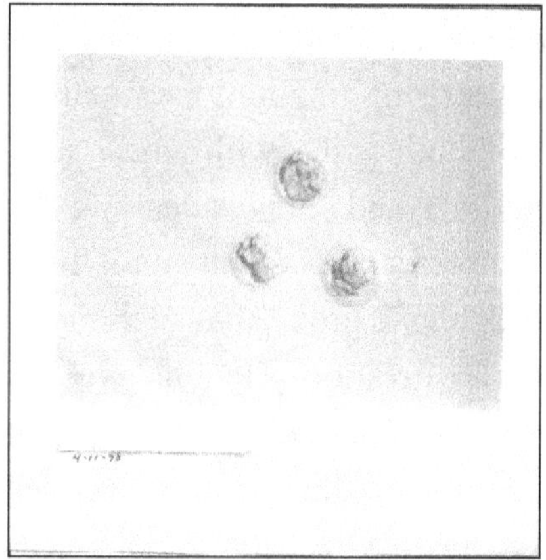

**Hannah and Two Siblings Outside the Womb
Day of Transfer**

The embryonic photos above are actual photos of Hannah, as an embryo, not ultrasounds. It is unknown which of the three embryos in the photos is Hannah. The first photo was taken on the day of the thaw, the second photo was taken the following day, before the transfer to Marlene's womb. Of note in looking closely at the photos is that **overnight, in a petri dish, the embryos advanced to their next stage of development.** This is called "compaction", when the cells start to move to one side and a fluid-filled sac is forming. This is a complete human **life** growing on its own. Not "a clump of cells," as abortion proponents frequently call embryos.

Thus was their journey. One that evolved from infertility to helping start a movement that allowed infertile couples to still experience pregnancies while helping alleviate a troublesome development in the in vitro fertilization industry. In couples' desperation to start a family, doctors were obliging them by helping create as many embryos as possible, often far more than they eventually might use, leaving a surplus of embryos in frozen storage.

Hannah's life proves life begins at fertilization. Hannah stands for the lives of all embryos in or out of the womb, especially those targeted for abortion.

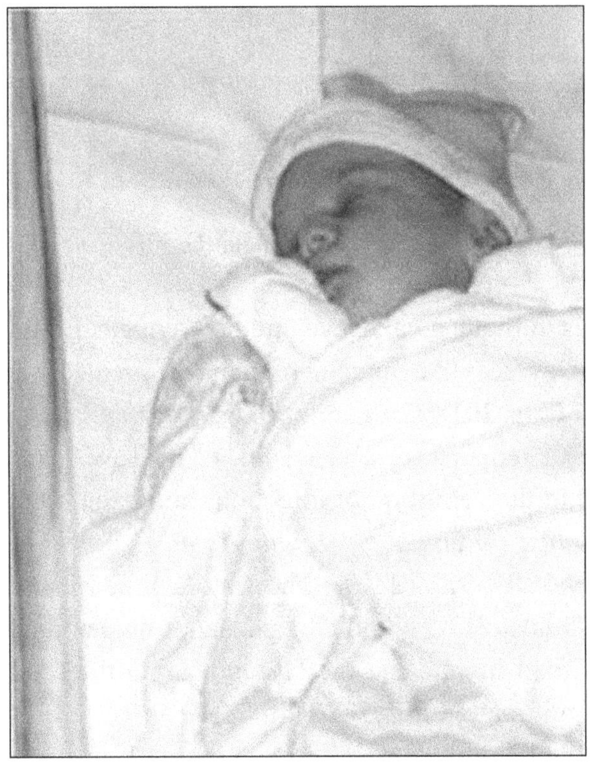

**Hannah After Birth**

**Hannah at 8 months**

Citizens in Indiana value even human remains from the womb. This Court agreed that human remains be treated with dignity by state law. In 2018, Indiana enacted a law related to the disposal of fetal remains. One provision of the law "excluded fetal remains from the definition of infectious and pathological waste." *Box v. Planned Parenthood of Indiana and Kentucky, Inc., et al.,* 129 S. Ct. 1780, 1781 (2019). The state claimed it had an interest in "the humane and dignified disposal of human remains". The Seventh Circuit invalidated the law indicating the state's interest was "not legitimate". *Id.* 1782. Citing *Akron v. Akron Center for Reproductive Health, Inc,* 462 U.S. 416, 452, n. 45, 103 S. Ct. 2481, 76 L.Ed.2d 687 (1983) this Court reversed, having "already acknowledged that a State has a 'legitimate interest in proper disposal of fetal remains.'" Id.

Further evidence that life has value, from inception, is found in Justice Thomas' concurring opinion in *Box,* at 1781-1793 (emphasis added):

"The use of abortion to achieve eugenic goals is not merely hypothetical. The foundations for legalizing abortion in America were laid during the early 20th-century birth-control movement. That movement developed alongside the American eugenics movement. And significantly, Planned Parenthood founder Margaret Sanger recognized the eugenic potential of her cause. She emphasized and embraced the notion that birth control 'opens the way to the eugenicist.' Sanger, Birth Control and Racial Betterment, Birth Control Rev., Feb. 1919, p. 12 (Racial Betterment). As a means of reducing the 'ever increasing, unceasingly spawning **class of human beings who never should have been born at all**,' Sanger argued that 'Birth Control ... is really the greatest and most truly eugenic method' of 'human generation.' M. Sanger, Pivot of Civilization 187, 189 (1922).

In her view, birth control had been 'accepted by the most clear thinking and far seeing of the Eugenists themselves as the most constructive and necessary of the means to racial health.' Id. , at 189. It is true that Sanger was not referring to abortion when she made these statements, at least not directly. She recognized a moral difference between 'contraceptives' and other, more 'extreme' ways for 'women to limit their families,'" such as "**the horrors of abortion and infanticide**.' M. Sanger, Woman and the New Race 25, 5 (1920) (Woman and the New Race). But Sanger's arguments about the eugenic value of birth control in securing 'the elimination of the unfit,' Racial Betterment 11, apply with even greater force to abortion, making it significantly more effective as a tool of eugenics. Whereas Sanger believed that birth control could prevent 'unfit' people from reproducing, abortion can prevent them from being born in the first place. Many eugenicists therefore supported legalizing abortion, and abortion advocates—including future Planned Parenthood President Alan Guttmacher—endorsed the use of abortion for eugenic reasons. Technological advances have only heightened the eugenic potential for abortion, as abortion can now be used to eliminate children with unwanted characteristics, such as a particular sex or disability."

This concurring opinion is a history lesson on the origins of Planned Parenthood and Margaret Sanger's intentional design to use birth control and abortion to foster a eugenics agenda. It is unlikely the *Roe* Court could even imagine the magnitude of "the horrors of abortion" as a form of birth control that we have today.

Once before, in our history, an entire class of people, African Americans, were unjustly considered property.[73] Today, human beings, capable of life outside their mother's womb, are considered

---

[73] "They [African Americans] had for more than a century before been regarded as beings of an inferior order, and altogether unfit to associate with the white race, either in social or political relations; and so far inferior, that they had no rights which the white man was bound to respect; and that the negro might justly and lawfully be reduced to slavery for his benefit. He was bought and sold, and treated as an ordinary article of merchandise and traffic, whenever a profit could be made by it. This opinion at that time was fixed and universal in the civilized portion of the white race. It was regarded as an axiom in morals as well as in politics, which no one thought of disputing, or supposed to be open to dispute; and men in every grade and position in society daily and habitually acted upon it in their private pursuits as well as in matters of public concern, without doubting for a moment the correctness of this opinion." *Dred Scott, Plaintiff in Error v. John Sanford, 60 U.S. 393*, at 408, 19 How. 15 L.Ed 691 (1856)

property, with "special characteristics" which can be bought and sold, dismembered and dissected, the subject of litigation, or placed in a mother's womb to bring forth a new human being.

Abortion is not contraception and any attempt to think of abortion as a contraceptive is wrong. Contraception prevents human life from starting. Abortion is the horrible killing of human life after it has begun. The Mississippi legislature made its perspective very clear. In section C of the Act: "(c) Based on the findings in paragraph (a) of this subsection, it is the intent of the Legislature, through this act and any regulations and policies promulgated hereunder, to restrict the practice of nontherapeutic or elective abortion to the period up to the fifteenth week of gestation."

**Hannah at her college graduation**

As in *The Emperor Has No Clothes,* it is time to admit life **does begin at fertilization**. Unlike the folktale, this is no laughing matter. It is logically evident that life begins at fertilization, as the example of Hannah clearly demonstrates. There is really no need to make something that is so simple complicated.

You see, a human is a human no matter how small.

A human is a human no matter which side of the uterine wall.[74]

It is truly an illusion to say that we cannot determine when life begins – it begins at the beginning.

## CONCLUSION

It is time for this Court to let the governed have a voice. It is time to get out of the business of forcing Americans, in every state, to pretend that the emperor has clothes – that abortion is okay because some people don't want to admit the obvious that abortion is infanticide. Many, many Americans already believe that life begins at fertilization. Science proves it is true. The life of Hannah proves it is true. It is time to let the citizen, through their elected representatives, pass enforceable laws that reflect that truth, that life begins at fertilization.

All "previability" prohibitions on elective abortions should be legal and enforceable. This Court has the ability, but does it have the courage and the will to right this wrong?

---

[74] Adapted from oft-quoted portion of Dr. Seuss's <u>Horton Hears a Who,</u> Random House Children's Books (1954) A Person Is A Person No Matter How Small <u>https://en.wikipedia.org/wiki/Horton_Hears_a_Who!</u>

## PRAYER

*Amici* respectfully pray this Court find that viability occurs upon fertilization and allow Mississippi's Gestational Act to take effect.

Mary J. Browning
Counsel of Record for
*Amici Curiae*
Allan E. Parker, Jr.
R. Clayton Trotter
The Justice Foundation

Further comments by Clayton Trotter – One other thing I want to share about the amazing Supreme Court briefs. There is an article from The New Yorker magazine highlighting the fact that Justice Amy Comedy Barrett questioned about Safe Haven laws. And this is what The New Yorker magazine said, "It's not clear what inspired Barrett's questions about Safe Haven laws. The brief filed by Mississippi in 2021 makes only a passing mention of them, and dozens of *Amicus* Briefs filed on behalf of Mississippi don't cite them at all. But two briefs, filed by relatively obscure organizations offer sunny assessments of Safe Havens as an antidote to abortion. A brief from the Justice Foundation, a Texas based litigation firm that handles anti-abortion cases, contends that 'As a matter of law, there are no more unwanted children in America because of the major change in circumstances known as Safe Haven laws. Even if states ban or restrict abortions completely or if only one abortion facility exists in a state, no longer would any woman have to parent a baby if she does not was to parent, or if she does not have the desire or ability to do so.' I just want everybody to know that The New Yorker magazine, by calling us obscure in that article, completely destroyed our obscurity. New Yorker magazine has a huge circulation, though I don't know how many, maybe millions. "We ain't obscure no more".

Allan Parker again – I want to highlight Mary Browning because she was the lead author on Hannah, Marlene, and John's brief. As she was writing, she put in an unusual literary device, a poem, well, just a prophetic statement. While writing the brief, she called me and said; "Al, can we put this in the brief? Can we say a person's a person, no matter how small." And I said yes. So she made it into a poem for the Supreme Court.

"You see, a human is a human, no matter how small.
A human is a human no matter which side of the uterine wall."

(Paraphrasing Dr. Seuss' "Horton Hears a Who")

We're just getting started. There may be roughly 150,000 to 170,000 babies alive this next year because *Roe v. Wade* was overturned.

# CHAPTER TEN

# How Can You Help Make Abortion Illegal in All 50 States?

I believe this message is for the Body of Christ. I am often just a reluctant witness; I confess to my shame. But I am one who is being trained by God to delight in doing His will. As I stated earlier, I resisted writing this book at first. After all, who am I to have anything to say, but the Lord made it very clear it was to be written. The February 11, 2000, Isaiah passages which contain the promise that *"your covenant with death will be annulled, and your agreement with Sheol (the place of the dead) shall not stand,"* (Isaiah 28:18 (Amplified Bible. Zondervan Publishing)) also contain several passages about writing a book. He says:

*"9 Now, go, write it on a tablet before them and inscribe it on a scroll. That it may serve in the time to come as a witness forever. For this is a rebellious people, false sons, sons who refuse to listen to the instruction of the Lord;*

*10 Who say to the seers; "you must not see visions"; and to the prophets. "You must not prophesy to us what is right! Speak to us pleasant words, prophesy illusions." Get out of the true way, turn aside out of the path, let us hear no more about the Holy One of Israel.*

*[12] Therefore, thus says the Holy One of Israel: Since you have rejected this word and have put your trust in oppression, and guile, and have relied on them.*

*[13] Therefore, this iniquity will be to you like a fall,*

*[14] whose crash will then come suddenly and swiftly, in an instant. And He shall break it as a potter's vessel is broken, breaking it in pieces without sparing so that there cannot be found among its pieces one large enough to carry coals of fire from the hearth or to dip water out of the cistern.*

*[15] For thus says the Lord God, the Holy One of Israel: In repentance and rest you shall be saved, in quietness and trust is your strength. But you were not willing....*

*[18] And therefore, the Lord earnestly waits to be gracious to you; and therefore He lifts Himself up, that He may have mercy on you and show loving kindness to you. For the Lord is a God of justice. Blessed are all those who wait for Him, who expect and long for Him."*

Isaiah 30:8-18

The final battle of The Moral Outcry To Make Abortion Illegal In All 50 States will not be won by man; it will not be won by TJF. It will not be won by smart lawyers. It can only be won by God. – And the first step – reversing *Roe v. Wade* has been accomplished by the Lord, the "Master of Breakthroughs." Isaiah 28:21, 2 Sam. 5:20. We have the promise of God in Isaiah 28:14-22, that the covenant with death will be cancelled, but that should be a spur to us to cry out to God to remind Him of His Word and His promise. Join us in this prayer of David,

*"O give us help against the adversary, for deliverance by man is in vain. Through God we shall do valiantly; and it is He who will tread down our adversaries."*

Psalm 108:12-13

When *Roe v. Wade* and *Doe v. Bolton* are overturned the Lord said this would happen, then:

*"<sup>18</sup> On that day the deaf will hear words of a book, And out of their gloom and darkness the eyes of the blind will see.*

*<sup>19</sup> The afflicted also will increase their gladness in the LORD, And the needy of mankind will rejoice in the Holy One of Israel.*

*<sup>20</sup> For the ruthless will come to an end and the scorner will be finished, Indeed all who are intent on doing evil will be cut off;*

*<sup>21</sup> Who cause a person to be indicted by a word, And ensnare him who adjudicates at the gate, And defraud the one in the right with meaningless arguments."*

Isaiah 29:18-21 (NASB)

Why does God wait so long to abolish evil? To give man time to repent, and then comes judgment, if there is no repentance. All of us in America must repent and be saved from the wrath of God.

## Contribute Testimonies of Abortion's Pain

The testimonies of the women hurt by abortion are figuratively worth their weight in gold. Their voices must be heard and amplified. It is hard to find courageous women willing to speak out. There is no national database, no phone listings. They do not stand on the street corners shouting how abortion affected them. The pain is hidden in secret, as their testimonies show over and over.

Second, a testimony is like gold in that it has to be refined and purified in a woman's heart, usually by time and pressure, sometimes in a furnace, before she is willing to speak out. Finally, it is like gold in that every woman's testimony is extremely precious and valuable.

If you would like to submit your testimony, you may use your full name, though if you have not told your family and gone through a healing class, we suggest you use your initials or first name only, to protect your identity. The courts have protected the identity of women who want to use initials or fictitious names in the past, so we will do everything in our power to protect the confidentiality of your name.

Giving your testimony in writing is all you have to do to be a part of *Operation Outcry* (www.operationoutcry.org). That is enough. Your testimony will be shared as and where needed. If you would like to also speak out publicly, we can help you share your stories with others. After healing, and if you feel led, we can help you to begin to speak out on talk radio, on pro-life programs, at church, and wherever you can tell the truth. One national abortion recovery program is even called "Surrendering the Secret," by Pat Layton. Call your local Christian radio or TV station, and secular talk shows or community programs, and tell them you want to tell your story. Do not be afraid to speak out!

# Find Abortion Recovery Programs Near You

1. **International Helpline for Abortion Recovery (based in the US):**

The International Helpline for Abortion Recovery trained phone consultants have experienced the pain of abortion and are ready to help you with your abortion recovery healing process.

- *They provide 24/7 confidential help and care.*
- *They listen to you and help you find the abortion recovery program nearest you.*
- *They mail resources and follow up to make sure you get the help you need.*

**If you have questions or need help after abortion, please call 1-866-482-LIFE (5433).**
**For more information go to <u>www.internationalhelpline.org.</u>**
**CALL NOW! The first step in the journey of healing can begin with your call.**

2. **Option Line:**

It doesn't matter if your abortion was yesterday or 20 years ago. Option Line provides emotional support after abortion through a hotline where you can speak to someone about the way you feel right away, or connect you with a group in your area that meets in person.

For help with your unplanned pregnancy visit:
- **<u>OptionLine.org</u> to chat,**
- **or call/text 800-712-4357.**

**Option Line also provides weekend retreats ready to help women sort through any difficult emotions from a past abortion. Option Line is here to help.**

### 3. Support After Abortion

In an atmosphere of acceptance and flexibility, Support After Abortion provides an options-based approach to emotional and spiritual healing. You can choose a program that best suits your needs. Over 800 agencies are available to help you.

- *Call Support After Abortion: 844-289-HOPE*
- *Visit Website: www.supportafterabortion.com*

**Their mission is "To end the demand for abortion through healing people impacted by abortion."**

### 4. H3 Helpline – Help, Hope, Healing

H3Helpline is a national after abortion helpline. They offer after abortion support and help, hope, healing for the pain of abortion.

- *Call 1-866-721-7881*
- *Visit Website: www.h3helpline.org*

**Call H3 Helpline and one of their Phone Coaches will provide you with healing information.**

It has been liberating for many women to be given "permission" to grieve the loss of their child. Many have found such relief to talk about it at last. The truth has finally set them free. Through Christ-centered healing programs, many are transformed. Giving testimony has deepened their healing and broken through layers of denial and a self-destructive lifestyle. If you have had more than one abortion, you can fill out one declaration for all or one for each abortion separately. See www.operationoutcry.org or www.thejusticefoundation.org.

We sincerely ask that you distribute these forms to your friends and other women who have experienced abortion. The testimonies of these women can impact America. Thank you for prayerfully considering supporting *Operation Outcry*. We need your help in finding and encouraging women to fill out the declaration. You may know a wife, a sister, aunt, niece, or friend, who has had an abortion. Tell them about *Operation Outcry* and how they can help end legalized abortion in America. Encourage them to put aside the pain, find healing, and help get out the truth. Be there for them in their grief and ask for their help.

If you work at a pregnancy resource center or an abortion recovery healing ministry, you should be able to encourage many women to come forward and tell their story. *Operation Outcry* has been endorsed by almost all of the national abortion recovery leaders. Some have even shared their own testimonies with us like Millie Lace, and Sheila Harper, author of "Save One."

## Share The Moral Outcry Petition to Make Abortion Illegal (And Unthinkable) in All 50 States

We need activists and churches throughout America to distribute the Petition or a link in the pews or in emails to every member of the church. It is important that post abortive women not be singled out for embarrassment, but women who have had abortion should be encouraged to find healing in a Christ centered abortion recovery program, then fill out the declaration later. Post abortion healing should be offered with names of local providers, if possible. All this is available at www.thejusticefoundation.org

# The Final Charge

## ABORTION SHOULD BE ILLEGAL AND UNTHINKABLE JUST LIKE SLAVERY AND SEGREGATION

Oswald Chambers certainly has it right when he says that we can lose the vision by spiritual leakage. We have to let God fulfill it, but we have to constantly look for it. In 2000, I certainly did not know exactly when the vision of Isaiah 28:18, that, *"...the covenant of death shall be canceled,"* would be fulfilled. But it was. I thought it might take three years, my wife thought seven. She was right in part; the first victory on the federal partial birth abortion ban came in seven years.

Neither of us thought it would take 22 years. But the Lord has strengthened and sustained us all along the journey. We must trust God. After giving us the extraordinary promise in Is. 28:14-22, and even stating that He will be the One to do the work to overturn *Roe v. Wade*, He says to us, His people:

*"And now do not carry on as scoffers, lest your fetters be made stronger; for I have heard from the Lord God of Hosts of decisive destruction on all the earth."*

Isaiah 28:22

I don't believe God gave us the *Roe v. Wade* reversal victory to see us lose the Final Battle to Make Abortion Illegal in all 50 States. Now that you have heard the message and the promise of God, is it time for you to become involved in the effort of *The Moral Outcry Petition* and *Operation Outcry*? Are you being asked by the Holy Spirit be involved? Do not say to yourself, "Well, there's not really a God or God's not really involved in this ending of abortion. I'm not going to do anything." Don't say "it can't be done." Nothing is impossible with God. It is time for you to arise and become involved. If you do not, if the women and the church do not heed this call, then the fetters, the iron prison chains which bind us at this time will become even stronger.

> *"[5] Blessed is he whose help is the God of Jacob,*
> *Whose hope is in the Lord his God,*
> *[6] The Maker of Heaven and earth, the sea,*
> *and everything in them —*
> *The Lord, who remains faithful forever.*
> *[7] He upholds the cause of the oppressed and gives*
> *food to the hungry.*
> *The Lord sets prisoners free,*
> *[8] the Lord gives sight to the blind,*
> *The Lord lifts up those who are bowed down,*
> *The Lord loves the righteous."*

Psalm 146:5-8 (NIV)

## He is Coming Soon!

*"[11] I saw heaven standing open and there before me was a white horse, whose rider is called Faithful and True. With justice He judges and makes war.*

*[12] His eyes are like blazing fire, and on His head are many crowns. He has a name written on Him that no one knows but He Himself.*

*[13] He is dressed in a robe dipped in blood, and His name is the Word of God."*

Revelations 19:11-13 (NIV)

Will you join us in the battle for Justice by prayer, testimony, signing The Petition, or financial donations? Everyone can share the good news!

# Acknowledgements

Ithank my beloved wife, Susan, who strengthens me and loves me along the journey wherever it goes. She is a diamond among women and greatly to be praised. I thank The Justice Foundation Board Members who through the years faithfully sought the Lord's direction and walked humbly wherever He said to go. (Jim Leininger, Fritz Steiger, Tim Lyles, Arch Bonnema, Mark Dorazio, Clayton Trotter, George Pond, and Danny Skaggs.)

I shall always honor and be grateful to our friends, our sisters and brothers in the Lord who allowed us to act on their behalf – Norma McCorvey (*Roe*), Sandra Cano (*Doe*), the Courageous **Women of *Operation Outcry*** (especially the national leaders and Board of Advisors – Susan Renne, Myra Myers, Molly White, Joyce Zounis-Brown, Cynthia Collins, Tracy Reynolds, Cecilia Sullivan, Luana Stoltenberg, Rebecca Streetman, Mayela Banks, Nona Ellington, Lisa Dudley, Millie Lace, Denise Seibert, Daria Monroe, Kay Painter, Karen Keitzman, Bernadette Roy, Sharon Blakeney, Missy Smith, Mary Lee Mason, Julie Thomas, Karen Bodle, Rhonda Arias, Paula Talley, Tammy Holly, Tina Brock, Karen Holdren, Cynthia Carney, Shari Richard, Heidi Swanson, Mary J. Browning, Serena Dye, Andrea Sosebee, Arlene Lehman, Susan Justice, Stacy Lynn Massey, Vicki Tucci-Krusel, Darlene Wood-Harvey, Angel Murchison, Kathy Rutledge, Saundra Decker, Virginia Lange, Lisa Skowron, Elsa Lopez, Sue Hooker,

Sharon McLendon, Theresa Bonapartis, Carla Stream, Kelly Roy-Williams, Lisa Stribling, Shanna Cates, Karen Elliott, Nona Ellington, Andrea Sosebee and many more. All this would not be complete without Melinda and Denny Thybault and the Signers of The Moral Outcry Petition; and Hannah and her mother and father, Marlene and John.

I also want to give special thanks to the saints, intercessors, prayer leaders, pastors and groups who prayed for me and my family, all of the employees of The Justice Foundation, especially Queta Aguilar and Marisol Aguilar, and for the reversal of *Roe v. Wade.*

I am thankful for all the **donors who gave** and **the intercessors** who prayed.

I also depended upon and am grateful for all the prayers from Eileen Vincent and Natalie Hardy, Dai Sup Han of Prayer Surge Now, The Heartland and Texas Apostolic Prayer Networks, Community Bible Church, The Signers of The Moral Outcry Petition, Tony and Lynette Abbott, the Noon Prayer Group, The Wailing Women, Alveda King, Walter Hoye, Catherine Davis, Connie Eller and other noble African-American Leaders, The Supreme Court Prayer Line, Prayer Surge Now, Pray California, Capitol Hill Prayer Partners, Matt Lockett and Bound4Life, Lou Engle and The Call, Maryal Boumann and Pray California, Art Remington, Barney Barnes, Pastor Phil Thompson and Ark Revival Ministries, The Men's Prayer Call, Mark and Sharon and the Passmore Sunday School Class, Paul and Carol Tondre, to name just a few.

May the Lord richly bless all of you who ever prayed or worked for the reversal of *Roe v. Wade!*

*[7] "And to the angel of the church in Philadelphia write: He who is holy, who is true, who has the key of David, who opens and no one will shut, and who shuts and no one opens, says this: [11] I am coming quickly; hold firmly to what*

*you have, so that no one will take your crown. [12]The one who overcomes, I will make him a pillar in the temple of My God, and he will not go out from it anymore; and I will write on him the name of My God, and the name of the city of My God, the new Jerusalem, which comes down out of heaven from My God, and My new name." Revelation 3:7,11,12*

# A COLD GLOW

# A COLD GLOW

Jason Sealy

Library of Congress Catalog Number: 2026906003

A Cold Glow / Jason Sealy
ISBNs: 979-8-9951777-9-1 (paperback)
       979-8-9951777-7-7 (ebook)

Cover art by Era Dervishi | IG: holyaphordite
Interior art by Steve Camillone | IG: steve.camillone

# DEDICATION

*To my family: Melvin & Stevie, who remind me to warm my heart on the coldest days.*

*Content warning & disclaimer: Depiction is not endorsement.*

# CONTENTS


**SUNRISE**......................................................................................1

1. OUR SYSTEM OF T-POSERS........................................................3
2. COUNCILMEMBER QUINN GERSHWIN.........................................15
3. VADA IKEBE'S SELECTION.........................................................21
4. ALCOHOLIC GETS LO.............................................................33
5. INFLUENCER ARTURO VASQUEZ................................................41
6. COUNCILMEMBER QUINN GERSHWIN.........................................49
7. VADA IKEBE'S SOLIPSISM........................................................57
8. TOO ALCOHOLIC GETS TOO LO................................................63
9. INFLUENCED ARTURO VASQUEZ...............................................71

**SOLAR NOON**.............................................................................81

10. WILLIAM TILLER AND DATES...................................................83
11. OUR SYSTEM, SIRENS SWEPT FROM THE TIDES OF TIME.............93
12. FUGITIVE QUINN GERSHWIN...................................................98
13. VADA IKEBE'S SIMULATION....................................................105
14. ALCOHOLIC GETS IT............................................................115
15. NUMBERS-MAXXING ARTURO VASQUEZ...................................125
16. OUR SYSTEM LACKS VERSTEHEN.............................................135
17. PREACHER ARTURO VASQUEZ.................................................143
18. RECOVERING ALCOHOLIC GETS LO..........................................157
19. VADA IKEBE'S SIMULACRA.....................................................169
20. QUINN GERSHWIN................................................................179
21. OUR SYSTEM IS CHIASTIC.....................................................193
22. WILLIAM TILLER AND FATE....................................................199

**SUNDOWN**................................................................................211

23. OUR SYSTEM IS ANY............................................................213
24. VADA IKEBE'S REIFICATION...................................................219
25. PROPHET ARTURO VASQUEZ..................................................235
26. RAPID RESPONDER GETS LO...................................................241
27. OUR SYSTEM IS ALL.............................................................247
28. GETS LO............................................................................253
29. ARTURO VASQUEZ...............................................................255
30. VADA IKEBE.......................................................................263
31. OUR SYSTEM IS ANY AND ALL................................................273
32. WILLIAM TILLER AND BOUNDARIES.........................................281

**TOMORROW**..............................................................................289

33. CASPER.............................................................................291

# SUNRISE

*WE ALL RUN TOGETHER AND IT'S OKAY.*

# 1

# OUR SYSTEM OF T-POSERS

Our routine is decades old and forced. The daybreak that scrolls up our eyelids is not the brightest light we've ever seen. 5:12 on the dot we're both conscious whether we like it or not—far too early, half-hungover—but it has nothing to do with those hot rays. It has to do with a brighter light and a cold glow.

We'd have to work to stay horizontal a few more hours. Sometimes we manage, and sometimes the stillness even feels okay. In spite of ourselves, we get its appeal. Today's the anniversary, though. Stillness is out of the cards.

5:12 becomes 5:13; we slap a story onto our encrypted messaging app Signal, for an audience of one: our other half.

Twin rotating skulls on a grainy black background, further instructions below. A proposal:

**T-Pose like it's 2010!**

T-Pose. Well, that's a Greatest Hit.

The T-Pose has been the default resting position of any 3D-generated human-shaped asset since 3D-generated assets became a thing. Whether a movie, a blueprint, a projection, or a videogame—whether it's motion captured by someone or entirely virtual, it's always the same stance. Existent only in some separate, entirely inaccessible realm. Uninhabited.

It's also the codename for one of our most successful anniversary ideas ever. We used to do it a lot in the early days. Feels like it's been forever.

You know when you work somewhere soaked in a specific scent, like a restaurant, how it becomes a part of you and you can only sometimes smell it? Clacking of brackish water on stone, tangy salt in the harbor, pink-orange sunrise clinging like froth to the air, the head-high of the tidewater Sitka spruce . . . there are certainly worse sensations in which to be immured.

It's easy to take it all for granted, is what we're saying.

We are George and Anne, and on Saturday, the first June 21st, 2025, of our lives, we each returned to our hometown of Liltin Yew, Washington for our high school Class of 2010's fifteen-year reunion. Covid had canceled the ten-year.

We must have thought there was some personal victory in finally attending the reunion. Like a cosmic rebuke to the stupid little maskless town of our childhoods, in the desperate hope that the rebuke would imbue our shattered post-pandemic lives with some meaning again.

We got something cosmic, all right: nothing but our old lives.

Actually, after we skinny dipped and slept together—

(Just slept—)

—in the marsh above the historic Mima Mounds, the UAP we saw *did not* have cosmic origins. It instead emerged in the runoff from the Duwamish River. In technical terms it was a whole-ass transmedium USO. After all these years, we remember how the only sound the massive craft made was its displacement of the river around it. Like an erratic tear across dawn-dyed water, behaving as if flung from a carnival ride, skipping like a saucer across the marsh before reversing back downward in a maneuver so impossibly sharp that a drone couldn't even swing it.

At the vertex of this impossible maneuver, something happened over us. Onto us. That's when we heard *a lot* of noise, and it was our blood screaming, bursting in our ears. Yet instead of burning, we froze.

Magneto-acoustic waves shattering all around us.

And then we wake separately in our respective beds; it's June 21st, 2025 for the second time; we've just flown in from Burbank and Miami, respectively; and that entire twenty-four hours has to have all been some dream, a vivid simulation conjured from travel fatigue and stress. Probably one of those weird, cryptic dreams that casually become absurd, cut out when the waking brain is aware enough of itself to blink.

*Why was that person from high school so prominent in it, though?* ask both the George and Anne of us, referring to the respective other. *How'd we subconsciously dig up such a random person from our pasts?*

Because we don't really know each other right now. Don't have each other's numbers, and we find each other blocked on our socials when we look each other up.

Half a decade back we'd gotten in a very public disagreement on the page for the initial 2020 high school reunion. The whole Facebook group had seen us go at it. In hindsight it was a funny little side note in the pandemic saga.

Anyway, that's why neither of us find it so strange that we were, ahem, in each other's dreams that night. We very soon, very seriously, will wish a dream was all it had been. It takes two subsequent iterations of the exact same June 21st, 2025: two subsequent experiences of *déjà-vu*, solipsism, hysteria, and mania before we each find the other one at the one spot we know where each has been: off the bank of the Budd inlet where the transradial whatever-the-fuck USO caught us.

We see it again. This time we watch from what we deem to be a safe distance—not in the splash zone, so to speak.

Again it flings itself from the water except, watching it closer, we realize something. A thin dark line anchors it all the way through the water, one long nail, the craft its fanning head. And the nail is stationary. All movement, even our own, is pulled into its gravitational matrix.

We hurtle into the stationary yet widening T and—this is literal, this part's no metaphor—we *feel* our eyes split at their roots, starting right along the optic nerves and then peeling forwards to push everything (the outer shells, corneas, the lenses, all the drooling mushy stuff) out of our faces. It's like switchblades clicking from inside our heads. White, agonizing light.

A cold glow, and then it's June 21st, 2025, and we're waking up in our respective beds on opposite ends of town still screaming.

No splash-free zone, after all. No matter how far we are from the craft (we test the limits), if we can see it, we will fall into it. That thin dark vertical line, it's like it clips through everything to anchor into our eyes.

We thought the first few days in the time hole were the worst but we've officially entered the nightmare proper. At least the first few days brought the gift of confusion. We have to endure ocular torture every time just to piece together more information on the craft from the sea. On the lead-up to June 22nd's inaccessible dawns, we're scrambling: searching the waters, warning people, and enlisting the townies, professors, Joint Base Wilkes-Boothe (newly named).

No one else follows us into the time hole's next day even if we show them the craft. We've lost track of time. Maybe it's been days, maybe a full month. Can't be longer than a month—please don't be longer than a month. We break down in each other's arms, begging not to go to the marshes and see what we must have seen the very first night.

So eventually, we don't. We take breaks from the hunt to break free. The pangs in our eyes dull. The immediate sense memory fades little by little. Although we should be refusing to look away, it might be time to kill just a *little* bit of hope for an occasional good night's sleep, for whatever sanity we can cling to.

The switch-over to resignation doesn't happen overnight (hah). We do more sleuthing, discover a thing or two—before hitting a brick wall, at least. It becomes harder to go back to the marshes and research. We establish an arbitrary "June 21st, 2025," and the tracking of days anchors us like the dreaded USO—anchors us like a ball and chain. We go fully around our makeshift calendar—again, and again.

Generations of the same Saturday pass as a laminar flow.

Once "annually" we saunter down the Mima Mounds to gaze bitterly at our aquatic Unmaker. We can't exactly call it a holiday. That's what it is, though. We're not even searching for clues anymore. The inside-out cleaving of our eyes is no less excruciating, but if we relegate it to just once every 365 Saturday, June 21$^{st}$, 2025s, we can almost fool ourselves into assigning it some kind of narrative.

Our anniversaries come to mean different things. Crafted celebrations, crafted crash-outs. Let's face it, crashing out seems a bit more attuned to our circumstances, doesn't it, George?

*Does it, Anne?*

"Happy anniversary," we say to one another over our burner phones. The one phone our she-half has borrowed from a drifter at the East 4th Food Mart, which is still six minutes and thirty-seven seconds from opening. That means its three leering cameras won't cycle on 'til 5:30. The other phone is the landline of George's dad, who is perpetually gone on a business trip. All across town today we will burn through a dozen burners.

"T-Pose?" we ask.

"Mhm," we say back.

"Well heck, George, that's clearly us going on Hard mode."

"Yeah. It's been a while."

"And so you're saying you're up for it?" Our Anne half.

"I've been practicing all year!"

"Yeeaaahhhh I don't believe you," Anne says.

"Well, past few months, though. For real. Think we can even pull off a no-kill run. Well, except for the one, obviously—"

"Medium. We're going medium on collateral, and that's a good compromise, and you should just take it."

Our male-half goes abruptly silent.

"Look, *you* wanna do the T-Pose run, right? That one's bloody. I'm not the one who chose it, you did."

Still no answer.

Maybe we should give a millimeter of ground.

"You still gonna download Tinder?"

"Already did."

". . . Fine," we both say. Almost a hiss.

"Plaza at 6:30," says George. "I'm taking it you'll want to be on meat duty?

"Mhm, I haven't been out in the forest for ages."

"Take it. I've got all the encryptions spoofed already."

"Ooo, sexy! You always forget those."

"Yeah, yeah, asshole. Like I said, I've been practicing. Anything else?"

"*Anything else?*"

"Oh. Yeah."

"The Insta post, George. It isolates him. You can't forget."

"I won't, Anne."

Call cut.

We won't jump to personal offense at the other. It was a simple negotiation. So all right, this hasn't been the smoothest start, but timewise we're still within every parameter. Forward.

What's important is that we both embody the motivation. Today just became quite the performance for one another. Stealing the store owner's unlocked electric sedan, taking it a mile down the road and jerking it to a stop to slip into a hardware store, Anne's heart is still only half. We can feel her doubt from the other side of town.

George's conviction certainly rang true on the phone. We'll admit, revisiting T-Pose was not an expected proposition from him—from *us*, we mean. So maybe it's time to put in our share of the work. From the hardware store's fridge we swipe the cuts of venison, the bucket of blood. As we ascend Liltin Yew's coast, cranes and thrum of harbor industry recede and a chaotic wall of rocky cliffs, haphazard evergreens, and painterly skies cradle us. We look to the left, spot brightly painted, rotting railroad tracks and smile.

Nature is everything, including people.

We halt at the base of Kaiser Woods behind the Black Hills, taking care to park in underbrush so that Officer Thaxton Pratt—presently speeding home two hours before shift change—passes right on by. A white sign warning hunters not to cook their kills (PFAS concentrations) is hidden from all but discerning eyes. Splashing the cold blood on the way, splattering the threshold of a long-abandoned mining passageway through the earth, and squeezing sick meat in slops from plastic, we note that kids used to work here.

When the first howl permeates the forest we won't be around, and in fact nobody will—not yet.

We're aligning.

Our male-half is hungover every single morning, and we'd never usually drank. Wouldn't have if we'd known the day before that Daisy was on death's door. Four furry legs a fit of quivers through the night, tiny heart flutters too sharp to let her sleep on her living room pillow; no strength to seek any family comfort, all family long gone anyways. She could've lain in our bed, we could've lain on her pillow. Our warmth may have calmed her.

In the early years of our sentence to the time hole we would take Daisy to the vet. Many days we'd take her together. But eventually the ritual of getting her high on overpriced drugs before the visit to juice her with an overpriced kiss became almost something masochistic: seeing some foreign entity hollow her out, unfocus her eyes, loosen her beyond the point of either working her little lungs or caring. She'd no longer be her. And only *then*—as if losing herself were the final requirement—would her eyes freeze.

We mostly ignore her now. Sometimes we'll end her quickly, but if we're trying to reprise T-Pose tonight, we don't have the free time.

George-half makes a move for business trip–daddy's safe to unsheathe exactly $4,500 of one $5,000 stack. Satisfaction lies in executing on a budget. One fewer way for people to see us coming. A blistering shower, a clean hole punched through a wall, and we're headed for the door. We know we'll hear it if we stop yet we stop anyway. The feeble wheezes from Daisy's pillow. Forward. Out the house, where we can't hear the wheezes.

Now we're one mind.

Two blocks down, a modded red 1989 Raider soft-top is gift-wrapped for us to jimmy into with one silken motion, its owner housebound for the day, locked into a true crime marathon hard-won by three straight Skateland doubles. Fresh disposable face masks are in the center console.

A Chao Xing at the window of the Dutch Bros Coffee beams when we ask if her brother's back in town for the overdue high school reunion. She says that yes, he's actually about to arrive with some much-needed breakfast burritos. When he shows up, he's with Liltin Yew's most successful part-time drug dealer, their movements giddily languid and eyes raw. Their partying is about to go one-on-one. After two minutes of effortless oleaginality, we wait for the brother to deliver the burritos; we then drop seven hundred into the dealer's jacket and mutter, "You won't know me. Twice the price not to ask how I know you've got Molly, Lucy, fenty, and K. Please."

After a beat the dealer snorts. Thrown by the deadpanned performance, so astonished this mysterious, handsome man is privy to the deal that's barely five hours' history, she almost skips to extract it from under her backseat. We need only say one thing to keep her, her daughter, even Chao Xing's brother happy outside town for the next 24 hours, and today, we say it. We settled on medium bodies, after all. "Warpaint's doing another secret show in Seattle."

We hope our Anne-half doesn't find out. All that should matter is we now have the 2mg of carfentanil—carfentanil clean enough to aerosolize for crowd control.

Not many cameras to be handled. We travel the most efficient routes and, approaching the Bay from the southwest and northeast respectively, we take care of each half of our sabotage with the rising sun to blow out our image. Of the three-dozen functional cameras along our routes, seventeen are wired and easily clipped from the ground. Six we obscure. The rest we simply reposition. A couple get paired with signal jammers—just in case. We didn't know how to do any of this before the USO. Now we know how to do everything we want.

We converge on Bay Plaza's sleepy south parking lot. It's been a while since we've shared the whole day. No one can hope to matter more to us than the other and that utterly circumstantial reality has grown to contain multitudes. Sure, it is a fucking problem. But it's never not grandiose.

On a bench with heads braced to the wind, we crack our energy drinks and cheers one another. We rub the smallest amount of carfentanil on our gums. We can't get addicted to any substance. Can't even experience its effects past twenty-four hours.

Digital information is crafted and repurposed for a thousand uses. Exactly eighty three boats bob and sway in the harbor, masts intersecting on the horizon without actually touching, as motionless as we are. At 6:52 a routine, distant boom from Joint Base Wilkes-Booth resounds, and in perfect synchronization with it, one of us whispers, "Pow."

Which one, though?

We both expected the pow. So which one of us actually whispered it?

Wait, how can we not know which one of us spoke? Was it both of us?

We stare blankly into each other, as if simple eye contact will unravel this maddening overlap. The exact opposite is achieved. An argument's swelling but we don't want one. So, back to Operation T-Pose: zero time to linger. Try to consolidate, to cohere again, and step into the soft-top Raider while leaving the stolen electric sedan there with its motor still running.

The rainbow tracks outside Liltin are the closest our town gets to tourism. A long-defunct railroad line intersects a trailhead nestled in the woods. We follow the tracks until they elevate onto a rickety wooden bridge. Salty wind gains insistence. Rocky cliffs overwrite evergreens until the ground falls away entirely. The Bay roils thirty feet below.

Just under half a football field's length away the tracks terminate at a mini-island, but not before each wooden beam turns a different color of the rainbow, painted to withstand the elements. It's the main attraction, the Instagram shot. Hundreds of iterations exist on locals' and visitors' profiles alike. A fall from this height doesn't render the water a solid. Low tide, though, pulls the surface just barely over mossy boulders of all sizes, their weathered points occasionally breaking above.

"Yo, aren't you Anne Oxendine?"

They know us from high school. There are five in total. Pietro and Barry, they're Liltin High sweethearts who finally got engaged after a decade apart. It was their idea to come out here. Nanno Sripariyattiwetti, leading this old clique, hops from beam to elevated beam. Rory, short for Aurora, is the one who's just called out to us. Her boyfriend, Ryan Holsey, hails from Tacoma. A tech sergeant when he was medically discharged, he helped evacuate Kabul in 2021.

He is the first one we discreetly steer ourselves towards.

"Wait, *the* Anne Oxendine?" Pietro is saying, hanging off his husband-to-be. "I subscribe to your CBD oils. And your free therapy app!"

"Mm . . . namaste," we nod, our male half smirking alongside us. The distance closed, we have the veteran triangulated. He's on 60mg of Prozac; he hasn't realized yet.

"You're here for the reunion! You're actually here!" Rory, short for Aurora, exclaims. "Anne, I've never been to Miami. Are there crocodiles everywhere? Or it's alligators, right? Which is it—"

"George? George Wheeler?" Barry is barely audible over sloshing waves. He stops on the orange wooden beam.

The George of us waves curtly.

"Y'all . . ." Barry and Pietro are confused. "Y'all know each other?"

"Who, Anne?" we say.

"George?" we say, too.

"Ah, yeah," we say, playing it off. "We've been . . . knowing each other for quite a bit, now." They're remembering the very public 2020 Reunion Page Debate we'd had. Lived history for them, a fictional universe for us. Anyway, together we shove the veteran off the lime-green colored wooden beam, his spine obliterating on the barely submerged rocks thirty feet down. Aurora next. She doesn't get the chance to turn from us and her scream snuffs as impact ruptures, water blinds. Barry and Pietro were tricky the first time we did this but we've learned the key is for George to duck Barry's grapple as Anne sweeps his feet; his head bounces off the yellow railroad support beam and George launches Pietro from the purple.

The rainbow road is exposed, visible from Bay Plaza to those paying attention. In fact, middle-aged parking attendant Cindy White *would* be viewing this entire 6.2-second massacre if not for the electric sedan we stole at the convenience store. She's already happily begun writing the citation.

Meanwhile, the leader of the railroad group, Nanno Sripariyattiwetti, is still about ten yards away on the blue-painted section of track. Her former classmates' screams have wheeled her around, and she's lowered to her knees, clutching to the blue beam like a leaf in a gale. We purse our lips and pretend to blow her over the side. She jumps into the Bay, mostly avoiding the jagged boulders.

We head back the way we came, watching Nanno swim like mad for the wooded coastline. The lone survivor thinks we're in hot pursuit but we're walking, not running. She'll make it to shore; she'll see us take her and the others' phones from their car at the trailhead; she'll get hopelessly lost in the Black Hills. She'll see us later.

Along the way we brush a Douglas fir free of one beefy assassin bug (*Rhynocoris iracundus*), and we lock the languid insect into our empty water bottle. Its bite is only potentially fatal to those with heart conditions. Like a steroid abuser.

There are campaign banners and illicit recordings to swipe.

A compromised officer, a town councilmember, and a Belarusian dance troupe touring Seattle to blackmail.

A generator to buy from Capitol Mall, which opens at ten.

An alcoholic to boot off the wagon.

And a live-streamed Saturday service to attend.

Before we split up to get all these plates spinning, we sideline ourselves. We must address this. We can't contain it anymore. "So when do we wanna figure out who said the *pow* back at Bay Plaza?" we ask ourselves.

"How 'bout tomorrow," we say.

# 2

# COUNCILMEMBER QUINN GERSHWIN

The skylight should have woken me.

Third Saturdays are typically the one schedule-less day I can afford. A whole different routine, one comforting and nostalgic. A personalized time machine.

Even cloudy, as it most often is, the skylight usually brightens enough to ignite my eyelids. By then it's typically about nine. Taylor, my high school sweetheart for a quarter century now, should be halfway through her stepmill exercise.

Not today. My work phone jolts my consciousness sloppily. Having just affixed her sweats and headband, Taylor exaggerates a groan before snatching it up from the dresser. The master bedroom is still very dark.

"Think fast." I hear the smirk in her voice as she readies her throw.

"Tall-ass order. Guuhhh." Eyes long tender from Lasik recovery, I miss the flying, screaming thing and shake down my silken quilt for it.

I breathe deep and sigh heavy. "Why're you calling me, Sarah?"

I'm suddenly very glad that Taylor has gone downstairs.

Three voices crackle on the end of my head of public affairs' office line. None of them belong to Sarah.

In fact, one of them is mine.

"Liltin Housing Now and the Nisqually tribe are obviously the loudest voices against this development, Mr. Gershwin." The voice is garbled. Recorded. Recorded from a conversation almost exactly three years ago, one which I recall all too well. Conducted in Seattle's Pike Place Market, between myself and two representatives from the Twice Loved Institute, or TLI for short.

"Obviously," Quinn Gershwin circa 2022 can be heard responding. "That area's barely south of Treaty Tree, that's all Billy Frank, Jr. Nature Preserve."

"Well, not *that* part —" the other voice says before another cuts in.

"Only 200 yards of its southwestern edge, which is flat and solid and provides natural drainage into the inlet."

Present-day me mumbles, *"Sarah,"* half a dozen times before accepting my head of PA's silence.

I know the rest of the recorded conversation by heart. The hairs on my nape tauten and I shoot up from bed.

It was the suits and I half-assedly debating the nebulous legality of private sector encroachment into national parks and refuges—flip-flopping presidential admins had left such smaller ones up to individual consideration, leaving Treaty Tree an exploitable gray—amidst crunches of lobster. *Which restaurant were we even at?* I ask myself by way of distraction. In the cold master bath I all but slap frigid water onto my face.

I'm not panicking. Not even when the recording reaches its most damning section. "You've done your homework, guys. Yes, I have extensively documented collaboration with Liltin Housing Now and the Nisqually," 2022 Quinn recites. "They have no current alternative to me on the council, they know it. Just as they know that no matter what they shout in public, your rehabilitation center—that's right, I did my homework too—is a matter of *when*, not *if*. Um, look, guys. I'm good at playing the begrudging fatalist. I really am. I imagine it's why you called me up here in the first place."

I'm so far from panicking that I opt to grab the bike from my three-car garage instead of the Volvo. I only have a couple weeks of ocular repair to go before I'm legally permitted to pilot a motorized vehicle. *But there's no hurry*, I self-soothe as I snatch my town hall keys. If Sarah is sharing this recording privately with me, it's yet unlikely she's taken it to publications. There is time to bargain. There is time to ask where she had gotten the recording in the first place.

"The hell? You're going in?"

Taylor pants in the garage's threshold, her glass of carrot water glistening like her forehead. I hadn't heard the stepmill pause.

"We're supposed to watch *Jurassic Park III*."

"I know, hon." I shake my head. No secrets. "There's something going on with Sarah."

My wife's panting subsides. "Your head of PA Sarah?" When I nod, she looks as if she's accessing some confidential document filed in a dark corner. Her gaze returns to me, reproachful now. "We vetted her."

"*You* vetted her."

Reproach becomes anger. "*We* vetted her."

"I—yes. I don't know why I," I trail off, not sure what to say. "So I shouldn't be long." I air up my bike's tires in silence and open one of the garage doors.

"I'm not answering any calls until you're back," Taylor says. "I love you."

"I love you."

Before the garage door closes completely I chance a backwards glance. She's still standing there.

Blurry, wooded suburbs steadily become blurry little offices. My bike shorts leave me chilly. I'm chewing through thick, but finite, grits of adrenaline, and a dull curiosity shades and shifts the corners of purely mechanical thoughts, *Tighten the helmet, turn right, downshift*, all leading through Capitol Campus to town hall for whichever equally blurry reality awaits me. My adoptive parents are no doubt proud of me from on high for my composure. No doubt, watching me right now.

I pedal past Capitol Apartments. As recently as last week I'd entertained the notion of leasing a loft there, once I won the September mayoral election. The first thrill of anxiety finds me like a needle to a cushion, and it pierces so deep that I actually gasp.

It lingers as a cramp in my side when I lock the bike beneath town hall's glass facade. Keying in the side entrance, I find my head turning to the left to view the distant old dome of the courthouse, an ugly beanie cemented like a still frame on dancing treetops.

Rows of empty desks before me, lenticular computer screens reflecting nothing. Sarah's office is adjacent to mine and, maddeningly, just as empty. I let myself in anyway. On her desk is a neat stack of paper.

My near sight has improved immensely since the Lasik. I peel away a Post-it with Sarah's unmistakable handwriting: *Live everywhere at 9 A.M.* Underneath, what appears to be an article.

*Toȷ Oïї Núẗ͡s ëť₄Rȁ̈ëȑ v̈v̈v̈ẁ͡s éd̈ú̈cëȑ h̤ëßi ȁ eȧȷhëŁ͡ȟȷ,aȷï h̤cȍ̈hȷhm̈ũ͡s aoȷ lös ȷ h̤ĩ͡s ȷ,ėßȍ̈dB ȷȍ̈ĩv̈ėßnȷ nᵗc̈ï ȷnȷcȷßȟȷ12.*

The author's name is censored. That's not what matters right now. Frantically, I flip through: Parts are highlighted in yellow.

*Councilmember Gershwin's office agreed to a figure roughly four times that of his rival, Mrs. Bonnie Cossio's. Accounting for 3%, the straw donations place Mr. Gershwin in the unlikely upper echelon of state individuals tied to the $2.5 mil total slush fund. Maintaining a rock-solid 8-pt edge among independents and voters over 35 in Thurston County since assuming office, he is clear proof that TLI acts quickly to poach stable and safe entities.*

I get a papercut.

"Sarah, where the fu—" I bite my tongue over my head of public affairs' cell phone voicemail; *conduct yourself as if everyone's listening, now.* "Where did all this come from? Did you *steal* this? Did a real person even write this? Sarah, come on, call me back."

I've barely disconnected when her text nudges the top of my screen.

### What's that in green highlighter? (48 mins left btw)

I start a reply, but shift back to the freshly printed article. Blood from my sliced index finger spots its corners. Green highlighter. Where. My viral speech lambasting TLI in 2023 for sending incarcerated firefighters to LA: highlighted yellow. The date of the recorded lunch on Pike Place Market: yellow. And . . . what? Placeholders in the article providing space for the accused—for *Quinn Gershwin*—to comment?

I couldn't give a shit about how much money my team allegedly accepted. No, I was told it was a high-five-figure sum of many individual PAC donations toward the impending election run. Wherever this article— or draft of a fucking article—has come from, it's less than half of the story. But the public won't care about that.

That Pike Place Market recording glaringly omits my insistence that TLI throw support for two more years of Thurston county's public lunch program, plus half a fleet of buses to reach less developed neighborhoods and reservation borders. Maybe that detail is negligible to whoever's writing this willfully blind hit piece, but to my constituents—

Finally. In a paragraph detailing the manageable pushback when I endorsed the new youth rehabilitation center, its address on the border of Nisqually tribal land: green highlighter.

"Sarah, help me understand," I type, and send.

A red exclamation appears immediately next to it. Her last message—*or the last message of whoever is spoofing her number,* I can't help but theorize with a horrid deflation—is the 48-minute countdown.

Still not panicking at all, I abandon town hall in a sprint. I punch in "TLI Black Hills" and estimate travel by bike: thirty-seven minutes. It's exactly 8:23.

3

# VADA IKEBE'S SELECTION

I haven't pulled an all-nighter since Amy's sleepover sophomore year—an accidental one at that, when fourteen inches of snow trapped her at my duplex.

Not quite *trapped* trapped: groggily I fall into the year-old memory of Amy dislodging the plastic lid to my dad's trash can, sledding it down the iced-over cul-de-sac. Streetlamps cast an amber glow on shoveled snow. My best friend's shivering laughter insulated the sleeping neighborhood.

So anyway, I'm pulling an all-nighter again.

All collision boxes in my devbuild's climactic mineshaft shootout demand 100% disentanglement. Grueling, tedious work for such an ambitious gauntlet. What else is new? Like, hello. Good morning. Ambition is the expectation. The foundation is all about execution. No excusing the technicalities when trying to draw attention—the higher the potential exposure, the higher the nitpicking.

Ambitious means no wonky physics before Sunday morning's demo, which is set to livestream for (by conservative estimates) thousands. *Definitely* no broken physics. With indie games first impressions reign supreme, and when the audience is the Internet, the window on that first impression is already closing the second you show up.

When I've finished, it's 3:30 A.M. Intelligent Vada Ikebe would now make the decision to lift her VR headset from her eye and knock out. But I still haven't rendered the individual texture-light mapping on the inspectable items. Could wait for the sun to rise but fuck it, I'm locked in.

Has to be done, and who else is gonna do it? Taek-su? Lead-developer Rundee? Kristen? Everybody clocked out hours ago—even Taek-su, sadly. When it comes to our indie FPS *Reify*, I am no procrastinator. Not like with my Honors Psych paper. My priorities are perfect.

An all-nighter before the big debut is my little secret, a surprising reconnection with the 8-year-old me whose anticipatory butterflies held sleep at bay on the eve of Potlatch (my mom's side) or Christmas (dad). Amidst a cavalcade of shit, a little private secret is what I need. It keeps my mind off Amy, off the ventilator that breathes for her, its plastic hiss barely registering in her frigid hospital corner.

6:46 A.M. I've deepened the textures in every inspectable item and rendered them out. *Reify* isn't my life's opus but that doesn't matter. All that matters is our team treats it as such, showcases our skills in front of some influential people—on Amy's behalf, and on the behalf of the futures we're trying to build for ourselves.

Need a quick decompression before I exit VR, some mental sugar, or I'll never fall asleep. I remove the thin glasses temporarily—the sky's all bright and painterly outside—and I squeeze a soothing drop of latanoprost onto my acrylic eyecap. I've had just the one intact eye since before I could remember; extended screentime really blooms the itch around my eyecap. But I've accepted the discomfort lately; it's crunch-time, baby, tech week. I'll have to refill my prescription hella early though. Dad will complain, but that won't be new.

Closing out of MarrowSDK devmode, I enter the YewVerse. This relic of 2022's metaverse bubble is so embarrassing that it's easy entertainment. It's packed with saturated, gyrating ads, devoid of users, and has pitiful draw distance. Username CYaVada, I float around an abhorrent ½-polygon rendering of the Mima Mounds, and behind the touchdown of a fake skybox, I once again find the avatars.

Legless, absolute budget builds the 6 of them, child-height with a low-res .jpeg smile plastered on each. The avatars are definitely real people in a real place—presumably somewhere in Washington.

They toil away, handing off assets invisible to my access, with clear practice to their movements. Doing . . . something? Something I've never been able to clue out all five times I've chanced upon them. I tried interacting with them early on but they were muted. Then, the skybox was erected. Easily bypassable for me.

One legless child notices me, then another. They wave with arms akin to 2x4s. I drift over; some of them float away from their stations and meet me halfway.

"Hoy," I try saying, but I don't think they're permitted to hear me. The ones not relegated to their mysterious dance are all crowded around, just looking at me.

No longer entertained, I cut the cord: *Disconnect from problem-solver mode, Vada.* I try not to focus on their pasted smiles as the last thing I see before I dock my VR.

In the shared bathroom down the hall opposite my bedroom I tap a lofi jazz mix (probably AI) and shower. Hair tied in two towels, I start a pre-bed skin routine with help from TikTok. Since Daniel "SalishUs" Deadwyler offered my friends and I a half-hour demo spot on his popular *SalishUs Sunday* stream, my impending camera appearance has forced an upgrade in my self-care routine. I'm even getting my nails done professionally tomorrow—first time ever. If only Mom were around to watch her little bisexual girl grow.

I take a break to tend to Chante while the bathroom airs. Chante's red-black scales glitter and refract depthless nebulae under the purple glow from his water tank's tight ceramic lid. At 7 A.M. he expectantly flits around his tank with all the agility of an old man pushing thirty inches. I love bonding with him at breakfast because I'm typically in extracurriculars through the night.

Home is where I sleep when all other options torpedo.

A burst of light from the sunken living room jolts me. I thought the TV was off. It illuminates my unconscious father, a formerly well-built white man. Home two hours early from the precinct for no other reason than lethargy, I'm guessing.

The sunshine, while cloying, torches the spotty sky, but you couldn't tell from Officer Pratt's couch. Pigs prefer shade.

I resume my facial cleanse with a heavy dollop of sugary snail slime for the fat that colonizes my weary-weakened under-eye tissue. My nightmare is to be middle-aged and passed out inches away from a screen like some exiled acolyte in a dark room, limbs atrophied, a brain of processed putties and cheeses. Dead or alive, an objective net negative to the human experiment. Retinol and dabs of cream lock in my bed face. I'm fading fast.

Ringtone explodes from my ceramic sink and ping-pongs off the tiles.

Breath caught, I hit *speaker*.

"Daniel? Hi?"

"Vada, girl!" SalishUs's Shaggy-like voice crackles. "So there's been a sorta gargantuan change of plan for this weekend, and before you flip, THE CHANGE IS GOOD."

—

His news wakes me so profoundly that I convene an emergency meeting with the team within an hour—held of course at our favorite café, Elonia, because caffeine must do its part.

The owners used to dawdle on opening but after our incessant bullying they now open on the dot, purely out of fear.

See, we're not *the good kids*. To our teachers, we're worse than bad kids—we're the ones they wish would like *them*, but don't. Smart means nerds, right? Maybe when you went to school. Do I need to dumb this down for you? Despite our grades, pretty much no one else likes us, and we'd have it no other way.

"Tonight? *Tonight?*" says Oh Taek-Su, rubbing his eyes, before slamming his chai.

"Tonight tonight," I say, channeling Mariah Carey behind my mug, scanning the in-house rentable TTRPGs and boardgames lining walls and bookshelves. Boba, coffees, teas, carrot water, they have it all, and we run them for it.

"He's really letting us do our campaign beforehand, while he does his streamin' thing?" Kristen (she/they), the sole senior among us juniors, swigs their why-bother like a soccer mom does wine, downplaying their excitement.

"Unrecorded, yeah. SalishUs has a community day or something to get through first." A play on the Salish Sea, the 28-year-old gamer personality and stepbrother to Amy exploded post-pandemic lockdown. His daily streams average over 5,000 viewers while bigger events/collabs sniff just shy of 20K.

"But changing days," Oh Taek-su jumping back in, "there's just something about it that seems *off*, isn't there?"

"What if I told you I'm ready for your social engineering?" I flick water from my still-damp hair at him. Oh Taek-su excels at leveraging perceived innocence to frame any and all dissensions as unreasonable, shocking even. Absolute tragedy that I have a crush on him.

He tries to appeal to Rundee now. "You know I'm happy they're platforming your game. Shit, happy don't begin to express it."

"*Reify*'s all of ours, but nice appeal to my ego," Rundee replies tersely. Then he looks down at his booth's cushion, distracted.

"But it's up in Tacoma, Rundee, it's a far drive," Taek-su says.

"I trust you behind the wheel." I bat my eyes. Taek-su's learner's permit is barely twenty hours old.

"Well you should, Vada. I'm literally gas. But in this case, we can just put off our tabletop campaign 'til tomorrow."

"No chance. Elonia closes early, I got kickboxing, Kristen babysits. Saturday's been our day."

"So you're ready to present, then."

Tomorrow would be most ideal. Launching the day after the celebration of summer equinox is the preferable option, from the standpoint of cozy spiritualism. And it'd be nice to attempt a final run through the demo as a player, not a dev.

But I know my blind spots. My all-nighter has proven prophetic. "Yes," I say, "it's ready."

"You sure about the collision boxes, Vay?" Rundee asks without skepticism or judgment. He's a good boss. He's fishing around the booth cushion for something.

"Whatever's left won't take more than an hour for us to iron out."

"Taek-su, you can't look at our campaign's cliffhanger last week and say, 'Oh, sure, let's put this off,'" Kristen muses in roundabout agreement. "I'd auto-deal you four damage just on principle but then your ass'd flatline and have to make a whole new character."

"I think he's just nervous," I smirk. "Not about driving us, but about meeting Daniel."

Taek-Su snorts. "SalishUs is a college dropout, motherfucker. I still see Daniel working at the theater. You think I'm jealous of the blood money he gets hawking PredictAct?"

"And look at him. Succeeding anyway." My edge softens. Taek-su isn't alone in envy. PredictAct is exactly how it sounds: a Seattle-based predictive market gathering enough legitimacy to run with Polymarket and Kalshi very soon. The influencer's pipe dream might tempt me if I didn't actually *want* to study biochem—or, well, analytical chem does pay significantly more so who knows—but the idea of getting paid by subscribers just for playing games and being funny? It's like cheating at the lottery and winning. The fantasy tugs at just about anyone.

"Anyway, while Vada's in her reverie," Kristen, as they do, takes point. "Vada says we can take Dan's kitchen. We won't be recorded or anything. It's gonna rock. Look, this group is a democracy."

"A social democracy," Oh Taek-su mumbles, defeated.

"And we have the numbers," I finish with a yawn. "Plus, I asked when we should head to their house, and Dan didn't seem to care. Y'all know him, he's scatter-brained."

"What about his girlfriend?" says Rundee, fishing around the booth's cushion now. "The Russian one."

"Ooo, she's hot." Taek-su coos.

"Shut up, Taek-su," I sigh. I look away. "She is hot," I admit.

Rundee pulls an ancient metal device from under his booth, turning it over in his fingers. It's a thumb drive.

"What's on that?" Kristen asks, trying to conceal their vape under their shirt, puffing out a cloud of strawberry flavored air as discreetly as possible.

Rundee sarcastically pretends to look inside the drive before shrugging and pocketing it.

—

The four of us part ways by the community center on State Ave. Oh Taek-Su does a double-take and stashes his own vape when he sees me following him, patting at my hair.

"Your mom okay with fitting me in a day early?" I ask, pointing in the direction of his umma's salon.

He collects himself, turns his face away from mine as we fall in step. Futile gesture: I catch the back of his neck flush red. "She does today."

Taek-Su's mother is one of my favorite people. She's frank and thoughtful and wields it all at once. Her beauty feels impossible given that she's forty. Her smiles are earned.

She lays an even seafoam base on my nails with barely a glance.

I summon every molecule of energy and muscle memory from the fifteen prior minutes of rehearsing. "Ta doe-wah-ju-shyuh-seoh kam-s-ahm-nida."

Taek-Su facepalms; his mother and her three employees (their tiny business survived the pandemic off sheer equity, north-of-livable wages, and ironclad word of mouth) all applaud.

"아까 말씀이 맞네 아들, 얘에 대한."

Oh Taek-su nods in response but his umma obviously needs more.

"여친인가?"

"그럴—놔둬 제발." Taek-su bounds away. His mother laughs herself into a coughing fit behind her mask. Just as quickly, she extracts the long two-toned translucent crumbles from the pod on her table and laser-focuses, placing them with just the right dimensionality and overlap of purple and red, the glass of her readers almost making contact. "So, apto . . . Aptomalia?"

"Anophthalmia, yes. My eye." I'm breathless at the sudden topic shift. This kinda shit is just funny, ill will nowhere to be found.

"아휴, etymology is hard." Taek-su's mother adjusts my right pinky as Taek-Su performs a thousand-yard stare. "This morning I learned a new word in my email. You wanna hear it?" She moves to the next hand.

"Naturally."

"*Sedulous*. Isn't that nice? Like, sounds nice."

"Huh. What's it mean?"

"I won't spoil, look it up! It's you."

The topcoat carries a subtly voluminous sheen. With a heavy discount I pay $65 for the shattered glass look. After my third goodbye I look up the word and gasp. It *is* me. I'm the one who blushes now, hot cheeks harboring a scare of tears behind real and prosthetic eye and sucking them in with a gooey sniff. A surface-level aspect I've picked up on and love from Korean language and culture is that if I called her *mom* no one would skip a beat.

"So, she said it was true, what I told her about you earlier." Taek-Su avoids my eye with a dumb smile.

"She's so good," I gush, revolving my nails in the sun. Maybe they'll draw Taek-su in for a closer inspection. "What'd you say?"

Instead, he backs up. "I said your Korean sounds like what reading romanization looks like."

"You fuckin' bitch," I say, but I quiet my cry far too late. We've barely left the building, wedged in the back alley.

He takes my hands now. Careful, soft, but moving my fingers individually.

"You sure you gonna be alright tonight?" He is hushed. I know what he's getting at. The Amy of it all.

"Y'know, I think I'll be alright tonight." As invisibly as I can I tug back on his fingers. "But I'll appreciate any support."

Our faces have only ever been closer by accident.

My rhythm suspends a moment as Taek-Su seems to lean in—and backs up again, walking up the tempered steps on the side of the salon to his home. "Heard."

I exhale.

"You should definitely nap before we go." From halfway up.

"You can tell I was tweaking the demo all night?"

"Nah, I just know *you*." The tip of his tongue between his teeth and he's gone. My man's getting bolder. Good news. I've been waiting.

I feel strong enough to visit Amy.

I'd been about 75% sure I'd visit before the demo. With the bump in the schedule it's only fitting; Amy's older stepbrother is the reason for tonight's opportunity after all. The other 25% is the usual hesitance of interfacing with a raw past that began in a warm 2020 summer and culminated in a cold 2025 ICU. I select a dandelion-heavy bouquet on the way to Providence Hospital.

—

I've visited enough over the past two weeks to be a familiar face. On the overcrowded second floor, I disturb the chained curtain to Amy's corner as little as possible, duck behind it, and immediately shudder. Another dark space, lit not by Amy's fleet of medical equipment but another near-soundless TV stapled to the wall and hardly facing her, as if that matters anyway. It's been proven that depending on the severity of the brain damage, the comatose can hear things from their peripherals. So I don't see how *that* translates to bombarding Amy's captive form with advertisements for Tide and shit—how could that lend any psychic motivation to Amy in the least? Hang in there for the Safeway discounts, girl!

I owe her many firsts. Two months after COVID took my mother I was dropped into a summer camp that was proud to flout emergency health regulations, to carry on like normal, put together by enthusiastic acquaintances of . . . who else? My dad. At 11 I'd tripped over plenty unsubtle hints, but summer 2020 was when it mentally cemented that Dad was simply not a good guy. The other seventeen children at camp were strung all along the phases of a similar recognition (including denial), or were just having fun splashing at murder hornets in the creek. Those of us who had lost someone were a bit closer to the sobering Awareness. For Amy it'd been her grandparents.

Summer camp inexplicably—certainly not miraculously—lasted two more summers before myriad safety violations shuttered it, garnering those in charge an incredibly pronounced, thorough slap on the wrist while some corporation snatched up the property. Amy and I formed a friendship outside. We went to different schools but slept over for days, even weeks at a time. After a high-adrenaline night of vandalizing our opps' houses with the whole gang, my first best friend became my first girlfriend. Fall of 2024 was us at our most inseparable. Amy's father and step-mother stole her from me to relocate all the way in Tacoma, a livelier town. Our brief romance may not have survived, but our friendship of course did. Tacoma was hard to get to, though. My vision disallows me from biking in low light.

Much as I love studying data, I sure hate its flattening implications. Teenage drug use has sharply declined relative to the generations before. But this data is macro. The boroughs under Puget Sound are stubbornly riding a line, no shift monumental enough either way, but there's another statistic. Teen drug *fatalities* have increased sharply due to the toxicity of drugs available and how often they're cut with the safer ones. Sometimes I wonder if Amy would have experimented if I were still able to visit as often. I know the answer is yes. Amy had found and developed the habit inside her step-mother's house.

The EKG beeps slow and steady. Amy Deadwyler, hypoxic since D-Day. That plasticky ventilator hiss. I shut off the TV and open the drawer under all the flowers next to Amy's bed. Amy's phone's fully charged. I key in the passcode (865137) and open her music player.

At that moment I feel reflexively the tiniest breath of pressure on one side of my face—like a floating foreign mote settling on my cheek hairs, tugging in a sourceless breeze. The familiar weight of what is unmistakably a stranger's gaze.

I turn to the curtain at my back. My stomach drops half an inch. The chains suspending it from the ceiling are swaying ever so slightly, soundlessly. The curtain seems to constrict, to close in. An entire wing of comatose patients, of long-term quiet sufferers, might have shuffled forward and gathered around, waiting for me to pull it open. Hospitals suck.

I imagine it's the mute child avatars from the town's YewVerse I saw last night, extracting themselves through some sleeping screen into meatspace to float, like ghosts, through town towards the only outsider who noticed them.

Impatience at myself surges with a fury. The phantasms in my mind might mellow if they listen to the playlist I'm about to put on, so I do it. Amy's custom ambient mix of Jeremy Soule.

"I'm gonna come back tomorrow and ask if I can cut your hair. I'll bring a replay of the stream, you can listen to me stutter through our demo. Your bro really carved out thirty minutes for me, can you believe how insane that is? Once the spot's done, it'll go up for sale right then." I'm willing a smile and stroking her hair. "And then we'll be able to get you whatever help you need."

Amy's parents aren't interested in saving her, just giving her up to a halfway house or something. No one is saving any of us. Raging in the face of all this manufactured doom is the point. I won't let the oldheads take more from my future, write my story for me. Even my anophthalmia, making me a likely statistic in development of early glaucoma, in total loss of vision, can fuck entirely off.

I'll mark this world before anyone or anything tells me otherwise, and *my* mark won't hurt those who come after.

"Love you, girly. See you tomorrow." I kiss Amy's forehead; my face rests there until I'm ready to leave. "You know, I don't know if I'll even be the same person. I'll tell you how it goes." I pull back the curtain. I've forgotten I was scared of it.

No one's there.

I thank the on-call nurse at the desk, who compliments my nails, and I head back into town. Liltin was supposed to be blanketed in rain by now, but it's as dry as my sleep-deprived eye.

I swear I'd have hung around if I'd known Amy's phone was about to be stolen.

# 4

# ALCOHOLIC GETS LO

Arturo isn't in the routine of showering before sleep, even when returning from a grotesquely elongated night of socializing, yet somehow he smells good. Well, no, definitely not good—*reassuring*, I decide with a groggy grin as I watch his chest rise and fall on the full-sized futon. I know for a fact I'd snored thunderously since knocking out at 2:00 A.M.; I'd woken myself up with a particularly violent one that left my throat crispy. Arturo hadn't stirred an inch. But I don't know if that's because he was sleeping or because he didn't want to talk to me.

Even though our relationship is far past fledgling, lately I can't help but mark the days since its start. My personal preamble to catastrophization. Slightly worrying, to understate.

Arturo hasn't revealed himself to be like other men. Since I touched down at SeaTac Airport less than twenty-four hours ago, however, I've clocked in him a . . . jumpier disposition. I insisted on taking driver's seat down to Liltin Yew—as a globe-trotting activist, this steep, wet, ancient wooded corridor of America is in my professional opinion among Earth's most magical—while Arturo spent the trip on a call to his parish, a call he seemed to be artificially inflating in his patented too-loud conversational tone. Wouldn't hold my gaze for over a second.

"What, Gets?"

I refocus my dull dawn psyche back to Arturo's trailer, to the imposter-bed, to see Arturo staring back, almost pleading. Instantly stressed.

Some find my figure, my frame, imposing. That isn't what stresses Arturo out; he actually quite likes that I dwarf him. Not many know I can be a big softie when I really try.

"Morning," I mumble with a half-apologetic head shake so quick my neck tweaks the wrong direction. Arturo rolls off his side and drops to the floor, crawls to his feet.

"You know an honest-to-God mattress is actually less expensive than years of back and neck problems."

Arturo doesn't respond.

He's a statue all of a sudden, bowed over with his phone only three inches from his face.

*Does he know I'm just joking?* "Arturo?"

"Yeah. I'm . . . sure. Need a drink." There is a flash of Instagram on his phone. He gets halfway to the kitchen before wheeling around to the bathroom to brush his teeth, moves his arms like he's swimming.

I sit up. The outlet on my side of the "bed" must not be live because *my* phone's battery hasn't budged. A silverfish skitters across the wall next to it. I cross the twenty feet to a trusty fake-wood-paneled fridge and forage through a couple hundred sauce bottles for the Brita gallon. Arturo doesn't believe in "fizzy water," which I've always tried not to judge him for.

There's no clean cup. I catch the water in my mouth.

I'm getting a markedly different version of my partner on this trip, one that has clearly never let anyone over, maybe ever. One who's trying to come across averse but seems to scrupulously evaluate himself every step.

Well, reticence was expected. It's about to be a big day for him: a high school reunion, an official tally on his "Queer Preacher" influencer persona. But I can now only guess into which territory that's spun Arturo's thoughts—he's not sharing them with me. Am I privileged for finally standing inside his home, or am I just a part of it now; part of the rest of what Arturo so often maligned as mediocre, as trash even; the futon, the stained and frayed rug, the stale air?

I have finally processed the vivid image of the six-pack of 9.2% ABV IPAs jammed into the front of Arturo's fridge.

Training's kicked in and I frame this surprise as the little victory it actually is: I'd seen the beer in there and glossed over it just like I did with the expired sriracha mayo to its immediate left. Good for me.

Then Arturo slumps in, a controlled beeline, opens the fridge, and grabs one.

"Swiped this from the party," he says as his fingertip touches the tab—but he stops, throws a cautionary glance at me, Gets Lo, Alcoholic, then lowers the beer and turns away. I give one of those polite smiles that mash chin to upper lip and auto-deduct a year off my lifespan.

Here's my training again: It's a sweet gesture from Arturo, actually. See, his agitation is clearly crescendoing—all the pressure he's put on himself for introducing me, his first "non-traditional" relationship since establishing his Queer Preacher brand a year ago, surely weighs heavy. Arturo finally told me he's secure enough to weather the initial dip in viewership which my announced existence will generate, and despite all that pressure, he even remembers to honor my alcohol sensitivity in the moment. Nice.

Or not. Arturo coughs to cover his cracking the beer open.

Fourteen months sober, a six-hour endurance test at a social gathering primarily of fundies the mere night before, what's another hour in front of my partner? I make for the sink and open the tap over the Brita jug, throw in some clean baby carrots, and breathe exclusively through my mouth to shut out the smell of hops.

That's not distraction enough. "I'm not tryna be that person, Arturo."

"You don't need to be."

My blood surges. "Is this how you're starting your big day?"

"It's not that deep," he says.

"You're streaming soon, down at Grace Cathedral. Then your reunion . . ."

"Not only the reunion—" Arturo upturns a finger, gulps half the can. "I'm sorry—Providence called." The hospital. "Last night."

"Your brother. Gabriel."

"They said Gabby's ready two days early. 'Ready.' You know what that means?"

"It means it's getting crowded in there, I'm gonna guess."

"Means they need a free spot, yeah. Same time as my stream they want me to pick 'im up." The first can already empty, he talks through gargling bubbles. "He's not ready, which I know for a fact. He's *not* ready."

"Whatchu want me to do?" I plop onto a squeaky barstool on the kitchen corner, chunks chewed out of its cushion. In my corner vision a pristine TV sagging off the living room wall chugs through *Trigun*. "It's your day."

Arturo exhales loudly and fishes another can out of his fridge.

"Well," he says, pretending to trail off in thought. "The reunion starts at 4:30 tonight." He's placing his fingers on his palms like working through an equation, but the gestures exaggerated, like an early 2000's CG character; like they're rehearsed. "6:00, really. But I'll be there at 4:30 at the door. My stream starts—well the service starts in like an hour . . ."

Is he about to ask me to pick up his brother?

*Craaaaack* goes his brand-new can.

I stare, dumbfounded, waiting for him to finish. Arturo's a different animal, alternately cool and cutting, so I don't understand how, after almost a year, he can believe I'm buying the pantomime. Which is so inelegant that it's immediately comical.

And I'm suddenly out of control, liable to be pulled along any which way by this stranger's next words. Some might characterize such a helpless panic as *adrift*, as *rudderless*, as *sinking* or some other seafaring term. To me, it is bespoke: It is careening in the backseat of a driverless car at night, a cliffside somewhere out there, somewhere close and closing in fast.

". . . I wanted you to come and watch. I know the Cathedral's not your vibe, but to watch me speak in person. I—I only have one car, though." And a pointed pause.

After all that song and dance, it is the most direct Arturo will get. I conceal a scoff. I too animate my motions, matching Arturo's performance, just to see if he'll notice. "So maybe halfway through, um, I just duck out. And . . . Providence Hospital, yeah? Just punch it in the ol' bleep bloop, probably a half hour there and back."

"Well the thing, about that," not at all noticing, "in Grace it gets kinda . . . Like leaving or coming in, in the middle of a service—"

"You don't want him there."

"Now it's not 'I don't want' him there. It'd be just, like, noticeable. Disruptive."

"Sure." My pointed judgment has broken the ignorant spell over him. I wasn't thinking. Or I was thinking too much. Past the point of walking back the bit, either way. "Arturo. Uh."

"Uh huh? Yeah, Gets?"

"Just stop for a sec and consider what you're asking me to do."

Arturo throws his hands up, Razzie-winning performance returned— the icicle of betrayal he's dropped onto the soft spot of my skull has long since thawed, however. We're both one mind now: *Let's just have it out.*

"You—Gets, you said what can you do to help."

"I said what do you want me to do."

"I—holy shit, Gets."

"You're not just asking me a favor!"

"It's the definition of a favor."

Heavyheaded, I stand. "How long've you known he was getting out today?"

"Are you kidding me, dude? Are you *this* paranoid about me?"

"It's no favor, it's family business. You're asking me to—you just said you know *for a fact* that your older brother, who has aggressive, drug-induced mania, who blew your family up—"

"*He* did *not*," Arturo positively spits. "Gabby did no such thing."

"Okay, so, well clearly you implied he's in distress," I'm gritting my teeth, giving just an inch, surprised at Arturo's authentic venom, digesting it unchewed for a future talk. "You'd rather a complete stranger, your secret little mangy enby crush, pick Gabriel up. And what, drop him back here? That right, dude?"

Arturo leans back on his palms, cracks his back, rolls his eyes under his eyelids. It's like I've forcibly astral-projected into a lower dimension, into the trailer park of another fucking hick masterminding some destined rise to the nourishing suns of a thousand influencers' eyes. "I just thought you said you were gonna help."

I laugh before I can stop myself. The rage intoxicates. "Well all of God's blessings to you, Arturo."

"Oh, so that makes you God's emissary right now, doesn't it Gets? Well—actually wait. Hold on . . . Oh, wow. Yeah, I feel Him in this very room." Arturo has never cynically wielded his preacher persona against me. This is very new. "He says He's proud of you, He says you're doing such good work. 'Keep it up, buddy!'"

He angles slightly into me so that I inhale his scent as he struts toward the narrow hall.

Arturo's a decent-looking guy. He's lean enough and average height. All he lets me know about his past is that he and his older brother at one point "disowned themselves" from their rich parents, who'd fucked off to their hometown of Trujillo Alto, and that his older brother Gabby had spiraled either during or shortly after. At one point Arturo had gotten them an okay apartment, but that changed after he quit his residency during Covid.

He's a cockroach. Started over and over and over and he's still kicking. Sometimes I'm convinced he'd never survive the life I've lived, sometimes I'm convinced vice versa.

I fight to stop myself from falling for him again. By the time he's naked in the shower, I realize I can't. Half a mind to overpower him in his own trailer, to cut the water and press his face against the bottom of his inlaid sink, to fuck him so hard he'll limp while emptying his reeling cock over the linoleum. Toe balancing on a knife's edge, I make peace with the cliffside approaching through the dark, but only because I've climbed behind the wheel, cackling as I slam the gas and send it over. I do it.

So Arturo is running slightly late after I let him shower, properly this time. With each article of clothing he affixes, he pulls away from me while dabbing his face on, steadying his hand, exhaling raggedly. "You're *not* my chauffeur. You're not my staff."

"Because that's not what I crossed coasts for, Arturo." Over a day in contentious layover waiting for the connecting flight's impromptu skeleton crew. Domestic airlines don't comp hotels anymore. "You know why I did?" With Arturo, I've learned to table my aftercare, stamped it down mostly to furtive smiles, but he's back to avoiding me like I've just arrived at SeaTac all over again. He peers blankly out his tiny window.

"So I'll just leave him. There's a lobby. Gabby can wait for me." He gives a cursory nod in my general direction. "It's a hospital. There're a lot of lobbies. He likes HGTV." Buttons his shirt.

He's moving too fast; I still haven't showered or changed. I telegraph a shift toward my open Kånken travel bag when . . . yep: "We'll just see you back here. You can meet him."

The miles flown and the extended gig in Europe I'd quietly rain checked for this promising weekend once again flit through my mind. Instead, here I am, bargaining. "Okay. I'll watch you on your TV." I'm not supposed to be getting this angry again so soon after what we just did. "It's a good TV."

Arturo grunts and gathers his gear: an APS-C camera and an affixed 70mm prime, a tripod, a Zoom H6, a bulky laptop bag, a cooling base extruding, and a mess of wires and plugs.

The low showerhead, calcification crusting its functional spouts, sputters to life as I strip the rest of my clothes.

I hear him open the front door to leave and I can't resist.

"You could've saved me a trip, man."

I feel the breeze across my face long enough to know that Arturo heard, Arturo considered, and Arturo didn't bother. A chilly *swoosh* and its accompanying *slam* usher me behind the curtain. The water pressure drills into me; I max out the temperature to match.

The second beer in the kitchen, full and open, waits just six paces away.

I've officially sent it over that cliff's edge, car wrecked and charring. The warpath has been outlined; stopping it now would render the whole day hollow, right? I am already at the bottom. The water's rushing in. Hey, a seafaring metaphor after all. Nothing left to prove. Come drown yourself, asshole. Shower beer! *You fucking bet.*

I catch myself, almost fall to my death in the tub. That IPA is no doubt gross, dubiously fermented, and all too "floral"—like bleu cheese shoved up the nose with half-chewed wheat paste funneled down the throat.

No way I break fourteen months with that.

I dress, slap the can into the sink with a heavy *clank*, unstick myself like a fly from a flytrap, and suddenly I'm racing across a gravel cul-de-sac. Hydrangeas glow in the blue hour. Black silhouettes of gulls skim across an eddy reflecting the thousands of shattered jewels of a blood-red sunrise. I wince as my retinas catch it directly. My feet rush me toward the cramped colony's outer edge. I think yesterday I saw a liquor store on the way in.

# 5

# INFLUENCER ARTURO VASQUEZ

I quit my residency in April of 2021 because I'd grown fond of watching people die. This wasn't gradual. It was an overnight thing, even though the quitting came months after. There was this pregnant woman who rushed in, ready to burst, and her husband wouldn't watch the delivery from a screen on the floor above. We all knew pandemic protocol; he very loudly insisted he was clean; we made the exception. He knew he had Covid; he exposed six newborns to the virus; one didn't make it.

Though hollowed by burnout, my sense of grief sharpened toward collateral. I wasn't me anymore—I was them. They reminded me of my brother Gabriel. And there was no escape. I slept on bags of mopheads in a maintenance closet instead of the on-call room. That way I couldn't hear them, or the phones, or my colleagues. The worst of the anti-vaxxers' whimpering deaths eventually lost their *schadenfreude* potency. I wanted to be the one to cause it, before they even landed in my hospital.

It wasn't like I was afraid to. But it would've left my big brother on his own. That'd just trade one injustice for another, one I'd fought against since the morning our parents decided to leave us on the mainland. So I never found out what I would've done.

I often wonder about that.

"To imagine hell is a privilege." The congregants don't catch my reference. "This past week, what was trending? Some of you help me out. 'Hell on Earth.' Alright—what's this 'Hell on Earth' in response to, hmm? The nuclear warhead that Iran is about to fire, any minute now? The socialists' destruction of the Atlantic Current, maybe? Of course not, it's about identity politics! A-gain."

I split commanding glances between Grace Cathedral's packed pews. The monitor hooked up to my camera distantly reflects me. "*Mi familia*, imagine for a second, wanting to co-opt the very idea of hell. Trying to overwrite our own learned knowledge of Revealed Truth." My audience groans to one another. "Because we know what it is. We've been *told*, by God, that's the whole point."

Scattered affirmation echoes across the magnified acoustics. "From the Bible of old the Hebrew word Sheol, 'the grave pit.'" I hope Gets is watching that part; Hakitía precursor, they'd taught me the word. "Death. Without everlasting life. Not a fiery pit but a hopelessness, a *despair*, a permanent state of being without the Holy Father's love." I begin to pace but I'm reminded of how little lube was left in my bathroom for Gets to use an hour ago; walking makes me wince. "2 Peter 2:19-22." I channel the pain, savor it. "Y'all might know this one. Hell is drawn from those 'who knew the way of righteousness, and turned away.' What was written next?"

Some in my crowd answer me, louder than before.

"Better they had never known the way."

"Yes. Let me ask you, do these so-called progressives with their trends, do they seem alone? Do they seem unloved? Eh, not really, you'd think. They clearly have numbers, oppressed as they want to make you believe. They have their online bubbles, their echo-chambers, don't they?" My audience shift in their seats. I hear the word "perverts". I have them.

"Now, I am not a straight man. I'm not ashamed of how my Lord made me and I stand before you knowing I am loved in *this* community, as Jesus loves me."

The lapse—the congregation's patience for my qualifier and anticipation of the *but*—I know by now to press through. For a moment I hear Gets in the shower again. *You could have saved me the trip, man.*

"I . . . would not think for a second to believe *this* house of love and acceptance was anything close to a hell, let alone to *use* that as a springboard. A springboard to call for the deaths of elected officials. And for free speech streamers like myself! For what? Because they uphold this nation's respect for religious autonomy? For liberty? Charlie Kirk's doing an excellent podcast about this, by the way." They're back. Nodding enthusiastically, *holy shit even he gets it,* nudging their restless kids to pay attention. I look back at the monitor. Its light remains a solid blue.

"*Mi familia*, they may look like they're united, but they're just alone on the Internet. Have these folks ever even known the way?" I pause for effect. "Is an innate love of the Father truly a guarantee anymore? You see how we're dwindling."

Standing in my trailer's doorway, I had responded to Gets. Said I was sorry. Had they heard me? Had I said it loud enough?

"They have been waylaid by decades of belief in a hateful agenda. So maybe, in that way, they *are* in hell. More than they know. With true, real, divine love unnurtured. No love for the Son, no love for the Spirit. Is that *not* already living in hell on earth?"

Grunts of solemn assertion ricochet into the walls, floors, vaulted ceiling. From the pulpit I see Father Malcolm nodding deeply. Everybody's eyes on Arturo Vasquez.

Suddenly it's difficult to look anywhere else but down the hall, at the monitor, at that faraway reflection. This happens sometimes, the dissonance getting in the way of my dissociation. It won't last long.

"For without the belief in an eternal, unconditional love by our own Creator, without the promise of returning to Him in the dawn of our next life, what is to stop them?" I'm shouting. "What is stopping *a single one of us* from reaching across our dinner table and murdering our family; from grooming and molesting our children; from torturing and laying waste to His Creation? This is the endgame of *el Diablo!*"

They're shouting too, almost wailing, to the point where I figure I don't even have to say the bit about Thanos in the critically acclaimed *Avengers: Endgame.* My ears ring.

"So maybe it *is* already happening. Maybe we *should* already be fighting. Should we wait for them to manifest this despair further? Where's that gotten us? What else is the Mission of God, but to repel the invasion of hell?"

I have to wait for half a minute. When the commotion recedes to a dull roar, fully possessed, some congregants still saying, "wow," I hold out my arms. Stupidly my mind flits to my brother's first arrest for possession, the quivering arms he held up at the traffic stop, blinded by the cop's floodlight. "*Gracias mi familia* for welcoming me into your house of worship. *Todos gracias.* All of God's blessings to you on this day of days."

I bite my tongue and resume my seat in the very front pew. "Thank you, Arturo Vasquez," Father Malcolm is saying breathlessly into the mic, "This is your house, too."

Cutting the broadcast, I see 782 viewers. The sub goal's been exceeded by 4. I breathe in deep through my nose, out long through my mouth. I flex my jaw and finally feel it pop.

Hands to shake, people to embrace, earnest sound bites to exchange. With genuine gratitude I indulge the dispersing crowd on the front veranda. I may hate them, but I'd hate them either way. At least they're paying me while I make them dumber. I peep my watch involuntarily; if I were actually going to pick up Gabriel, I'd be an hour late.

"There he is! *Mi familia,* hilarious. Good touch." A radiantly tanned woman around my age is charging me, pulling me into a bear-hug. "Arturo Vasquez, my guy. Class of 2010's gonna be thrilled tonight. Your *energy,* man."

"Wait, Anne?" I can barely process. "Anne Oxendine? What're you doing here?"

"Seeing the prophet work his magic in person!" Her voice muffles against my shoulder. Pure disbelief, I return the hug as if testing that she's solid.

Anne Oxendine is a controversial legend among 2010's alumni; personally, I adore her. Yuppie extraordinaire, she began working at her mother's company right out of high school and colonized every self-starting self-help business imaginable: yoga, free therapy, CBD oils, the works. She had the money and clout to rise above MLM reproach. Over the past decade her Miami lavishness has never strayed far from any screen I've used.

This is the first time we've ever purposely interacted, and it can only mean one thing: she's been watching me.

"How you likin' it back up here? The good old PNW." I glance down real quick and yep: my feet still touch the ground.

"Oh, I'll tell ya. It feels like I never left." She laughs as if we're sharing an inside joke. It's the kind of performance that's for everyone around, not us.

"Hah, sure, sure, I bet." I want to say something else, but I don't even know what. I want to say, *We're peers now?* But in the commotion, Father Malcolm noticed me from the vestibule and he's started to hobble over with a predatory smile.

"Oh, uh-oh. The clergy." Anne must have somehow read the darkness on my face. "You don't want to talk about virtual bingo and TL Osborn. Come on, I'll show you something instead." She takes my hand, leads me away.

There's a sizable Sitka spruce grazing the bell tower at Grace Cathedral's edge. With each step our shoes sink slightly into the mossy grass.

In person, Anne is bewildering. She's taller than I remember. Her tan is so deep it's practically body paint. The BBL and buccal fat removal are subtle but noticeable, her natural brunette obliterated by the color of bleach. She's wearing sweats. "You're into birds, right, Arturo?"

"Uh. Yeah, back in high school I . . . was into 'em, yeah." Young Arturo was actually interested in pursuing ornithology. Covertly I applied to Cornell for wildlife biology and was actually accepted, but my parents (who definitely could afford it) laughed in my face. They told me such a major was too competitive, idealistic, and wouldn't really be helping anybody but me at the end of the day. "You?"

"Of course. And I know something you don't. There. That near corner on the bell tower's base."

I look. There's a mess of twigs jammed into a crack between stone blocks. Anne holds up her fingers. "Three . . . two . . ." And she snaps: A blue-striped feathery face with a long bill pokes out, below its chin a bright sunfire that winds to its belly.

"Red-breasted nuthatch," we both say, and then Anne gives me a nudge. "Don't see *that* anywhere near your fancy-ass birdfeeders."

"No, I do not." She knows about my custom birdfeeders?

"I actually applied to Cornell University," Anne whispers, "for wildlife bio. And was accepted! But my parents (who *definitely* could afford it) laughed in my face. Told me it was too competitive, idealistic, and at the end of the day who'd I really be helping?"

The smile tugs uncomfortably at my face. "Who are you, Anne?"

"Well, I'm not a stalker. I'd have to start *pretty early* to know that in 10th grade you and Jose Castaño were the ones to climb up this bell tower and spray-paint it. I hadn't even transferred to Liltin High by then, remember? I got here in the spring of '09."

She's closed the short distance between us.

"Of course, that isn't all you two did up there, is it?" She passes and disappears around the bell tower.

I shake dust and grime off old memories. Jose and I hadn't told anyone. My legs are heavy. There's a light *squawk* from above and I twitch; the brilliant nuthatch spreads its wings and glides over to the Sitka spruce.

"*. . . Squawk,*" I repeat, a futile effort to decode the world around me. My ankles are suddenly cold and wet. I've sunk too far.

I bound back to the Cathedral's face. The Miami yuppie leans on the veranda's wrought-iron banister. Taps away on an oddly cheap phone. "Can I kidnap you now? Or would you like to see something else first?"

I'm just watching her. Dramatically, as if I'm a child, she waves me over.

Yeah, I was coming anyway.

"You were. Sh." With a tip of her head she bids me to peer through the church's open doors. "It's not just you."

Father Malcolm is visible gathering leftover materials from the tabernacle. Altar boy position long vacant, he's alone in there.

"He starts with the left collection plate then stacks it on the right. It makes a louder sound than he expected. He thinks he folds the linen cloth tight, but it comes loose in the back and his heel catches it on the way down the altar."

I watch Father Malcolm. Left, then right. Clang. The long cloth unfurls and for a moment the priest has a linen tail. He's descending the shallow steps, an old man; a fall from ground height could kill him—

"He catches himself. He's fine."

The cloth pulls tight and Father Malcolm stumbles, barely makes the last step.

"But he stubs his toe on the first pew and says, 'Oh mercy me,' it's pretty cute."

She's interrupted by him doing the exact same thing. It is kind of cute. Blithering, the priest catches me standing in the doorway.

"Er—*Hasta luego padre,*" I hoarsely call with my right hand awkwardly extended. Anne is mimicking me.

I like to imagine I have a good poker face. After all, I'm a streamer. But when she asks, "Now you wanna take a ride with me, don't ya?", she's already flashed her too-white smile and turned heel by the time I sputter, "How'd you know?"

# 6

# COUNCILMEMBER QUINN GERSHWIN

A fake house hugs county limits.

One of a handful of fake houses across town slapped together in the spring of 2024, it is a rush job. I co-signed its existence. Liltin Yew at the time underwent a rash of petty infrastructure attacks. Power grid sabotage of the drive-by shooting variety. We joked about how the bullets were home-grown; the reality is that no one's ever been caught.

Public works got creative with the budget surplus to devise protection for substations that the county deemed critical. The costliest part was hiring outside contractors since we couldn't officially trust our own. The overwhelming majority of contractors around here are veterans, which is entertaining when you observe how they price-gouge the fine folks at Joint Base Wilkes-Booth. No one tells you the robbers of the Department of War are so often its own offspring. Or no one used to.

My muscles scream and tear atop this bike. Morning chill flays my lungs. Luckily my phone's Map rewards my efforts with a fifteen-minute cut to my ETA. I know shortcuts. I guess I've trained for this.

The bay's fog burns away, dissipates. I can see the Duwamish River to my right now. It smells awful. The green-highlighted Twice Loved Institute's new youth rehabilitation center draws frighteningly nearer.

So does a jogger with a reflective belt, who is descending the steady grade as I ascend, and his eyes lock onto me.

"Hello!"

*Fuck him.* I play deaf, make the whirring of my bike go harder, my breath louder.

"Hey, Mister Gershwin!" he says with an animated wave.

*Fuck you.* I grunt an approximation of a chuckle and grit my teeth as I pedal past.

So that's why the fake house is on my mind: Each second out here exposes me further as I play right into my blackmailer's hands by racing to this very damning address. No wonder the author of my incendiary hit-piece was blacked out. They're probably waiting in TLI's vestibule with a shotgun mic and a rolling camera.

It unfurls around a curve of evergreens. A mile upriver, a silhouette in the glowing mist. Will Sarah be with them? It was her handwriting next to the article. Handwriting can be forged. I don't know why, though. I just don't want to believe it's her. We vetted her. *We.* Us.

At any rate, I won't simply waltz into the end of my career.

I wait for a garbage truck to pass and then I zip across the road to the wooded side. An overgrown gate is barely fifty meters down a dirt turnoff to the left. I'm off my bike, its back wheel still spinning as I hop the fence.

The fake house is long with a flat front of tan bricks, two stories tall, and black plywood behind every window. One of the blackboards has a pot of flowers and desk drawn on it. No doubt a convincing facade from the other side of that gate. Public works doesn't get paid nearly enough.

It's a water treatment satellite retrofitted to manage most of TLI. Not only will I get a clearer view of the rehabilitation center, but I'm also betting that there'll be some live information to access in there. I know for a fact it's fully autonomous on weekends.

I circle the well-cut lawn to a driveway. The back-left of the house has large, caged openings on the upper walls beneath its roof, and weather-worn metal mesh doors at its base that are chained, but I push one, pull the other, and squeeze right on through. 1311 disables security systems for basically every municipal utility station.

8:47 A.M.

A back door into TLI, a shutdown valve, a visitor schedule . . . I'm not certain what I'll find, but I have just enough time to look. Another reason I doubt Sarah is the mastermind: She knows me, knows I'm never caught with my pants down. I grew up in foster care then spent my entire young adult life in Thurston County, among people who'd try all sorts of things on account of my skin being just a few shades darker than theirs, or in some cases, not dark enough. I didn't just luck into where I am without knowing how to push back in a pinch.

A tinny hum undergirds the swirling and slushing of a dozen little waterfalls above me. They hide behind huge, cement-encased tanks which burrow deep into the gravel ground. The power switches hide as well, faraway details unreadable to my post-Lasik vision. Enough light comes in from the gaps below the roofing to render the noisy cavern dim but navigable.

I try calling the reclusive CFO whisperer to TLI with my phone while also using it as a flashlight, making my progression stumbly and awkward.

"Gerry Mercer's office," says a chatbot. "How may I help you?"

"Hey—this is Quinn Gershwin." My exhalation pushes against clamped teeth. I think I see a hollowed cone hanging down from a tank's corner. "Mayoral frontrunner for Liltin Yew. I'll need to speak to Gerry directly, urgently."

"Thank you, Mr. Gershwin. She is on another call at the moment." The voice is metallic, like a dozen people and no one at all speaking at the same time.

"It's more urgent than the call she's on."

It's 8:50 now.

"I cannot override Mrs. Mercer's current call, sir."

"Flash an alert or something." I am pleading with a goddamned robot. "This is highly relevant to TLI and, by extension, Gerry."

I reach the corner next to a trilling sediment monitor and I grasp a mounted plastic casing and unlatch it, then flip the switch inside. The click of the overhead light is louder than I expected.

"We are aware of the developing story questioning partial origin of your campaign funds, Mr. Gershwin, and will make a statement at the beginning of the business week."

A scraping of metal against gravel reverberates from the entrance I'd snuck in. Someone's here.

Very slowly, I take a step backwards and then another, out from under the light. The call is dead silent on the chatbot's side.

8:51.

"Are you . . . *Who* am I speaking with?"

For a second there's nothing, save for distant footsteps within the facility retracing my own. Then there's a chuckle in my ear. I swear I hear a chuckle. I hang up.

Whoever is in here with me is not being quiet. Although it can technically be anyone on account of my disabling the alarm, logically it must be a sanitation worker. The presence of anybody malicious or not is very bad news—I have yet to even find anything in here.

So I crouch into a nest of oversized piping. Rivets as big as my hands. 8:53. I see white-yellow running shoes first, then the whole person. It's not a sanitation worker.

Bonnie Cossio is the Republican favorite and my projected opposition; her primary is in two Tuesdays. Some months ago she "made a joke" which my legal team interpreted as credible incitement to violence against me. Lo and behold, just a week later, neighboring Olympia PD found an out-of-state fentanyl addict in a stolen car with a rifle and a Quinn-Gershwin-centric manifesto. That's not why Bonnie is the favorite, though. After labeling the suspect a Jewish psy-op, she had another joke for me: "Maybe our future Mayor could try *not* being antifa?"

She's half my age, and she looks like Jim Henson made her. Crossfit ugly with black and bright-red joggers two sizes too small—just like Laura Loomer, crafted in the Grinch's image. She'd look natural riding a little tricycle in *Saw.* But her joggers aren't the only reason I'm suddenly seeing red.

8:54.

"Quinn, I already know you're here." Her voice is a nail to my skull. I'm staring straight at her as I duck under a pipe, then step over another. I'm aware how aggressive it looks. But my pulse is pounding. Of course it's her. Of course it's Bonnie.

"Why are you doing this?" It's her asking, not me.

I straighten my posture and feel my brow slacken. "Doing what?" I ask.

"Don't you dare bullshit me."

"Explain yourself, Bonnie."

Disbelief colors Bonnie's sigh. She clutches something in her right hand. I see her fingers tighten around it. "You're clearly not my husband, which I've gotta say doesn't shock me. Look, I got here nice and early. So now *I'm* giving *you* five minutes."

8:56. A chill shoots through me. I'm equally flustered and—I'll admit it now—panicked. "No. No, I've got five minutes to . . ." TLI. The youth rehabilitation center, up the road . . . "You got a message from your husband's phone?"

With an imperceptible windup she lets loose what she clutched: gravel. Far too late I wince but she's thrown them wide on purpose. They clatter against the water tank.

"Now I can hit you with something a lot smaller and a lot more dangerous. Wanna see?" She's reaching in her bag.

"Goddammit. Don't shoot me. Take a breath."

She trembles with adrenaline. "You're at five seconds now, Quinn, not minutes."

"I received messages too." I can close the distance between us and rip her arm away from that bag, but she is strong. It could get real bad real quick. "I'm supposed to be somewhere by 9 too, and it's not even here."

Apart from her snarl, her expression goes inscrutable. She stops reaching for what I can only assume is a handgun. 8:57.

"Who messaged you?" she asks.

I shake my head. "No clue, same as you. But they pretended to be one of my team." Is the speed of the sloshing water above us increasing? And where did that tinny hum go?

"What did they tell you to . . ." And then she clearly figures something out. "Where were you told to go?"

"Um."

"Twice Loved Institute." She nods for me. An eyebrow raises. I didn't know her face had that much articulation after all the Botox. "How much?"

*Right,* I think. *She took money for herself.* "I'm not sure I follow."

Bonnie actually laughs. She revolves on the spot, digging into her own hips. "Get sure." She stops, freezes, faces down the facility toward our entry. The metal mesh doors are jiggling and there's a human silhouette.

We move as one toward it. Bonnie's hand is back in her bag. I bring up the rear. The water tank nearest me emits a low buzzing.

"Sir? Sir!"

Refocusing on the metal mesh doors, I look over Bonnie's head and a trapdoor may as well have opened and shit me to hell: a cop. Skin-tight Oakleys hide his eyes, and a coyote brown cloth conceals the rest of his face. He's undone the padlock on the chains but only to pull them tighter.

"Officer, I'm asking you to tell us what's going on." Bonnie's voice goes up an octave.

"Sir," I say calmly, neutrally, "what's your name? I don't see your badge."

He clicks the lock shut before Bonnie can reach it. No give on the chains.

"Maybe your Captain will tell us?" She is outraged.

The cop cocks his head at her bag, back up to her, and then he walks down the driveway. "G'luck with that," he says. He's laughing.

A klaxon blares. The surging of water stops. I brace for a flood. I try and fail to make sense of my surroundings, of my situation. I've forgotten how to think.

Bonnie turns slowly towards me like an over-tightened screw. "Call LYPD. I hate to say it but it'll mean more if it's coming from you."

My work phone's on red. It's a Saturday, I wasn't supposed to be leaning on it. The flashlight's still on and shining through my shorts. Bringing forth the lock screen, I blink.

9:01.

Notifications stack with the torrential speed of a slot machine. Bonnie's is practically strobing. Our eyes bounce off one another and I register her confusion, terror. She probably sees the same on me.

"I . . . I mean, I shared my location," she manages.

We really are business partners now.

<h1 style="text-align:center">7</h1>

# VADA IKEBE'S SOLIPSISM

Two people at least twice my age overpower the windowless beige hall to the hospital elevator. One of them is very clearly drunk and trying to convince the nurses that they're a family friend of the other, a rail-thin man with a purple DNR wristband stretched thin and loose from liberation attempts.

Shoving past the drawling enby, all salmon and beige techwear, demands suppression of my gag reflex. They're clearly drunk. They stink like my dad.

"Mr. Vasquez." The nurses can't conceal palpable alarm. "You know we won't just hand you out to a stranger."

The wristbanded man's wide eyes bely a frozen posture. "Oh boy," he says to himself.

Yeah, I take the stairs.

Onto both organic and acrylic I blink in my respective eyedrops; an artificial tear is snatched by the bay wind. All this walking around town bright and early, my hair's finally dry. Stashing the vials in my purse I catch a notification hitting my phone.

Fumbling it free with my new nails, briefly dropping it onto the bricks that peek beneath cracked asphalt, I swipe it open.

Daniel "SalishUs" Deadwyler seems to be having as eventful of a morning as I am. He'll be out of his apartment until an hour or two before stream, but he assures me his girlfriend, Katyusha (or OMGrozny, as she's known online), will let us in early. She's really hot. I think that came up earlier.

"u sure u want us presenting tn n not tmrw?" I offer one last time. "just seems like a stacked day for u already."

**Vay YES it literally needs to be today. Wish it didn't take us waiting outside her ER to hear about u and Amy's game but i'm glad i did. It sounds insane. We sell it tonight, it'll do numbers, it'll help her & all of us out. Abt to have maybe my best view count ever so the iron gonna be hot**

Puzzled, I ask him why.

**ye shall seeee :D**

I send him some emojis I know his late-twenties ass won't understand and then make for Kristen's mom's house. Rundee just posted a Snap working on *Reify* in the unfinished basement, along with a Snap of the grey USB he'd found in Elonia with the caption "#foundmedia." Once I'm there I can catch a nap and get grinding.

There's ageless charm in this mini city flanked by nature's near-vertical, green-black walls. Storefronts emblazoned with the owners' names; historic stone facades paired with stubborn vinyl single-family units; hardly a parking lot covered or otherwise. I pass a VCR repair shop for fuck's sake. Although I'm not trying to stay in Liltin Yew, I can't imagine I'll go far— geographically, that is. Seattle would be good if it's not underwater in 10 years.

Kristen opens their broken basement screen door for me. Rundee jostles back and forth in the obnoxious, RGB-lit gaming chair banging out some finance homework; Kristen's gargantuan, L-shaped PC build displays our game's menu screen with blistering fidelity.

Me, I'm entering rest mode. No need to ditch my shoes on the dirty cement floor, I unfurl over the slipcover couch.

"It's a PowerPoint slideshow." Kristen points at the furthest of their three lenticular monitors. "For our school's Class of 2010 reunion tonight."

"The flash drive you found?" When they nod I *mmmmm,* in what I hope is a very, "cool, now leave me alone" kind of way.

"Kristen tried to plug it right into their computer without testing," Rundee smirks.

"Bitch it wasn't like that."

They click the space bar and I watch a WordArt star-wipe over an expanding image of Liltin High circa 2010. Ooo, it still had the old gym back then.

"Hope whoever lost this had backups," I grunt. My phone's dying.

"It's actually pretty impressive for PowerPoint." It's cycling through graduates: a still from their senior year, then a picture purportedly from the present, with brief screeds personal enough to defy decoding. Must be inside jokes.

Kristen's kitty Jinx jumps and plants right on my solar plexus and just like that, my fate's decided. I extend my phone to the gang. "Charge this." The exposed low ceiling seems to yawn and wrap itself around me like putty. I'm cool from tips to core, then I'm nothing.

Spirited discussion by the computer wakes me up. I'm rested but I won't lie, I feel icky: A specific moment floated to my forethought while my brain cooled down. "We sell it tonight, it'll do numbers, it'll help her & all of us out," SalishUs said to me almost two hours ago—I confirm 9:47 on my blessedly charged phone—and it just sits funny. Like, exploitative.

They're all talking some fresh scandal; I hear the letters "TLI" repeatedly while I stretch; it's not just Rundee and Kristen anymore, it's Oh Taek-su! Oversized shirt, gentle eyes, the works. I inhale so sharp it pricks my heart. When'd he get here? He saw me sleeping. People fart in their sleep, Jesus fucking Christ.

In spite of myself, I curse in Lushootseed. Taek-su perks his head up, beams and waves. I groan.

"*Reify*'s all ready to go, Vay," says Rundee, holding two thumbs up. "Thank you for your service."

I mirror half his gesture but with my other thumb rubbing my eye.

"So it's a TLI slush fund of just five accounts that made up *all* the 'small donations,' and don't even get me started on TLI's founder." Taek-su is wilding. He's very passionate. "We're talking GEO ties, Nestlé ties . . ."

"Any of the funds from a-a 503(c)?"

"Rundee, just because your AP Econ teacher actually likes you..." Kristen, wearing Jinx like a scarf, turns to me. "Some exposé got leaked. Our Democratic and Republican hopefuls for Mayor apparently take bribes from the same shady-ass company."

"*Severely* shocking shit." I roll my eyes. "I don't think my headset dock's plugged in, I should get going."

"This breaking news is above you, Vada?" Taek-su's teasing, but I detect a trace of exasperation in his voice. Embarrassment stings my face as I imagine points subtracted from my respectability but also, yeah, guy. Back off. "I don't follow politics like that."

"And you've never told us why."

"*This* is why. How much surprise that everyone sucks do ya think I have in me?"

Rundee nods in the hazy corner. They all know my lore—the Covid camp and Dad and my mom dying. Taek-su clamps his jaw.

"Want a ride back?" he says finally.

I can't agree quickly enough.

—

He steers his hand-me-down hatchback slowly, fearfully, adorably.

"Y'know, I'm second gen," Taek-su tries. "My parents emigrated in '04."

"And I'm native. We about to square up?"

"Dumbass. Where they're from, politics are crazy hostile." He flicks a hastily 3D-printed *K-Pop Demon Hunters* charm on his rearview. "Like don't talk to my mom on May 18th."

"Mhm."

"Just saying, there's reason to—"

"Pay attention, yeah. I hear ya, junior. How about tomorrow I'll start."

"After SalishUs makes us rich and famous."

I shift in the passenger seat. "Don't even." Maybe it's because I'm finally awake enough, but the nerves set in for the first time. The effort. The thousands watching: Maybe one of them a well-connected game dev themself. The stakes. Amy's hospital bills. The care we could get her if—*when*—she wakes up.

An old red Raider with a soft-top fishtails past us; we almost hit a light pole.

"젠 장—"

I grip my knees hard. The SUV's whooping bleach-blonde driver stabs a thumb out her window and rockets past.

"Taek-su."

"That wasn't my fault!"

"I know," I breathe unsteadily, and then give a little, "*oh,*" as I notice my hand's landed on his arm.

He's staring straight ahead like a good driver, not daring to comment. I lift my hand. That was way too awkward. I, uh, give his shoulder two pats and nod. There. Fixed.

He clears his throat. "That was somethin'."

"What?"

"The . . ."

"Car. Yeah." The outside of my window is suddenly super interesting. A bird could fly into my frozen mouth right now.

"So I'll pick you up later," he says at the tip of my cul-de-sac. I walk halfway up the steep steps to my duplex before he barely audibly adds, "I mean I'm picking all of you up, later, um." and drives off, considerably faster than usual.

My heart's pounding so hard that I feel it beating in my smile. I struggle with my house keys, I struggle accepting that this is real life, and the incoming two-pulse notification from my phone doesn't anchor my swimming head.

Those two pulses are a custom notification tied to only one of my Contacts.

I freeze at my front door.

**u r still dreaming, girly.**

It's from Amy.

8

# TOO ALCOHOLIC GETS TOO LO

Feels good to walk with purpose.

There are those who pretend their real lives freeze when they travel. Think they can set it all aside to soak in the sights and experiences. Hit pause.

I think the truest potential for change occurs when we're somewhere new, foreign, uncomfortable. With my floor management gig in my hometown's warehouse screeching to an end devastating enough to banish it from my mind, I've been transient since the 2012 encampment at Zuccotti Park. Moving with the seasons from city to city, showering in whichever gym I could, I tended bars and exorcised my helplessness on the chanting streets. 2016 I was bankrolled by Crowds On Demand for the Wetlands Coalition and American Environmental Foundation, and by 2018 I was getting pepper-sprayed in France during *ethical pipelines* demos for EIKE, planting trees on behalf of VW in Stockholm to pull press from their emissions scandal, chaining myself to trust fund kiddos' brownstones and cashing subsequent checks from their fathers.

I can duck plainclothes police and tweakers—can group shots in center mass if I need to. I can get over a guilt-obsessed partner who lies about his strength, who in crunch-time withdraws all promised commitment at the nadir of my personal and professional lives.

It's no liquor store guarding the trailer park but a gas station. It'll do. Browsing the back aisle of the tungsten-orange convenience store is harmless; state law locks all alcohol shelving. Just looking, that's all I'm doing. Just thinking.

I am rushing to Acceptance, I know it. Anger's all I truly feel.

"That's my favorite," says a gruff voice that's incredibly close to me.

Snapping to the present, I step wide of an abrasive man wearing the gas station's uniform sans nametag. One hand on hip, the other running through stylishly clipped brown curls. Freshly bruised cuts on two of his knuckles, like he punched through a wall.

"The powder blue gin," he continues, and points. I know the one. There's a white-outlined topless mermaid on the blue gin bottle, reaching out as if from a better place. That better place being Big Sur, where it's imported.

"Mine too," I mutter.

The clerk brandishes some keys. "Kismet. Want me to get it for you . . . sir . . . ?"

I watch the guy's expression change as he fully takes in my appearance. But rather than a momentary flit, the expression settles there and sours. His nose is upturned, clearly affronted that he has to humor what is *obviously* some attention-seeking joke. Imagine: He's the one offended.

"Uhh, no, sir, I'll be fine." I cringe and turn heel. This day just keeps getting better.

"Sorry, partner. It's—just, shit. At first you look like, but then you sound—"

"You sound like you're from Ohio, and 78," I call on my way out the chiming door.

I flex my fists in the Bay's chill. I wonder what else I could have called him instead of old, since he clearly wasn't. Not my best work. It's high time to be anywhere but this trailer park. I admire an old soft-top red Raider parked in front of me before opening my Kick account to the waiting screen for Trad-Queer Preacher Arturo Vasquez's stream.

"Heh. So, you used to people not hittin' you 'cuz you act like a girl?" The store clerk again. He's followed me out.

With a disbelieving scoff I square my stance. "You gonna teach me otherwise?"

This may be just what I need.

But the handsome asshole retreats a step, my subtle change in posture not lost on him. "Look, it's early," he says. "Haven't had my pick-me-up! Y'know how it is." He tips a vinyl bag in his hand, then on the ice machine next to me, he sets it down.

It makes a familiar heavy *clink*.

"Truce. Enjoy the PNW. I got another under my seat." And then into the pristine Raider he goes, roaring away.

When one is directly at the edge, simply move the tips of your tippy-toes one centimeter up or down and you're over. Through magical amounts of talent and luck you *might* stay completely still while puzzling out the *safe* way to back away. All the while, a gust of wind can take you. A breeze can make you die.

Dude even threw in a 32oz container. Liltin Yew-emblazoned, of course. I transfer the liquid, then shatter the glass with its shrapnel showering me. The Sitka spruces smell so nice, and there's barely a passing car. Birdsong all around. I take another look at Arturo's live stream on my phone.

Woke-Christian DeviantArt and lo-fi music as a countdown flips south of thirty seconds; 300 viewers are in the queue. Going off recent channel analytics, that's likely half of what today's audience will average.

Arturo at last promised that he could finally make us official, that his following was stable enough—and in front of his old high school class that he never cared about, he could accept one more incremental bit of who he was, without care "for blowback." But I guess I know him better, now. He danced over so many of my lines in the process of lying to himself. I shouldn't have fucked him in his bathroom this morning. One way or another, I've given him what he wants: not his manic older brother Gabriel quietly handled, but the guilt for having asked. No one runs on guilt like Arturo.

The first sip's bitter, delicious shockwaves spread from my mouth, through my gums to douse my brainstem, dump chemicals, and drip down my body which is now shivering with the sudden change in temperature. The hot antidote.

Don't make too big of a deal about it. The older brother Gabriel. *There's* something to stop me recalling my sponsor's first and last name. Another sinus-clearing swig and the bottle absorbs my quiet little moan.

"Well, no doubt this'll be an adventure," I mutter to no one. Arturo started this stupid game; his last expectation will be compliance. If he's so averse to Gabriel in the first place, well, Gabriel is likely a chill guy. Chill or not he won't wait all day.

*He might even spill about what happened with their parents*, I think half a mile later, my legs tightening with the steady uphill grade. I grin openly not just at the thought but at the welcome onset of my quickening pulse: I have a heart still. It's not dried out back in Arturo's silverfish-skittering trailer.

A whole lot of harbor lies between me and downtown. That's enough exercise for now! Calling a RideShare shouldn't be this fun.

"Can you put on Poppy?"

"Eh?" My driver's already annoyed that I made such a fuss about the seatbelt.

"Poppy. You got a music app? Your car do music?"

"Pop's not my thing."

"No," no, no, that's not what I said at all. And I should be frustrated but everything's okay. I'm still chuckling about it at Providence Hospital, staring down the stabbing fluorescent lights. The lights blink first.

Psych wards are typically not a first-floor fit. If they were, people like me would just hop out a window. I was unlucky enough to hit my worst bender a week before I was set to leave the States for an extended greenwashing gig a year and a half ago. Rehabs in most of Europe would've been free.

Instead, I was thrown into a place not unlike this one and into a giant heap of debt; after a colorful one-week tenure, Arturo, livestreaming a needle exchange, noticed me on my way out. Not a cute meet. He's never seen me anything but sober.

"Boy oh boy, things come 'round." The nurse isn't humoring me. Okay, this person does not deserve me at my worst. "Gabriel Vasquez," I repeat over and over to the packed reception room.

A man my age rises, slowly. The resemblance is there. Gabriel is thinner than in the limited pictures Arturo allows me to see. Shirt and shorts wrinkled, likely last worn on the day he was admitted. He has on Target sandals.

"Gabby V., I shall be your envoy."

Expressionlessly the man dips his head. There's no surprise, or if there is, he's just glad to leave.

The nurses should be glad he's leaving, too, but they're following right behind us with a clipboard.

"I *know* him, motherfuckers. I'm dating his brother. Don't tell him I said that, though! Oh, oh Jesus fucking Christ, y'all were two seconds from chucking him out on his own anyway. I know how this works. We go way back, Gabriel and me."

"Yep," Gabby rasps helpfully.

The orderlies are all but putting their hands on us and I sigh, I shoot my little look towards them, and they're suddenly keyed into the fact that they're way better off not doing that, actually. Security's gonna be next. They keep calling Gabby "Mr. Vasquez" and I watch him brace, brace—

"I'mma call 'im," I announce. Maybe they'll listen to Arutro.

My maybe-ex-boyfriend's phone audio is battered by loud static and blaring commotion. The Puget Sound? All I can glean from his voice is that it's shaking.

"Hey babe. You still want your brother? They're tryna euthanize him, I think. Does that do anything for you, preacher?"

The call just keeps getting weirder and the blaring noise seems to infest my phone and crawl out its speaker, which stops me from objecting to the orderlies' requests to hand it over.

But now they have my phone. "C'mon. C'mon," I'm muttering. They have to hear me. So, "Give it back, now," I enunciate. I hear me echo down the hall.

A rough grip tugs my salmon tech jacket. "Come on, dude."

Hey, he's stronger than he looks. *Meth-head energy?* I laugh at myself. The elevator enclosing the two of us, I'm breathing like we've climbed a hill. The bottle of gin barely yields against my vise-like grip. At first I thought it's just because I'm drunk but it really does seem like he stands, moves, even talks without breathing.

"That was one bizarre phone call," he says.

No shit. I brain-dump the confusing conversation, fearing the furious spin of my morning may be threatening to toss. The sinking elevator lifts my gut.

Ground-floor *ding* and I'm power-walking toward the automatic entrance doors. "So whatchu wanna do?" I power-walk directly into a standing vase. "Your li'l bro wanted me to drop you off in your trailer but I'm—ahhah, ow fuck—I'm betting you want a day in the wild? Get some of that red-blooded freedom back in, uh, your blood." The salty air greets us. I gulp hard.

"I want to go home." Gabby shudders in the dull wind.

"You want to go home. Psshhh, oh-kay. Wellll we are not walking."

The entire world sways.

"There's a bench over here."

I realize I shouldn't be sitting on the hospital curb, shoot up and replant. "I saw there's an arcade three blocks away, it's like an arcade bar. And we don't have to—you don't gotta do the bar part, I'll keep you to that. Mhm. Straight and narrow."

Gabby spins around, scanning our surroundings.

I have to focus much, much harder this time to confirm the RideShare. I decide to head off the spinning by meeting its pace. Cough-gasp as the full-throated gin swill clears my esophagus.

"Mmm. No walking to the arcade then, too bad. Walking'd do us good—"

"So you're, what, Arturo's . . . partner? Significant other?"

"Partner. Enbyfriend, if you're feelin' dangerous. I mean it doesn't matter, it—"

"No, sorry."

"Not everyone can take the terms straight. Can *get 'em* straight I mean. People have trouble sometimes. Other things to deal with."

Gabby doesn't blink as he looks at me. "It matters. I'm sorry."

"Naw," I sing. "Psh. See? I knew you were a chill guy. Arturo don't know the fuck he's talkin' about."

I finally see Gabby exhale—then he takes off, measured but fast. "Actually! Cancel that ride."

"That's more like it!" One more sip and I join with renewed vigor.

We pass two blocks of tightly-stacked shops, blighted houses, a ballet studio. I have long since given up looking for an eruv, keeping my eyes off the sky. Christian-ass town.

"How was it? Two weeks, right? Or no it was eleven days." When Gabby nods: "No epiphanies, life lessons or anything? Hah I'm not being a dick. I've just had the same . . . I been in a rehab like that. If you want to like, talk."

"Less people I recognized this time around."

"Oh, yeah? Good, yeah."

"Is it!"

He lingers at a crowded corner. I pace a few tight circles before registering I'm not going anywhere.

"Are we . . . Y'know how to get there? It says we're half a block away." Oh shit, I didn't cancel the RideShare. It says the driver's still waiting at the hospital. I'm losing stars *plural* today. "I figured since you live around here."

"That arcade opened up in the spring," Gabby says, "it'll probably close next year." Then he recoils as if shot, his gaze fixed up the hill.

Where there's a man running. Face contorted in effort. Sprinting, really. Right at the two of us.

I recognize him. Devilishly handsome guy, scuffed knuckles, handing out gin bottles at convenience stores with abandon.

A piercing squeal of brakes and hydraulic *tssk* and there's a bus sidling into our corner.

"Wait!" the running man calls.

"What?!" I scream at him, arms out; Gabby tries to pull me away. "What, man?"

That stops the guy for a second. He's slackjawed, like he can't come up with a response. Then he's briskly walking, running, sprinting once more, face furious and closing.

I get pulled onto the bus. Gabby thrusts a fistful of coins at the driver and murmurs something as I half-intentionally fall onto a seat.

The running man makes it to the bus stop and pounds on the bus; the driver ignores this and pulls away.

"You see that guy?" I pant.

"Yep! Saw that guy." Arturo's older brother seems to slacken in relief. "So, he's real." A horrible realization appears to dawn on him. His eyes lock back onto me, unblinking, fully dilated. "Oh boy . . . He's real."

"Yeah, second time I've seen him today," I scratch my chin. "Wonder why—"

"That would be George," Gabby interrupts. "That is not a good guy, Gets. Barely even a guy anymore, trust me."

9

# INFLUENCED ARTURO VASQUEZ

Compared to my beater Corolla, Anne's vintage red Raider is no simple upgrade; it is iconic. Her seamless moving in and out of gears gives the SUV an illusion of gliding. The soft-top roof whips satisfying low purrs in the wind as we roll down the steep forest hill.

"Father Malcolm said it was your house, too. That's why I thought of the bell tower thing. What would you do to it, if it actually were your home?"

"What do you mean?"

"Like, would you renovate? You can put some music on if you want, there's an AUX in the cupholder."

"Anne? Uh-Miss Oxendine?"

She explodes with laughter. "Anne."

"What's the bit here?"

"The bit's long. It is a looooong bit," she turns her head sideways at me, freckles dark against her skin. Are they even real? "You were right when I hugged you. About me watching you, seeing opportunity. It's your opportunity, too. And no one—no one *I* know, on Earth, has ever gotten this opportunity or ever will again."

She's not looking away from me.

And we're actually going really fast.

"I'll be telling you a lot more. But first, how're we doing, Artie?" Her words becoming suddenly much clearer, pointed. "Are you in so far?"

Haven't drifted an inch out of our lane. About 400 meters ahead, a sharp right turn denotes the edge of the hill.

I refocus back to Anne. "In so far."

Her contentment gives 2010s-era Obama. "Not bad," she says. I flex my palms and close them. Breath quickens as I try to extricate my gaze. She blinks at me, then clears her throat. "Hey," she says with a cock of her head. "What's with this turn up here, huh?"

We are on top of it.

I cry out "What?" and don't have time to grab the roll bar, or the seat or the dashboard, before a crashing *whine* splits my ears and I am off the ground.

Everything yanks in a blur to the left and flailing I feel myself leave the orbit of Earth. Only the blueing sky is out my window, the road almost directly below Anne's.

Then my stomach lurches up to my lungs. Two wheels on my side collide with asphalt and my neck folds under the Raider's soft-top before I'm dumped lopsided back onto my seat. One eye pushed open from inertia, Anne dropping the e-brake and the crashing *whine* returning—we haven't even stopped, we're fishtailing over a spit of rocks on her side, grazing the border of life and death. She downshifts and we level out.

"So, I'm your Guardian Angel!" Her mouth a thrown-open guffaw as she slaps on a pair of sunglasses. "And you're gonna be made a god for a day."

"How in the fuck—you crazy—*aagh*—" I'm contorting in pain. She's accelerating again.

"Trust exercise, Arturo. Tighten that seatbelt, but go limp. If you tense your neck right now, it's gonna be too tender," she shouts over engine roar. Her hand dances over the clutch with no hint of grind.

"Get through this," she continues and hair-pins left, crossing directly into an oncoming van, ducking it with a split-second scrape across its driver-side bumper; I hear children scream.

My car—"My car!"—my equipment left in the Cathedral, my brother Gabriel in Providence Hospital, sitting outside the psych wing in a waiting room without a clue—

"Gabriel. Yasss. Speaking of Guardian Angels." Anne twists to me again as she takes a turn so hard her sunglasses fly off and hit my ribs, land on my lap. "We're taking care of that right now. Not you 'n me! Sort of you 'n me. Cell reception's bunk. I'm taking us—ooooooo, right to the open."

Her turn has sent us above the Bay. The trees blow away and I hear the sea. A winding route sprawls along the cliff below. Mercifully, no cars. "No cars," she echoes encouragingly and the Raider's needle passes 55. At the far base of the road, a scenic turnoff. "Yep, that right there. Mile tops."

I close my eyes, lurching so violently that I know I'll tip over. Something latches to the bridge of my nose and pokes my ear as I flinch. I open my eyes again: she is affixing her sunglasses to me, both hands off the wheel.

"Now we're sleepin'." She closes her eyes too.

"OH MY GOD—" The taut seatbelt stops me from lunging forward.

"Touch me and I'll really kill us. Yo," she says, scrunching her already closed eyes to make a face for my benefit, "is that . . . the *loons?*"

"The loo—" Chancing a forward glance, there are five of them, spear-shaped bills full of fish, mistaken for ducks but for their far-back feet, wholly unable to walk quickly on land, crossing down the center line. *"The loons—?!"*

"OH MY GOD NOT THE LOONS," as if Anne is being murdered, she stomps the brake, sightlessly spins the wheel over, me calling for Gets as I throw my hands over my tear-streaked face, losing control of my body, the tires punching up to my seat, I hear a *squawk.*

Then, we are slowing. Weight is shifting to the back, the decline less steep. "Oh," I croak as I lower my hands. Anne emits a probing drone, "*mmmmmm*," until "*hm*," then she swerves gently into the scenic turnoff. Her eyes are still shut. I notice and don't.

Her eyes finally open, she blinks several times at the churning water now surrounding us. "It's more of a bay than the actual sea." She unclips the seatbelt and leaves the car idling. I follow her out. I fall on all fours and my legs wobble as I pick myself up.

"Right?" Anne exhales loudly, shaking out her knees. "Shake 'em out." She looks at her watch. There is no blood nor feathers on the Raider.

"I'm dead." I wipe snot and tears. I flail around trying to spot the hidden cameras. I pat my chest, my biceps, I press down on my pulse. "I have to be dead."

"No one's dead. We're all still here."

"My neck—"

"You'll be okay tomorrow. Can you make it on over?" She's at the center of the overlook now, stretching her calves on a log. "It's kinda loud."

I stay put.

"How did you do that?"

"I said I'd be telling you more after this. Here it comes. You're about to see. Ten seconds."

I can't catch my breath. The encompassing rush of the water smudges me into static. I am vibrating.

I *am* vibrating. My right pocket, to be specific.

"That's Gets Lo. Arturo, can you hear me?"

I pull my phone out. Of course she's right.

"Can you hear me?" she asks again.

"What—yeah, what do you want?" I shout, aggressively. She smiles.

"Just try answering that phone, but don't hold it to your ear. Don't listen. And just . . . talk to me the whole time. Focus only on *me*. You get it?"

I don't get it.

Anne waves her hands impatiently. "You don't have to get it yet, but do you, like, get the instructions?"

I close my eyes, finally riding my heart-rate. I scoff. "I do. Yeah."

"Fuckin' perfect!" The smile becomes a beam. "You got this, Artie. Go."

With a right swipe, I answer the phone.

Over the rushing waves I can parse Gets' tone but not their words—calm, cool, collected, maybe too much so, but definitely not under duress, when,

"Okay, are you with me, man?" Anne says.

"Yeah."

She puts her hand to her ear.

"Yes, I'm here," more forcefully.

"Okay, so we were talking about your brother."

"Gabby?"

"Call him Gabriel for this if you don't mind," she chirps politely with a what-can-you-do wave of her wrist.

"Gabriel."

"Did what I just did to you remind you of anything?"

"I . . . I don't follow." The sounds from the phone are overlapping, maybe arguing?

"Come on. You were ten. It was your first R-rated movie. He smuggled it in from college."

"I . . . Yeah, he brought his *Fight Club* DVD. He showed me *Fight Club* I think when I was ten. We watched it together."

I hear faint laughter from my palm. Familiar. Gabby's.

Anne nods. "Yeah, that's what . . . that's all I was doing. Just an itty bitty recreation of that famous car scene for ya." A stately-sounding voice I can't place asserts itself on the phone, but, "Arturo. You focus on only me."

"Okay."

"Was it wrong for Gabriel to show you that movie when you were ten? If you had to choose, was there something *wrong* with that? Or was he just trying to help you out?"

"Help me out?"

"Yeah, like expand your horizons. And all that."

It is a nonsensical conversation. And it's hard to hear her.

"Sure."

"Sure what, Arturo?"

"Yes, trying to help me out. Is that what you want me to say?"

Anne brushes the bleached hair from her eyes. She puts her hands together. "Okay, that's the whole conversation outta the way. This next part's kinda boring. Are you ready? Just nod."

I sigh, gawk at her blankly.

She bounces. "Just repeat what I say once I've said it. Ready? Or." On her fingers, like back at the Cathedral, she counts down, three, two, one. "Here we go. Arturo, still with me?"

"*Yes*, I'm here." I hear that stately voice in my hand again. Not Gabby's, not Gets'.

"Stellar. Say, 'Whatever, yeah, it's clearly fine.'"

"Yeah, whatever, it's clearly fine."

A pause. "Say, 'Send that to my email. He's in good hands.'" A hand parallel to her mouth and an octave higher: "Like All-State."

"Uh, send that to my email. He's . . . in good hands?"

"Now this one, you relate to: 'Just get on with it.'"

"Just get on with it," I say.

"Hang up."

"Hang up. Oh." I thumb the disconnect.

Anne paces leisurely over and holds her hand out for my phone. "Trust me one minute longer."

I wouldn't call it trust. She makes a few clicks and shows the location of Gets' phone at time of call. Providence St. Peter's Hospital. "Go ahead. What do you think just happened?"

"Gets got Gabby."

"My alliterative friend, that's the long 'n short. They did what you wanted them to this morning, and you just helped."

Under natural circumstances, I'd be infuriated. To go rogue after a fight and pick up my mentally unsound hermano mayor *out of spite* while Gets was supposed to be waiting at home, moderating my stream.

To talk shit with Gabriel about how toxic, probably, how damaging I've become. To divulge far too much family history . . . maybe even tell how his little brother got stuck with him in the first place.

I'm never concerned for Gets' safety—Gets is tough as weathered leather, they can beat up a bouncer. No, I'm concerned about keeping my goddamn dignity.

So I guess I am a little furious. But natural circumstances aren't anywhere near. I grip myself in the windy chill. It has been inexcusably long since I last got out by the water.

As if reading my mind—as if?

Anne looks me up and down. "Gets just takes Gabriel right home. Where Gabriel will stay for the rest of the day. Far out of our way. You don't go home. Well," she looks away slightly. "Not until you're all done."

"*Can* you read my mind?" I ask.

"Eh. It'll just seem like it sometimes. I know a lot of what you want to say, because on a lot of days, you say it."

No compunction for being rude anymore, I eye her pointedly, waiting.

"If this *whole day* were your house, what would you do?" She is moving toward the idling Raider. She climbs in as I follow, as I pause at the passenger door. "You don't realize this, but from sun-up to sun-up it's yours, man. We know everything that happens today, virtually everywhere. And with that, we can do a *whole* lot of . . . I mean, whatever you want, really. And I'm tellin' you, mark that down. You'll be surprised how little a day limits."

I lean into the window.

"You've been here before? So, you're a time traveler."

With a "Bless your heart," Anne shakes her head and says, "No, Arturo. I'm not a time traveler." I drum my fingers on the car door with one hand, rub my temples with the other. "I'm a time prisoner."

I stop drumming. That certainly can't be original. Someone has said that before. But our gazes hold one another, and it seems real. I've completely forgotten that Anne pocketed my phone. I should do something about that.

"Um, you're entering into a fugue state, by the way. You've spent about half an hour witnessing what seems like literal magic. Your brain's rejecting it. Even if you don't want to. You should get in the car."

"I actually . . . think I should, yeah." I'm fine. I'm fine, but the car door does feel heavier and slower to open than estimated. I need to be in here to get my phone back, though.

"It doesn't last long," Anne goes on while I gingerly sit. "You've had an episode before. When Gabby attacked your mom and dad with a kitchen knife nine years ago, you disassociated. So you know what it's like. This won't be as intense. You'll be responsive enough to get settled with me over the next two hours, but if you want it gone completely in 30 minutes . . . Glove compartment."

*My phone.* I open the glove compartment. My fingers begin to feel noodly. A small baggy of white powder is smashed into the corner.

"Obviously, it's your choice. You've done it before, you don't mind."

I attempt to shake my head. "No I haven't. I've never."

For the first time in my life since I ever purposely interacted with Anne Oxendine, she appears to hold her tongue. To bite it.

"You can put together what I said now. I'll give you some time."

Was I trying to get something back from her? I can't concentrate so I look out to the roiling bay. I feel chilly. Clumsily I work the hand-crank on the car door and the window stutters closed.

*We know everything about what happens today.*

*You don't realize this but . . .*

*I'll give you some time.*

I slither slowly back towards Anne's direction, the soreness in my neck bursting. I feel I can't meet her eyes, just as back at the Cathedral when I could only gaze into the distant, almost unseeable reflection of myself.

"I'm . . . I . . ."

"You're a prisoner, too. We all are, I think. Some just see the cage."

But, what? That is not anything. What in that is a metaphor, what is a literal thing? A literal thing?

I know I'm begging myself to ask questions, simple ones too, but each leaves my mind as I try. Somewhere, Anne is pulling the car into motion again. My brain is slowing. Face hot. I shouldn't have rolled up the window.

"God. Here." The white baggy lands on my chest and clings to my shirt. "Use a finger. I don't care, there's more. Do something with it."

I do it.

She really is a fantastic driver. All jerkiness gone, that gauntlet ran, she looks like no small part of her cherishes how cleanly she can throw it around. My hand stays atop my chest, terrified less of its beat against my palm than the idea of abandoning it. I have a vision that I've been shot and hold my intestines in. Except my intestines are oddly cozy.

"What was that?" Anne is purring.

"I said," I drawl, but press on, "Why didn't I just believe you were my Guardian Angel."

She laughs the first laugh that seems to contain just the two of us, and there is a touch of bitterness. "Maybe, if we play it right, we can be each other's."

With numbed befuddlement, I register that her eyes are glassy. There's a steeliness behind the tears. "Maybe we can break each other free."

"Prison break, baby," I garble, and then I have to go to sleep for a little while.

# SOLAR NOON

*WE CAN SKIP AROUND, IF WE WANT.*

# 10

# WILLIAM TILLER AND DATES

William Tiller had no clue bomb threats were still taken so seriously. His point of contact's voice from the Twice Loved Institute explains that, while most likely AI, this particular call-in also displays some uncanny knowledge of the rehabilitation center's floor plan. As a result, they are pushing today's server installation to Sunday or Monday, whichever Bill prefers.

"I already extended your per diem," the TLI employee says brightly.

"Oh, well, okay." Free hand running slowly down his thick, black Viking mohawk, Bill wishes they'd just led with that. "Bet."

The 11:00 A.M. call woke him and he tries to keep his attention on the installation delay, instead of searching for his absent Tinder date. On one hand he's saved the trouble of covertly checking their in-app messages to remember her name. On the other he now has a whole day, possibly two, of PNW tourism ahead, and nobody to do it with.

On a map—a real map, since Bill is an unashamed Luddite—he plots out a trip to Cape Flattery. Two and a half hours. He loves road trips, especially in such a dramatically new place. His testosterone gel feels cool on his side in an overtly motel-mini-fridge-chilled kinda way, and there is

83

enough time now to run blood pressure and jot levels into his worn little notepad. Heart problems run in William's broadly supportive family, so a pre-existing adherence to diet and exercise helps him heaps after the double mastectomy, even more so post-ALT phalloplasty saga.

Pressure readings hold normal.

Leaning his meaty shoulder on peeling wallpaper, he opens the dating app. A couple refresh attempts confirm his Tinder hookup, whatever her name, unmatched. He rolls his eyes, wondering if he satisfied some based progressive's fetish.

If she knew in advance she'd get an opportunity to travel the coast with him the next day, would she stay? She did say she was off all weekend; they clearly clicked enough. What was her name?

Maybe he talked in his sleep again.

*We're not going there today*, he thinks, and indiscriminately swipes right until the artificially scarce free likes deplete.

Morning workout via the necessity to carry, not roll, his tightly packed server-build components. The sidewalk is far too mottled for William's liking; rolling the equipment would loosen something. It's not a full installation, just a bit of a tear-out and upgrade, with a large emphasis by the TLI on aesthetic improvements. Why a youth rehabilitation center needs a bleeding-edge server, he doesn't care to ask. Maybe ray tracing is their therapy.

Loading each case of segmented racks into his rental 2024 Ford Focus, he starts the ignition before realizing he has nowhere to stay.

"Just in the event that I have to come back here tonight," he says with maximum charisma to 70-year-old Susan, the Bull Elk Motel's manager sitting behind a reception booth outlined in worn dreamcatchers, "is there a room to hold?"

"Normally you'd leave a deposit and we'd go ahead and wire it back if you find somewhere else, but we're fully booked through the weekend." She nods through medicated tremors of Parkinson's, extra "mhmm"s emanating somewhere from her interior. "Besides Room 203, of course." She sees his confusion. "There's some high school reunion going on or something."

"Ah, I see. You said Room 203?"

"Oh," she says feebly, "you don't want that room, sir. Nobody wants that room."

He cocks an eyebrow. Local tea alert. "There a murder there or something?"

Lucratively ping-ponging around America to install all kinds of practical or artistic tech fixtures, Bill keeps a lookout for motels with unsavory histories. Those have the best rates, and their stories make better keepsakes than fridge magnets—though he has plenty of those, too.

"Heavens, no no no. There were cameras, though. Clyde—he's my husband—he must have removed a dozen hidden cameras from 203 over the years. Word spread, unfortunately. Now it just gathers dust."

"That *is* unfortunate!" Pocketing his business debit, he scrawls a 40% tip on the motel's receipt copy.

"Oh, honey no, that is far too much."

"We're profiting off a domestic terror threat today, Susan. Live an inch."

She flashes an achingly coy smile and says with a terrified little whisper, "Fuck the feds."

—

He's a personable guy. Most travelers he'd met on the drive from his hometown of Omaha, Nebraska, had never heard of little Liltin Yew, Washington. The 2 who did highly recommended Line 9 Diner and even stressed the need to book a reservation. Bill did—not online, but over the phone, with a real human being—for 11:30 A.M. today.

Before engaging the Focus' clutch, Bill finally checks Tinder again. He's matched with a woman named Anne.

**By necessity or princess-ity I'll never stop being pretty**

**Don't ask me to drive**

Loads of emojis that are impressively baffling. At 33, she is 6 years older than he. She's a blue collar dock work at the harbor, fit, in one picture striking a pose on a mountainside. Book lover. Green flags, but she looks oddly familiar. He can't place it. He knows no one here.

She's already messaging him.

**Morning, traveler. I'm passing thru for the day. Abt 2 be on my way to Cape Flattery, wanna come?**

Now this *might* elicit a spike in his blood pressure.

"That's astonishing," he writes, "I was literally about to head out there now! Picked out the CDs for the trip 'n everything." A moment of deliberation, and then a follow-up: "But not before going to my reservation at Line 9, wanna meet there . . .?"

A heart from Anne appears under his first message, an ellipsis under his second.

**Bet. Maybe when this day's over you can fuck me so hard I'll feel it tomorrow.**

Bill reminds himself multiple times not to speed on his way to the diner.

Sunlight stiffens behind the dissipating bay fog and reflects off the converted, pastel-painted train car's corrugated roof. The parking lot is noisy. Bill swallows his mint, covers his server build's crates with his coat, and eagerly joins the fray.

His booth is in the back corner of the car, not a problem since the only restrooms are outside across a patio. Mahogany lines the walls, shaded lights hanging a few inches below overhead storage. Ducking and bobbing around waiters, boisterous clientele, and an Arcade Fire playlist, he notes a glass moonroof cutting the car's narrow center, painted over in places with thorny vines. A rich espresso scent clings to him and he secretly hopes it will saturate his clothes forever.

He is first to arrive. *Fuck me so hard I'll feel it tomorrow*, his narrator voice repeats almost in singsong, as he orders two carrot waters and a black coffee to start, eyes darting to the front entrance. He reopens the app and begins to type, "In the back booth."

"Hi. George?"

He looks to his left, and there she is.

Matted blow-out falls slightly curly just above her chest, which works with nervous rapidity. A burnt orange graphic tee pokes out from under a camo jacket. Her left knee is dancing.

"Uh, what? Hi! Bill. I'm Bill."

Her hand plays up and down her long, thin purse strap as she fumbles for her phone.

"What—sorry, your name's not George?"

"Is yours Anne?"

She looks at him blankly. She holds out her phone and William's eyes narrow on a profile that is not his. But this is his picture—one of his rarer pictures, taken in his old shop, by his ex-girlfriend whom he devoted 4 years of his life to.

"Uh, what's going on—" He makes to scroll to the next pictures, but she yanks the phone away.

"I'm Hunter." She waits.

"Um . . . Nice to meet you." Bill shows her the profile he matched with.

"Your drinks," the waiter shuffles in next to them with a tray from which he deposits the waters, the carrot juices, the pot of coffee, and a mug.

"Get me a mug too when you can, please, Pranav."

"Yo, Hunter! What's good? Thought that was you. Yeah, gimme a sec."

She sits opposite Bill. "So what the heck." Her voice flecks with cigarette rasp.

Bill looks around, unsure for what. "Is this a catfish?"

"But these are pictures of us."

"I don't get it. Well, I mean, what did yours say?"

She blinks. "Just to meet here. We matched, and we, like—you're here for a day and, y'know, to meet here at 11:30. What'd they say to you?"

*Fuck me so hard I'll feel it tomorrow.*

Bill gulps. "Same." He clears his throat. "Same here. You bet."

He can't remember ever feeling more awkward, can't presently remember much of anything. He only realizes he's pushed the one coffee mug to her side of the table because she now looks pointedly down at it.

"I'm gonna message this person. See if it dings on your end, okay?" he says.

She nods.

He finally presses send on the message he'd written: "In the back booth."

The profile of 'Anne' disappears from his matched conversations entirely. Hunter hasn't touched her phone.

"Did you just—I'm really bad at technology, could you check it now, please."

Her thumbs work furiously. He watches her mouth open then close. Then she locks and drops the phone on the welded-down table.

They sit wordlessly. At some point, the music shifts to Wolf Alice's *Blue Weekend*.

"So your name's . . . Bill?"

"Short for William. Uh, are you also here for a day?"

Still looking down, "No. I live here."

"That's what you'd said, so I—that's what *Anne* said. This is the weirdest . . . I'm a little confused."

"Oh, yeah?" She snaps back up to him. His breath catches in his throat. Her face is distraught, but her eyes? Searching. Bemused? She waits for a punchline.

Pranav the waiter returns with another mug, asks her if she is supposed to be on shift. Waving him off, she slides Bill's empty mug right back to him and pours coffee into the new one. "Confused, I think, is mutual."

*On shift* . . . William's gaze moves from her to the booth's window: A defunct bar lay across the street, its yellow neon sign inert in the daylight. "Wait, you bartend at the Barking Shark. I was just there last night. I remember you."

Hunter nods slowly. "Every other weekend. You were with an old high school buddy of mine."

Bill shakes his head for about seven seconds. "Is this a—"

"How'd it go?"

"Is this a setup, or is this a catfish?"

"Uhhh, yes." She shrugs. "I don't know, man."

"Jesus fuckin'—sorry." Head light, he grabs the pot of coffee.

"Jesus fuckin' forgives, relax." She sips and he sips. The coffee is almost too good. "I wanna know what more this Anne said to you."

"Why do you think there's more? What'd I say to you?"

"What did *George* say to me?"

"I'm Bill. Keep up."

Hunter flashes her teeth. Not badly stained by smokers' standards. "Where are you from, you son of a bitch?"

"N'braska. My mom—my mom's a beautiful soul, how dare you."

"I'm just wondering who ends up with a name like William anymore."

"You are literally *Hunter*."

"'Scuse me?"

"No, like it's a common-ass name, too, but . . ."

"Out with it."

He appraises her camo, "You don't need to dress the part *that* much."

"Cougar season's two months away. And counting." She clings to her mug. "Guns must not do it for you."

The caffeine influx doesn't help his present situation; his voice is wavering. "I've been on a lot of dating apps. But never once—"

"Yeah this is a bit of a new scenario for me too, friend. Tied for weirdest thing that's happened to me so far." It is his turn to stare at her blankly. "Uh, about four months ago, I was hittin' it off with this dude when some girl crashed our date, asked if she could sit with us. She wasn't old enough to get into some concert with her friends. We end up all walking around Liltin in thirty-degree weather. Two strangers babysitting her basically."

"Don't know if that sounds fun or frustrating."

"Fun. We had to like . . . work together. Saw him for a little while after that." She grimaces. "Yeah, that one was fun for a bit."

Wait, for the first time in this conversation the pause is a natural one. *Collect yourself, Bill.* And, *Okay, your turn.* "I just—I get some interesting ones. I travel for work, so lots of one 'n dones."

"Hm. Not always my speed, but I respect it."

"And everyone says guys don't read the profiles, but it ain't just guys. I've gotten a few, 'Oh, *trans*-masc? That's awesome, slay,' just—woefully unprepared." He chuckles. "It's just," he trails off. "Really funny stuff."

A momentary tug at the corner of her lip. He has no idea what the fuck he is saying. "And so how did it go last night with Maria?"

"Maria? Oh, yeah, no, last night w—"

"Wow, dude."

"Look, I'm frazzled, okay."

Hunter puts her hands up behind her mug. Her nails aren't painted.

"Um, you know," Bill's voice strains an octave higher, "I mean, are you friends?" She shakes her head violently. "Well, I don't want you pegging me a misogynist."

"Just say it."

Pranav the waiter makes his way from the kitchen to the back of the train car.

"She's that, 'looking for something serious, NOT here for hookups' type, right. So like clockwork she's asking my height and dick size five messages in."

Hunter's laugh comes like a jump-scare. She finishes her coffee and pours more. "Well, that could've gone badly, but no, I will not be pegging you."

Bill scoffs, chuckles. Running a hand through his Viking mohawk, he ventures his gaze back to her eyes and holds it before being interrupted by Pranav.

"Sorry fam, it's busier than usual right now. What're you getting?"

The menus lay untouched next to the napkins. "Err. Hunter's gonna take this."

The booth whines as Hunter leans back. "Slammer specials, two. And the poutine. Pranav, before you go. Y'all still doing that thing where you meet up at one?"

"It's a Saturday and it's the summer solstice, 'course we are," Pranav says.

"Good to know."

Pranav raises an eyebrow at the two of them, "Okay, then," he says and walks back to the front.

Bill leans in. "You forgot to ask about my dietary restrictions." Hunter nods, blinks again, this time slowly. "So what's at one?" Bill asks.

"I guess you could say it's a jam session. We'll stop by before we head out of town."

"Out of town?"

"Yeah. Cape Flattery *is* still the plan, right?" Off Bill's look, she points at her phone. "George. Told me all about you."

"Oh." He thinks of Hunter's bio—or *Anne's* bio. *Don't ask me to drive.* Fine by him. He wonders what else she knows about him already. "Uh, I mean, yeah. You bet."

*Fuck me so hard I'll feel it tomorrow.*

There's still hope.

# 11

# OUR SYSTEM, SIRENS SWEPT FROM THE TIDES OF TIME

Our physiologies reset as they were on the first June 21ˢᵗ, the one which trapped us. We only ever sleep by choice. Sometimes we're awake for months or years.

While at first the Anne of us tried hard to leave the time hole, the George of us lauded our radical circumstance as an opportunity. A break, a recharge. Self-improve and emerge on the other side a champion, for once. Learn guitar. Learn the whole symphony. Learn a language. Polyglot. Meet idols. Private flights. Prolifically consume. Prolifically create?

No, Anne reminds us. Our slate wipes clean constantly. Hardly exists. Can't take it with us, nor with accuracy refer back. Filling our heads with too many new talents guarantees we'll unlearn others, eventually. That, and our dog's dying every day. That we don't forget. We hear the wheezes.

So, sleep's great when craved. Pretend *we* don't exist either. A break from the break; they never last long. Base cravings, complex cravings, brand-new cravings rise and fall through 3,000 iterations of June 21ˢᵗ, 2025, and more or less flatten.

We can, with practice, make the amazing happen. Solve so many problems in each iteration, make them worse—all the same when we never glimpse an outcome, let alone sit in one. And every iteration reminds us how much we can't change.

For a while we go loud in the thinking that we'll at least do right by the Georges and Annes whose futures we can't inhabit. That thinking flattens, too. In fact those hypothetical tomorrows flatten *us*. How do we know they're even there? If they are, how can we be anything but jealous? We become dulled down, diluted little things. We accept that those Georges, those Annes, are fictions we will never meet. Our space for dreaming fills up quick.

We stick through the good long enough that it becomes the bad; we wonder if there's anything that can't go bad.

We learn that there is just one thing.

It's no suicide—though we've crossed into that territory more than once by now. More on that later. No, our she-half is busy hiking with, funnily enough, Nanno Sripariyattiwetti just while an ignorant miscalculation of the tides and foot placement on Liltin Yew's rainbow bridge makes mincemeat of our male half on jagged rocks below. It's an accidental death.

This final feeling of being shot through from everywhere. Nothing, then too much.

And we glimpse something.

We wait a full day to tell our she-half, just lying in bed, staring at the ceiling until it goes dark. Definitely not sleeping.

The ceiling faintly glows blue with dawn and *there it is* again at 5:12 A.M.—a flash, a furling, a fractaling overlap. A glistening lattice.

The whole time in bed we've been trying to place how something so insane could seem so terminally familiar. But seeing it again confirms its actual origin: the transmedium USO's piercing *T*, back when we fell into its calcifying burst. The last thing each sense felt before the time hole: the living insides of our Unmaker. Come to think of it, our eyes didn't peel open then, and they certainly aren't now, while moreover . . .

Well, there's simply no comprehension, no sufficient description to share. Not at first.

Not until about 5:12:09 A.M. when Anne calls us, shouting, "Did you *see that?*"

Haven't slept for generations since.

—

"Astronauts at the ISS refer to a shift in perspective, in cognition, upon seeing Earth from the outside," we tell Arturo Vasquez in our Raider, 17,000-ish iterations after discovering the stutter between the dawns. "It's a multiple of that."

"Ooo, oh, okay," he says. He's trying to become the passenger seat, closed eyelids fluttering as if in REM mode, lolling. Hand on his chest, his tongue is practically out.

"So that's why killing ourselves doesn't work, like you asked," we continue, half truthfully: "Because with the hope of our exit, there's no need." The charade of freely offering information is crucial, even though he doesn't remember asking—isn't hearing our response.

We can get closer than family to almost anybody, change lives in so many directions, and with our reset, we're forgotten. We alone know each other's history and not even we can totally keep track anymore. Days become years, years become days.

—

Speaking of our other half, the exact moment we're driving our little preacher uptown as intended, the George of us races through downtown's streets to stop Gets Lo and Gabby at all cost, and fails. Let's put that another way. While half of Operation T-Pose hums along immaculately, the other half has already begun to come apart.

T-Pose's big picture, conversations, places, even timing are typically not issues. But we're not good on timing when we forget a comatose child's simple 6-digit passcode, almost get caught by her one-eyed friend trying to peek it, and have to fumble through multiple enforced lock-out periods on our way to remembering. This is what we mean by not keeping track, and while a hangover that returns each day with the same vigor might be spiritually conquered—grudgingly accepted as a state of existence after a year, or two or six—it doesn't un-handicap our literal brain matter.

We did well at the railroad tracks, let Nanno live to run to the woods to find the politicians. We dropped the assassin bug and locked the town sideshow into the wastewater satellite. We blackmailed Vada Ikebe's father, Officer Pratt. As Vada herself lay passed out in her friend's basement, we infiltrated *Reify* and planted our three surprise assets in the game with ease.

But because of a simple 6-digit passcode, we are not there to stop Gabriel Vasquez from neglecting Gets' RideShare.

And we missed their bus.

Knowing them both, as we do more than themselves, Gabby will nonetheless wind up in his trailer, squarely out of the way, but the question becomes, *When?* and, *What happens to Gets?* Their drunk ass is now in the wind, which simply can't be allowed for a soul so solecistic.

We do not yet inform our she-half of the hitch we created. We take the long route to our next destination. Wind past a handful of bars frequented by Gets in other iterations of our laminar flow. Something has to give—we abandon our plans for the Tinder couple for the time being. The alcoholic is nowhere to be found.

So on we drive, to end up at Liltin High's newly remodeled gym.

And we're also uptown with Preacher Arturo. We make him record the live video and it's as funny as always. He's so out of breath he can barely try to escape. Our he-half hasn't texted us in a bit, though. Regular check-ins aren't mandated but after everything we've been through lately, silence seems a strange choice.

That pit in our gut amplifies in the echoey remodeled gym, George-half masked up and signing for every ostentatious order. A bounce castle, a 16-ft slide, Liltin High silver-and-blue, each an express rental fee on a separate swiped card from those happy few who can afford it. Even after tonight's events their fragile banks likely won't cover our fraud. Every signature we sign is an exact replication of either Quinn Gershwin's or Bonnie Cossio's.

Maybe, we both think, we've been a little fixated on the thing in the morning. That routine detonation from the joint military base.

We both knew when it was coming: We know when most variations of most things do. And we were both expecting the detonation: it's loud. But as to which one verbalized it . . . well, we still haven't asked.

That overlap between us. Half-sacred, half-abhorrent.

—

Eight blocks from Liltin High is low-income housing complex Firwood Manor beneath some foothills. Time to visit our favorite doomsday prepper. Texting Vada as her comatose friend, the reason George-half so easily remembers *this* particular code is that it's simply a reverse of the complex's emblazoned building number plus an extra zero.

In the nylon carpeted hall we knock and proclaim that we're sent by the smelly, agoraphobic prepper's uncle; he cracks his door just wide enough to catch a plunging knife into his belly, dislodging a rib and unzipping him all the way to his sternum, while mentally we flip through any of Gets Lo's favorite bars that we might have missed. The old slob, stumbling back, spills all over his apartment and we hopscotch over writhing lower intestinal knots. Living insides spellbind only the first couple thousand times.

We make ourselves half at home in the converted living room-turned-laboratory/warchest. We'll handle Gets soon. The clock is ticking (a hilarious thought). Flush the ultrasonic LVN and compressor kits. It's time to turn carfentanil into a gas.

12

# FUGITIVE QUINN GERSHWIN

Shoot the lock."

"You really are a fucking idiot."

Not being an expert on firearms is but one of a myriad factors indicative of my moral standing over Republican Bonnie Cossio. She thinks she's my rival for Mayor. She goes low, I go high: Her insult rolls right off me.

"With whom did you share your location, Bonnie?" I try.

"Your mom." She's pushing on the rigid metal mesh doors, then pulling, then pushing again. "My husband and I moderate a local forum. Grassroots patriots. Would you help me open this thing?"

My nose wrinkles as I turn back toward the cavernous water treatment plant and I feel pressure in Lasik laser-cut eyes, a building headache. I try not to imagine my wife reading the leaked article. Taylor said she wouldn't answer calls from anyone until I returned.

"Both of us won't make a difference," I hear myself saying. It drains my battery to keep checking (I'm on 4% and it's physically hot in my palm), but I check again.

Bonnie's voice is heavy with effort. "You're not even gonna try?" she asks.

Taylor hasn't called or texted. *That's my girl*, I observe with an influx of melancholy, inexpressibly and suddenly all alone; I divert attention to the caged openings between the satellite facility's wall and ceiling. They look segmented, latched. And if I reach them they will be locked too.

"These places never have just one entry or exit." I announce. I start to wander. Not through the center of the plant like when I came in, but around its perimeter. "Otherwise, it's a county code violation."

Bonnie trails me. "No way," she hisses, pantomiming an interested schoolgirl. She silences the hundredth call to her cell in as many seconds. "So how much kickback money did your team take from TLI?"

"'Kickbacks' is an incendiary term. Are you pretending you didn't receive an advanced copy of the exposé? Wouldn't exactly jive with what you told me ten minutes ago."

Bonnie kicks more gravel. It clangs weakly against thick piping. She is an amateur. "Yes, I got the article. Was the author's name redacted on yours as well?"

"Yes. I'm guessing someone must have leaked it."

"Info-terrorism. Cue me sharing my location. My hacker boys from my forum are still trying to confirm who sent it."

As if her cue were literal, there are bangs from the metal mesh doors.

I can distinguish at least three of them calling her name, their voices straining against the metal.

"Would those happen to be the same hacker boys who investigated the out-of-towner plotting to kill me?" I spit.

"Sure, bring that up again now. Play victim. Y'all always do."

*I was literally an intended victim, you bitch,* I almost yell. *Y'all? Y'ALL?* My head pangs. Taylor taught me to do breathing exercises to help stave off my painful headaches. I try. But this is no ideal environment.

I notice she glances furtively at her purported fan club without rushing to meet them.

"It's only that if they are, I question their accuracy," I manage.

I hear a very gruff voice from outside the fake house shout, "Does anyone have bolt cutters?"

Bonnie's jaw sets at that, and she quickens her patrol around the forest of clanging pipes and valves. I grab her arm and she shakes me off, but wheels around. "What, Quinn?"

"Are they loyal to you," I speak low and slow for her, "or are they loyal to your cause?"

Judging by the non-reaction, she's starting to catch on, if she hadn't already. She compulsively summoned a gang of fascists to dig into a highly damning hit piece. 50/50 on if they buoy or burn her.

"They're wolves, the public," I offer anyway, unwilling to contain my smirk, "especially your crowd. And wolves eat their own."

She looks me up and down. Her contempt is evident, no mere performance for the press. "There's a door, over there." She gestures casually over my shoulder.

The grated storm door is at first invisible in the low light and my hackneyed vision. The cold draft it emits, however, that's very detectable. It is propped open.

I am no fan of dark passages beneath the dirt. Yet as we approach it we hear behind us an echoing shift of chains, a *snap*, and cheering as Bonnie's crowd lay siege.

"Flood it, flood it," one chants as if in a war film.

By the time it's clarified not to literally flood the waste water treatment plant, Bonnie closes the storm door softly behind us. She breathes fast. The first steps are soft wood under my sustainably sourced sneakers. Too pliant. If only I could properly see in the dark already.

Why couldn't this career-altering article have waited two more weeks, when my vision fully heals? How do I deserve any part of this situation to begin with? Because I fought for free student meals? Better transportation from the reservation? It's outrageous, I think as my foot slides forward on the dirt-covered weak wood, as my face hits mossy ground at the bottom of the stairs. It's unfair. I curse and spit a pebble.

Towering over me, Bonnie fumbles in her purse. Why do I *hope* she's grabbing her gun, ending me like a dog, hauling my carcass up to her Klan friends?

Instead I'm blinded by her phone's flashlight. She's holding out a hand. With remarkable ease, HIIT unwasted, she helps me stand. "Sh."

I nod.

She continues, "Is there a fucking exit?"

The passage is wide, frigid. Vines. Little legs scampering for cover. It stretches far into the distance and slopes down.

My right ankle is scraped and twinging. Five feet away, I notice the thoroughly cracked screen of my work phone light up.

## TAYLOR GERSHWIN

Breathlessly, I scurry with no care for the detonation in my ankle, but the phone goes dark one last time, dies. Bonnie clears her throat, averts her whole body, and starts to walk down the drain.

"Where is it?" one of the voices from the satellite facility's ground level asks. "Looks like it'd be in this corner."

"Found it," says another almost directly above me.

"What is it?"

"A live-streaming GoPro, kid. Look, he got the blinking red light all covered up. Hey there, Wong! We live?"

"What are they talking about?" I whisper. Bonnie is too far to hear.

"Hooo, is that a Sennheiser? A RODE? Whoops, red light's off."

"Remote stop?"

"So we definitely made the stream."

They're all laughing now.

I'm more than a bit confused. I begin to more loudly reiterate my question—I'm interrupted by the clearing of a throat and a figure stepping out from behind the cellar stairs.

I'm only mildly shocked. Truthfully I expected a boogeyman to be down here with us, but here is just a young man with a vaguely familiar face. Meanwhile my Republican rival stifles a high-pitched gasp, loud enough for the excessively bulky man to put a finger to his meaty lips—loud enough for the footsteps above us to stop.

Emails. The guy's bespectacled face is from my emails. Recent ones. He reaches up to the closed doors, latches them locked from the inside. Athletic build straining his self-branded WONG'S RIGHTS shirt, he bounds down towards us.

"I know you," I say.

"Nah, you know of me. Y'all wanna get outta here?" He smiles: Adult braces.

"Arnold Wong?" Bonnie has finally come around.

"From Seattle," Bonnie and I say in unison. Wong nods.

"Y'all both had interviews scheduled with me," he says, beaming, then he scrambles his arms and shakes his head, one frantic *Undo* button. "*Have.* Of course. Err—I came in this way."

Arnold Wong of Wong's Rights Podcast squeezes past us and shines a much brighter handheld light; I see the slopes in the concrete walls and ceilings. Tubular. An emergency drain. The commotion of upstairs acolytes fades as we descend.

"I heard y'all got an advanced look at the article that just dropped," the young broadcaster tries as we wind a wet, shadowy turn. His cartoonish biceps, too large to be natural, flex as he adjusts his glasses. I try hard to remember those damned emails.

"You made a video about lab leak deniers."

"That's right, Councilmember Gershwin! 'Exit stage Left.' That put me on the map."

"Just tell me how you knew we'd be here, Wong," Bonnie cuts in.

"Well I didn't know y'all'd come down where I was posted up, if that's what you're asking!" Wong chuckles.

"That is not what I'm asking."

A *clang* resounds all the way from the storm door, echoing abrasively enough to jolt. The uncounted crowd from the satellite plant are banging on it.

"Oh, well, y'know, I was clubbing in Q when a friend sent me the article and address."

"Aren't you 20?" Bonnie asks, arms crossed over her red/black jogging wear.

"Which would make you a divorced cougar," Wong responds.

"How 'bout you not," she snipes while I try to defuse. Divorced?

"Who's your friend?" My impatience quiets them. I'm typically good at restraining my tone, so this mannered outburst gets them to listen. "Who tipped you off about this? About us?"

The young podcaster readjusts his thick-framed glasses. His steroid-muscle silhouette is like a caricature. I am surrounded by garish caricatures. "A journalist never reveals sources, bro."

"So you don't know."

"What I know is you, Councilmember Gershwin, sat down with TLI execs in my freakin' hometown and agreed to support a private prison for kids." A breathtaking mischaracterization. Wong tries for a standoff now, several inches shorter than me. His squiggly neck veins are popping.

And at first I think that the six-legged, sickly-red bug with black lines checkering its sides, clutched onto his neck, is a tattoo. But then it crawls.

"And partly on Native American land!" Wong is saying. He takes my backing away as me backing down, gloats.

"Wong, there's a—"

But Bonnie raises a hand, locks eyes with me and shakes her head. "Arnold, you know I've expressed admiration for your journalistic integrity.

I frankly don't know why I'm here, who wrote this article, or what's actually going on. Is the exit close?" She's talking like he doesn't have a spindly monster slowly scaling his throat. She's talking like . . .

"Why are you talking like you're being recorded, Bonnie?"

"Because he's recording us, Quinn. Look at his glasses."

The kid angles away. "Uhh," he stutters. "Exit. Right. It's deadass just over —"

Then he flinches; the grotesquely large bug shudders before he brushes it off. His hand stays over the bite, applying pressure so hard his knuckles go white.

"*Ow,*" he says.

# 13

# VADA IKEBE'S SIMULATION

I dial Amy's number immediately.

Four hollow rings and then a disembodied voicemail from my unconscious best friend, cheery and confident.

I remember that feeling of being watched at Providence Hospital. My duplex is surrounded by nice enough neighbors, warming air, a view almost to the town center—and suddenly every inch, far and near, even the air itself has turned into that constricting curtain in Amy's hissing hospital corner. The lurking presence behind it has snaked its way into my reality.

Is it reality? Am I dreaming? No quicker after screenshotting the text from "Amy" do I get another one.

**ur gonna delete that screenshot.**

"Hello? Hello?" The nurse from Amy's floor repeats himself twice before I realize I've called the hospital.

"Hey, it's Vada Ikebe—Vada Pratt, whichever shows up." With leaden limbs I pull myself indoors. Dad's keys and shoes aren't here. "Um. Calling about Amy Deadwyler in your ICU."

"Oh, yes, hi. You were back this morning, weren't you? The nurse right next to me just re-upped her fluids."

". . . So she's still there?

"Err . . . The nurse, or the comatose patient, Miss?"

"Amy," I gulp. The house is soundless. My red arowana fish's soft thumps and water sloshes against his glass amplify the thundering of my heart.

"Well, yes, she's still here."

"Right, right. Check her phone. Could you check for her phone please?"

"Uh."

"I don't know, it's doing something weird." I desperately need this man to check this phone.

"Sure . . . ?"

"All right, I'll stay on the line."

"—You mean now. Okay, well, hold one moment."

Some watered-down Sabrina Carpenter Muzak fills my speaker as two more pulses herald another dreadful text.

**tell anyone at all about me, and i will never wake up.**

I fight the impulse to toss it at the wall as if it's acidified. "Who the," my new nails stab my screen, "who the fuck are you?"

Before I can hit send there's a response.

**just ur best friend.**

"Hello? Ma'am? Vada?" The nurse returns.

"Yeah," I all but scream.

"Usually we keep patients' phones inside their drawer. I'm not . . . seeing it here."

"Okay someone stole it. Can you check the cameras?" *Buzz buzz*. I might throw up. "Check the cameras and I'll call back." I disconnect.

**remember what i said, Vada.**

"What do you mean you'll never wake up," I text. "What'll you do to her?"

Whoever has the phone reacts to my text with a stupid little drooling face emoji. Nothing more. Furiously I close banner notifications from *Reify*'s Discord chat. "This is no ducking joke," no need to battle autocorrect, "return this phone NOW or you'll be behind bars by sunset."

**why? bc daddy's a cop? heyyy do u know where ol pork belly is?**

The inner voice that usually urges me to *calm down* is stunned speechless. "Pork Belly" is how Amy and I have referred to my dad since Summer Camp 2020. And Amy's phone doesn't stop there. Whoever is on the other end shares a link—to *Reify*'s Discord chat.

**no more training wheels. tell no one, girl.**

For whatever good it'll do, I've locked myself in my room. I shutter my window. My jaw is clamped shut, clamped hard. My desktop's not right. Someone touched it. I go cold.

Dad knows not to fuck with it. Least of all the VR headset, which I know beyond a shadow of a doubt that I docked before sprinting over to Elonia. It's turned around on my chair, the wristlet peripherals splayed out on either side, like it has gained autonomy, inviting me.

The thief's link is not just to the Discord but to a specific message within. An image. A portion of an article shared by Oh Taek-su. Oh God, the local politician scandal thing again.

*Years ago, an employee of Twice Loved Institute made unsubstantiated allegations that their residential treatment centers regularly used its children as free labor under the guise of a 'job training game' performed in virtual reality.*

Amy has been in a coma for 10 days. She is still in all of our group chats, and as assistant narrative lead on *Reify*, she messaged often before she started swiping her stepmother's pills. I'm only reminded of this because I see her profile icon flash a momentary *Like* on the image—and then instantly vanish.

I launch into a frenzy. Scour for the TLI employee's ghastly testimony while I run the Institute's website and socials. Search local papers and come up empty as a sliver of afternoon sunlight peaks through my closed shutters and casts a glare on my OLED monitor.

TLI's youth outreach, their field days . . . their residential treatment centers. Centers which draw a Southeastward-sloping belt scraping Nevada, 16 in total. The closest is 40 minutes, in Vail, Oregon.

Tumalo, Washington is the fifth notch on the belt. That's the place I find the referenced story in the local paper's digital archives.

Now I'm half reading, half unearthing recordings from my time in the decrepit YewVerse. The plucked article is just three paragraphs, sickly-thin newspaper paragraphs at that. A furtive story told in a bar with corroboration that the storyteller was in fact an employee, and the reason it made the paper was that the man stole money before resigning. I keyword through the entire subsequent year. There is nothing more.

But here are those 6 legless child avatars on my logs, moving repetitively and in clear sync. Encrypting digital assets? Dumping files or corrupting code two tech-generations old and frequented less than SeaWorld? Paid jobs in virtual spaces aren't uncommon recently. The Nebraskan slaughterhouses' and Tyson's vast child labor law abuses at the turn of the decade aren't a new thing either.

I plunge into the ugly salmon-orange YewVerse.

Past the Mima Mounds again and under the skybox. The poorly-concealed play space is there and the smiling, legless children aren't. Come to think of it, I've only seen them on weekends. Making their absence all the stranger.

I drift to a large mirrored surface and, equipping my pen tool, write,

"Vail, OR?

Tumalo, WA?"

But when I finish with the latter the former disappears.

The entire world blinks white and I see through the ground. Falling. I'm deposited outside the play space. The false skybox touchdown is now an impassable solid.

Three real-life raps on the door jolt me from my headset; lifting it, its padding leaves an outline of cold sweat on my face. The knocks on my duplex door are quick, impatient, loud enough to hear from my room.

I lean out into the hallway. My eye itches. I want to call out but there's no shaking the feeling that someone, something, awaits one false move on my part, poised to pounce. Then I see the time on my kitchen-hallway wall. 3:16 P.M.

"Oh Taek-su?" I try.

"Even better. Rundee," states my muffled front door. I rip it open. "He did want to come up and get you, but we're sorta parked illegally and you . . . are not ready at all, are you?"

"Get your camera up," I manage. "Take a picture of these messages, Rundee. Please."

I thrust out my phone and he, baby-face full concern, positions his variable lens. "Wait. Just that?"

I look down. The exchange with Amy's phone yields only one message: mine. "No ducking joke." The thief wiped it all.

Below my front porch Taek-su's hatchback idles on the street, everyone else vibing inside. With admirably minimal grousing Rundee packs up my tech while I speed-run a wash-up. I stare so long into the mirror that I hardly recognize me.

When I was a kid I'd experience what's called *Alice in Wonderland* syndrome, probably from my anophthalmic migraines. Shapes and sizes would go so wonky that I'd cry. I'd desperately try to stop derealizing. Mom always hugged me to her, helped. I think the last time was when I was like 7; the sensations I'm fighting today, they're scarily familiar.

I remember very little of my mother's language but I whisper *sk'wuy* for protection as I lock my duplex. I hardly view it as my home but part of me wants to just sleep for the rest of the day, sleep through every impending big moment, shake this dream-nightmare.

"You okay, Vada?" Rundee asks on the way down the steep front stairs.

I nod. "How 'bout you? *Reify*'s hours from going live."

He sighs. "What will be will be, y'know."

We head out. Taek-su keeps uncharacteristically quiet. I feel a kind of kinsmanship here: both of us lost in our thoughts as we cross Liltin Yew's border. I do my eye drops, open my messages, check my erased conversation with *Amy*.

Only to see *Amy is typing* . . . for barely a Mississippi second before disappearing.

*Her phone*. It's been hours since my last call to Providence. I sigh in relief when the same nurse answers me now. "Hey, uh." I angle into the window, lower my voice. "I called about a lost phone earlier. Any word on that?"

"Right. Well, Miss Pratt—er, Miss Ikebe, it's proving hard to pinpoint. Lots of people wear facemasks around here. You tried Find My Phone, I take it?"

I'm not quite sure what I mumble as I hang up. Kristen and Rundee haven't noticed.

Taek-su is staring at me in his rearview. That's uncharacteristic too. And it's not playful. It's searching, serious. It's confused.

Twenty minutes later the hatchback parks in front of Daniel "SalishUs" Deadwyler's address, a little red-brick apartment overlooking the windswept bay. Blackout curtains give away the gamer couple's unit. Rundee and Kristen compliment Taek-su's driving.

He pulls lightly at my sweater as I pass. "Do you have a sec?"

He's suspended my rhythm again, even in spite of everything else today is bringing. I look up into him; too embarrassed to hold his eyes, I fall to his Adam's apple and realize that's actually worse.

He doesn't seem to notice. "This'll sound . . . severely strange. I know you've barely been on it today, but did you notice anything strange in our Discord earlier?"

My mouth drops. The phone thief's explicit instructions: *tell no one.* "I—like what?"

He shakes his head. "It was luck that I even caught it. But an image I shared, from the whole TLI thing. For a second it said someone Liked it . . ." Rubbing his eyes, he looks out to the glittering bay. "Nothing. I don't think I saw what I thought I saw."

"Oh." I feel as if I'm about to cry from sheer helplessness. He unlocks his hand-me-down Subaru's trunk, gathers some of our bags. My opportunity's almost gone. I blurt out, "What'd you think you saw?"

Immediately my phone pulses twice.

He says her name I'm sure, but I can't hear it. Can't even hear the bay. I hear only a staggered exhalation caught in my throat, stopping my breath. I chance one quick glance at my lock screen.

**u really shouldn't be this comfortable in gray areas, Vada.**

"Who were you talking to in my car earlier, Vay?"

How could Amy's thief even know what we're talking about right now? Am I bugged?

**dream logic, remember?**

"The fuck." I actually drop my phone. Can't bug someone's brain.

Taek-su's confusion borders on alarm. "Vay?"

A dial tone and heavy unlatching come from SalishUs' apartment complex lobby. Daniel's girlfriend must have buzzed us in. Kristen and Rundee wave us over.

Amy's messages delete themselves as they go: they've been set to a 10-second timer. "Huh?" I say. "Ah, I was just talking to my pharmacist. My meds. You know, um, that's really weird about Amy. Sounds . . . I mean, sounds impossible, man."

I can feel Taek-su receding into himself. "No, I know. Yeah."

I strap the rest of the tech bags to myself and waddle behind his sullen form into the dingy apartment hallway. Partly out of guilt, partly because the weight anchors me to the earth. Sometimes, when I'm dreaming, I'll float up and into a whole other dream entirely.

And I'm definitely dreaming right now. There's no mistaking, there's no other explanation. I am in a dream.

Haven't had one this vivid in ages. It's exciting. Must be because of my all-nighter. It's not great so far but it's building to something. It's certainly not horrible. But in my (short) lived experience, awareness of a dream state will send it toppling around me. So I focus not on my state of consciousness, but instead on the thundering of videogame gunfire, metalcore, and stomping that shakes the apartment.

—

Katyusha, known online as OMGrozny, has an earmuffed infant who clings to a playpen's struts out of camera view. Katyusha streams herself attempting a first-person survival-horror with a dancepad. She's doing really well, unsurprisingly.

"Ладно, прыгай. Прыгай, ублюдок. Альтернативный огонь." Sweating through her tank, she leaps back and forth with pronounced violence. "Ребята, я не пройду мимо этого. Нет, это невозможно. Вертеться как уж на сковородке."

She notices us in her doorway. Katyusha stares long at my face before jutting a manicured finger at my acrylic eye, says, "hard," and flicks her orange hair unstuck from a side-buzzed temple. "пять сек."

Stepping away from her 3,400-odd viewers, Kat pauses everything to throw a towel over her slick torso, then cradles her earmuffed baby against it.

"Welcome. Daniel leave note for me to give. Uh, water?"

Rundee and Kristen nod reverently.

"Me too." Kat launches an expedition into her kitchen.

What would real-life Vada Ikebe do if this weren't a dream? I mean, this *is* real-life Vada Ikebe's dream. I would fight, that's what I would do. Rage against those trying to pull me down. Taek-su sets his heavy bags in the RGB-lit living room, his aura morose.

"I'm not saying I don't believe you." He may be a little lanky but his shoulder feels sculpted, surprisingly hard, as my hand settles on it. Eyes wide, he flushes. "The Discord thing. Text her stepbrother! If they're on the same plan he can Find My Phone."

He releases the strap of his last bag, straightens. A flame reignites in his eyes. "I know it's ridiculous . . . Can I have his number?"

I say "of course" in flawless Korean and he tilts his head, guffaws at the personality swerve. I want the fun Taek-su. I'm ready for Amy's text this time.


**overconfidence is a slow and insidious killer.**


"Doing quotes now?" I put my palm over my phone and whisper. "This is me playing by your rules. Quote that, bitch."


**u just chose ur own adventure.**

I instruct whatever part of my subconscious dreamed up such a phantom, "Fuck you."

"Ah. Here is note." Her baby clubbing her face, Katyusha stretches to hand a folded paper to Taek-su before finishing an entire water bottle in three gulps. "Don't make too at home, yeah?"

Its scrawled writing I can identify from the past week-and-change of witnessing Daniel sign all sorts of medical forms on my comatose best friend's behalf. Taek-su's brow creases deeply as he reads. Then he holds the note up to Kat, clears his throat. I forgive his shyness; she's gorgeous. "What is this?"

"Address of streaming tonight. Daniel get new sponsorship in morning."

"Uh huh. Uh huh." He looks around the room, face blank.

"What, dude?" say Kristen and Rundee as one.

"Anyone happen to give SalishUs a sneak peek of our game?"

We all shake our heads but I can guess as to where, quite literally, this is going.

All the information I ever really shared with Daniel in the ICU was from the technical side of *Reify*: its clean TAAU upsampling; its node-based geometry; the novel ways in which we calibrated movement and combat. I never told him where our game is set. I never told him the real-life location we ransacked a dozen different times for 3D scans and reference media.

"... It's you and Amy's shady-ass old summer camp," Taek-su utters in disbelief.

"Well. Um, that's a little devious." I say this with as much neutrality, as little excitement as humanly possible.

# 14

# ALCOHOLIC GETS IT

I'm starting to think it wasn't a great idea to ditch our RideShare.

"We're so lucky we ditched the RideShare. Public transpo's anonymous." Gabby grips the bus railing as if wringing a neck. "Support your local infrastructure. Never do ride apps. That's how the fascists track 'dividuals' like ourselves. Then they know when we're going to call a ride and where. Do you really think every driver who picks you up is a private citizen?"

Years of experience manning protests alongside some particularly passionate folk, I hold my tongue and wait for him to get it all out.

"Who was that chasing us, Gabby?" I say over an animated family in the back. "You know him? George?"

"Not until this morning." His stare grips me.

"In the psych ward—uh, in the mental health . . .?"

"The waiting room. I was there a while and he sat right across from me." I can tell by the slow shift of his irises that I'm swaying. "He said he's a siren swept from the tides of time. He was like, 'I've been in the same day for sixty years,' and he was keeping track and had an inner calendar and today was some kind of anniversary and so he flew down here to wear his person costume. Did you know sirens started out as bird-people?"

"A siren, huh. A bird siren."

"Yeah! Yes. Why, that mean something to you?" He does not blink.

I hold up my half-full bottle. "That's just what's on the label of my favorite gin. He gave it to me outside your trailer p—your neighborhood this morning."

Gabby pinches and drags along his forehead. "I can't parse it."

"Simple: sirens all the way down. Ya hungry?" I unscrew my siren-bequeathed siren gin. "You could go for a bite. I can go for a bite."

"But George is probably following us!"

"Then he won't be the worst guy I've lain the fuck out. Sooner the better. Best not run for long, it gives people the chance to flank you." Speaking of flanks, I go for a sip, and the image of Arturo in his trailer's kitchen carelessly with the beer cold cocks me. "I'm . . . sorry. I been drinkin' this in front of you the whole time. That's not cool. I . . . shit."

Gabby shakes his head, blinks just once but it is long and hard, like a tic. "Alcohol disgusts me, man."

"Heh. Same here." I swill and shudder.

"Arturo did say once you're in the program. No AA, God-bothering, abusive stuff. Just some program, for AUD."

Well that was certainly a dramatic descriptor. *Another atheist Latino, noted.* "Yeah, well. Y'know. It's nice he actually told someone about me, and, uh, it's funny that's what he told you about me."

Elonia is a rustic boardgame cafe, deceptively large on the inside, with bagels and boba. I pay for everything plus some branded hats for disguise and we sit on stools by the window. Gabby gets extra sugar, scans the streets.

In the hospital I'd doubted he'd divulge Vasquez family history unless I applied some serious finesse. But I'm relieved. He's no Arturo. While Gabby may look like a lanky dog braced for a kick, his mouth's loose. There's a lot he wants to say.

"So, you and Arturo close?" I open as softly as possible.

That halts his scanning. "He sent you to pick me up. That should tell you all you need."

"That's why we had a whole fight. I mean I'm sure you can tell we fought. That's why . . ." I think I'm underestimating how much I drank. Rusty. I sneak a bit into my boba. "But honestly it was already decided. I was half lookin' forward to it when I woke up." I massage my brow. "I thought by announcing me to his pathetic high school friends, it could be this li'l victory for him, and I'd have one Negroni to join that. As an apéritif. To commemorate. Like for *me*, just one. And for *him*, to show him I could be normal. To add to the . . . triumph."

"You wanted to drink." His attention phases back to the town.

"Well. Everyone drank at his li'l Christofascist party last night, I didn't say shit."

I can tell I earn some points. I get a half-smile. "You gotta. See something say something. Don't ask don't tell." He speaks around his straw. "You wanted to transcend your addiction but you're an addict! It's not slaying a dragon, it's keeping it at the gates." He gets a brain freeze.

"Heh. Dragon . . . or siren."

"We're done saying that word."

I laugh and sip my boba and almost throw up.

We make the next bus. I get blurry. "Gets, you're leaking," I hear him say. I check face and crotch before seeing that my George Bottle is not exactly secure. Warm, clear liquid runs down my hand onto the metal floor. "Yo."

—

We must be here. Gabby motions me to stand and leads me out to a wide-open, windswept road. I spot a cliff edge; I have to see the view. Have to see how high up we are.

The water far below plateaus in the shape of a teardrop: We are on the deepest carve of a bight. Lots of bights in Europe, not many here. "Thought you said we were going home," I say. I'm rendered mute in the gale. There goes my Elonia hat.

I really was fine without a literalization of my morning's cliff-related musings. I really could have gone without this today.

Over 15 years ago at my local sortation warehouse one of my employees was this kid with a goatee named Nick. He was 22 at the time and older than me. Chronically late, full of excuses, and otherwise quiet. I had to lodge a complaint with my floor supervisor to protect the 2B3 team and my slightly elevated position above them. The old kid kept showing late, unfired—I was never told why. Instead of checking on Nick, I theorized with my other employees. Snickered softly, signaled tacit approval, then said not to make light, that he was a real issue going unaddressed.

One 12-hour evening he didn't return from his 30-minute break, causing us six hours of unmitigated stress and quota shortfall. Dental records nailed him in a compacted pickup at the bottom of a cliff. I wouldn't know until next shift. When I first saw Nick's Facebook obit he was unfamiliar to me: He was smiling.

Gabby makes me turn and walk inland.

We ascend a slope of knotted grass. Massive clouds soar over us like they're pulled along an invisible conveyer belt.

"It's why I ditched the RideShare. This leads home, but there's a stop along the way I have to make." Gabby's wiry frame appears more eased in the sun.

"What we stoppin' for?"

"Personal effects."

I shoot him a look. "Do they produce narcotic effects?"

"They—no, not those kind. It's just stuff. Money and things to sell."

"You going somewhere?" I pant.

"If I have enough scrap, yep! Alberta."

". . . Canada?"

He nods and picks up the pace.

At the outskirts of a forest two minutes later lay the overgrown remains of a small scrapyard and burn pit, mostly piles of crumbled rust.

But a white-painted school bus from the 1990's stands intact, facing out toward the bay, a gleaming sentry against 100-foot-tall evergreens, inexplicably free of graffiti. I hear seagulls cry around me.

Pretty quickly, I get it. "You come here a lot."

"More when I was a kid." Gabby approaches the old doorless entry, out of which some weeds spring. "Arturo said I basically lived here! I can't really remember far back anymore, though."

I feel the specter of the sortation warehouse. "Doesn't sound all bad to be honest."

Gabby climbs aboard. "I guess it depends on what you remember."

I hesitate at boarding, decide against. I've spilled most of my goddamn gin. Just a little sip—the regrettable boba concoction soured an immediate want for more, anyway.

"But this place," Gabby continues, emerging with a dirty metal box, "is good. This place I'll miss."

"You got a reason for leaving? I mean, Arturo'd probably have some questions. And the people here, they probably don't want you to leave right away."

"'They.' Sinister use of that pronoun, Gets."

"Aw you're so funny."

"This hasn't been my home for longer than it has." He says this to his metal box.

"You better have some inflatable coats in there."

"Winterwear's in the trailer." Gabby clicks through a combination lock, first carefully and then insistently. "Hmm. Darnit."

I extricate multipurpose pliers from my rolled-up tech jacket and unfold a needle nose. Clipping the clamps' thin arms surprisingly reveals no heroin, fenty, or meth, but a stack of bills, a National Parks 2025-2026 membership, and about twenty plastic-encased trading cards ranging from baseball to Gen-1 Pokémon.

It occurs to me that Gabriel Vasquez is almost 40 years old.

"Have you entirely thought this through, man? I mean more power to you, but maybe tell Arturo first—"

"I'm leaving a letter I wrote two years ago." Gabby goes to pocket the contents but puts them back in the broken box and carries it up the hill. The evergreens accept him, their shadows snaking over his gaunt face. "You know Arturo. Goal-oriented. Pathologically mendacious. Bludgeoning audiences with his Trad-Queer Preacher grift."

I look back toward the bus. I can see far over the distant bight now and make out several boats on the water and in harbor. *Should save this spot to my Map,* I think agreeably.

"Now that's a bit much," I rejoin after tapping my phone. "He's just talking. Fillin' a li'l market niche. People get to feel seen."

"The wrong people. Christofascists. You don't think it's dangerous to normalize what they're doing? You don't believe indirect harm is harm?"

I shake my head in exasperation, realize too late that Gabby won't extrapolate exasperation as the motivator.

"It justifies atrocity, trust me!" His eyes bore through me again. "And I'm not just talking ICE. You know what my parents let happen to me? To us both?"

It's what I've been waiting for. Scrubbing a spiderweb with my hand, I prepare—and then I very much don't want it anymore. I knew this would cross some kind of Rubicon, banishment by Arturo forever, and frankly that didn't bother me an hour ago, the idea of shooting off a final cliff with no handholds to crawl up. But I've had enough of falling for the time being. This simply cannot be how I learn it.

"So, what, you're saying little bro just needs some therapy instead?" I clear my throat.

"So my youth minister molested me," Sing-songy, Gabby ignores me completely, cleaves my heart, "more than once, and when I told Mom and Dad, they said not to make shit up, but they at least pulled me from the program—"

"That's—sorry. Hey, I can't really hear this stuff right now, I'm not doin' too hot—"

"And it would've been fine left right there, I mean not *fine* but . . . But when Arturo gets old enough my parents say they're going to put *him* in the same program, okay? So, I freak out a little, I pay the youth minister a visit, I get a really good hit in. I mean *really* good. Arturo didn't know what happened 'till way after high school. Mom and Dad, though, they knew."

He expects me to say something. I'm perfectly okay continuing through the grove in silence. Waist-high fireweed is extremely common in the PNW. I sift it through my palms.

"Leaving is helping him," Gabby says definitively. "Always having to look after his big brother. Should be the other way around."

"Mm." I pluck a violet petal, crush its juices into the grooves of my fingerprints.

A few trailers are dimly visible in a clearing a quarter mile ahead, even the puff of smoke from the convenience store at which I chose today's turgid path.

"You probably want some water, right?"

I do, but returning to that trailer is not the vibe. "I'm gonna head back down to civilization, I think." I look sideways at Gabby. "Unless you'd rather have me around?"

"I'm good, *camarada*!" Gabby smiles. "I'm just gonna organize some stuff. Probably finish GTA. I see why Arturo loves you. You're a good person. Get some water, though."

I wince. "Thanks, brother. You . . ." I exhale. "I mean I'm sure you had plenty of time to think things over. Safe travels."

Unprompted, Gabby hugs me. "Maybe I'll stay the night! I'm sure I'll see you later." Some of the trading cards fall from his box. He gathers them.

"Okay." This is goodbye.

—

For a while I watch him wade through brush in his sandals. A lone egret unsticks itself from a high branch and with two beats of its wings retreats.

It's nice in these woods. Sweet oxidation. Quiet. Rich droves and matted layers of Douglas fir and hemlock obstruct the scantest spits of rainfall. But I'm no botanical expert. Liltin's crisp wind is generous. Drifting seeds smell like spearmint dyed with dirt. It's a good place to empty half my lunch from my stomach. When I'm done, I think a little clearer. I wander. My phone's not close to dead, I'll be okay.

Third call dumped to Arturo's voicemail. I sigh in frustration. I hear the crunch of brambles under heavy boots.

There are seven people in total. Some cover the lower half of their faces and carry bags that clatter. All are young. "You find anything, bud?" one asks me.

"What am I lookin' for?" I lose balance as I sink a foot into a decayed log.

"The town sideshow," the same one jeers helpfully.

"Um, I'm just out for a walk, really."

"You can help us look," says another.

"I'll need a more informed perspective first, y'all."

"They don't know, Braeden." One of the masked searchers pulls down their balaclava. "Our mayoral candidates are fighting to the death out here or running away or something. No one knows why but it's not AI."

I nod like I get it. "Wild, wild. Well, hope you find 'em."

There are shrugs as the group reach and pass me. "Better us than others, that's for sure."

"We ain't finding them. We're mad far from where the livestream dropped." Braeden? I think? Cracks a 12oz of Cutwater. 12.5% ABV.

"That's why we'll find 'em, Braeden. The crazies flush 'em out, they'll have no choice but to head downriver."

"Want one, unc?" Braeden hands the open can to me.

Overpowering the forest's spearmint, I smell lime. Slowly, I sigh.

"You have any water?" I push it back.

"Got a couple for ya. Catch. If you're not trying to run into Delulu Platoon out here, though, check the phone."

Delulu Platoon. That's good. "Okay, folks, I'll . . . do my own research." I chuckle at my own joke, but Braeden's funnier than me. "Happy hunting."

I chug a water bottle while they leave, crush and store it with the sealed one in my tech coat. Imagining George the Siren still sprinting after me somewhere, I feel a little foolish for not seeking safety in numbers. I mean, I could take him. But I don't know. I'm not sure what I'm doing here. I haven't been sure since the hospital.

I test the nearest log before I sit. I run a search for Liltin Yew local news. For a moment I scroll results.

The moment elongates before I can accept what I'm reading. I lean forward.

The State Department has just posted about Arturo Vasquez.

# 15

# NUMBERS-MAXXING ARTURO VASQUEZ

I need everything to slow down.

Thankfully, things seem to be doing just that. I'm brought lucid from my powder-induced reverie by Anne calling, "Arturo. Arturo." in succession, asking me what I want. That's quite the question. Then I ascertain that we're idling in a fast-food drive through. With every word of my response, I dump the word prior.

A smile takes progressive residence along her face the further we leave downtown. Tastefully distributed conifers and boulders on all sides, Anne pulls level to a stunted column, leans her whole body out the Raider, and punches a sequence into a keypad. We roll quietly through a covered gate that closes behind us.

"You know where we are," she says, parking the SUV. I decide to take her at her word for the moment. We get out and walk toward a house. Rounding the corner of the twin garage, I notice a basket of a few blue flowers. Then I gasp.

714 Percival Lane is a massive French Colonial on a lush estate built in the Roaring Twenties, both floors wrapped in vintage taupe split siding, two wide chimneys protruding from its west and east. I first saw it Orientation Day at Evergreen State. Dreams for wildlife biology freshly dashed, I admired the distant house and imagined its view of Mt. Rainier.

Resolved to own one just like it someday. But a nurse's wage proved it another misinformed resolution in a growing line, and the pandemic in Portland robbed me of all my medical ambition, thus driving me ultimately back here to reunite with my mess of a brother. I never sought the view again.

"The owners are in Tuscany," Anne explains. Together we cross a long, mossy walkway composed of the same brick as the driveway, making it to the French double doors. "They come back in . . . well, three days. For them."

I'm still not fully returned to my body. I am the immediate residue, the question marks following just behind my firing nerves. "Three days for them? So they're not . . . what'd you call us again? Time prisoners."

"The time hole swallowed Liltin and surrounding marshes. Imagine a small grain inside a 5D brick, a localized calcification from one superposited spatial-instant. That's us. Tuscany's way more beautiful. I've only been there a few hours at a time, though. Takes the majority of the day just getting there. Worth it, though, for the sights."

She procures keys from an untraceable when and where and we're through the front door, Anne disabling the alarm with a litheness.

Now that I'm fully fantasizing, I want to take Gets' hand and lead them into this two-story foyer that looks like it's wearing a sundress, to show *them* some place new for a change: glossy maple wooden floor and white stucco in every room, a panda marble pillar built into the kitchen island, and an inlaid bookshelf crowned with travel mugs next to the dining room's cushioned bench. I panic for a moment at the thought of tracking mud, see with relief that I've already removed my shoes.

"24-hour time loop, Arturo, remember? The mud would be gone anyway tomorrow. Like it never happened."

*Right. Sometimes it's like she'll read my mind.* I shut my eyes. My fingertips finally slide and curl exactly when and how I tell them; my toes flex against the hardwood through my socks. It smells like pine here. Just how I imagined. "Can I talk to my parents?"

I open my eyes and she's looking back at me with a shockingly sincere frown.

"No matter what you do today, they don't talk to you. They're done with both Gabriel and you, ever since he told you what really happened to him."

I nod.

She plucks a vibrator-looking remote from a regal coffee table and hits a button: A massive TV rises slowly from a slit in the living room's floor.

I resume my kitchen tour, inspecting the large sink closely, blinking stinging eyes. "What about Gets?"

"Well, after your quality time in the trailer Gets went ahead and somersaulted off the wagon."

I feel a part of me die a little. Maybe more than just one part.

"They're terrorizing the local underworld by now." She has dipped down a side hall with lower, vaulted ceilings. Her voice is made a choir. "You're lucky you're in a town of 34,000 people. There isn't a lot of serious damage they can cause. Hey, set up your streaming equipment."

I dislodge from the kitchen island to spot my tripod, camera, laptop, and stream deck bags all waiting by the coffee table in front of the fully risen, paper-thin TV.

"Surprised?" Anne calls. "Only took 80 seconds to pack up and fasten down while you were shaking all those veiny hands at Grace." Every piece of equipment is packed exactly how I pack it. "But don't sweat Gets, or Gabby while you're at it. Those ones you definitely couldn't have helped."

Why couldn't *she* have done anything? She knows everything that goes on today, after all, if she's to be believed. I free my tripod and extend its legs to match my height.

"My main focus today is *you*, Arturo. I got to you as soon as you'd allow me." There are clatters from the sun-drenched room at the end of the hall—

Anne is moving something. "If I cold-call you first thing in the morning, you think I'm crazy and avoid me. Worse yet, I could overload you."

"Overload me, huh." My frustration must be plain. I don't like that she can anticipate my thoughts from the next room over, no need to go off my expression or body language.

"In-deed, *ese*. What, you forget you passed out in my ride an hour ago? We got you to have a seizure once. Yeah, you died on your grimy fuckin' trailer floor."

I try to ground myself once more. My jaw, tightly clenched, resists.

A racket of rolling rubber wheels. Anne pushes an exercise machine into the living room, its wire looped from her shoulder to forearm. She's smiling innocently at me.

"So how does this work? With you seeming to read my mind?"

"Like I said, on other days you say it, so we've developed a kind of shorthand."

"You can hit the 'skip ahead' button." I grimace. Why is she saying *we*? "But how many times have you . . . tried *this* kind of day? You said you could break us free—"

"I said nothing of the sort. I said we can break each *other* free." She releases the machine; it slams hard onto the hardwood. It is a stepmill. With a whip of her unruly bob, Anne walks its wire toward my bags, plugs it into my 12-port power outlet. "And that's because in all of Liltin Yew, Arturo, I strongly believe you're the only one who can help pull it off. You have the most potential of anyone in this town. Stop standing around, help me with this."

She chuckles to herself when I muse over how bossy she is.

I position the tripod, attach the camera and angle it at the tall, sturdy stepmill. No doubt it cost thousands.

"Um. Okay, then your time loop—"

"*Our.*"

"Is it more *Lazarus Project, Palm Springs,* or *Edge of Tomorrow*?"

"*Groundhog Day,* you uncultured baby."

A glimmer of hope. "First of all, we're the same age. Or were, I guess. Second of all, do you mean it's *we just have to do some selfless deeds and restore our karma* type shit?"

She holds up a wire splitter for dramatic effect. "It's a two-pronged approach. You have to flood the time hole with your own energy. You need to pour all of yourself into it. So," she ties both wires together, "*positive* energy on one day, and *negative* energy on the other. Play it whichever order you want, but no matter where you start, the days have got to be one after the other. Overload the time hole, and the system as you experience it will short-circuit."

She connects my camera and stream deck. "That's what all this is," she continues matter-of-factly. "Whether you choose this day as your Trick-or-Treat or your Mischief Night, so to speak, our little livestream gets you up onto the largest stage possible. Your energy will be felt." Wickedly, she laughs at my raised eyebrows. "Trust. I'm about to push your get-famous button. You'll see! Couple hours, you'll be quoted by the President."

Again, I need everything to slow down. I gulp in air. "Well—but I was doing just fine today, Anne. I—I hit my subscriber goals. The reunion's coming up. Everything was on track until you came in with all of this."

I try not to picture Gets day-drinking in the unfamiliar town I'd dragged them to after 14 months of hard-fought sobriety. Dragged here under the promise that I was finally mature enough to be publicly honest with myself, that I could weather the ire of my audience, of the Liltin Yew Church-goers, a few of whom used to know my parents.

"Of course that's what you think, Arturo. Your awareness hasn't shaken the loop! You've had the same dream, the same goals of fame, money; somewhere out of this dump; of being respected, appreciated for the sacrifices, the pain you've endured. While for the past 23,280-odd days, you've woken up on that same broken futon with the bugs. And no future."

How many years are 23,000 days? School and residency cost me north of 1,400 and that was 4 years in all. I multiply, round up to 1,500 for cleaner numbers. It's over a proper generation . . . over two. I consider what that many decades on my futon would do to my back—truthfully, it's already done a number.

I wish I hadn't woken up to that random Instagram *Like*. Anxiety-wracked already, all it took was seeing my parents' horrendous, smiling faces. And Gabby's. Still ruining my day all this time later.

Anne watches expectantly, eyes still glittering, almost 90 years old if my math's right. "You're wondering if I already know which one you're gonna choose. It's a 50/50 choice, so no, I really don't. A million different little things outside of my control could've changed your mind on any given iteration of the loop. Hey, do you mind if I run a PredictAct ad on-stream? My original Anne has a brand partnership we can leverage."

"Yeah, let's just start this." I begin the stream.

I'm on Mile 26 of my 30-Mile Walk to Redemption Challenge. It's a bog-standard month-long initiative to promote fitness and forgiveness— through Christ, of course. Neither of those could ever be achieved on one's own, apparently.

They're popular streams. I wasn't planning on continuing until days after Liltin High's reunion, but the production value of this French Colonial and stepmill have swayed me. Plus, I need to move. There is a fire in me that outpaces even my usual restlessness.

Anne monitors the camera but doesn't touch it. Hers is a silent role.

"*Bienvenidos*," I say with an enormous smile. My phone buzzes in the stepmill's cup holder—my phone! When was the last time I even saw it? Quickly, I check for calls.

Nobody.

**Repeat after me :)**

Unknown number. I can puzzle it out, however: Anne winks over the equipment.

We start with game scores on Mile 26.3. Based on Anne's prompting I ask if anyone has kept up with the Men's World College Series. "Finals start today, right?" Then I give the final score and the broad strokes of how it'll go down.

Mile 27 I touch on my morning pulpit speech and say, "On the topic of Hell on Earth, in two hours Congress will deny a motion to reconvene on Monday and, in 4 hours 9 minutes, will by a margin of 243-178 uphold the repeal of 29 CFR Part 570.2."

Chatting while perpetually walking uphill winds me. I take a quick break. Anne keys me some coke off camera. I cannot believe I feared drugs mere hours ago, certain that if I tried any I'd wind up, like Gabriel, spiraling into innate, violent psychosis. No. Genetics aren't everything. I am the next iteration. The upgrade.

She hands me a sealed envelope. "Open this when I say." She slaps me on the shoulder.

Mile 27.4. "Though the oarfish is a cosmopolitan species, it's extremely rare to see one above 600 ft depth, let alone close to shore. Residents of Puerto Vallarta, check out Magico, namely 20.65259, -105.25028 at 1:32 P.M. to glance not just one, but two!"

The enormous TV behind me screens a POV hiking video, a reverse view. Eyeballs on my stream accumulate. Lo-fi Christian tunes play softly.

We get into the heavy hitters. I inform the camera that I leaked an article about mayoral candidates Quinn Gershwin and Bonnie Cossio, whoever they are. 2,000 plus and counting concurrent viewers. I'm whistleblowing on ICE raids that haven't happened yet. My base is losing their minds.

A notion sprouts: I really don't care about my base. I mean, obviously not, but now I find myself actively, consciously, not caring. It starts to horseshoe. I'm starting to like watching them squirm.

Mile 28.1. I'm no Sisyphus. I can't go on much longer. Anne prompts me to pick up the envelope. "Okay, *mi familia*, I know you have plenty of questions in the chat. All I can say just yet is that my Walk to Redemption is no joke. Let Christ in, and He works through you. It's time for the grand finale."

Sweat drips onto the envelope as I tear the top off. I open the generic card, read it, and my saintly composure breaks for just a moment. I disguise my laugh as a coughing fit.

"God bless our troops. US CENTCOM forces are readying for strikes on Iranian nuclear facilities Fordow, Natanz, and Isfahan. Codename Midnight Hammer."

I sign off with the promise of more streams, more predictions, and one wild high school reunion. I've gained hundreds of subscribers.

"You'll want to be careful around that phone, now," Anne chuckles. "CIA's about to backdoor in, try to find how you got TS/SCI access."

"Well, I won't be here tomorrow, will I? Let 'em." I turn off my camera and begin breaking down the setup.

"Going somewhere, Mr. Preacher?" She surveys me like a meal. Lets the silence lengthen.

I nod. "Mischief Night it is." Her stare turns analytical; I pack my tripod. My legs burn pleasantly. "I'd explain why, but you already know what I'm gonna say, don't you?"

"Well, *you* don't fully. Talk it through, it'll help."

*Thanks so much for the permission.* "It has to be a bad day. A good day would involve Gets. Maybe even Gabby, I don't know."

"I mean, I know ways you can make it up to them by nightfall. We can quite literally throw a party right here with celebrity guests flown in. You're very welcome, by the way."

"I just don't think a perfect day would start with me pushing anyone away," I admit.

Anne nods at the floor, then goes to the kitchen. She returns with food—and not just any food, but my favorite trashy Tex-Mex drive-through. She must have memorized every word I likely forgot to say back at the window: Shrimp Diablo, cotija, habanero pepper sliced lengthwise.

Sauce dribbles and runs across the expensive kitchen island. "Don't be afraid to go dark with it," she says between mouthfuls. "Everyone'll be here tomorrow. They'll feel it today, like you felt that seizure I gave you. But do *you* know what a seizure feels like? No? See? Never actually happened. I think it happened to the *you* in my mind, if we're being honest."

"Whatchu mean?" It's hot. "Like everyone in the time hole's consciousness is in some kind of holding—?"

"Until activated, yeah." Anne chugs mineral water from the French Colonial's closet-sized fridge. "It's like constructs in here until they're chosen. Just the same day repeating over and over without 'em realizing. Empty pincushions. You'll make it up to them on the Good Day. Like, repentance. In my opinion, you chose the right order, Arturo. This is why I chose *you*." She wipes her face with her entire forearm. "Whether you grasp it or not, you see through the systemic bullshit."

I still have far too much energy. From the wall-length window I can see Mt. Rainier, as I'd hypothesized a decade ago. I'm on its peak, the Aurora swirling around me, pounding against me. My knee bounces. I want to make my audience squirm. My phone is in my pocket.

"Our high school reunion tonight," I say. "I'm getting a few ideas. Like a . . . presentation, so to speak. Done in old 2007 PowerPoint."

*My phone is in my pocket.*

She is responding, but from nowhere an invisible vise grips me. The shaking of my knee becomes the shaking of my core but I can't shake the vise; sitting here, it's about to crush me.

I'm scared, I realize as I throw open the front French doors, scramble down the brick driveway in my socks and leap over the gate to Percival Lane: I'm fucking terrified.

# 16

# OUR SYSTEM LACKS VERSTEHEN

In our time hole's overture we daytrip down the West Coast to CalTech.

Fables of sealed documents containing Feynman's more outlandish theories fill our heads. Outlandish, dangerous. They are real, but that is a discovery that takes us the better part of 8 months to confirm.

Next 22 months are recon. At SeaTac we clock the earliest private jet we can con our way onto or, once we've learned flight, to commandeer. We virtually attend weekend lectures (it's Saturday, after all) across the globe, test each other until we have a cursory grasp on evolving theoretical physics. We map all applicable CalTech faculty/staff routines and interior lives.

Predating the stutters in our dawn, this dark academia era grips us around the time that we start trying on suicides. Doesn't matter if our George or Anne half goes through with it first—we've both been curious about this "final" rule, and at this frozen point, we're trying to leave anyway we can. Ages later, we allow ourselves the decency of forgetting who kicked it off. What, too raw of a memory to forget? Time heals all wounds, pal.

And eventually time equates the prospect of a voluntary death to the prospect of grabbing Dutch Bros down the road. Suicide's just riffing if we wake up the next day. We're infinitely pain-tolerant when we know in seconds all we'll feel is half hungover. It even gets academic in itself: we didn't know we could feel in *that* way, or that way, or *that* . . .

Is it falling in love if it's trauma-bonding? Is cold obligation all that motivates the last woman and man on Earth to procreate? Given the parameters is *any* of it, any of it at all, honest? Would we accept one another—every major action that led us to Liltin Yew, Washington—if there were anyone else to accept?

We didn't even fuck on that original night with the booze cruise. Just stargazed and confided and kissed and slept. Maybe we should've. Who knows where it could've made us go next? We begin to meet more regularly. Doesn't feel so much like obligation anymore. Our old he-half's firing from his dev job the week after helping finish a Game of the Year contender; our old she-half's massive credit card debt (of which 70% is from her mom's familial identity theft)—they have never been who we are to each other, and they certainly aren't who we can be to ourselves, not now.

Because there's no *now* here. Or there's *only now*; to us these distinctions mean nothing.

The simple fact remains that we are the only ones who know the other's history.

Amidst the seemingly impossible campaign to win a glimpse at Feynman's sealed documents from our CalTech friends (to which we're utter strangers), our first involuntary death and subsequent glimpse of the stuttering dawn instead of the afterlife—that is imbued with enough weight to be spiritual.

Will that shared glimpse of the USO's living insides be more readable, or vary, if our bodies and minds are radically different in the lead-up? Might we get longer glimpses? We poke, we prod. We limit each other's oxygen. We shoot up. We slice. Stab. Drown. Burn. Maim one another. Strum each other's nerves like guitar strings, snip tendons. Still spiritual.

The electrifying stutter between the dawns will not be held still. No secrets dislodge from this. And there is no high to chase when the high is a cipher that always cuts short.

Yes, we lose track of just how long we grind suicide. We do not yet know what spirit we are channeling. Throughout, however, we are more glad to have one another than we can express.

Just in case, we express it every way possible. We learn many new ways.

Fourth old stolen car set to neutral and perusing the underbrush, our male half sets up the outdoor generator and mosquito-netted streamer tent at Vada and Amy's overgrown summer camp. On the knife's edge of summer solstice spiderwebs are millions of interwoven silken threads, draped thickly as a town at the turn of the 20th might have draped its power lines; on these lines crackle an aurora-like rainbow, reflecting the post-solar noon.

—

A miniature lattice. In spite of this anniversary's continued proximity to embarrassing failure, we're comforted. If we've truly fucked Operation T-Pose, we'll just own up to our she-half and we'll both eventually move on. What's the other option?

Daniel Deadwyler approaches the perimeter lugging his equipment. We gesture broadly around us. "SalishUs, this setup enough for ya?"

He carefully sets everything down, surveys the LED lights strung between the wooden camping barracks, the smoke machines under the picnic tables. "Yeah, man. It's great! So. What is this, who are you, wh—" He flinches at an echoing *crunch*. "Eyy. What was that?"

"My burner car," our George-half offers.

Daniel's eyebrow jolts and he gives us a theatrical once-over. "You're not actually one of Councilmember Gershwin's guys, huh?"

"Nah. It's his dirty money, but not his show. Have you heard about who leaked the exposé on him and Cunt Cossio?"

"Yah, boi! Only my favorite local streamer! That . . ." He stares slack jawed. Expectant.

"Viva la Vasquez, hombre."

"Holy *shit!*" He punches the sky. "I knew it—well I didn't, but I *wanted* it! Are you memeing? You're not memeing?"

The ultrasonic LVN and compressors at the prepper's should be capping centrifugation about now. It's time to slash some tires at the precinct, return to Liltin High's remodeled gym, and fucking search for Gets more. "Vasquez and I are deadly serious," we say, grinning.

We assure Daniel not to worry about Oh Taek-su's text concerning his stepsister's stolen phone, and invisibly we slip that stolen phone into his laptop bag (no need for her hardware when we're in her cloud) as he dials what we claim to be Arturo's number.

The real Arturo Vasquez, not the one Daniel is calling, has fled far enough away from the estates that he feels as exposed as he is winded. Through the stupor he remembers the number of eyeballs on his latest stream.

On cue, in rolls Officer Thaxton Pratt, thinking he's spotted enough leverage to wiggle out from under the blackmail. Staring down red and blue lights, Arturo's fears of endangerment are now coming to fruition. How very lucky, then, that the Anne of us drifts our Raider around the corner, does a full doughnut inches from Pratt, stares him down, and denies his curly-tailed, truffle-trifling ass with a closed-eyed wave.

Is Arturo ever glad to see us.

Our Voice Bot's AI Vasquez clone tells Daniel "SalishUs" Deadwyler everything that he wants to hear. Cryptically it tells him that a hidden USB thumb drive will play an important role tonight; that once he finds it, it must be delivered immediately to Liltin High's 15-year reunion. It explicitly enlists him in The Cause. "It's chaos, isn't it?" Daniel asks the bot ecstatically.

"Oh, it's chaos."

As AI-ordered, he gives us his pickup; we're off to feed Chaos some more.

"Get your steps in?" we ask the real Arturo.

"Fuck off, Anne. You making me your hostage?"

"I'm helping *you* broaden your reach! Could you not run? You don't normally do that." He does. He always does that. But he must believe he has agency. "But maybe it's good you did. You see firsthand fame comes with haters. In case you've forgotten how the law treats Hispanic folk foiling ICE raids, leaking military maneuvers real-time."

"Haters I can deal with." The man who hates himself harder than any of them buckles into our passenger seat. Brain molded heavily Catholic, eternally convinced his magical thinking grasps an underlying truth, Arturo is predisposed to filling himself into any and all gaps. He's not just one threat to consider—he's all and none of them. "Haters are my fuel." He can be more honest than he realizes.

We lead him into Firwood Manor apartments.

Something new happens when he sees the dead prepper's unzipped body.

Nurses see and smell some particularly foul death. No matter how often he may fantasize about murders, though, he's never seen a murder victim dead on the spot. The freshness (~90-120 minutes) and aggression of our kill will quickly absolve us of suspicion in his mind. Anyway, he stifles a shout and he bounds for the hallway behind him—or he is supposed to.

This time, he backs halfway up, but doesn't slam into the wall. And his face is different. Mouth covered, his eyes should look at us all bugging out–like. This time they just lock onto the corpse.

"Estranged son got him. He's a piece of shit, so I never save him anymore. You really don't know what goes on in your neighborhood, trust." We stick to the script, but our rhythm's gone unsteady. "He'll be alive tomorrow anyway, sadly. Or . . . maybe he's waking up right now . . ."

The corpse's unzipped torso sits upright.

Then, mechanically, it settles back down. Cadaveric spasm. It's one of our mutual top three T-Pose gags, for both she-half and he-, and that makes it a big moment.

But Arturo's non-reaction completely ruins it. More frozen than the prepper, he just keeps on watching.

"It's—uh, it's one of our favorites—"

"What do you mean, 'our,' Anne? That was fucking mean." Our breath stops entirely. For a moment, there's no thought. No processing. We feel the shockwave like it's the maddening *pow* again from this morning that neither half could claim. "Just say that's *your* favorite, because if you know me so well, you'd know this disgusts me. This is inhuman. This was inconsiderate of you to do to me. Shut the fuck up."

Something has gone very wrong.

T-Pose is erected around a simulation of catharsis. It is designed to reignite our distant emotions, and should our many spinning plates fall and shatter, it opens in us a vulnerability. This is not a day for accruing more anger.

Reminding ourselves that, of course, makes us angrier. The If Only Things Could Be Different of it all. That is not for today. That is not for *ever*.

Arturo finds the basement. Our dry aerosolization has completed. Sleeping gas, that's how we describe the pressurized canisters filled with thick beige vapor. Stick to the script. Slide both canisters into the shock-absorbent backpack we make him fetch off the corkboard wall. Except this time, we watch him closely, ensuring the mounted knives and pistols by the cushioned backpack's side stay in their place.

He confirms he's being monitored before abandoning them, slowly. He's unafraid of getting close to us despite claiming only minutes ago that he's outraged by the prepper prank.

That's got plenty to do with us chatting up Jay from the Tex-Mex drive thru window, requesting for $20 extra that he wrap the Shrimp Diablo

Cotija with more than veggie spices. He had all the right tools to crush our MDMA into a fine chalk, only half of it necessary to garnish the guacamole. The rest he got to keep for himself. He asked for our number.

God fucking dammit, we wanted *verstehen, schadenfreude,* petrichor. We needed them. *Those* are sorely missed emotions.

Infuriation? Cheap.

It's our baseline. Imagining hell is a privilege we don't have. Our anniversaries excise anger. For a moment, we get to pretend we excise our anger.

On balance, it *is* hard to remember the last time our thoughts were completely halted. That was at least semi-gripping.

We suppose it's not the end of the world. For today, though, goodbye to a complex run. "Medium collateral," George-half insisted all the way at the top. Yeah, no.

If only there were anybody to live for but each other. We're not allowed. We're all we have. Kill us for it.

# 17

# PREACHER ARTURO VASQUEZ

Is that too much to ask for?" I load the doomsday prepper's kitchenware into his microwave. I've always wanted to explode one of these. "A little PowerPoint presentation about each of my classmates that we can hook up in the gym? You should know what I think about them if we're such good friends."

In no time sparks morph from yellow to a pretty green and pink, from flickering to spouting. An arcing and a loud *boom* strain the apartment's dingy windows. The machine is a misshapen smolder. "You have no idea how little of an ask that is. Just wait 'till you see the venue."

"Good. Well, get to it."

I step out to the hallway and smoke follows me. Anne has assured me no one else dies on these grounds, but the Liltin Yew Fire Department will take far too long to slum it down here. The roof will end up in the basement; evidence will be burned and buried.

I feel a little bad ordering her around. The purportedly patricided bum and the cadaveric spasm were tasteless, but she has been spot on about everything else. Turning the red Raider around in the cul-de-sac, I glimpse sooty smoke choking the low-income apartment hall.

What I do not feel bad about is fleeing Percival Lane to catch a text from Gets, asking if I was okay. I asked them to meet me at the high school

143

reunion tonight, said I'll explain what I can, and that I was sorry I made them drink. Even though I deleted our message history directly after, the CIA and FBI and DHS probably see it all, and I couldn't care less. All that matters is that Anne can't know.

On the drive up and down our little downtown, she tells me where I'll place the canisters in the gym. I may have overdone it when I yelled at her. I feel a swell of empathy.

"I'm sorry."

She navigates out of Capitol Campus and drifts to an abrupt halt at a marketplace's overhanging ceiling, a deep inlet of hidden employee parking. We're across the street from Liltin Yew High School.

She rolls her eyes.

"You've said and done worse. Keep that energy focused on the time hole. Flood it, remember? Mischief Night."

Blood swimming pleasantly through my veins, pushed smoothly by my breath, I close my eyes and allow myself to drink in the comfort, to store it.

"Go get 'em, Prophet. Can't be seen walking in with anyone. You're doing all this through the grace of God, yeah?"

"Yeah."

"You'll see a familiar face at the gym entrance. Don't worry, he'll let you in."

What's that mean?

"Phone."

I open my eyes.

She shrugs lazily in her grey sweater. "Now's the real meat 'n potatoes. No 19-year-old Pentagon cryptologist wired off Monster gets to listen in and ruin your night."

Relief. Thank absolute fuck that I deleted my texts with Gets. Palm held out, Anne's smile falters for just a nanosecond. She looks me up and down.

"Ain't I gonna be livestreaming or something?"

Her head turns side-to-side like an automaton. "Won't have to. Everybody will be livestreaming *you*."

A thrill sparks like lit iron wool through my lungs. "Ah. Right." I give the phone over. Her hand is soft. She shoves the cushioned backpack of sleeping gas onto my lap.

"One last thing." She reaches to the backseat and closes some distance between us while doing so—she smells really good. Clear plastic crinkles as she holds a tailored suit by its wire hanger. "I know everyone in town with your measurements."

"See you in there."

Her surgically lifted lips tighten. I think she expected a different reaction, so I give her a grateful smile. "Hop-skip-and-a-jump away," she says.

—

Poking out the low alley, warmth hugs me from all around. I take a moment to watch clouds lumber on by. Liltin High sits just uphill of town center. In the '50's the wealthiest family around handsomely funded state-of-the-art education facilities. With the courthouse and library it is the only classical-looking building, and certainly its most impressive.

I cross the quiet street and keep my distance as I circle around back. By contrast, the remodeled gym behind the school, its own building, is all too modern. The only windows line the top of the flat, tanned brick facade, connecting to its shallow white roof. It's like if a small warehouse were a perfect square—a warehouse cut in half. Pretty ugly.

Birdsong pulls my attention to a northern shrike, a rare sighting on the edge of summer. It dives close to the ground and catches a red-legged grasshopper in midair, thrashing it back and forth. That bug has a tough few hours ahead: shrikes don't kill slow. After the great egret, they're my second favorite bird. Good omen.

The police officer who almost snatched me up is waiting at the entrance.

His all-black, heavily tinted '26 pickup stews on the curb. His gleaming bald head is almost crimson, that's how angry he looks. There are no identifiers on his navy uniform.

*Don't worry, he'll let you in.*

"Some shit you pulled earlier, Vasquez. You know Trump posted about you?"

I stare ahead as I walk past.

"I give it another hour before this town is crawling with plain-clothes agents. Hear that?" His every muscle strains not to pin me by the throat. "They're very interested in you."

I'm in the gym. The officer catches the heavy metal door before it shuts:

"Think your junkie brother will be able to hide? We know where y'all live."

"Watch this." I let down my tailored suit and backpack, sprint into the center of the gym, cartwheel, chain into a somersault, off the ground like my morning Raider ride except this time, I'm in full control. I hear the door slam.

The gym was remodeled a year after I graduated. I only ever saw the new look in pictures—and it looked nothing like this.

The eight-spot lighting rig on the ceiling engages a blue-infused spectrum from pink to violet. Furling all over every surface are spirals constricting to singularities that reset back to their widest irises. The back-center of the gym is made into a dance floor. Around the dance floor is packed with over a dozen circular, flower-adorned tables. Quivering turrets of an inflatable adult bouncy house, an equally adult-sized ball pit, and a giant, twisting metal slide that feeds into it. A table buckling under copious beer and jungle juice. It's all silver and blue.

I deposit our backpack under the DJ table. Following the gym's old layout in my mind I find the showers in the locker room behind the bleachers to be relatively unchanged.

I'll give the believers a belief their time to shine has finally come—and in front of the wider world I'll show them, unequivocally, just how easy they are to dupe. For forcing me to play their "trad-queer" game for acceptance as only half of who I am, the half they approve of. My audience are the people who violated my brother and tried to destroy me for sticking with him as a result. My audience are those who twisted my parents to allow it. They are my parents, who shoved their kids aside in service of a beneficial, shared religious psychosis. They enable and enact all the violence I have ever known.

I look great in this suit.

Anne, tiptoeing off a ladder, screws one of the canisters into a bulky device fixed to the retracted central basketball backboard right overtop the dance floor. It looks like an air quality monitor. Pointed directly down. She salutes.

"Check the laptop!"

It's on the DJ table by the mixer and a live wireless mic.

My PowerPoint presentation. All 103 of my classmates accounted for, with the statements next to each—musings, observations—perfectly distilled, and 100% in my voice.

I grab the mic and press it to my lips. "You came through."

"Keep reading!" she calls and folds the ladder. "Some Russian girl comes in halfway through the party to deliver a thumb drive to you, by the way. It's the OG copy of this presentation. Just accept it and she'll go away."

"Uh, whatever, sure." My tongue along the mic's head scrapes loudly over the speakers as I scroll through. But then I understand that maybe this Russian woman is where Anne got so much of her intel: I gasp. Jared Saunders took out a second mortgage on 200 PS5s right when they cracked down on scalpers? Manuel Zegarra laid off his whole team for AI? Raul Nalzany locked up his wife? *He was having an affair on the side?*

Laughing, slow dancing at the DJ table, I look around for Anne. "This is perfect!"

Anne is gone.

Across the gym a trickle of incoming guests hush their voices as they notice me, their shoes clacking off the reflective hardwood.

Oh God. All right, here we go. A momentary desire to sleep for the rest of the day almost flattens me on the spot. But it's the last time I'll have that thought tonight. I know that, because it's what I promise myself. "Action," I mutter.

They all but lunge at me in succession. Showing me videos of the oarfish in Vallarta, the Midnight Hammer mess, the scores of the College World Series. Some names or faces I recognize from my cagey, isolated teen years. Most not. I recognize Cierra Alrose from so many investigative reports on the local news. I quickly stop tallying all the, "Wow, been so long, couldn't wait to see you, how're you?"s—baldly perfidious. Nobody remembers me.

Many younger attendees make me a prop. "If it's Hell on Earth is this Heaven?" "Our prophet!" "Acceleration time, darlings." They hit all their best angles while reciting these. "Class reunion! EXPOSE THE PATTERN!" That last kid is definitely still in Liltin High.

Feels like forever before the unmarked officer closes the entrance behind him and ushers my saccharine acolytes into the party space proper. I'd thank him, but he's just doing his job as a good piggie. Stragglers sneak in through a propped back entrance next to the lockers, which must be where Anne went off to, because I spot her in the crowd: she's stunningly made-up and her burgundy dress must be a pilfered collector's item. A whole different person. I try to catch her eye but she cluelessly heads to the drinks.

The gigantic speakers shout to life and *Elevate* blasts over everyone. A dozen dancers rush the floor, definitely European, silver mesh fabrics over spaghetti straps, hair in buns, and all moving in perfect synchronization. On the giant slide and in the bounce castle the already nonplussed attendees freeze and gawk. Irregular meters, leaping over one another, then folding to the center and undulating in one resolved, explosive beat, the song ends and confetti blows laterally from all four corners.

"That's . . . that was exciting," I'm saying into the wireless mic. Oh, good, I'm holding the mic. Wow, when'd that happen! "Everybody, give it up for the Bolshoi ballet."

There is hearty applause but it's surprisingly scattered. The buzz of the audience is now a confused roar.

How do I separate my former classmates from the acolytes and media? I step into the reeling crowd in search of Anne. If I could get her somewhere . . . I know it has to look like I'm the one doing all of this but . . . Are drugs supposed to last this long?

Some of the audience parts for me. Everybody is so overdressed. Someone loudly asks where the food is. That could be an issue.

I can't find her. The gym is so packed it's practically creaking, people stacked on each other like ants. I'm feeling more than I'm thinking. There's too much going on.

A woman stops me in my tracks.

"Oh, hey, Cierra. What brings you here?" I ask.

The local reporter muscles through her surprise. "Um, Mr. Vasquez—"

"Yes?"

"Are you aware that there are reports of Department of Homeland Security agents entering Liltin Yew? This directly after comments you made on top-secret military movements were verified by Iran?"

Not the time. I finally spot Anne at the base of the bleachers about twenty yards away, chatting with other alums.

"Some are even saying they've seen uniformed individuals, *active duty* troops coming in from Joint Base Wilkes-Booth."

A perimeter has formed around me of pointed phones with their flash on.

"I, um." Anne and the alums are casually strolling the crowd's perimeter. I refocus to Cierra Alrose, clear my throat. "I could throw you a story from the Old Testament. Passover, the night where God's punishing plagues descended upon the city. Those faithful to Hashem stayed inside and marked the threshold of their dwellings with blood, and in marking their doors as such they uh, y'know, they survived the night." I realize once again that I'm holding the live microphone. "Those who didn't, didn't."

The perimeter of recorders and live streamers stare blankly. I shrug and push through the crowd.

Some follow as I bound towards Anne. I switch the live mic off and pocket it. Late-aughts awful indie pop echoes.

"Hey," I call after her. "Um, ma'am? Excuse me?"

She takes a step back; I've gotten closer to her than I intended. "Hi?"

"Hi." I straighten. "I was wondering if I could have a word."

Anne looks sideways at the three classmates around her. I recognize them vaguely. They were her old high school clique. "You are?"

"Well, I'm Arturo. I'm . . . a fan!" I laugh. I get the front she's putting up, but she has to know I need to talk to her. And it's not like this pretend-Anne wouldn't know who I am today . . . Who doesn't at this point? "I took all your free therapy classes. Just wondering—"

"Okay? *Namaste*. You used to go here too?" She gestures around, her expression severely perturbed.

"Yeah . . . Heh, you don't know me? I'm kind of a big deal today," I try to nudge her in the right direction. Hadn't she planned for everything today? That's certainly what it sounded like.

Anne just furrows her brow and backs up further.

"You okay, Anne?" One of her classmates shuffles herself between us.

"Wait. Lemme just . . ." Then I remember a loophole, a good code. "Jose Castaño! Do you remember when he and I, uh, we snuck up the bell tower in Grace Cathedral?"

"Bro," Anne snaps, "what the *fuck* are you talking about?"

The classmate between us holds up her hand to keep me in place while Anne and the others retreat. Half of the phone cameras go with them, the other half stay on me.

A wandering fractal projection from the light rig blinds me. Blinking, I croak, "My mistake," and find now to be a good time to check out the slide into the ball pit.

Why isn't she talking to me? What did I do wrong? It has to be because of the cameras, the people. It has to be. But I can't get her expression out of my head. She looked completely different, like the Anne Oxendine I knew from her social media, completely unaware of who I am. It has to be acting. She's had decades to train, after all.

From the top of the metal slide, I see the dance floor filling. Can't tell which ones are Liltin High '10 and which are the opportunists. I need to be able to. If my plans for the slideshow, the naming and shaming, have any chance of coming to pass . . .

*Passover.* Its Hebrew name is *Pesach.* Gets taught me that.

Holy shit, I told Gets to meet me here.

I grip the slide's handles and push off, land in the pit below. I flip the mic on and send silver-blue balls spilling onto the gym floor.

"Hey, *todos, escúchame.*" The roaring dips to murmurs as I find my way back to the platform with the DJ table. "Cutting the music for just a sec. Don't know who put The Shins on. So, since we're beginning . . ."

"Where the food at?" someone bellows to rising cries of agreement.

"Soon," I pray. "Since we're beginning, I wanna officially welcome the Liltin High Class of 2010. Long overdue!" I wait for the applause to die down. "We're gonna start off with a quick roll call. I swear I'll be, uh, *muy rápido,* to my real ones in the audience."

I take care not to descend the projector from the ceiling while I open the PowerPoint presentation. It's in alphabetical order, thankfully. Just doing names for now. "All right, here we go! Shout 'present!'"

I get through it all in about four minutes. "Anne Oxendine," I call.

"Here."

65 of 104 respond with varying levels of enthusiasm. They're good sports.

I pretend to count. "Now, lemme see if my math's correct. I'm pretty sure even if all 66 of us brought a plus-one, this place wouldn't be nearly so crowded! Hmm? Do we happen to have complete strangers among us?"

There are grumbles of agreement; the 150-odd remainder seem to shrink.

"Yeah, I know the freakin' media's here. Just talked to 'em, actually. Hey, look, all are welcome. I wanna say you have a place here. Safe space, eh? And on a campus, too. Just like you people always want! Here's my hang-up. My class, many of them came from far and wide to be here. Darn near a pilgrimage. Forty days and forty nights type stuff. Tonight, it's not like all other nights."

I cough, collect my thoughts. *Why am I so hung up on Passover?*

"These tables all around me? The tables have *their* names on them. We missed our 10-year because the whole nation was on lockdown, remember?" Louder agreement this time. "So, I'm gonna make a request and I'm afraid that if you wanna see how my li'l show progresses, well, then it's non-negotiable."

The only sound is my echo. Everybody's eyes are stuck to me. I'm outside my body once more, but on so many of their screens. I'm doing just fine.

"For the time being, y'all are gonna have a seat up on the bleachers back there. You don't have to sit down actually, just . . . stay there, okay? Fear not, it's temporary."

Surveying the gym stoically for a good 10 seconds, I lift my eyebrows as if offended.

I resume the music. "Go."

I grind my teeth as the audience sorts itself out. Some try to stay on the floor, only for others to usher them impatiently to the back. My classmates are hooting in approval. Funny. Fifteen years ago they didn't know my name.

I scan the bleachers as they file in. No Gets. I hope they saw me just now. Is that what caused this disruption? Me telling Gets to meet me here? Did Gets do something? Throw something off with the Anne plan?

Circling the gym like I'm in PE all over again, I'm sweating. People follow in hot pursuit and they're asking me what is going on, how I'm predicting the day's events, what's coming next. "Stay tuned," I say a million times before I leave them behind: Some of my bigger classmates hold them back.

"You heard him," one of them says.

The vestibule is much less populated. Maybe Gets is here, maybe I can peek outside into town. Or maybe I can just get some fresh air. I pass a fairly spartan trophy display.

I'm grabbed by the elbow and next thing I know I'm inside a maintenance closet.

Anne Oxendine is pulling the suit jacket off of me.

"Oof, thanks," I gasp in relief. "It's hot as hell out there!"

"No better in here." She hangs my jacket over the small window on the door.

"The fuck was that earlier? Embarrassing me part of our big Mischief Night plan?"

"Mischief Night? Um, well, you were right." She smirks shyly . . . shyly? Her hands run up my arms for some reason. She still smells really good. "I do know who you are."

Her fingers drift from my biceps to my chest and, before I can begin to process, lower. Lower. She presses her burgundy dress against me and I tell myself to back away—but I don't move.

"Umm. Hey now."

"Not until 30 minutes ago, I'll admit. But I was like, 'Hey, this motherfucker follows me,' and I did a little sleuthing." She's whispering, but it's directly into my ear, it's all I can hear aside from my pounding blood. "You like almost all of my posts, don't you?"

Her breath lands on me and her perfume fills my nostrils. This is not the Anne I've met. Her knee wedges between both of mine, gently but firmly plying, and she leans in. One hand on the back of my neck, the other slips below my belt, steadily kneads.

"W-wait," I manage, and I knock a broom aside as she pushes me onto the wall.

"Yeah, I don't know how you're doing all these things to go viral, preacher, but there's strength in numbers. I just want to make it clear I'm on your side."

Her cheek along my neck, hand still working rhythmically, I feel a stirring despite myself. I try to think but the sensation pushes to the forefront.

"Yeah, I'm on your side," she croons.

"What are you—*ehehheh*," as if being tickled, "Anne, I'm not even straight, wha—"

With a *zip* my pants drop and she's squeezing me hard from base and tightening balls, staring up into my eyes as I engorge in her smooth palm. Still whispering, eyes heavy: "You think I can't spot a trendy public persona? Sure, Arturo, you're queer. Where's your boyfriend? I'm not seeing one, not in your entire post history."

I can't exhale.

"Well-well they're an enbyfriend . . ."

"A what?" she asks. "Nevermind. Don't care." Her chin and her brow lift in some kind of precious amusement, the tip of my cock jumps as she traces it, and then she's on her knees. Straining, I protest, but Anne doesn't hear. She flicks her tongue on it and then I fully sink into her mouth. I try for the broom I knocked aside, but it clatters to the floor. I can't just kick her. That, *that* would be so *fucked up*.

I push against her head. I suck in what little air I can and when I finally exhale, a whimper slips out.

That seems to please her. Her hair is soft. It glitters, ripples.

*I don't know what's happening.* My mind clings desperately to the horrible, muffled music outside. My vision swims and fills with splotches of color. No, I know. I stop trying. Frozen in place, every screaming inch massaged into compliance, I don't know *how* this can feel identical to the best head I've ever received in my life, all the best I've ever given, all the way back to . . .

"Jose," I blurt. Jose Castaño in the bell tower, 10th grade.

With her puffy lips she makes an exaggerated *smack* as she momentarily unlatches.

"From our class?" she pants.

"You . . . were doing it just like him for a second." The tension she'd been drawing hovers achingly and the all-consuming shame overpowers: disgusted, my cock flexes involuntarily, begging her to finish. She lets it quiver next to her swinging earring as she grins, eyes blazing, both hands reaching around behind me.

"Should we go get him in here, preacher?"

She doesn't wait for an answer. She's hungry.

By the time she stifles my crying out, fully defeated, I notice my suit jacket has fallen from the maintenance closet door and someone is looking in.

Found Gets.

# 18

# RECOVERING ALCOHOLIC GETS LO

*assover, the night when God's punishing plagues descended upon the city. Those faithful to Hashem stayed inside and marked the threshold of their dwellings with blood..."*

I minimize LYTV's local livestream and check the Map: thirty minutes away. I huff loudly, resume the *brat* remixes, and get to jogging. Arturo and I enabled location sharing months ago, but I never checked before today. Much to my irritation, he's ping-ponged around town twice since I reached out.

I actually screamed at the top of my lungs when I saw his pin abandon Firwood Manor apartments. Shortly after, though, there was a distant plume of dark smoke rising from the direction of the housing complex.

While walking to Arturo's seemingly permanent new location of Liltin High Gym, firetrucks zoom past me at full speed.

Some horrible trebuchet is clicking into place, and the more I think into it the less I can guess its trajectory.

Sunlight has dyed the world orange; rectangular shadows link into pools of indigo on asphalt. To passersby there's no denying that I look like a gaudy drunk, but it's not like I've a local reputation to uphold.

The ugly gym hides (as it should) behind the high school's main facility. I've been walking all day. It's a surprisingly vertical little area. Great for partly sobering up, but I'm winded and a headache is blooming. I rest on a bench for a moment. My salmon tech jacket hangs from its shoulder straps and bunches up behind my back.

There is no proper amount of preparation. No earthly explanation for how the Arturo of this morning is the Arturo of tonight. How is he predicting the future? How the hell does he know I drank earlier?

An urge spikes to either text him again or recheck the internet's chronicling of his messianic proclamations. I am a slave to twin urges: Arturo limerence, and if not Arturo, then more alcohol to numb. The same urge, I admit, head thrown back to the cable-choked sky. The same urge. A tug of war with a hula hoop.

There's a cop patrolling the main entrance, because of course there is. I can see from my bench that his pickup is a private vehicle with a whirling LED beacon suction-cupped to its roof.

When he takes his very serious patrol around the far corner, I spring and make a beeline for the entrance. It's like when I smuggled paint cans all the way onto that famous Van Gogh in Stockholm three summers back. I smile.

Although the inside may not approach the most crowded venue I've crashed, the vibe is instantly the most hostile. All courtesy of my boyfriend. He's splitting them up. Separating the many onlookers and the Class of 2010.

It's my first time standing directly among his crowd. The deep passion that is his anger, I've seen it on his streams, but this is something new. Here he barely disguises it, and they're all the more enthralled for it. I think of what Gabby said earlier: *indirect harm.* Not many people get this chance to work on such a scale. Arturo wields power.

—

"He looks good in that suit, huh?" I say by way of conversation between stomps in the adult bounce castle.

"You're not an alum," an attendee with a flat-top responds. "You're holding up the line to get in."

"Oh, no I am. My name's uhh . . ." I give up, finger-gun and fuck off. I swipe a can from the overburdened alcohol table on the way to the bleachers.

Everyone over there is not having the greatest time. I slink into the vestibule to check my phone and hear what sounds like a struggle from an offhand broom closet. Oh, it has a window. Oh, there's Arturo getting deepthroated by a glitzy *woman with her finger halfway up his ass.*

I plant there, watch in detached disbelief. She's enthusiastic. He seems really into it. I'm acutely aware of what both horror and despair can do to me right now so instead, I will focus on the confusion. There is enough confusion here to occupy me for years.

It occupies me for about fifteen seconds. I lose my will. He notices me and starts; the woman half-turns her dripping face. I can do nothing but tip my can at them and leave.

There is less sunlight out here and somehow no air. I trip on a root. Don't hear Arturo's voice until he's a few feet behind me, and I forbid myself from processing a single word.

"What's next?" I spin around and he crashes into me, stumbles back. The closest I can look to his face is his tie. Retaining as much of my composure as possible, I breathe through my nose, but it gets more difficult by the second. The woman sucking him dry has emerged from the gym, too, spectating. How high school this all is. He's trying to say something, but I'm talking over him.

"Flew to Washington. Braved your fundie mixer. Picked up your neglected older brother. Sat in the cuck seat for your girlfriend reveal. It takes a second to kill someone, Arturo, just point and shoot. What'd I do for you to make a whole day out of it? Tell me what's next."

He's shaking. I think he's pleading. Fuck him. I hold up my hand to say *stop* and look anywhere else—and from the same bench I'd rested on, George the Siren looks back.

It's no hallucination. There he is, slumped comfortably with his hands in his pockets. Found me at last. His eyes flit from me to the woman behind Arturo.

"Look, how 'bout you skip ahead and get it over with," I snarl at Arturo over his pathetic cries and I walk to the street corner.

"No, I didn't fucking want that!"

Those words get through.

"I didn't fucking want it!"

In truly degrading moments like these it's best to remember you still have yourself. When you're so obviously the one who's been wronged, it can make the other party's most lunatic attempts at justification just sound like the ravings of madmen. No hindsight needed, it's immediately comic. Maybe even pathetic.

The sad laugh I give is genuine as I cross the street. Arturo doesn't give chase.

I sip the beer once before throwing it at the side of a building: 5% ABV. A shower of droplets lands in my hair.

"I mean, has he always been that kind of guy?" I ask George the Siren, who currently walks abreast of me, his eyes on the sidewalk but his face angled slightly my way. "He pawned his tweaker brother onto me, two people who never met each other . . . And don't get me wrong, Gabby's cool. Actually, he's great. But that's not the point."

"The point is," George cuts in, "trying to empathize with Arturo's choices clearly won't lead anywhere good. It's about as safe as running at a wall."

*Or driving off a cliff.* I punctuate the thought with a sharp inhalation.

George is steering us through town. At least the curiosity of his inevitable presence makes for some distraction. On 4th Avenue we pass a dive bar that had intrigued me on the way over.

"Hey, I'm going in here." I stop and point in.

George looks further down the street. "But we …" He sighs. "It's all the same now. You haven't been where you were supposed to be all day."

The bar is a combination of goth (aged wood and purple drapery adorned in crosses and buff Baphomets), and LGBTQIA+ sensibilities, its dim chamber lighting all colors of the rainbow. Tall candles of slanting elevations stand like organ pipes at the front by the bar where George and I order a double London mule.

"I'm buying," he winks.

"So where would you prefer I be?" I ask in the best faith I can, which ain't much. Behind low-hanging Crystorama chandeliers toward the bar's back a busking-dressed duo run sound tests on their guitar and amp.

"Oh, my preference doesn't enter into it, Getty. It's just where things go. You were supposed to be face-down in Le Voyeur like two hours ago."

I return the gaze from his gleaming eyes. He knows my full first name. "That the art-deco one up the block? I considered that. Looked a li'l arch if I'm keeping it a stack."

"Interesting," mulls George. "That *is* what you think. That's what you think on days when you … when we don't let you … Hmm. The normal days, non-anniversary days."

The busking duo issue forth some subtle folk offering that sounds like a breezy Midwest cornfield on the edge of a thunderstorm. The affable bartender gives us each our double mules in cold, copper mugs.

"What do you mean anniversary days?" Mint lime, just the right bite. What are a few sips?

"But here works too," he plows on. "Far as we're concerned, when it comes to you it's not location that matters, it's intent …"

"What're you saying *we* for?" When he stays silent, I try, "Hey, I've been meaning to ask. Are you more of a mermaid kinda siren or a bird-person kinda siren?"

"Transmedium," he says without hesitation.

A group of impeccably dressed drag queen patrons to my left urgently mutter amongst themselves about Trad-Queer Preacher Arturo Vasquez—or I guess just preacher:

"He gave some kinda speech about Passover?" one of them cringes. "To stop the feds from entering town or something?"

"Too late on that," says another, phone held out. "People were filming the base gates just in case. Look, count how many black SUVs that is! That's from like ten minutes ago."

"It's gonna be like this wherever we go, if you're wondering," George tells me, picking at the legions of band stickers on the sticky bar. "Everybody's talking about Arturo at this point. Well, either it's about him or about our Mayoral candidates. That's heating up too."

I'm not wondering. I'm actually looking at Arturo's saved photo in my Contacts. It's from our sunny trip to the Golden Gate, not the standard angle overlooking it, but from the pier below, suicide-level where it towered above: him literally carrying me on his back, masks pulled under chins and both faces alight. I don't remember the tourist who took our picture but for no real reason I hope the tourist still remembers us.

"Of course, it was *you* who was supposed to embarrass themself at the reunion, not Mr. Man of the Hour. That had to've been an improvisation. We're good at improv. *Half*-good," he says, laughing at some joke clearly not meant for me. George takes a swig. "I fucked up again, Getty. Six numbers. 'S'all it took."

"Oh, for real? Six numbers did all this?"

"Yeah dude."

"That's—how?"

"Oh, I forgot 'em."

"Yo. No shit?"

"At like a crucial fuckin' moment." He almost slams the table but stops, mime-slams instead.

"Okay. Wow. Dang. Well don't, uh, get too hard on yourself."

"I can't not sometimes, Gets!"

"I get that. Sure."

"I wake up every goddamn day hungover! It's like I'm on retard mode."

The approaching bartender turns to serve the other side.

"You should consider not drinking," I say.

He laughs at that, almost cries. "You get to not wake up that way."

"You're a bit dick-heavy, you know that?"

That snaps George back. Bemused, the siren mouths soundlessly as if flipping through a script, trying to remember his spot on a dialogue tree. I give him a once-over and clock a long, thin *something* bulging from his pocket, slightly rounded at the ends: a foldable knife. Can't tell what kind of blade.

"I had a dog," he says, "she was a beagle. Daisy. Our neighbor had this whole litter my senior year of high school. I went to community college at first, so I still lived here. Housebroke her, took her for walks, put 'er in my twin bed all the time."

Word by word George's neck bends as if under some amassing weight, leaning a bit into the dim light. "Dad kept her in the divorce. And after years when I get back up here for the reunion," he chuckles darkly, turning his head to the side, "first day it takes her a minute to remember me. The excitement of, like, seeing me again . . . it mighta gotten to her. And I forgot how old she is. She actually died. While I was here in Liltin Yew, but out of the house, not here for *her*, you know."

I take another sip.

"I get to re-live that failure every day. As much or as little as I want, to be sure, but it's always there. A reminder, my forever state. And that gives us something in common, Getty."

I narrow my gaze at him, half-shake my head.

"Oh, come on. The sortation warehouse. Nick, idiot! Nick Valento. That employee you killed in 2010."

I forgot his last name.

The edges of my vision contract further, forming a tunnel out of which the siren's face slowly morphs into a leer. I feel the labor in my breath.

"That's when you decided to become a ghost. Not a girl, not a guy. Barely a they." He's sending me over.

As slowly as I can, I lift the copper mug of London mule to my mouth for another, much longer sip. The siren leans back, fully beaming now, as if I've proven him a point.

I halt the gin right there, thoughts racing.

*You haven't been where you're supposed to be.*

*You were supposed to embarrass yourself at the reunion, not Arturo.*

*We're good at improv.*

He wants me drunk. A lot drunker than I am right now.

*"I didn't fucking want it!"*

This demon is trying to pull all of our strings. Somehow it's aware of our thoughts, and it's poking us, prodding us. Trying to set us off.

And then it actually hits me.

*We.*

The woman behind Arturo with the finger up his ass.

Staring into George, I see the performance. Clumsily tying my very identity to personal brokenness, to some trauma instead of a limiting, binary system chugging along perfectly as intended. Maybe I'd buy it if more of my brain cells were numbed. As it stands, it's all a little tacky.

With effort I summon a smile. "Nah."

Satisfaction freezes and fades in the siren's eyes as he watches me table my gin. There's the confirmation. My tunnel vision falls away like an exhalation.

"Nah?" George intones quietly. All of a sudden, a captive audience.

"'Life is not made of what life was.' NLE Choppa."

"I see." Reduced, visibly recalibrating. Glaring.

"Plus, buddy, you've missed a very important part of me."

"What'd that be?"

"It'd be fuck you." A much more welcome old habit than my gin, his anger is giving me fuel. "Because let's be clear," I lean in, "whatever this is you're doing, whatever region-wide game you're playing with us, you . . . You *are* cheating, right? Rushin' through shortcuts. A tool-assisted speedrun. This ain't a level playing field. I mean, where's the talent in it?"

"That'd be the finding the shortcuts in the first place," he hisses. "I know *all* the ways to connect with you." He is well-built, lean, and worked up. It won't be an easy fight unless I get an initial upper hand. "You have no clue exactly how easy it is to take *anybody* at *any* headspace, and *bend them* into something else."

"Something else, huh? See, I don't think people change at all." I stop myself from adding, "Prove me wrong!" I take one big, performative swig, swallowing only the smallest fraction just to buy time.

"Maybe not long term, I'll give you that, but moment-to-moment you're all so pliant. You're a canvas reacting to whatever sensation splashes on ya. We just puzzle out the most effective paint and—"

I lean forward and throw up on the base of his barstool.

"Gosh, I am so sorry," I cough. "Think I'm faded, man. Gimme a sec." I wipe my face and dart into the belly of the bar. "This is super fascinating," I call as I pass the folk duo humbly bowing and breaking down their equipment, "you gimme one sec."

George shoots up to tail me, but he's given me about three seconds' head start and the queens are in his way. An exit sign flickers at the end of the narrow restroom hall; I clocked it the moment we arrived.

I throw it open and slam it shut, then hide wide of it. Dusk descending, the automated exit light not yet engaged, the vaguely sweet scent of decomposing trash. An old couple far ahead at the alley's edge smokes. They won't interfere.

With a fat, private grin, heart racing at my evening's fortune, I hear the racing feet from inside, and the moment the siren clears the door, I thrust into motion.

He turns into my right hook, spins around on his cheekbone and slams face-first into the sticky brick wall. My knee finds his back and the jab sends him far from me. I turn to catch the closing exit door. A heavy metal song is blasting inside.

But a scuffed hand catches my arm and rips me back, George already on his feet in an inhuman rally, and I duck a fist to catch a knee myself.

Pain cleaves my face in two. I kneel on cracked pavement. George isn't done. His face snarls in the dark, open skin along where it slapped the bricks; he picks me up and throws me into the opposing wall.

"Fuck it," I hear him mumble, and next I hear the knife click open in the siren's hands. Tanto blade. Turn off the pain. Push off the wall and launch fully into him.

I quicken through a rip that feels electric, pull his forward shoulder to twist and there's a *snap*, clatter, bark.

My legs are swept from underneath. My head bounces and I'm breathless on my back.

Frantically down stroking, butterflying, I put distance on his last known position but no assault bears down. The small of my back protests as I rise. Backing up further, further, almost out of the alley. George leans on a leaking trashcan with a hand tucked to his chest, muck sliding down his bleeding temple as if a laconic lava flow.

His Tanto lay between us.

We both eye it.

He points a crooked thumb all the way back to the bar's bass-boosted exit door. "You like metal?"

"You tell me," I rasp, back-step out and around the corner. My nose is broken. With the help of the old smokers, I stem my blood onto a bar napkin and tampon, howling like a raccoon as I manually reset it.

My salmon tech coat's outer layer is slashed under the left armpit. Staggering through the funk, vision regaining as I wipe away tears, I cast back glances at the alley.

A blurry figure stands there, just watching.

I scarf down the old couple's sympathy cigarette. Like 30 seconds, it's a new record.

George and the mystery woman know Arturo and me. Quick information deduction from the midday tells me that they must know Gabby, too. And definitely the politicians in the fucking woods.

Whatever is about to happen to all of us, I don't know my size in it, and I fear Arturo least of all is filled in on the details.

A distant scraping scuffle behind me and I hear the old couple cry out— then abrupt silence.

The streets are empty.

Desperately I scan downtown Liltin Yew, its quaint offices, apartments, corner stores. Some are marked with a thick, reddish-brown brushstroke on their front doors.

# 19

# VADA IKEBE'S SIMULACRA

I try to fly.

My late mother showed me Lucid Dreaming 101 when I had my *Alice in Wonderland* issues, and pre-high school it developed into one of my more niche hobbies. I still have my dream journal somewhere. If I know the dream is changing location, I'm typically able to do a little hop, flutter my hands a bit, and then off I go.

"What this one is doing?" asks Katyusha/OMGrozny, baby safely loaded in her Scion. Kat watches me strain for the sky with real concern next to Oh Taek-su's Subaru.

My friends are at as much of a loss.

With a huff, I climb into the backseat's middle. "Forget it. It's an aura thing I guess."

It is an aura thing. In-dream flight requires confidence, and a part of me is over-investing in the imminent demo. I suffer the long drive that winds around the western-most tip of the Hoh Rainforest and through the Black Hills. Obsessively I check my phone for more texts from Amy. Given that she's fast asleep in her coma, I'd love to think this is actually her communicating with me through some primal plane.

"U there?" I type. Nothing.

Taek-su passes a gated fence, behind which sits a solitary house. It looks like it hasn't finished loading in, like it's fake. Everyone else in the car is conveniently looking the other direction; anything is normal in a dream.

Our campgrounds are littered at the tail of an overgrown gravel road, carved, sometimes sloppily, through jagged wooded hills. The curiosity with which I first viewed this passage, when Dad drove me 5 years ago, came to foreshadow dread and resignation. Once Amy and I connected, though, it felt like home.

We're stepping right into our videogame.

SalishUs and his viewers may not be ready for how photoreal we rendered this place, but Rundee, Kristen, Taek-su, and I aren't ready for the reality. The last time we 3D-scanned around camp was back in February. All four cabins now choke on weeds.

A maroon canopy tent takes up residence in the middle by the well, overtop the reclaimed road. Katyusha runs her baby under its mosquito screens and hugs Daniel, who's finished his streaming setup. They speak in hushed tones. Cables run from the canopy's zipper into a bulky generator parked between two splintered picnic tables.

On this Duwamish-hugging side of Liltin Yew, far removed from the bay of the Budd inlet, sunlight gets blocked behind hills. A hush seems to have settled among nature in the premature dusk, and it's tough not to feel its influence. One deep, anticipatory breath.

"Vada, y'all's game takes place right here?" Daniel ducks to step out from the canopy.

I'm still looking around, so Kristen answers for me. "Yeah, and it took almost a year for us to make. Did you really have no clue it's set here?"

"Nope!"

"Is weird, no?" Kat says to her boyfriend.

Daniel shrugs. "What it is is *kismet*. Destiny!"

I smile privately, grab the loose railing up to the old girls' barracks like I'm 11 again. I shoo a spider out of my way to peek inside. The skeleton of mine and Amy's bunk still sits in the back.

"Everything about today is destined. Y'all arrived right after I shooed away more of those Gershwin/Cossio hunters," Daniel tells my friends. "I put the fear of Jesus in 'em."

"What's the word on that anyway?" asks Rundee, extracting his tech from a blanket.

"No one knows," Taek-su mumbles before Daniel can. "The second Wong's Rights stream was uploaded an hour ago. It's set to Live Premiere so no one can skip ahead." He approaches SalishUs without the nervousness I would expect from him. "Hey, Dan. I have a quick question about your sister's phone."

A knot forms in my chest. I move closer to rejoin the others' setup, my ears pricked.

"Oh yeah?"

"I was wondering if you'd mind doing a quick Find My Phone on it."

"Uh, I'm about to start stream, kid. It's Just Chatting hour coming up."

"It's just . . . I don't think it takes long. Did you get my text earlier?"

". . . You must not have texted the right number. You think Amy's phone's not gonna be sitting in the hospital with her?"

I plug my backup battery into my VR kit.

Taek-su shifts uncomfortably. "Well, uh, we just may have noticed something weird earlier, so we kind of want to just make sure? Right, Vay?"

Acting surprised, and actually a little surprised he'd enlist me as backup, I offer a stilted nod. "Mm."

"Daniel," Kat touches his shoulder. "Your truck. Where is it?"

"It's safe." He keeps his focus on Taek-su, broadens it to include me. "It's safe like Amy's phone and Amy are safe. Look, maybe something weird happened with her phone, I don't know. But I've been assured directly that it's nothing to worry about."

"Assured by whom?"

With a patented, toothy SalishUs grin: "Our real benefactor. Y'all want anything to drink, kids? I'll even look the other way if you want some hard seltzers!"

"Er—no," I say. That's enough for me. It's my dream after all, so I'm probably the *benefactor* he's alluding to with his code-speech. I hum a tune as I try to fit Rundee's blanket on the picnic table. Taek-su seems all the more baffled.

"That blanket'll never cover the whole thing." Daniel gives Kat a pat and skips over some knotted thorns to our table. "Trade. I'm gonna use yours for sound dampening, just FYI."

He hands Rundee and Kristen a blanket; they cover the table with it.

"Bro," I say. It's a giant Washington Redskins logo.

"What? Oh, uh. Heh. It's an old blanket."

"You sure?" Kristen asks him. "Looks in really good condition to me."

"Yeah? Well," SalishUs stammers, "I take good care of my shit, what can I say?"

"It's 2025, dude," I mutter. I spread our TTRPG atop the giant offensive face. The grin on the logo feels like it's just for me, like it's laughing at me. I want to tell it to shut the fuck up, that this is *my* dream, but I restrain myself.

"Okay, and what if it has some sentimental value? What if my mom gave it to me as a kid or something?"

"Then maybe you can ask PredictAct to bet on you burning it live. That symbol certainly has sentimental value to *me*." I shake my head, just as I would if I were actually awake—only in my dream, I am much more confident doing so. "Not a positive one."

"I'm sorry, Vada." He throws his hands up in surrender. "Look, you kids covered it all up with your DnD stuff. There! That's like . . . symbolic." We watch him recede into his canopy tent. I can still feel the grin through our TTRPG spread. He hangs Rundee's blanket behind him, entertains the crawling baby.

"Sure took him a while to shut up," Taek-su muses.

"Input lag," says Katyusha, who has been listening next to her idling Scion the whole time. She shuts off the engine.

I must look so cool to my friends. I'm playing it like I don't care if he kicks us out before we even feature, and that's because I don't. This isn't reality, but even if it were, I don't think my behavior would be wildly far off. I don't need him. We don't need him. We just need us. I'm so cool I shiver in the breeze.

We sit down and resume our weekly Cyberpunk RED campaign. It's a street-level story about the normal folk affected by bloody corporate espionage over Kang Tao's smart gun blueprints; I'm our team's Solo. "I'm sorry," sputters Taek-su when he miscounts a skill-check roll. "Is this not weird to anybody else? Being here, acting all normal."

Rundee and Kristen don't know what to do. I'm sitting next to him, willing myself to psychically quell his spiking nerves. He doesn't know he is just a part of my dream.

My pocket buzzes, twice.

***Reify*'s first checkpoint.**

It's fake Amy. I swivel in my seat, lean to look at the spot in my old camp that we turned into *Reify*'s first checkpoint: the well.

"Pause." I stand and walk over to it.

In 2020 the well was caving in. I remember we'd find the biggest rocks that could fit, drop them in to hear the *thunk!*, the youngest of us claiming they felt a water droplet or two splash up at them. It was a risk; the well was right outside the furthest cabin where the adults slept. Amy and I would tell the others that we'd found a way into the rumored mineshafts below, made it to the ground water.

Now it only drops about 8 inches down before meeting a mess of brick, dirt, twigs—and one very recent addition, judging by the SalishUs-branded sticker on the hidden Beretta handgun case.

It's not even locked. I re-cover it and stab my eye toward Daniel's canopy tent. He's streaming live. I don't really care.

Katyusha exits it, stands in my way, flashes a warm smile that brags a diamond-encrusted cage on the bottom incisor.

"You want makeup? For tonight."

She applies foundation matching my skin tone as I do my best to sit still on a tree stump. I wonder why she even has something this tone. Daniel's not particularly known for the diversity of his guests.

"Daniel say he put fear of Jesus in trespassers earlier. That is what case in well is for."

I hum annoyedly, jaw static for Kat to smear contour and brush in a radiant blush.

"You know my child's name?" she asks gently.

I stutter and reach back in my thoughts. "I think Daniel told me y'all named him Max?"

"Not Daniel's baby, not *my* baby." Carefully she applies a matte heliotrope lipstick. "I have aunt in Russia. She receive Mother Heroine award. Beautiful son, fiercely loyal. Would kill to protect her. She hear he not survive 12 hours in Bakhmut. Puts gun in her mouth. It doesn't finish it right away."

She signals me to close my eyelids and I feel eyeshadow, lash thickener. "Nurses—this I hear in next room—tell her reason she miss brain is that her dead son punish her, for dare attempt such a thing. His name is Maxim. They use him. She is gone next morning. Open."

I meet her phone's front camera as I do. I'm glitching between admiring my reflection, a reflection that looks like I've profoundly leveled up, and Kat's parable. She doesn't seem to regard the dissonance.

"He has one son. He had named him same name. Maxim II. I bring him with me to America. Now, he *is* my baby." She puts her makeup kit into an oversized handbag, then reaches in. Between thumb and pinky she dangles the barrel of a pistol herself, diamond cage gleaming in her wide grin. "I see you are fighter. You should be. The world kills. I am ready to fight too." She lets it drop. "Daniel—"

She struggles with her phrasing here. I am taken aback. She is telling me something important to her. "He hides it from you, he is not showing you. It is for him to feel safe only." She abruptly rubs my shoulders with enthusiasm. "You look like snack!"

"Th-thanks." Hesitantly I hit a couple of my angles for her camera. The dream has taken a weird turn.

She nods and heads back to the tent. "Tell friends about guns, or do not. Is not big deal either way. Your choice."

**interesting.**

"Very," I respond aloud.

*Amy is typing . . .*

**but do u think he rly brought a Redskins blanket by accident??**

Taek-su, Rundee, and Kristen are packing away the TTRPG. "You were so set on getting us to play this morning . . ." Kristen grouses loud enough for me to hear as I approach.

"Vay," Taek-su says, "Seriously, what's . . ." He takes in my appearance. I've quite literally stunned him speechless.

"Incandescent." Rundee applauds. "Bioluminescent."

I glance at the collapsed well, at the streamers' canopy tent. It's now or never.

"Um . . . does anyone know where I put my eyecaps? The cool ones for the demo."

**kinda weird that he offered a bunch of kids alc right?**

"Oh. I bagged your stuff." Rundee dips into my bag and pulls out my case of cosplay eyecaps. "I put all the small stuff up top. This, your adapters, the 2010 USB, I don't know why I took it, but it felt right. Lucky thumb drive."

"Thumb drive?"

I didn't hear Daniel leave the tent; he's on break, a caffeinated carrot water in his hand.

"You have a thumb drive?"

"Huh? Well, it's not ours." Rundee turns the silver thing in his fingers. "I found it in Elonia."

"You said 2010 USB? Like the year 2010?"

"Yeah, it's a slide show for the reunion."

Daniel lurches forward.

"I think I might know where that came from."

"Like who it belongs to?" Kristen takes over for Rundee, who's flustered by Daniel's sudden insistence.

Daniel just nods. "Can I have a look?"

Rundee hands him the drive and hands me my case of eyes. Choosing between the lime-green eyecap and the black/purple one, I also watch SalishUs behind his mosquito nets, searching for a free USB port on his rig.

Taek-su clears his throat. The others have gone off to pack the TTRPG.

I point to mine and Amy's cabin. "I slept in there three summers in a row. Surreal."

"What's going on with you?"

I gulp.

"You're acting like you know something." He looks guilty as fuck for saying it. I feel that swell of helplessness again. It's not a good feeling. "Like you're in on something."

I hate it. I can't stand the feeling of actively harming him, confusing him, condemning even a simulacrum of him to the dark. Do I crash the dream around me? Do I shatter the illusion by speaking it out loud? He watches me with increasing alarm; it must be all over my face.

Okay. This sucks, but now's as good a time as any to tap out.

"I'm dreaming," I whisper, and even though I'm bracing, it's like my soul unclenches. "I'm in a dream."

The world doesn't blink white like in the VR YewVerse. I'm not falling through the ground. I'm still here, looking in Taek-su's eyes, and they've softened.

"I feel like I am too," he says quietly. "I stopped looking at my phone because nothing I'm seeing on it makes goddamned sense."

"What, like it turned into hieroglyphs or something?" This happens to me sometimes.

"Like it was all a bunch of hyper-specific stuff about our town, and none of it can be true . . ." Shakily he sighs. "Ever since the thing about some American airstrike in Iran this onslaught of shit started hitting town. It's like some sort of coordinated media blitz, like an info assault. That's how invasions start, Vada. I tried looking if different countries were covering this and everyone is just reflecting it back and saying it's really going on, to the point where it's like I don't know if they're bots? I'm scared, Vay. Are we locked down? Is everywhere else getting isolated right now?" He is just about hyperventilating.

"Taek-su, it's okay."

"You don't . . ." He faces away to wipe his nose. ". . . think that's what's happening right now?"

"I don't think so . . . I don't hope so. Er," I search. "It wouldn't explain everything. Like the demo, where and when we're doing it." *Like Amy.*

The gentle chaos of rustling leaves. Bugs chirring. The summer sky darkening. I finally let my awareness expand, just a little. Off his mention of phones, I look to mine reflexively:

**ur dreams are stronger than you think.**

That's very nice of her to say. She can stop chaperoning us, though. Given our history it's a little problematic.

"Well, I know *I'm* real." I push that same sturdy shoulder.

"I think *I* am too," he says in relative disbelief. "I won't push a lady, though."

"You're fine," I assure him.

"*You're* fine." His chuckle turns to dread. "I mean, you, you know."

"Hm." I lift an eyebrow. We allow ourselves to laugh at one another.

"Hey, I think I'm gonna steal Daniel's phone to find Amy's."

"Oh!" I consider. "Okay." Amy's on my side now, that I know. And I can feel it in my gut: If I wanted to, I could fly right now. I'm in full control. "I think I know just when I can buy you some time to do that."

Taek-su's bewilderment at my approval gives way to something like muted awe. "When will that be?"

Daniel and Katyusha are silhouettes in their canopy tent. They are locked in a heated discussion; he holds the USB drive up to her as if in offering. I watch them intently. "Around when I humiliate SalishUs on his own stream," I say. "Tell Rundee and Kristen."

# 20

# QUINN GERSHWIN

Assurance of an unspoken understanding has proven my swiftest guarantor of failure.

First and most damning is my 2022 TLI meeting in Seattle. Strutting into whatever restaurant that was, thinking I'd assessed the risks and had them figured. Of course it would be recorded, but I had this expectation for others' awareness of their own self-interest, their capacity to maintain some collectively beneficial privacy. I was asking for too much professionalism, because it's undoubtedly been bombarding the news for hours.

Next is Taylor. I should have voiced my misgivings at the straw donations instead of sealing them and pretending they didn't exist. The campaign was—*was*, I reflect grimly—still fledgling. We hadn't even started canvassing in earnest. Hadn't even considered opening that warchest, not yet. I still should have told her. She could have pulled me back to Earth.

And now it's Bonnie Cossio and Arnold Wong. I follow them underground as the dark passage splits. One tunnel angles upwards, the other down. The three of us reach a curt agreement. Fifty paces each way, then double back to the fork to compare notes. Bonnie elects to go by herself.

We do this in front of what I assume are many thousands of witnesses peering through the young streamer's transition lenses. At mine and Bonnie's protests he, and I quote, "shut it off." It most certainly is insulting that he'd expect us to believe him, but he's only 20 years old. She and I don't display our frustrations. People are watching, after all.

The upwards-sloping passage terminates at the bottom of a storm drain. We can't reach its lowest rebar handhold. At any rate the temperamental sunlight 30 feet above is caged by thick, braided steel—Wong and I double back.

He sounds exceptionally winded. This is not much of a surprise; cardio is my specialty, his is steroids. Still, my tender right ankle twinges when I catch the ground wrong, and given that we're sometimes feeling blindly in the dark, it's happening far too often.

I find the fork in the passage just in time to see Bonnie's flashlight return up the other route. It occurs to me that when we split, I accepted she was probably not coming back. It's what I would have done. I can't tell if I'm humbled or exasperated.

"This one keeps going." She points behind her.

"Ours didn't. Downhill's the answer anyway, especially a diversion drain like this."

"Diversion drain, huh?" Wong catches up, laboring, and we all descend together. Bonnie's phone's GPS is no help. The connection is fitful and has us jumping around a wide block of green.

"Why aren't you calling your ex-husband?" Wong talks through gulps that aren't quite heaves, turns to me. "Or your wife?"

I let him think that question through: the townies in pursuit, his own live stream. The shame of it all. "Why haven't you found the way you came in?" I say simply. Bonnie snorts.

Muggy air steadily gathers locomotion. I walk abreast of Bonnie, but we have to slow several times; Arnold is lagging behind. What is wrong with him? Two of him still wouldn't equal my age. He mutters to himself with a hand on his heart. Must be talking to his viewers.

A low horizontal slit harshly shines around a twist in the passage. Weighted drain cover, I wager. The basement's basement. I let it burn my pupils taut.

Bonnie and I find the center latch, shoulder the weight, and push.

Thanklessly Wong slides under the drain cover. We follow him in unison—*in unison*, I think with disgust—and into a thin drain, dry as a spent vein, all dead roots and buzzing puddles. Its cement walls slope to meet the ground fifty or so meters ahead. I see the tops of a churning tree perimeter beyond.

Head bent to the sky, Wong furiously taps at the temple of his glasses. He leans on the crumbling walls for support. "Gyuh. Finally. Signal. Okay . . ."

"You didn't have a signal?" I ask.

"Ngh. 'S underground, idiot." He is wheezing. "I could only record."

Bonnie looks at him, then me. "He's uploading it."

I find myself walking a little faster to catch up with him.

"When did you switch from your livestream to start recording, Wong?" I ask him. He turns to look at me, tapping once on his glasses' rim this time. Startled, I take one step back, and not because he is recording me again.

His neck looks almost necrotic. The spot where the six-legged bug had sunk its fangs is a sickly purplish red, bulging outward, all around it yellow as if a weeks-old bruise. Behind the tinted glasses Wong's eyelids droop, his face pained and gasping for air. The knuckles of the hand over his heart are white.

"Mr. Gershwin, didja use any slush fund to fund opposition research?" he slurs.

"Wong," I gasp, "The bug bite . . . something's wrong with—"

"Didja tell any of your team whatchu, whatchu . . ."

He slumps against the now waist-high wall. I help him sit.

"Don't talk about any of that right now, Wong. Why didn't you say anything? We've got to airlift you or something."

"Phone died," he speaks as if chewing gravel, "ages ago. Got the tip 'bout y'all on the road." He winces. "Gas station . . . outta charging blocks."

"All right, all right." I curse under my breath. Gnats lash at our faces. The kid is having a heart attack. "Let's keep you upright. You should stop talking."

He hacks, "What about your position on Israel?"

I rip the glasses off of his face and press the same rim button he did moments ago. "I—what? Don't talk."

Bonnie laughs heartily before reaching us, then stops and jumps backwards. "Jesus, what the fuck?"

"The bug," I stutter. "Poisoned him or something."

"'M fine."

"You very much the fuck aren't." Bonnie whips out her dying phone.

I put the glasses on, find the video I've just stopped, and delete it.

Three melodious taps and Bonnie's dialing someone.

"Bonnie," Massaging my forehead, I force my face and jaw to slacken once more, Taylor's meditative training a lifeline that stops me from shouting. I delete the video from the trash can, too. "It's fine. Don't try and game out the consequences. We're not getting elected to so much as a school board after today. We're done. If anything, saving him will help both of us going forward. Call 911."

She's not listening.

She is pale, her gaze fixed behind and just above me.

Where a bloodied, sunburnt woman in torn clothes crawls close enough for me to count the twigs in her hair.

Her breath hits my face. Alarm beams like reeking waves from her eyes and mine and crashes into the sliver of space between us.

Through quicksand, I leap to the opposite side of the drain, detonating my right ankle as the woman hoarsely croaks, *"You."* Her voice is fried. Attempts to will out more lock her in a veiny, silent scream. Dirty fingers find the wall's edge and she raises herself shaking to a crouch, a rabid gargoyle.

"*You.*"

"Stay back!" Bonnie's hand is suddenly in her purse.

"We can hear you out," I'm saying. "What's going on? The others looking for us, did they do this to you? Did you fall from something?"

A death rattle resolves as a dry cough; she gawks at Bonnie and me. "*Y-you murdered my friends.*"

"Ma'am?"

Lacerated chest flaring, she points a red hand squarely at me. "*George . . . Anne . . . the rainbow tracks . . .*" The intruder falls into the narrow drain with us. "*How could you?*"

"Ma'am, please, *what are you saying?* The rainbow tracks? Just help me understand."

When she rights herself, dry-sobbing, her head splits open out the back in a crimson fissure, a solid object suddenly ribbons and jelly with a slack mouth; the body seems to reverse-step, then crumples haphazardly onto the low wall.

Nitroglycerin stings my nostrils. Retroactive sense recognition of the *crack* blooms right-to-left, a blaring deafness. Bonnie does not lower her compact pistol; her elbows lock.

Several things happen very quickly. She shouts challenges at the tall grass; Wong tries to lift his head and fails; I've crushed his glasses in my hand. Everything is muffled. I flinch as Bonnie flags me. She's suddenly wiping the handle and trigger on her joggers and placing it in Wong's hand. She sprints from the drain and into the perimeter of churning trees.

My gaze cannot dislodge from the body. Sludge is sliding out its soft top.

"Hello?" someone is saying as if from another universe. "Hello?"

Bonnie's abandoned phone lies between roots. Her call to 911 did in fact go through.

I wring breath like water from a beach towel.

So does Wong, but louder.

I could just stay here.

"Hello?"

"It's me!" I call uphill, out of breath from running, to Bonnie after finally catching up with her. She is peering behind a thicket. We're fully shaded by the forest now. My ankle feels like it might fall off, and at this point, I kind of want it to.

"I killed her," she says through shivers. "Oh my God, it's a prank, right? I didn't kill someone. I did not just kill someone."

I stagger up to her, then stop. Out of nowhere, I taste something sweet.

A horrid *whirring* from above fills the undergrowth, like a massive cloud of wasps. Dread overwrites all. I starred in an advertisement for Liltin "Yew-tilities" a year back, I know the sound of spinning drone blades.

Launching under the ferns at a maple tree's base, tucking my legs, the *whir* abruptly magnifies and cuts above, recedes toward the valley from where we ran.

Aggressively, I gulp, muscle down the gag reflex, as I swivel to spot my mayoral rival. She's hiding too. The relief I feel is violent: At least someone still has a sense of self-preservation. I part the ferns at their base to get a sightline.

Distant shouts and engines echo up from the diversion drain's valley. From way up here I can spot the empty retention pond we passed under less than an hour ago. I wait, eyes glued. "You killed someone," I inform Bonnie.

I would have stayed.

I would have stayed, but there was a groyper mob on the way, a mostly headless corpse, a political streamer in cardiac arrest, a loaded gun, a murderous bimbo, and me. Me, too black to survive this situation. Bonnie wasted no time in shooting the intruder; I was mere inches from her face. Darker-skinned herself, Asian, Southeast Asian—what mattered in the moment was not that she was terrified, but that she did not look like Bonnie Cossio.

I was talking with her.

My head is in my hands.

Down in the valley, a pristine Gladiator pickup with the license plate DEVST8R rocks across the tall grass and stops at the drain head. Half a dozen folks pour forth as it idles, rolling coal in place. Every one of them camo-clad.

If these people want *us* to spot *them*, why would they wear camo?

More Cossio crazies. Maybe Wong's Rights die-hards or opportunists. None mutually exclusive, none appeal.

They find the kill box. Everybody converges. Their voices turn shrill. The FPV drone pilot is a kid with a grey VR block over his eyes in the pickup's bed; when the pickup lurches forward to the drainhead, the goggled kid screams.

"They'll find Wong," I hear behind me. No shit. Already did. I observe a minute longer. Arnold Wong is loaded onto the pickup while the kid is helped off. The DEVST8R lumbers off the way it came. The rest fan out.

I hear a sucking-in of air and stand to see Bonnie already on the move.

We trek upwards then downwards uninterrupted for a full twenty minutes. Bonnie has an Adderall pill in the bottom of her purse. We split it.

Ankle pulling uncomfortably, I lead us laterally across a hill. We're skimming past the Hoh Rainforest. The search party thickens all the while, and the resilient drone makes regular passes. It takes time.

We accumulate scrapes. Bonnie's joggers are unrecognizable under mud. I keep replaying the moment she wiped her gun on them.

Our mutual shares in TLI's slush fund are undeniable. Our actions on the day of exposure will finish this story, for better and for worse.

"Were you waiting for me?" I ask.

"What?" Scant drizzling from the clouds and tree cover above, Bonnie tries to catch water on her tongue.

Drops land hot on my sunburned neck. "After you left the drain, were you waiting?"

She sighs. "Waiting and watching."

I pick up a deer trail and decide to follow it.

"Hey, you don't have my phone, do you?"

I shake my head. "They have it."

After a minute she nods. "Good. Let them look. I have nothing to hide."

Fresh off a slaughter and a staged crime scene, Bonnie is moving with purpose. Escaping a roided-out political streamer, maybe, who gunned down an innocent fan of hers. A *Chinese* American streamer at that. She's betting on the story of today to claw her way out of the scandal. It's like she's willing a future and following it.

She bets a lot on Wong not surviving, though. His flashy glasses, albeit cracked in two, are still stuffed in my biker shorts. Only the right lens displays a screen on its inner plate.

## —PLOADED via Cloud

Over a peaceful blue background.

I successfully suppressed his last recording when he wanted my boilerplate *Israel has a right to exist* response—which they don't, to be clear, but you'll never hear me saying it. The recording in the tunnels, however, made it through.

My ankle is swollen. I hobble. Shockingly, Bonnie slows to accommodate. We keep low and hide often as Earth's rotation bends the sun under wild vistas, the gathering darkness affecting my unhealed Lasik vision. We swap the ridgeline deer trail for one more traveled, which delves further into shade, taking us inwards. It traces a lush green spine for a mile or two. The whirs of the drone come further and further at our backs now, flora a shield.

Maybe she doesn't care if Wong lives. If the kid has any accurate recollections, they're compromised in a court of law by way of undergoing a severe health crisis at the time. Even if admissible, whispered stories of

Bonnie being the one to valiantly shoot a brown-skinned vagrant, saving both her *and* the Democrat, why, that's bipartisan. Feeds her base too. Fattens them, actually. She might emerge from this with public sentiment.

I don't think she remembers the camera from the morning. The hidden one planted by Wong in the satellite treatment plant before we arrived, the one that her acolytes busted in on. Of the two of us, I may have been the only one to hear them clearly; I'd remained at the cellar door longer. Wait, I *was* the only one: I remember now. When the mob broke into the facility, she'd already started down the drain.

*Do I say anything?* I think. *Do I remind her she threatened me with a gun when we were secretly livestreamed?*

"Quinn, what's going on? Why are you laughing?"

"It's a trauma response. Ignore it."

She looks like she wants to say something, her expression hollow, raw. I close my eyes and watch that girl's face shred into ribbons once more. Bonnie turns around.

The moment she perceives freedom from the thorns she will try to kick me back into them. But my story—the full truth—likely already circulates, while Bonnie will publicly act under the assumption that no one has seen this morning's recording, at least for long enough to damn herself. It will be like that one horrible girl from *Love Island* who was exposed for incessant racial bullying.

Very soon there will be time to watch reality shows with Taylor again.

If she lets me.

Eventually the natural passageway plummets. The lopsided hillside levels to a low-grade landing halved by a rivulet. We remain elevated, however, and for the first time in hours there is a distant sign of civilization.

Through a near-vertical cascade of trees is a cluster of lights far below, widely spaced, a considerable compound overhanging the sunset-drenched Duwamish River.

"That's not TLI, is it?"

"It must be," I say.

Incredulous, she scoffs. "God sure has a sense of humor, doesn't She?"

I exhale sharply as the branch I lean on snaps.

"Look at this, Quinn." Head cocked to the side, she points with a silent *ohh* to a broad hole that burrows into our hillside. It is no cave. Caves are not traditionally buttressed by wooden planks.

"It's a portal. This is where the mines used to be," Bonnie says with awe. "Hm. Do you see that? Above the threshold there."

"I do not." I squint at the mine's mouth, but the forest is too dark; my blurred vision can't detect anything.

When Bonnie is flush with the entrance, she exclaims, bends down.

She's holding something. "The fuck are the odds," I hear her mutter. Her hand ignites and I almost think she's shooting me now. It's a flashlight. She points it.

A huge swab of reddish-brown, some dried viscera, stands out on the threshold of the ancient mine. Dried, but not anywhere near as crusty as the wood beneath. Somewhat new. My hands are on my hips. "What is that?"

"Graffiti. I'm thinking we cut through here, Quinn. We have a flashlight now!"

"We'll get lost again."

"I know mines. This is the slope. Main adits and shafts are straightforward." She paints the threshold herself with light. "We can give it a look, make sure nothing's collapsed. This will save us hours and be easier on your foot."

I deliberate. "Let me guess, your family used to oversee these mines way back when?"

"Of course not." Bonnie starts into the mouth with that same semi-wired energy. "That was my ex-husband's great-grandparents."

It's the last straw.

She doesn't immediately notice I'm stationary. The beam of light hits me from deep inside the mine. "I was thinking about the ol' tree octopi."

Citing an old PNW joke, our regional subset of Sasquatch, I go maximum politician mode: smile easy, tone conversational. "It's so elusive. It could be anywhere. I'm thinking, maybe that's what's responsible for what happened to that girl. The girl who was coming at us in the valley. A tree octopus."

The light beam lowers to the ground in front of me like a drooped head.

My ocular handicap makes reading her face impossible. The pause is pronounced, though. I imagine a frightened girl, tears welling, maybe. I'll never know. "It could've been anyone," I hear an uneven mix of slyness and hesitance like she's trying something on for the first time.

My facade stays right where it's supposed to. "Right. Well, I will see you down there." I limp wide of the mine's mouth.

"Quinn."

She would rather navigate the descent with company. "Bonnie, I'm tapped out of enclosed spaces for the day, maybe the year. If it's caved in you just double back and follow the path that got us here. I'm sure you'll see me. I can't exactly hustle."

With no answer nor pursuit, I've undoubtedly filed myself back into her old, familiar hatred; I am free of her.

—

I was hoping that her absence would lift more than just my spirits and I'm not disappointed. Second wind. I'm lighter. My screaming ankle lowers its dial to a dull roar. And it's all downhill from here.

Protecting my compromised eyes, I wrap Wong's bisected glasses together with twine. They must have transitioned back to clear frames when Wong was face-down in the drain.

What if Wong's hidden camera in the satellite treatment plant had been too far away to detect audio? Bonnie is not aware of the thing at all, while I in turn may be over-investing in it. It was a highly noisy facility. I suppose all will be revealed in a couple of hours when I emerge in front of TLI. I don't plan on sticking around there.

The sharp *snap* of a twig spins me around and I catch four scurrying legs. A deer lags behind me, blending in and out of the foliage. I'm woven by my path into a gully twice as wide as that fatal drain head, but with higher walls of dirt and thick, eye-level knotted roots.

My adoptive parents took me in at 5 years old; I lived just long enough before that to be surprised when my first official school charged me for a meal. My parents looked just like me. Not many knew I was adopted. They told me matter-of-factly that it's just how things went here. The paid meals, to be specific.

For decades I kept in contact with a few of my friends from foster care. Most were white or native. Some were consumed by the system in so many ways, others like myself hit the lottery. I never forget any of them.

"School lunches and buses" will be the most charitable motivator assigned to my backing of TLI's rehabilitation center. If the public is anything like Wong and runs with the "private prison for kids" narrative—which sounds absurd, but I simply don't know anymore—charitability won't be in the cards for me. Stifling a shout at a sudden tweak in my ankle, I know the latter will be my lot. I've known charity exactly once, as a child, and the parents who showed me it died within 8 months of one another.

A spurt of vines shudders along the gully's ridge as the deer trots above, hurries quickly past. There's a heavier crunch from further away over the opposing ridge. Must be time for the whole family to come home. I empathize.

I miss Taylor. She entertained my pursuit in Liltin High Class of '99, by allowing such a kid into her world. I guess I've known charitability twice. Her family was a nuisance. Through college we white-knuckled life's roughest patches, buried our parents, cheated a couple times, closed our disparities in earnest and then that was it: we won each other for life. I don't think that's all going to change in a day.

The gully gives way to a clearing. Monochromatic navy-blue forest on all sides, shadows which fuse. With an effort I discern the shape of the deer ahead; it stands still. Firs, evergreens climb high toward clouds which burn orange, red and deep purple, far above.

At the age of eleven the first proper PG-13 premiere my parents let me attend was *Jurassic Park*. I still remember the bullying from dressing up as Mr. Arnold for freshman Halloween. It was a formative moment that dulled my enthusiasm for paleontology. But in '96, Taylor and I first met alongside mutual friends at a drive-in re-release, two years before we'd actually start dating.

A series of soft *thuds* land in the gully behind me. The second deer has bounded down the ridge, bringing itself level with me.

It's closer than the first; I can see it better and am forced to admit that for the past 5-odd minutes, I've assured myself of an unspoken understanding between me and these deer: namely, that they are in fact deer, and aren't stalking me. The quiet, deep growl may as well emit a centimeter from my ear.

Just like *Jurassic Park*'s heavily fictionalized version of velociraptors, a wolf often draws attention to its prey's front, serving as distraction while another, hidden wolf, strikes the unguarded angle.

He's no longer hiding, forelegs planted slightly wider than hind, head bowed and locked impassively to my every movement. Pupils dilated, fur matted—this one is huge.

I need to be able to see them both. I have to let them triangulate me. I make myself large, back up slowly, every footfall, half of which are painful, an oscillating decision. Nothing sudden.

Then my right heel meets the faintest divot in the earth and my ankle gives out completely.

As the huge one springs, I beg my mind to flee its body, and a deafening *crack* cleaves the forest. I land hard on my back.

I part my trembling hands—both wolves are now bolting into the blurry darkness, the sudden sound sending them fleeing.

The sudden sound exactly like the one back in the fatal drain head.

My chest is burning. Splitting. My arms turn to lead and I can't cover the hole between my ribs.

"Holy shit," I hear someone say, "Did you get that? I fucking nailed him!"

# 21

# OUR SYSTEM IS CHIASTIC

We'll be tender babies.

The fabled Feynman papers are finally accessed through years of finesse. It remains the hardest thing we've done. The first time we see them, 7 hours remain in our day, which proves insufficient. We try to access them 5 more times, with a 60% success rate. The last time we get a peak, we smuggle them out and reveal them to the world out of spite. That's a fun day.

With help from the new proofs, we classify our transmedium USO's cold glow as a faster-than-light "photonic fluid," for lack of a better term, which is kinetically blasting and reconfiguring our neurons in the split-second it is piercing the original Us. We transform our projected time hole into a Mandelbrot and determine its duration relative to two observers. Our findings' ramifications dawning, dread shading our hearts, we seek a second opinion.

We find Nanno Sripariyattiwetti, as she is every 7:00 A.M. bar our interference, with her friends on the rainbow tracks. Otherworldly charisma redirects her attention towards the two new faces carrying a notebook of fresh equations. She is a CalTech grad herself.

"So, this one's actually not too bad in terms of iterations," Nanno ponders. "Standard depth. I like that you make it look like a recursive sunspot."

"But cold." We nod. The three of us are sat on the bridge's edge, six legs swinging off purple-colored planks. "Garden-variety fractal curve," we offer.

"Only because it's doubled. Which you guys were right to do." Holding whipping bangs from her eyes Nanno pours over our scrawlings. "Would've been a small divot if not for that." She doesn't catch our smile at each other. "63,528 iterations is what I'm getting. Is that close to what you guys got?"

"Yes," we laugh. "Roughly." 63,000-odd iterations total north of 174 years. 174 years of the same day—

"And," Nanno reminds us on a subsequent visit—this time we make it to the small island at the end of the bridge—"your calculations make it chiastic. So what you traverse *into* the Mandelbrot you'll reverse *out* of."

"Relive every iteration in reverse?"

"Entropy, folks," Nanno says, then furrows her brow. "This is just a hypothetical though. I mean these are astounding equations, some of the wildest I've ever seen—"

"Well, right," we reassure.

"But no, wouldn't exactly mirror the same rate," she goes on, plucking green thorns from her leggings. "I imagine the trip backwards would be sort of erratic, haphazard. Like skipping around as it retraces."

"Fun." We breathe into our diaphragms, calming ourselves by force.

"Hey, don't I know you? Aren't you Anne Oxendine?"

We pick up where we left off the next morning.

"If these proofs of yours are real," Nanno says, once more a stranger, "then the observer can't actually *experience* this without an equal and opposite charge to pull from."

"Feynman's proofs," we remind her. "Not ours."

"Okay," she says doubtfully.

A full 24-hour iteration doesn't steal a full 24 hours at a time. No, if Einstein and Feynman are right then one iteration robs the most recent 4-

ish hours' experience from pre-time hole George and Anne. Those stolen hours reach further into our linear pasts each time.

"When we reverse, we'd get those hours back, right?"

"Uh-uh. Energy's already transferred. You'll flow backwards through what's already been created."

The ugly truth is that eventually the time hole will consume decades' worth. When the USO's cold glow has finally traversed our brains' many-worlds, we will emerge collapsed back into the observable one. But we will do so having lost almost our entire lived experiences.

"Someone like that could maybe retain motor functions," Nanno muses the next morning, suntanning with us on the orange tracks long after her friend group has left. "A baby elk falls out of its mother's cooch and it's already walking around."

"Wouldn't have its sea legs, though," we rejoin, "this hypothetical newborn adult." What little our senses retain will no doubt be bathed in horror; we'll be whimpering, wet things in need of immediate care. We'll instead be all alone for miles on the edge of a dirty river.

"Would they comprehend who they are at all? Would they have any awareness?"

Nanno shakes her head. "I'm no ontologist."

So we'll be tender babies. We could die *for real* mere minutes after the lobotomized versions of us tumble from the time hole into the wild.

"Not quite." Nanno interjects, pointing with the mug of tea we've bought her the next afternoon. This time we've told her our entire story and she entertains it as a thought experiment. "This 'photonic fluid' you were talking about earlier. Tell me more."

"Well, we thought at first it's just the craft's propulsion. Then we figured, with how quickly the craft moves, it *could* be a kind of LiDAR, a directional mapping—"

"Like something thrown not just ahead but behind," we interrupt ourselves, "that freezes physical dimensions of its trajectory, allowing it to zip around unbound by their rules."

"And we think," we interrupt ourselves again, "the craft's emergence from the water, the photonic radiation in the sunrise—"

"Given we're locked in a dawn-to-dawn loop—"

"Factor into it," Nanno finishes. "Right. You said 'freezing.' And that it felt cold."

"Mhm." We sip our coffees. Our Unmaker's rays are, as we speak, flexing and pounding and pulsing and smoothing the wrinkles in our brains, out there in the first dawn of '25's summer solstice.

"So, a cooling effect. Who's to say that's not preserving the interiors of your brains?"

"... Like some magic cryo-stasis."

"Exactly," she says. "And you know what they say about magic."

That evening our she-half and he-half borrow a pair of cellos from a retired pit player in Liltin's suburbs. Via duet, we work through it: if George and Anne on the other side understand the danger of the river, remember how to use a phone even, then our immediate crisis will disappear. Our minds would regrow and relearn a version of who we really are. Not the self-murdering sadomasochists. We secretly hope that we get to retain an instrument, or an extra language or two.

The humans in us might survive this.

"Unless you've broken the equal-and-opposite-force law, that is!" declares Nanno off-handedly as we walk through town with her the next day.

"How's that?" We're squinting in the sun.

"Well, just don't push back too hard. Don't add to the clock."

"But how would we do that?" we ask, as one.

"Forcing a day reset, I imagine. Distorting the natural duration." She shrugs. "Because the situation you're describing, it's borderline nonsense, but that just makes it a natural event that hasn't been studied. It has rules."

The three of us turn a corner and close in on some bustling outdoor dining. "Suicide could force a day reset."

"If suicide doesn't just delete you altogether, then yeah."

"It doesn't," our she-half says.

"Right, well," Nanno inhales the savory smells from the restaurant. "Don't do that, then. You may even think it'd fast-forward the iterations, but it'd probably just compound this 'time hole' of yours further."

Before a waiter can seat a couple at the only empty spot we pick up its chairs and throw them through the window. We flip food-laden tables and send plates spinning into passing cars. We push screaming people away from us and flee.

We can avoid cops. Not like it matters if we're arrested. We trudge through Liltin Yew's clamoring harbor, about ten paces from each other. We're seeing ourselves from behind, and we hate it.

At 5:12 P.M. we duck into a mill freshly emptied of its workers and we beat each other up. It begins as a furious fight. It becomes an equal trading of blows. We're broken open, inches from another death, leaking.

"Don't," we tell ourselves through a lopsided jaw.

Panting, sighing, we watch the light drain from the mill's frosted windows.

"This isn't working," we groan.

By way of *no shit*, our feral cry fills what's left of our hearts. We didn't know what we didn't know. We stopped counting suicides long ago. There was a whole month there where half of us woke up, got the rifle from our closet, and blasted ourselves into tomorrow just to see what would happen. We thought that nothing happened. When we make it out of the time hole, we may not be babies. We may be braindead on the spot.

The silent mill is pitch-black. We've hurt each other too deeply. One of us bleeds out, then the other. It's the last time we will, maybe the last time we'll feel anything novel. The stutter in the dawn carries us away as if in disgust.

Downstairs our dog is wheezing.

# 22

# WILLIAM TILLER AND FATE

William Tiller usually approaches these kinds of things with an agenda. A mutually understood agenda that is (if dealing with actual adults) very straightforward. But parking under the balcony of a two-floor house in a shared alley, telling his new acquaintance Hunter Dames that he needs a minute before joining her inside, watching her wave to smoking neighbors across low-fenced back porches, Bill realizes that he didn't angle into a compliment, a flirt, for the whole car ride. They both just talked and gave each other space to answer. Like dipping a toe into a hot tub in winter.

She trusts him to find the back entrance. The house is no longer a house, Every little room is a part of one sprawling, dusty record shop. Not just vinyls. Not just cassettes and CDs. Turntables, amps, phonographs, a shrine to Tomita and Electronico Fantastico. Signed KIRARA and ManicPixieBoyToy shirts behind glass. Plants everywhere feeding on the ample sunlight from the open windows.

As Hunter leads him upstairs Bill counts more wires, coils, a Zipdisk or two; other specialized junk to the untrained eye which, in actuality, is a tinkerer's paradise. Over a dozen cathode-ray TVs in various states of undress. Soldering boards and irons. Clunky box fans, microphones, kickstands.

Bill spots a price tag on a mimeograph and dives hungrily on it. "I can qualify this as a business expense."

By self-labeling as *Luddite*, he really means that his affinity for technology drops off past the mid-2000s shedding of tactility. After passing through a balcony door the first oddity that meets his gaze is a row of upward-angled late-'90s CRT TVs parked on the painted wood, each switched on and displaying a different solid color with frozen black tracking bars. Next, he sees a mint-hued Hitachi stand fan from the 1980s, strapped around the shoulders of the record store's owner, a bespectacled Japanese woman with lavender-ash hair and a facemask. The fan blades and cage are tipped down.

An active A/C unit leans on the distressed siding of the overtaken balcony but a blinking white light below its vent signals its true re-purpose. Pranav the waiter in a fresh change of clothes wraps a coil around two fingers and waves his hand over the wind-gushing grate; an ethereal high warbling comes from the amp by the A/C's side. He and the store owner move into position on the second story balcony, preparing for some kind of performance.

Bill looks over the railing and sees people on the neighboring lawns below, pulling up plastic chairs and settling in.

"We ready?" calls Pranav.

"When you are," says the store owner.

One hoodied man behind the rainbow row of large CRT TVs pounds on them, pitch modulating uniquely by the screens' lines, stomping Wah pedals as percussion; the facemasked woman clicks a Speco push-to-talk along the spinning fan's sides and center to lay the bass loop; another joins, distorting static by swiping barcodes with a scanner. Pranav stabs the air over the air conditioner and drifts, harpsichordal liltings over every other downbeat.

They rock around as one, instruments all gussied up with amps 'n wires. Below, the aged audience whoops, clapping along with their spouses amidst raised beers and blunts. A most PNW-ass venture.

For their set's last song, Pranav drops instruments in Hunter's and William's hands. William is given a smaller CRT TV out of which a wooden neck springs, RGB buttons all up it. "Shred her, man."

This song comes faster, louder. Covers his mistakes. The rest of the band of course hears, but grace is all they give in return. They are all warm and intense, livid IQs, at ease exploding into the spotty sun. "Well, shoot," buzzes Bill at the song's conclusion, eyeing the guitar-TV dotingly, "could see myself makin' one of these."

They breakdown the equipment. "Hunter and I didn't speak for, what was it? Almost a year," Pranav says, laughing between grunts. He sets the transcendental A/C unit inside all on his own.

"Don't tell 'im that," Hunter grins.

"My boy wasn't leaving her daughter alone," Pranav says, ignoring her, "her first year of middle school. And in response I was apparently being . . . How'd you phrase it?"

"I used an expression I've these days risen above," Hunter clasps her hands. "Bill, it's time to leave."

She is tense in the passenger seat of his rental car, her hands clenched over her knees. "Err," Bill tries, "so what's the best beer the Barking Shark serves?"

"Salt & Seed Gosé," she responds enthusiastically, looking thankful for the resumed conversation. "My favorite, period. Acquired taste for sure."

"'Gosé'? Never even heard of it. Now I'm curious." He switches highways; they are halfway to the Cape. The hilly journey feels like one long, winding rollercoaster, but the chill version. Canyons of green trees and pillar-like stone.

"All right, Bill. You started it. Some Higher Power arranged our meet-cute and it's our duty to burn through every dead date ritual to figure out who. Gimme your cringiest pickup line."

"I'll do you one better, it used to be my Tinder bio."

"Oh god."

"'Just looking for my needle in a hoestack.'"

"You're somehow both basic *and* a sociopath."

"Dad jokes hit in the flyover states, girl. What's your cringiest?"

"Hell no. Too embarrassing. Furthest you've traveled?" she asks, cute creases in the corners of her mouth. He tries not to look for too long.

"Astoria from Wall. My first serious commission was a megabuilding replica out of a Series X, I didn't trust the shippers. One of the few smart business moves I made startin' out. You?"

"Greenland," she wistfully whispers. She won't unstick her gaze from the front windshield, as if the moment she does, they'll crash. "Laid at the base of a sundog for 15 minutes. Transformed me, dude. What if you could settle down somewhere? Anywhere."

"Oh, a good patch of farm would be fulfilling. South, maybe North Dakota. Land's still cheap enough to offset some upfront on the solar grazing setup. Your turn."

"Aluminum pod in whichever lunar colony's completed first."

He laughs. "We'll unpack that later. So, why the fear of driving? If you don't mind me asking." It takes one second of silence to realize that Hunter very much does.

Her expression is blank, more shocked than offended. Bill flushes. "Sorry, it's just the thing from your bio."

"Thing?" Her voice has turned serious. "My bio?"

"Er, *Anne's* bio, I mean." He takes a deep breath. "The . . . it said 'don't ask me to drive', or something."

Hunter takes her eyes from the windshield for the first time, drops them to her feet. "Yours said you talk in your sleep."

Very slowly William's stomach flips, descends.

Not only is it an *extremely* personal dig, but a dig that no person could know to make against him. Not outside of him and, of course, his ex-girlfriend, who left him in his sleep at blue hour. After 4 years of dating and a CD opened to save for an engagement ring. "But you weren't told what that means either," he says, diplomatically.

Hunter shakes her head. "And I'm okay keeping it that way."

"Me too," he agrees quickly, then under his breath says, "what the heck."

"*Ahem.* Forks, Washington is just the other way, you know. You ever get into *Twilight*?"

"My ex made me read them." She doesn't know, but her subject pivot is less of a change than she'd like. But he honors the intent. "I quit at book two."

The two strangers pass the trip's last half hour in silence—a silence which, while contemplative, is not tense. It's like they are starring in some kind of mystery, Bill observes, snatching for the invisible strings that pulled them together.

Cape Flattery's interior is a marvel. Towering tree trunks with branches that begin at least halfway up, it is both wooded and bright, a tang of salt and white noise teasing the ocean just out of sight. Bill's wonder spreads to the passenger side.

They park at a trailhead. "There might be some more maps in the glovebox," he says to Hunter. "It's a rental, it comes with loads of maps."

"We got two living maps in our hands." She smirks but checks the glove all the same—and freezes. "The hell?"

"Huh? What's up?"

She pulls a slip of paper out of the compartment and holds it up. It is a handwritten set of numbers: 7330. "No, wait," she says and fumbles for a pen in her purse. Flipping the paper over, she scribbles and shows me again. Same numbers, but:

"That looks like the same handwriting," Bill breathes.

Hunter nods, jaw clenched.

Bill exits the Focus and leans on its roof. Hunter joins him after a moment.

"You're *not* catfishing me, are you?" he asks. "Or messing with me in any way?"

She tucks her closed lips under her front teeth, pushes them against each other as if biting, then rolls them out slowly—a nervous tic, her eyes averting coastwards. Bill gasps instinctively against a deep, yearning twinge.

"Wouldn't dream of it," she says.

They pass couples and families and a leashless dog on the short, low-grade hike. A few years back William took part in a high-budget scavenger hunt via a Larian sponsorship which encompassed a chunk of the Northeast. He followed clues and encountered young creators and techies throughout. Today bears similar shades. He cannot help but expect some kind of prize waiting at Cape Flattery's peninsula overlook.

"You ever date any of those guys at the concert this afternoon?" Bill wonders too late if she'll bounce off the non-sequitur.

"My friends?" Hunter doesn't find it the least bit strange.

"Yeah, like Pranav. Single, active, good with his hands."

The views roll in and keep on coming: glimpses at the frothy Pacific below all knotted up with half-submerged trees and blade-sharp rocks. Swirling inlets, dripping caves, all-around enchantment. "Y'all work your second jobs right across the street from each other . . ."

"Probably why we've each stayed much longer than we should've to be honest." Hunter is snapping a few photos.

"Your kids are friends . . ."

"Their colleges aren't far from each other, either. Nah, Pranav and I never got too messy. Not that flavor of soulmates." Their trail ducks slightly upwards, lined in glistening slate. The wildflowers are real nice. Yellow kind, blue kind . . . He doesn't know flowers. "There've generally been plenty of guys before." Bill doesn't doubt that. "Plenty of chances . . . You know what I feel like? I see the good things I could do." She splays her open hands as if measuring, shaking first a start point, and then an end: "I don't do them."

"And do you have any idea why you—?"

"Course I do. Fear of good things. And each time I let one pass by is just further confirmation that I *should*. Part of me thinks I'm happy enough, no need to go any further. I'm tripping I know."

"Eh. I've always preferred basket cases. Where else am I gonna put all my baggage?"

"Oh!" Hunter shoots him her nebula eyes. "Another pickup line."

The hallway of sighing spruces unclasps, yields to a field of sky and an infinite ocean. Cliffsides are all around, and high islands of rock that hold little terraria on their tops. The water is a tri-toned emerald, richer even than what it reflects above. Breathing deep against the whipping wind, Bill grins.

Hunter points. "Look."

A family at the overlook moves out of the way to reveal a square black box, sat in the center of a shallow pool of accumulated wave water. Inching closer: there is a combination lock on it. The prize at the end, maybe.

Hunter leads Bill to the edge of the overlook.

"I don't know about this," he grumbles.

She laughs at him. "You've a li'l trust aversion, don't you, Bill?"

"Easy," he says as playfully as he can manage.

"Okay." A small nod, a tenderness empty of condescension. As she goes to pluck the box from the outcropping she squeezes his wrist. His blood pressure spikes again.

"It's kinda heavy. 7330, right?" Hunter clicks the numbers into place before Bill can respond and *click*, the lock opens. Rather than crane to look he watches her face as she lifts the top. Her eyes seem to unfocus for a second, and she sits on the mossy rock. "Want a beer?"

Salt & Seed Gosés, a 6-pack.

"Aight." As Hunter tries to decipher its delivery receipt he takes a few steps into the center of Cape Flattery's picturesque overlook, then calls out: "*Hellooooo.* Come on out now. We won't bite! This is seriously well done! For real."

Cawing crows, skittering squirrels, befuddled tourists.

The cap is tightly affixed to the bottle, not a screw-off. No way for anyone to put anything funny in it and repackage it to keep its carbonation. Sitting next to his date Bill tries to decide if he is overthinking or underthinking. "You have a bottle opener?"

"Sure," she jiggles her keyring, "but so do you."

Hunter positions the jagged lip of the nearest jutting rock between bottle's mouth and bottlecap. Her second pound does it. He catches the suds before it's overflowing.

"I'm not just trying to play into the moment when I say I love this taste."

They sit and watch the horizon, no heed paid to the Cape's alcohol ban. They finish two beers each.

"I think we've been given all the clues, about today," mutters Hunter when the last of the tourists clear. "We just have to share them."

William opens his third bottle. The clouds dye hues of aging parchment.

"My little girl, I didn't give birth to her. My ex husband had her in a marriage before ours." The rest comes with a clear, mighty effort. "It's been eight years without him. Birthday was just last month. He would've been . . ." Her mouth is open. "He um, was a delivery driver. Started when he was nineteen." She bites her bottom lip. "Hmm." Tears welling in her eyes. She looks away and flinches her whole face in the effort to suppress. By the time she angles back they are clung to her lashes.

Hunter doesn't like cars.

This isn't the kind of date that Bill deals with—he is not equipped. He feels the urge expanding in his brain, his own voice screaming to run back down the trail he ascended.

But the thing about one's narrator voice is it's just another sense, like smell or taste or touch. Limited control over input. Not the core of an identity.

Bill gulps.

Outward pity doesn't seem of interest to Hunter, so he instead elects to return the favor.

"I talked in my sleep ever since I was, like, knee-high to a pig's eye. Way before I started to socially transition. Sometimes I'd wake up to my own voice carrying on some conversation. It was always fun to me, like passing by somebody else handing me back the controls. But then my girl and I— we were real on-again, off-again, well . . . at the moment we were *really* on. I was saving up for a ring. Then one morning . . . um." He takes a long swig. "Well, she up and left, no note. And I couldn't really tell my family what happened because I didn't know, myself. My guy friends don't ask unless we're all shitfaced, like they can only be vulnerable when heavily sedated . . ."

He can feel the low sun's warmth very directly. "Thing is I remember mumbling something that morning, half-awake. Something that must've scared her."

One tear releases to trace a fiery reflection of Golden Hour down Hunter's cheek as she scoots next to him, puts her head on his shoulder.

He doesn't know what to feel. Her springy hair certainly is nice on the back of his neck. But an unmistakable element at play is the profound lightness that comes with finally talking to someone. "I'm so sorry about your husband, Hunter."

When the moment of stillness—stillness all over the world, he swears— ends, Hunter lifts her head to look at him. The tear is dried; Golden Hour has moved to her whole face, lending it the glow of an unflickering bonfire. "Holy shit. I think I know what you said that morning."

"Uh, I don't follow."

"Your bio this morning. Or . . . what was the name. George's bio. On Tinder." She stands up. "There was this text on your—on *his* last picture and I screenshot it."

He knows Hunter is readying herself to continue. He readies himself to hear. Strangely enough, he isn't impatient. Sitting there, he shifts back to the sea with his mouth slightly open.

"I don't know how this George person would know a thing like this. Or if it's true."

"Me neither. But what'd he say?" He senses the shyness in his smile. "What'd I say?"

She reads from her phone. "'She heard me mumbling half-asleep. So she asked me what I thought of us. I told her, *It'll last.*'"

"*It'll last?*"

Hunter nods. "Initially I thought it was a poem or something." Her expression softens as she sits back down. "Lucky for you, I'm into that shit."

Bill nods too, at his knees.

In his subconscious, the atavistic affirmation: whoever "George" is, *what* he is is telling the truth.

She asks if he is good; he nods one last time.

They drain their beers and decide to leave the black box where they found it. Halfway down the trail, around where they saw the leashless dog, she quickens her step to take his hand. He pulls her in and they kiss, one long, steady inhale of nose against nose, their arms climbing each other's backs. They walk down the rest of the trail to the rental.

"So what now?" Bill kicks some gravel at his rental's wheels as they approach.

"Night's young baby." They've taken the glow of the peninsula with them. "I'd say come to my place back in Liltin Yew, watch a movie, drink some more," she continues, "but my daughter's got her girlfriend over. Where are you staying?"

Bill thumbs the ignition. "Eh, nowhere. Was at the Bull Elk Motel last night, but there's a high school reunion. Place is full."

"Yeah, *my* high school reunion. Hard to believe people are turning up for that. But Bull Elk, perfect. Susan'll give us Room 203!"

He cocks his eyebrow. "The camera room?"

"Oh, she told you? That's just town legend," Hunter laughs. "We'll swing by my place for the wine and head right over."

William's heart thuds, and he takes the chance to follow Fate on its wavelength, "Hey maybe, if we play our cards right, I can 'fuck you so hard you'll feel it tomorrow.'"

"*No.*" Hunter's jaw drops. "You knew my cringe pickup line? You knew what it was all along?"

He points at his phone, at Tinder, and shrugs, "Not *right* away but . . ." He lifts his well-defined chin. "It fell into place."

Astonished, Hunter just shakes her head. And then, "Not a chance, buck-o."

They'll check Room 203 thoroughly, Bill promises to himself, if it is still available. Anywhere she wants to go, he's going to follow. It is honestly difficult to imagine the night getting any better.

# SUNDOWN

*WE DANCE BY OURSELVES.*

# 23

# OUR SYSTEM IS ANY

Uberwall is a recent addition to our grab bag of tricks. Four, maybe five years old. It formulated as we expanded the scope of our simulated anniversary catharses.

After the abrupt halt to our casual bodily experiments, we arrive at three formative conclusions in quick succession.

First, there is no conceivable way to break the loop. With no positive forecast for our mental states post-time hole, we resign the rest of our lives to its duration. Like a DMT dump extended beyond our capacity to combat. We must become Russian cosmonauts, turn the tapping into song.

Second, we have relied on increasingly creative suicides to hear said music. Learning new professions and unearthing new corners of June 21st, 2025's world has great novelty and significance. We know Hegel, Derrida, Deleuze, de Beauvoir, in their own native tongues no less. We shift our focus on physics from the macro to the micro: how far must we push the dumpster into 6th Street's alley to alter Pranav Kahsay's on-foot commute so that we can meet him organically and yap about Bergman and yews?

Nothing approximates the very specific sensations of ripping each other open and touching what's inside. Bursting as one on a frozen lake after pencil diving arm-in-arm. None of that anymore.

Third and final is that every piece of every citizen of Liltin Yew—those time-bound citizens whom we've taken care to respect—can be used to disassemble. Hell, we *already* use them. Put them where we want, discuss what we want, do what we want. We create wondrous town-wide events when we crave positivity. So what if exorcising a little resentment is unfair towards them? Unfairness doesn't stop a thing from being the way it is, and they're fine the next June 21st, 2025. Like furniture that forgets our weight.

Murders become sprees, direct killings a Rube Goldberg trap. There are ways we can kill the whole town without having to look at a single one of them all day. Turns out an entire *new* world springs forth, though, from someone you think you know when you watch them die. We stop throwing up so much and get to work on an authorial voice. Less to do with killing than with destroying. It is a spiritual enough endeavor to scratch the old itch. On our anniversaries the brightly latticed dawn-stutters of 5:12 A.M. come to represent a kind of macabre scoreboard.

Half of us gets disillusioned while the other doesn't, like a see-saw, and the cycle repeats. Sometimes our disgust overlaps and we take breaks. Many times we both really enjoy it. We're often interchangeable. We Mischief Night, we Trick-or-Treat; some years we reverse the order. A whole town's evil sirens, a whole town's guardian angels, we're any and all. But lately our she-half is *really* pouring us into Mischief. Like we said, it resonates more with our circumstance.

Mischief is chaotic, so it requires mastery. It's ambitious puzzling: How do you expand a Hell Simulation beyond town to the whole of the country? Of course we can do nukes and leaks and any old way to heat Cold War II into WWIII, but they're too easy. And they mostly get us killed before 5:12, which we now figure counts as suicide and adds another, what, 4-ish hours to our time hole? To make further putty of our shared plasticities?

Of course we do a handful anyway at our most masochistic. Get drunk, whatnot.

No, it has to tie back into *us* somehow. We develop the authorial voice—that's the real intrigue. If, through all engineered positives and negatives, we find there's still something we can tell ourselves? That is an assurance some human part in us lives.

—

Uberwall is trialed and succeeds.

It's work one can purposely get lost inside. Anne-half is lost in work on purpose. Maybe it's not a problem at all, we don't know; it's a wholly new scale of this phase. It is kind of exciting, to be sure. What we know is we're more tired now. Can never get enough sleep but sleeping for years anyway, our George-half, while Anne-half tinkers, plans. We hang out a lot together still, but at our house with the wheezes from you-know-who. It is when we have both halves of ourselves that we find the courage to end Daisy's suffering painlessly.

We both hope that one day, through our positives and negatives, something might get said, but to neither of us.

We voice this feeling less than we probably should.

With moderate caution we can harness a manageable chunk of military aggression for our Rube Goldberg machine. A top-secret decapitation strike on Iran's highest profile nuclear enrichment and research facilities, for example, doesn't seem to accomplish much in the first place. But unveiling Operation Midnight Hammer to the world makes its ineffectiveness a certainty, the War Department's Department of PR Defense running meth-fueled damage control.

The current administration is looking for any reason to deploy National Guardsfolk. Major cities are in their crosshairs, but they'd like something trial-sized and under the radar first. Now the national population is on considerable alert over Iran—a non-threat pushed forth by dubious propaganda, but the admin, with its fatherly words of protection, keeps hundreds of millions misinformed even now—keeps them on-edge and liable to pull those closest to them down, their thoughts on survival instead of corrupt bureaucracy. Unredacted files on which billionaires are eating babies and raping kids are easier to obtain than Feynman's research, by the way.

And if you're wondering, everyone's guilty.

So the admin's just as eager for a crisis as it is furious at the leaks. Turns out, Arturo Vasquez briefed the world on Midnight Hammer a full forty minutes before the bunker buster bombs fell. Knowing this current Commander in Chief, things are about to get vindictive.

The Army National Guard has a platoon in Joint-Base Wilkes-Booth. The Washington governor is told to fuck off *verbatim* as federal orders issue forth. It takes a while to call in every boot and get the real go-ahead. Liltin's Chief of Police confirms the station's cars are all crippled. One off-duty cop, though, is already just a dozen yards from the offender, the epicenter, Vasquez. His name is Thaxton Pratt and he's their new point of contact.

He's ordered not to let anybody inside the high school gym leave.

Among the Guardsfolk are a few good apples, but they certainly don't ripen the bunch. That's not how that saying goes, as we recall it.

They're in a great many ways Thaxton Pratt variants. Some of the only people in a 30-mile radius we don't know deeply and that's fine with us. Can't say we didn't try.

At 7:02 P.M. they convoy in from the Northwest on US-2 East. Sundown's an hour off but no sun reaches the town's buildings. Liltin has two off-ramps; the whole convoy takes the first because it's not like there's an active threat. Strength in numbers. Show of force more than anything; "Hope y'all have been working out because we got ourselves a photo op!" one jokes before his sergeant first class shuts him up.

Uberwall was born out of accident and circumstance, like all our greatest hits. Like us! We were doing some fiddling with the military and frustrating them any way possible (it made for entertaining skillbuilding) and once we notice they all enter as one, we block them. We block them with several dozen RideShares and food delivery apps' worth of supernaturally spaced appointments to the same cluster of addresses at the start of the urban sprawl. If left alone, the simultaneous arrival of unwilling workers, their cars big and small, creates a 180-second hitch wherein the military gains situational awareness (which they abbreviate as SA) on the pileup. "They're definitely sitting ducks," we observe, and nod at a tall parking complex at the end of the block. "A lotta these workers are *real* anti-government too. Interesting."

—

It's one of our easiest orchestrated mass casualty events, one of the more convenient. It's totally optional. He-half must hilariously believe we're still operating under the medium-casualty rule, because we're alone on the parking lot's top level. The high school gym is a quick drive; we're the last person Arturo wants to see right now, so he doesn't notice.

A sergeant waddles off the convoy to yell at the frightened gig workers (some of whom are active duty themselves). We waste no time in beginning. Most of these drivers are below the poverty line. Many sleep in their cars. Aligned with national trends, 56% of Liltin Yew's unhoused hold down jobs, gig work or/and otherwise. The 14 obliterated by rifle fire after we snipe the sergeant into Tomorrow do sometimes weigh on our minds. More innocents will die if we stop now, so we hit the convoy with three more headshots before giving away our position.

The convoy breaks through, their panicked distress cries dampening from the signal jammers we placed next to the camera feeds we cut all along our present escape route. It won't hold back their comms for long.

Scooting the Raider past blood-covered doors hiding screaming families, we stand straight up on the brake pedal: our he-half. He's wandering the middle of the street sporting a busted face and broken hand.

"Uberwall," we observe flatly to she-half.

We shrug. "Your fault."

"Could use a lift."

"You forgot Amy's passcode again," we say just as flatly, not a question, as we're climbing in. "And this face? What else did you do?"

"What's it look like? Improvised." We smile over approaching gunfire. Some brave Americans have stormed from their unmarked doors off of US-2 East to address the military's slaughter. "That clearly remains your forte."

# 24

# VADA IKEBE'S REIFICATION

I record audio from my pocket at 6:24 P.M., watching Katyusha/OMGrozny buckle her baby into the Scion's slim backseat. Daniel drums on its roof. The baby doesn't like it. "It's important, Kat," he's saying, "the USB. Factors into our benefactor. That's all I can know for sure."

"You have explained yourself." Single-mindedly she settles into the driver's side.

"I wish it could be me delivering this, you don't even know how much . . ." He tries not to glance back at us teens. Something about it rings performative. I think he's right where he wants to be.

"And so do I. Daniel," she gives him a look now, "You are responsible for them now."

I watch his back twitch and brace, bitter at the reminder. He finally nods. Kat shuts her door, tips the thumb drive at him before pocketing and—a flutter fills my gut—finds my made-up face in the party.

"You are eating! Make sure they leave you tip, yeah?" She flashes her diamond-studded incisor and the car labors away, 4 mini cylinders battling the grassy road. Little Maxim is earmuffed up as she blasts house music. I'm sad to see her go. My dreaming subconscious has likely tricked itself into thinking I'm not mature enough for someone like her in my life.

She's wrong, this atavistic Vada. AtaVada needs to quiet her fretting. I'm more than ready for a burst of good. The death spiral of a world outside me will worsen either way. I deserve the smallest reprieve, the comfort of a meaningful night or two and some recognition that my work led to something. Recognition, fame, whatever. It's all branding, even professional development, and its proverbial fifteen minutes would be a goddamn vacation.

"Vada, you ready for your intro?" Daniel asks me. He's changed into one of his $30 burnt orange SalishUs tees. His vibe is confident.

I take a deep breath, exhale. "Let's get it."

He leads me to the canopy tent as I drop latanoprost onto my sci-fi eyecap. "First thirty minutes is just hanging with Chat, getting to know you. Seven sharp we're onto your demo, got it?"

"Cake."

"That's the attitude." With a pat to the back he ushers me inside. Kristen sits in front of the SalishUs cameras while Taek-su runs light tests. Rundee fiddles through *Reify* on my VR set.

"You know what *camera obscura* is?" Daniel taps away at his plugged-in laptop atop a fold-out table.

I brush off the one mosquito that made it through the tent's entrance. "Uh, a band?"

"It's the idea of how your behavior changes when you know you're being recorded, like the Hawthorne effect. People expect that now, though. Don't be afraid to perform."

"Well, I'm not in theater class or anything."

Daniel brings up his channel and prepares the stream. "You're going to be having a conversation with me, only heightened. A performative version of me. Just follow my lead."

I nod. Sure, I'm nervous, but only slightly. If this weren't all just my dream I would maybe care. Instead, I maneuver over the disparate wires to reach Taek-su. "Keep a lookout for his phone," I whisper. "Find Amy."

With a smile he tips his head. I really want to kiss him, so I do.

It's just a few seconds but it's electric. When I step back, he gawks at me.

"Oh my *God* Vada." Kristen is beaming at me from her seat.

"What? What happened?" Rundee flails from inside my headset.

"Nothing," Kristen and I chirp, Taek-su still stunlocked.

Daniel has us fixed in a peculiar gaze. "Live in forty-five. Seconds, that is. Mic up."

It's brighter in the hotseat than I expected, and whiter like a frozen flashbang, a cold glow with a clinical camera allegedly somewhere in the center. I'm the best of us four at presenting, even if the teachers yell at me for the odd inappropriate joke. Rundee only ever wants to be behind a camera, and Taek-su and Kristen would rather die. And *Reify*'s setting and story are rooted in my experience. Amy's, too. We *were* angling for the two of us to be handling general promotion together, but then she just had to go and overdose on June 10th.

**u 100% got this vada. Rip it to shreds.**

Amy herself says, on my phone, through my dream. *Shared dream, Amy*, I think to myself.

**shared dream :)**

I glow from within.

"Kid, you're in the shot," I hear Daniel/SalishUs say.

Taek-su still stands there, behind me now. A big red light flicks on from the camera. We go live. I just stay turned to Taek-su, grinning. He returns it, saunters out of frame slowly. Squeezes my shoulders. "Knock it out, Vay." He's got courage now.

SalishUs looks annoyed as he intros stream. He gets past a horrific ad read for the betting app PredictAct, which I cover my face from the camera for, and introduces me as his stepsister's best friend. Apparently most of Chat didn't know SalishUs had a sister, to which he says, "more on that in a bit." He doesn't show me what the commenters are typing, just reads them off his phone, which is a relief.

I expect the "more on that" connects to an eventual discussion of Amy's medical condition, asking for donos via our game. But for now we run through the basics: *Reify*, VR extraction horror, inspired by LSD Dream Emulator and Slave of God; TAAU upscaling and gaussian splatting; the works.

"But why make it?" asks SalishUs. "What's this about?"

"Sure. So in 2020 I came to this summer camp with your stepsister, and—"

"No, I didn't mean that. I mean what makes y'all want to develop games?"

"Oh, well for *me* at least it's—"

"Because there's a poll in chat about the youngest age you should be before being allowed to use a VR set," he continues.

"Uh. Hah," I mumble, off-guard. "Who knows."

"No, I mean, like, are you kids touching grass these days?" SalishUs says, to me, but he's facing slightly toward the center of those lights. "Just checking to make sure. Don't be in a rush to glue your whole face to a screen. Trust me, there'll be plenty of time for that!" I twitch. My dad in front of his giant living room TV and Amy being blasted with ads in Providence, enter my mind unwanted. "Ain't beating life to the punch, that's right, well put, flesh_bunny."

I grit my teeth. "I guess we just love doing it. Playing games."

"Mm." Daniel's head is bowed to his Chat in his hand. "Oh, *that's* a good question. Did you folks use any AI to help make it?"

"There's no AI in it," I gasp.

Daniel smiles in curiosity—and I know he knows I'm technically lying. He's part of *my* dream, after all. The curiosity's a show. *Camera obscura* type shit. He's about to talk. I can't let him break it first.

"I mean, I may run my own program to proofread some code, but—"

"Uh-oh," he can't help but say in front of thousands. "Kinda sounds like a yes . . ."

"I have a disability, Dan."

"Oh, you have a disability!" SalishUs turns to his camera, all cloying smiles again, and the whiplash is so insane I can't keep up. "Chat *was* wondering about that eyecap of yours. Would you like to tell us about it? Or—"

I see red.

"Whoa, whoa, whoa, Jesus fucking Christ, Vada," he's saying, and I realize I can't breathe. "Crippled? I would *never*—and I don't come across as . . . as *that*, what do you—let's just take a breather, maybe? There's, there's water, right there. Jesus fucking Christ."

What did I say? I can't remember exactly what I said, I just gave it up to the moment. I don't feel awful? But I feel slightly silly. What did I say?

Amy texts me. I ignore Daniel's softer prompts, close off from the interview to check.

**and i quote "OMG you're really joking about a disability right now? Was that whole concerned stepbrother persona Daniel and now this is SalishUs tryna to lulcow me in front of his boys? Like 'ooo, diversity, look at the crippled girl, buy her game lol'? Shut your bitch-ass up, creep.**

I read it through as Daniel tries to divert the mogging of me from thousands. They're just dream-thousands, though. They're not real. On a quicker reread I nod my head, hold in the tears then chuckle, negotiating with myself.

So, that is a lot, but not horrible. A lot of how that lands will depend on my delivery, if I stuttered a lot but I don't think I did. Maybe I shouted or something here and there but overall,

**YOU SLAYEDDD**

And even if I didn't, too late. I have to pretend I planned that now. Gotta own it.

"But I'd just like to make a finer point if that's okay, SalishUs."

"—Oh," he says, surprised, and shoots a warning glance at his camera— "Of course, Vay. But I mean—"

"No, there's no generative AI in *Reify*. We did not have bots create assets or write code. I trained a bot on *my code* to look through *my code* after every half hour to flag potential failures. It saves me, with *my one eye*, hours of eye strain a day. Plenty of times it's wrong, plenty of times it helps. Because of it I work twice as fast. There's a difference between generative and non-generative AI. Y'all've got such thick skin but cry like bitches when you hear two letters. Maybe study what you're hating on, be a good student like me, and you won't show your whole ass, okay?"

There can be no subtlety. I'm so lucky my dream is letting me trial this kind of exchange. I know for certain that I'll remember this interaction when I wake up. It's how my brain works—a way it learns.

In sleep my cooling brain speaks wisdom. My mom could tell. She's the one who gave me the dream journal. It's why I never pull an all-nighter: They're truly addictive and they harm brain matter, especially young brains. Every kid thinks they can afford all-nighters precisely because of their age. In truth, it will be worse for their development.

At first, I think SalishUs' laugh is in disbelief that I'm doubling down. Then I look deeper. He's not checking Chat on his phone anymore—that signifies a little victory for me. He's just my projection of him, anyways, right? I don't need to be scared; I need to study him. Scout my opp, police my preconceived notions, write down any blind spots.

From his lap under the camera's sightline he lifts a card, angled at me: *Well Done!*

I give him no more, just wait on his response.

"You know what? Respect. No, you genuinely schooled me. Chat, I'm deadass. I'm deceased." He gestures to me then claps as if I've won a streamer award.

He goes on about how important disability representation and accessibility in games are, and how he has always said so, and his Chat cools off. With that he announces we'll be back in a bit. He steps over to his laptop, taps a red button on his stream deck. A SalishUs graphic fullscreens on-stream; he's cut the live feed.

"Ey, Vada, can I talk to you for a second?" Daniel clears his throat.

"Sure, let's go out here." I unzip the canopy tent and he obliges. I follow him, but only after I get Oh Taek-su's attention to nod at Daniel's unlocked iPhone on his vacant seat.

He hands me a water as we sit on a reclaimed picnic table.

"Sure you don't want a seltzer?" He says, holding them out.

"One of your hard seltzers?"

"I won't tell anyone," he says, smiles with his hands up. I smile, too.

"Yeah, I'm good."

"I'm so glad you doubled down!" He pounds an entire can. "Not a theater kid? Sheesh, fooled me!"

"You really mean that?" I look as inconspicuously as possible behind him: Through the tent, Taek-su has commandeered SalishUs' phone.

"Hell yeah! Drama sells, conflict on-screen always sells. We're all about to get a lot of money from your game—Amy included. As long as you know you can weather it! Chat ain't shit. I promise they ain't shit. I'll protect you."

"Wow, thanks!" I say, musing on how he doesn't apologize for anything.

"I got more cue cards if you need 'em. Look, this is just the language Chat understands. I'm glad you get it." He puts a hand on my shoulder. "And if you're always this fun of a guest, I might have to have you on more often, huh?"

He lets his fingertips pull slightly down my arm as he lifts his hand and grabs another seltzer.

"Ah, I see. Hey, maybe!"

SalishUs nods, stands and stretches.

Of course he is a pedophile. Private texts, offering alcohol, shooing Kat away, getting combative on the vod. I know how I look to him: a cute little Cyclops he can make his impression on. That he's a disgusting beta-human isn't a surprise. I'm just glad I'm still recording audio.

He turns to head to the canopy tent and Taek-su still hasn't put down the stolen phone.

"H-hey!" Kristen steps in front of Taek-su. "We got Vada's VR set paired to your WiFi. The net's, like, so wide and stable here! How'd you pull that off?"

"Oh," Daniel looks around the run-down, darkening camp. "Someone from our stream's, er, *benefactor* came by earlier and set everything up, it's a wide net here. In fact..."

He goes to the bulky generator and plugs in a half-dozen cords I didn't notice were even here. Strings of colored lights ignite across the camp. All over the trees a laser light show dances through a preset. That lessens the tax on my vision's low-light impairment.

It's 6:57. I check my makeup, take a picture, and send it to Amy over Signal, where it's instantly hearted.

"Did you find her phone?" I ask Taek-su, who glowers by my side at the streamer.

"Sure did. You wouldn't guess where it is."

"Where?"

He unlocks his arms to gesture all around. "Right here. Probably in this tent."

My eye searches the little space for a moment. I try not to scowl.

"The hell is actually going on here, Vay."

"Time to find out. Tell Rundee and Kristen we're about to take control."

Eyebrow raised, Taek-su smacks his lips. "We'll be ready."

My VR headset is paired to SalishUs' laptop; a couple keystrokes will share its A/V with viewers, of which there are 20.7k and climbing.

"Welcome back, beautiful babies," Daniel grunts in full SalishUs mode, tossing an empty seltzer under the camera. "I see a lotta chatter about Arturo Vasquez and the livestreams of him in Liltin High right now, and I must say that yes, he *is* involved in tonight's stream, but don't take my word for it! The game demo for . . . what's it called again, Vay?"

"*Reify.*"

"Yes, *Reify*. We kind of got into it earlier, but now it's showtime. Right, Vay?"

"Right you are, SalishUs!" I say in my presenter voice. The cold lights blind but I can hear my friends giggle. "And it's time to reveal why we're out in the boonies, isn't it?"

"Indeed! So, on the subject of Arturo Vasquez and *kismet*. This morning I took a sponsorship from what I thought was Future Mayor Gershwin's team." I don't know why he's talking about whoever Arturo Vasquez is all of a sudden, let alone that politician. Everyone is obsessed with these politicians. "It was only after I saw the location where I'd be streaming that I started to wonder who my *real* benefactor was. And as it turns out: Vada, where does this game of yours, the one we're about to dive into, take place?"

I take a sip of water. "So, yeah, it actually is based on this exact summer camp."

SalishUs faces the camera smugly, and his smirk grows wider the longer he reads Chat in his hand.

I hold up my VR headset and continue. "We talked about how we did a 1:1 recreation of a physical space. Well, this is the physical space. Theoretically, if our connection's stable, I'll even be able to walk around the space as I use my joysticks to walk in-game. No boring old standing in place." I cue SalishUs to share my headset's screen.

"Err, that'd be cool," he says after doing so, "but who'll run camera?"

"I can," offers Rundee. "It'll be like a hybrid IRL slash gaming stream."

"I'm not sure . . ."

"SalishUs. Don't you think our *benefactor* wants everyone watching to see how cool this space looks? It's all lit up out there, and you said you're not even the one who did it."

He considers, nods. "Yeah, sure. *¡Viva la Vasquez!*"

I promptly exit the canopy tent; SalishUs orders Kristen to take over the stream deck and runs after me. Rundee has removed the livestreaming camera from its stilts to go handheld.

The laser show and lights throw a synthwave glow over the abandoned forest camp. The wall between reality and simulation, between waking life and dreams, has evaporated. It's time I lock in.

"So, *Reify* starts at the front of the camp counselors' quarters." I slip on my headset and flip to one-eyed display.

Our game's title drips down like blue honey onto inky blackness. I've practically lived in this game for nine months, dreamed of it more times than I can count. This time the fidelity is even more impressive. I can smell the Sitka spruce, feel the tug of warm air.

Calmly I explain my actions: With a blowtorch-like weapon I paint the 3D *Reify* title until it fades into the blackness. An intuitive tutorial. "And now we're feeling in the dark. We use the headset's haptics to simulate a kind of echolocation . . ."

In the blackness is a dotted wireframe. With a thumb to the joystick my character steps forward—and I step forward myself. It's wonky, like parallax, even with my one eye, and awkwardly I get my sea legs. "Make sure I don't trip over anything," I tell SalishUs.

"Uh—not sure how you want me to do that," I hear him mutter somewhere behind me.

Walking carefully to the base of the camp counselors' quarters both in-game and IRL, I aim the blowtorch at its rippling dots and fire, painting it with a white-blue light. "The more I paint the closer it gets to illuminating permanently," I explain, "but the blowtorch attracts enemies that are hiding in the dark. Rundee, you getting all this?"

"Yep," I hear.

"Okay. Hey, Taek-su?"

"Yeah?"

"Would you mind going to the location of our first checkpoint and grabbing what's inside? Don't open it though."

"Uh . . . sure."

SalishUs doesn't understand that I'm referring to the caved-in well. I'm sending Taek-su to retrieve the gun.

As I inch around the wooden counselors' quarters, illuminating it further and wondering why there haven't been enemy AIs yet, I stumble on a root.

"Catch me, man!" I shout.

"Vada, I'm not gonna just put my hands on you," SalishUs says, falling seamlessly into my trap.

"No? Well, that doesn't sound like you." With a tap to my headset I minimize *Reify* and enter camera mode so that I can see my phone as I take it out. I hold it to my headset's speakers and roll the audio I've recorded.

"This is you offering me alcohol," I say quickly, "and if we jump ahead a bit, here you are offering to have me on the stream more since I'm 'such a good guest.' Chat, for reference, his hand is on my shoulder as he's saying this—"

"You recorded me without consent."

I bring the game back up and continue painting. "Hell yeah, I did. Conflict sells."

"Chat . . . Vada, that isn't what that meant. I was joking about the alcohol—"

"16 years old, by the way, folks." In-game I paint enough of the building to convert it: It becomes a shining render of the real thing that casts light onto its surroundings, showing the way forward. But why aren't there enemies? I'm supposed to be having a much harder time here. This is not an exciting demo.

Maybe the game (and my dream) can sense my one real-life opp, the one who's currently huffing through the weeds next to me. "You—I was just being supportive, I didn't mean anything by it. You're like a little sister to me, Vada."

"Uh-huh."

"Just like Amy!"

"Amy, who you still haven't told your followers about?" I minimize the game again: SalishUs' face is bright red. He looks like he wants to cry. Before he can respond, though, he looks over my shoulder and freaks.

"YOU, KID, GIVE ME THAT."

Taek-su has returned with the streamer's handgun case. "Is this what I think it is?"

"Don't give it to him, Taek-su. It's a gun, Chat, if you were wondering."

SalishUs lunges for his camera but Rundee pulls away from him; he tries to grab his stream deck but Kristen is too quick.

"GIVE ME THE GUN OR ELSE YOU ARE THREATENING ME WITH IT, KID."

"'Kid,'" Taek-su snorts. "이름이 뭐죠?"

"I don't speak *Squid Game*!"

"Why'd you bring this gun, SalishUs?" Taek-su, unphased, continues.

"FOR PROTECTION. We are IN THE WOODS. There are BEARS AND WOLVES."

Rundee pushes in with the red-glowing camera. "I don't buy it. This is hella fuckin' weird. What's really going on with this stream, Daniel? Why're we doing this a day early? Why are we out here when you claim you didn't know about our game's setting?"

At this point I'm watching the show. Taek-su steps forward. "And Amy. You lied about not knowing where her phone was."

Two pulses from my phone: seems like Amy wants to chime in.

"What are you talking about?" SalishUs is exasperated, embarrassed, astounded.

"I took your phone while you were creeping on Vada. Did a Find My Phone for Amy's. Says you've had it right here, with us, whole time."

SalishUs looks like he's about to start swinging.

I eat up Amy's text and smirk as I repeat it, like uttering a spell. "*Camera obscura*, right pal?" A spell of remembrance. SalishUs looks sideways at his hijacked livestreaming camera, then seems to recede into himself.

"I don't have Amy's phone," he mutters.

"You're lying," I immediately rejoin.

"No, I swear. I was just told not to worry about it."

"Told? Who by?" Kristen spits, but I hold up a hand as I fully remove my VR headset.

"What is tonight's stream actually about, Daniel?"

"I . . . *I don't know*, okay? I'm just doing what I'm told and I'm *trying* to sell your goddamn videogame in the meantime so I can stop my mom and my stepdad from throwing *your* best friend in a rehab when she's out of her coma. We were on track to hit it big tonight."

"And you thought you could do anything," I muse. He's just like me in that regard. He *is* me, of course—just a dream's projection. I have the rare opportunity to interrogate my subconscious, here. "How do you feel now?"

He must think I'm gloating, because he puts his head in his hands. Convincing projection, this. "I—I'm *not* a pedo, Vada, okay? You can't just go around and accuse—"

"Hold up." Taek-su's grip on the handgun case tightens. "Your parents want to dump Amy in rehab?"

"Yes, kid, and a *bad* one. That's a big reason why I'm doing—"

"Would that rehab by any chance be the Twice Loved Institute? TLI for short."

Through SalishUs' panting red face, I see Daniel Deadwyler. The scared, morose Daniel that I got to know in Amy's ICU. I almost feel pity.

"Why would you know that?" he says. "What's that got to do with anything?"

Taek-su shoots me a stunned expression, and I too connect the dots. The news article from the afternoon: the buried accusation of virtual child labor. The legless child avatars in the YewVerse. "Uh-oh," I say.

The colored lights in the summer camp flicker.

"Holy shit," Daniel is saying, almost sobbing. "Oh, oh no."

"What?" my friends ask all at once.

"We're at 50,000 views. No, it's 60,000."

This stuns everyone but me. My thoughts are once again consumed by the legless children. Daniel scrolls furiously through his Chat. "People are saying the internet in town is completely down," he mumbles. "Like, *turned off.*"

"Then how do we still have it?" Rundee asks.

"I don't know," Daniel says.

"Just who was your benefactor?" I ask, but he ignores me.

My dream has officially gone off the rails. I check my phone once more as Daniel argues with Taek-su and Chat about needing his gun back. Still have a clear signal out here.

That very moment, Amy texts.

**aaaaand *Rjdn*'s final checkpoint.**

Slightly uphill from the campgrounds, hidden to all but the discerning eye behind thick evergreens, is a tunnel through the earth. An old mineshaft. Amy and I found it back in 2020; it was our secret hang spot, our little cave.

I can't see shit in the dark. Going off nothing but intuition, I hold my VR headset to my eye, position my in-game self to look where I'm looking.

The player is supposed to end up in that tunneling mineshaft for a tense final gauntlet against many enemy NPCs.

And they are all still missing. I haven't paused the game once since I started, and not a single enemy AI has wandered over to deal damage to my character.

The distant mouth of the mineshaft, however, is not totally empty—at least not in our game. Though it should be. None of the *Reify* team planted or even programmed the asset that presently hovers at its entrance. Despite the Summer Solstice heat, my blood chills. From even this distance I can make it out clearly. A blocky, legless blonde woman wearing what looks like black and red joggers. Her arms are out as if beckoning me, only me, over.

## 25

# PROPHET ARTURO VASQUEZ

I'm nearing the summit of my lifelong, uphill battle. The post-parents, post-nurse life; the Trad-Queer Preacher path. Everything.

With each upward step countless people have tried to pull me off that mountain. Liberals outraged that the queer part of me would sell out to conservative religion; "real Christians" outraged at my queerness; and then me, holding myself back from unleashing my fury on all of them. Now, my enemies rally one final time with my peak finally in sight—that's logical. But tonight is Mischief Night. I'm more than ready to flip the script.

Anne Oxendine is off somewhere, having ghosted the moment Gets did. Fuck them both. Gets had to have done something to mess with the time loop. I hope Anne really *did* glitch out and become unaware of her prison, because if not, then she's just playing head games with me. Double entendre intended.

And it would make what she did to me Gets' fault, wouldn't it?

I weave through dancing alumni and party-crashers toward the low DJ stage up front. The latter have largely descended from the bleachers to mingle with the former. Thrums and pulses slaughter the stringing of complex thought. I can tell that investigative reporter Cierra Alrose and her local news crew are trailing me.

There remains no food, which supports my hope that Gets actually did cause Anne to glitch out of today's awareness. The Anne I know—my fast friend who truly knows and believes in me—would've arranged for some kind of catering. As it stands everyone is swiftly getting more and more pissed off. As well as drunk.

A most advantageous feedback loop.

I duck a dozen leering cameras and step onto the DJ stand. It's slideshow time. A remote next to the tethered laptop is for the projector; I turn it on. Unnoticed by most, the projector screen unrolls mechanically from above.

Patiently I watch it extend. I'll set the slideshow to Rebecca Black's "Friday." In terms of quality, it's far behind her current output, but it's 2010-appropriate. Checking the laptop's BlueTooth connections, I see one named *AIR PURIFIER*. I remember Anne's words about the AQI-like device containing our sleeping gas, the device hiding in plain sight.

"Whaddaya know," I mumble. I click. A panel lights up the laptop's lefthand corner. Two simple prompts: *Run* and *Dismiss*.

I leave the panel open.

"Time for more magic, *mi familia*," I breathe into my mic. "Utilizing my undisputed God-given prescience, I will show in detail just how far our Class of 2010 has come!"

I hit play and let it rip.

I'm already sweating. I want to sweat more. I jump onto the dance floor and let loose, my mind instantly becoming my body, the thought to guess or care how I may look a universe removed. My arms undulate over my shifting face, hips opening and rolling—and then I jump, stamp my feet so hard my ankles scream. Pound down. Purge.

And all the while most of the 250 or so attendees are transfixed by the Slideshow. Still processing. The loud laughs steadily turn more baffled. I take the opportunity to sprint to the back for a good view.

There's valedictorian Strom Legge, pictured riding a podium next to a graphic tallying his AIPAC donations. I'm not the only one who whistles at that.

As fate would have it, my phone lies abandoned on an empty bleacher. Another hopeful sign that Anne, who previously confiscated it, truly did glitch out: why would she hold onto a phone that isn't hers? Greedily, I scoop it up.

It's 7:05 P.M. My battery's about dead from its unending notifications; it's hot in my hand. A hundred missed calls from area codes I don't recognize.

"Vasquez!" comes a cry from the crowd.

"What's up?" I say, then bring the mic up and say again.

"The hell is this?" I hear the same voice from the crowd, which seem to run the gamut from hysterically furious to hysterical. Many, panicked, insist the slideshow is lying. The non-alumni, the party-crashers, seem to be laughing the most. There are even a few cheers.

"This is nothing," I insist with a massive effort to keep from smiling. "We're catching up. This is just a, uh, the Great Equalizer."

"Mr. Vasquez!" A woman steps forward authoritatively: It's the reporter again, Cierra Alrose. "I want a statement from you."

"You don't get a slide, Cierra, you don't even go here! Oh look, folks, it's the cop from outside the gym."

Thaxton Pratt's name and bald visage appears on the projector screen— wow, I forgot he graduated with us. Crazy what that much hate will do to your hair and skin.

**Not even ICE is letting him join.**

it reads.

"Mr. Vasquez," Cierra plows on, and one of her disguised crew makes it onto the DJ platform, turns down the music.

"Hey now," I growl. "You're overstaying your welcome."

Some attendees brace at my tone.

"We just got word that a gunfight broke out at the edge of town off the highway," Cierra continues gravely, projecting her voice. "Uniformed troops opened fire on a mass of civilians. Do you know what caused this?"

The audience murmurs, shifts.

"Um," I utter.

"Did you tell people to congregate there? Is—" Cierra suddenly stops, two fingers to her right ear, and I watch her face warp into an alarmed disbelief like she's been punched. "It's not stopping. There's reports of gunfire advancing through town."

"No, it's not," I say matter-of-factly. "Here? Or if it is I've, like . . . I didn't do that."

People are checking for themselves. Looking at their screens then at one another, blanching. I hear muffled *pows* from multiple phones across the wide gym.

"*Mi familia*, if that's true it's not me. I just predict things—"

Music explodes back onto the speakers. Wincing, I look into the crowd and I see Anne.

Stretching shadows chase insane patterns across her. Stance wide, a jagged krump races from fingers down to ribs until she arches a liquid spine that resolves with snake agility over her wining waist. Anne's messy bob smacks her upturned chin as she folds a knee, reverse-twerks, side-semis, some alien prototype disassembling its limbs north of lightspeed to reassemble into more unwritten fusions. A 33-year-old body caged in a near-infinite day can probably retain some muscle memory. My stomach drops.

Someone near me says, "Yo, that bitch got 57k in credit card debt."

"*Her*," I yell into the mic and point, as others make for the gym's side exits. "She fed me all those predictions today! She's playing some sick supernatural game with us! It's her doing!" My throat cracks and burns.

Anne, who noticed me halfway through my tirade, looks around, swaying in her beautiful dress. "Fuck you say?" I hear.

"*You're* the orchestrator," I rasp. I can feel my eyes bulging.

She takes a step back, and at first, I think her dizzy from dancing, but evidently she is very drunk. "Lemme get this straight. An hour and a half ago you're holding my head in place and making me choke down your cum, and now you're tryna call *me* out on some bullshit right now!?"

The onlookers, alumni and no, swivel their heads back to me and their dronings rise.

"I've got video!" She screams as it rises still. "I recorded it!"

"ENOUGH!" I scream against searing feedback from the mic, and Rebecca Black's cheery song ends.

In the following seconds of absolute silence we all finally hear the real gunfire outside the gym. Not virtual, not recorded. Real.

I search for Anne, but she's gone. The droning becomes a din. The gym's center empties as gasping throngs break away in all directions. Some people are already at the exits, arms flailing madly, shouting, *It's locked, it's locked*, as the muffled *cracks* magnify in volume. "All Star" is next on the music queue.

Each metal door shudders under collective ramming efforts. Cierra Alrose has left me and is shouting to her crew that her broadcast has lost connection.

A realization clicks. Sleeping gas. Stationary bodies won't tempt itchy trigger fingers.

Am I following Anne's plan after all? Is she looking out for me even now?

"We're fine!" I'm saying through waves of ramping adrenaline. I will my synapses to administer electric shock to my legs. Salvation's on the other side of the gym. "We'll be fine. This is why I'm here! Believe in me!" As if I've discerned the one divine path through chaos. Maybe this preacher thing holds water.

I make it off the bleachers and, from the gym's four corners, half the crowd turns to my voice. The thudding of their shoes on the polished hardwood is like several basketball teams at once racing towards me.

"Oh fuck." I drop the mic, "Oh fuck *oh fuck*," adrenaline finally reaching my limbs and propelling me so violently forward that I trip.

I can't hear the squeaking of my sweating hands pushing me up over blasting gunfire, gunfire right outside now. It shakes the walls. I can't breathe and I run anyway, DJ stage closing, howling crowd closer; I feel their heat.

Smash Mouth and assault rifles deafen but I'm behind the laptop. "Wait!" I throw out a commanding arm. The rabid throngs stop just long enough. All back in the center, all under the AQI lookalike device.

"Part of me wishes you'll remember this," I pant and click *Run* on the screen's bottom corner. Elbow over face as I fly, an all-consuming *hiss* and the dance floor is instantly bombed by thick, beige smoke.

# 26

# RAPID RESPONDER GETS LO

Agony excavates every lobe of my brain, digs with persistence and scoops a motor function here, a sliver of consciousness there. I shake out my limbs to force a factory reset. Must keep moving. The siren's not far behind. I can't see him anywhere—a horrible sign.

But I've stomped these streets three times now; even though drunk for two of them I have it mapped out in its entirety. It's no Friedrichshain-Kreuzberg or Mitte, no Glasgow West End. I'm only a half mile from Liltin High. I try to run there.

A distant *crack* whips me 90 degrees. It's clear, loud, and elevated. The following cavalcade of *pop, pop, pops* are more muffled, sound waves crashing on urban exterior, ground level. And three more of those clearer *cracks* punctuate the air above, closer than the ground-level ones.

"What the fuck," I mutter, then yell. I've been on the receiving end of flashbangs, rubber bullets, all manner of riot dispersal. These sounds would qualify if not for their rapid succession. It is automatic fire.

The goth bar queens said something about American troops from a neighboring base. I can't be 100% sure where they're headed but the Homeland Security tweet about Arturo is a goddamn good lead.

Streetlights flick on all at once. I avoid them as best I can. The *pop, pop, pops* get louder and seem to be butting up against other, intermittent fire. Shotgun blasts? Semi-auto rifles? Civil war?

My cell signal symbol is an empty outline with a black line cutting diagonally through.

Two teens rush from a family storefront as their father, chasing after, stops at the glass door to hastily mark it with something red. The crook of his elbow is wrapped in gauze: it's blood. From across the street a family stands watching aghast in a window, their door marked too. Passover, Arturo called it. Or *Pesach* if he ever bothered to learn Christianity's Jewish roots.

"Hey, what's happening?" I try. "My phone's not working. What's going on?" But the teens see my swollen nose and scurry into a car, spirit away. I press forward.

Gunfire no longer muffles but echoes, resounds.

I look behind in time to see George the Siren round the nearest corner and it's like I'm jolted by 300 joules. Stray bullets atomize the freshly red-marked storefront's glass behind him. I dive behind pruned shrubs.

I hear the screaming of brakes and risk a glance. Wiping more involuntary tears I catch an old racer-red Dodge Raider skidding to a stop an inch from the siren; he walks around its front, climbs in the passenger seat like nothing's going on. The driver is the fucking blowjob girl. Called it.

*We're all going to the same place*, I realize as they speed past my cover. I've evaded patrols but never a military with live rounds. Still, I have experience. I can shelter in place somewhere, I can flee town before they truly box me in. I don't need to go to the gym.

But Arturo needs me now more than ever.

Bracing myself on a booted car I massage around my severed nose bridge. From inside a window of the nearest red-swabbed house comes a sudden flash, a sound like bubble wrap and a horrific shriek.

I run.

A flow of masked men with shotguns and elbow pads and flagwear spills out an alley and brushes past me. They open fire on the uniformed soldiers pushing down the street and every sound becomes one solitary note. I take cover in the alley from which they emerged—

Almost a dozen townsfolk cower behind recycling bins, and some scream as I enter. They're kids. I crouch. "Y'all can't stay here," I think I'm saying—I hear neither me nor them but their frantic pointing down the alley's rear communicates the message: We're pinned.

I lift a bin and bludgeon a high window above us till it breaks; there's screaming again. I bow into my tech jacket as shards shower me and bring the bin back down to the ground. I waste no time propping it under the makeshift escape. Climbing up and in I call, "We're friendly!" to a dark, blessedly vacant apartment, and with a sweeping motion I clear the window frame of all its jagged protrusions.

Arm out, I pull in the first townsperson and shout in their ear to do the same for the next. "Where you going!?" they call as if from underwater. I'm out into the apartment's hall.

I yank a mounted fire extinguisher and crash out an emergency exit. The facade is pelted by strays, horizontal hail, mini-explosions raining brick matter. I have to run.

My mind is nothing but *Please, please, almost, please* for what feels like minutes as I conquer the street adjacent to Liltin Yew High. A car's tire deflates less than five yards from me. The barrage intensifies.

"Fuck you, fascists!" someone shouts on a bullhorn.

I kneel behind a newspaper stand. Shrill screams draw my focus and, purely from adrenaline, I look: the soldiers not laying down suppressive fire are pointing at red-marked doors and knocking them open. They think it's some kind of protest symbol, a faction sign.

They're immolated in a Molotov's pool of fire.

More townsfolk pressed onto the sidewalk move as if to break across the lit-up street.

"Stop!" I scream. "Fuck you doing?!"

Tab pulled on the fire extinguisher, I aim around the newspaper stand, hold my breath, spray. Mercifully it's not expired. A grainy cloud obscures me, obscures the townsfolk, but I motion for them to keep their faces on the pavement, and it proves prophetic; whistles cut through the billowing cloud to my left. The response ends. Coughing, I dart down the sidewalk and make a beeline to a bar's locked storm door.

Four times I bring the extinguisher down on rusty chains, but I'm weakened, heaving. A man whose keffiyeh tightly obscures his nose and mouth grabs it, knocks the chains' lock sideways until it bursts, claps my back and pushes his friends inside.

I slam the door closed for them and sprint to follow my traveling cloud. Liltin High, finally. Like a WWII fortress. No one's reached it yet.

Clutching a stitch in my side, I recoil: that's not quite true. "Shit."

The red Raider idles by the modern gym's corner bench, but it's empty of sirens, its doors thrown open. My head flails in all directions but there's no slowing, not now. All that's stopping me is the inexplicably badgeless cop at the entrance—

Who is arguing with an orange-haired woman pleading in a thick Russian accent. Her earmuffed baby cries on the passenger side.

"Let them out!" the woman shouts in a fury.

"Ma'am, clear the building!" the cop screams in her face. "It ain't safe!"

And I notice the metal front door is shaking, shuddering like it's being pounded on from the inside.

The Russian lands a blow on the cop and reaches the locked door, sputtering. The cop unclips his holster. "You bitch."

No time to think. No further courses of action to weigh. Ears ringing, I channel my inner Belal Muhammad and barrel forward the last few meters.

Though I've disarmed zealous protestors before it's never involved closing such a range. But the pig's elbows are locked, a rookie mistake born of panic and incompetence. With a mighty exhale I fling my arms forward and up while bodying him. His iron hits concrete—still set to safety. I roll once before hopping and regaining my breath. The pig makes an all-fours scurry toward his Glock; I've rolled too far to stop him.

The Russian woman shoots a stream of pepper spray, and the pig folds immediately into a heaping, ugly mess. Slightly singed by the spray but no stranger to the sensation, I scoop up his gun, and stuff it deep into my tech coat.

"Goddamn," I spit out: The woman is kicking the shit out of him.

I undo the bolts on the double door and pull. They give an inch before the weight of piled bodies flings them fully open. The cuts on my face tingle and my eyes burn as dozens of attendees burst forth hacking out their lungs. I squint into the large gym.

Through the vestibule I see arms hanging off bleachers. Plastic balls from the ball pit roll everywhere. The dance floor is blanketed in a thick, settling haze and in its center twitches a massive knot of people, lain flat, dripping.

A far exit opens and through the haze I place the silhouette of my boyfriend Arturo Vasquez stumbling out the other end of the gym.

Too late I hear a huff, a wind-up. The female siren bludgeons my skull and the world blinks white into deep, panicked black. I forget who and what I am long enough for her to tie me tightly to the Raider's backseat.

# 27

# OUR SYSTEM IS ALL

With a simple hex key we Irish Goodbye just before the idea of leaving the gym becomes popular. Mere minutes hence the retching Trad-Queer Preacher comes charging for the back-right exit after chemical-bombing his peers; our male half unlocks it just in time, curtly nods at Arturo's pleasant surprise. It's re-locked before a single screaming attendee can follow.

Gets Lo has flouted our course-correction attempts. It's our fault—or Amy's passcode's fault, or a hangover's fault, whatever—but it produces an unplanned conclusion to Patrol Sergeant Thaxton Pratt's feeble excuse for a story, one truly better than the plan in place. Awestruck, our she-half watches.

Blackmailing Vada's deadbeat father takes minimal effort. In the A.M. we simply present evidence of the marital abuse of his late wife (our negative motivator), while dangling an opportunity to engage in heroics worthy of recognition by the FBI, DOJ, and ICE (our positive motivator). Our only condition is that he must remove all identifiers from his uniform, something he happily accepts under the presumption of going undercover.

Officer Pratt thinks he's schemed behind our backs, wiggled free of our blackmail. He's already called ICE on Arturo's home address where older brother Gabriel Vasquez half-heartedly packs his valuables, unaware of the approaching maelstrom. Pratt has already informed his boss and now follows federal orders. Ecstatic, he's locked every door to Liltin Yew High's gymnasium and, against his better judgment as the screams begin, continues to keep them locked.

This is normally when he murders Katyusha at the entrance, something he'll regret after spotting the sad, white baby crying for its dead white mother. He'll nonetheless scream self-defense to National Guardsfolk rounding the corner; with no identifying markers of a police officer, this is typically when he is turned into Swiss cheese.

But Gets Lo's butterfly effect is immense; its wings spread across town. This is the Integration Hell we feared, but shockingly, it's a kind of heaven.

Gets tackles the loser, bounces his bald head off the curb, and steals his gun. Katyusha pepper sprays and breaks several of his ribs. As she speeds her Scion far from the soldiers Officer Pratt crawls cursing down the street; he's pissed himself.

After we load our favorite enby into the Raider, we stroll back to spectate the pig. He's dragged his lard to the neighboring establishment, pounding on its red-swabbed door, hollering that he needs to be let in. The old MAGAt who answers is as Thin Blue Line and ICE-fondling as they come. But again, no badge, no identifiers.

We laugh ourselves lightheaded. Almost as light a head as the pig who's just had his blasted into sauce by a dusty double-barrel. One of the old shells is a dud—it blackens the shooter's face like a cartoon character, dumb expression and all as he puts down Pratt.

How can we repeat this on our next anniversary? That was such a satisfying, wholesome iteration. We're much less furious at our male half, who has now made it to the Raider's front. "You accidentally made some art," we say.

"Yeah?" we also say.

"I'll tell you on the morning debrief. Goddamn. The jazz is in the accidents, for real."

We beam at ourselves. "Lookin' forward to it! Breakfast at Line 9 Diner?"

Our gaze falls to the ground and we nod expressionlessly.

"Well, better get going. Arturo should be circling back to Pratt's car right about now."

We consider showing our male half the late officer's stolen Glock in Gets' tech coat. It's not like Gets can reach in and grab it, but it might be good for both halves of us to know.

Then again, why?

For us 18 months is basically a week and a half. Approximately 550 June 21ˢᵗ, 2025s prior, we were high off smack trading COVID stories: the time the old George worked on a Game of the Year contender socially isolated in his San Francisco apartment; the time the old Anne had entire stretches of Miami beach all to herself. All the death back then was so abstract and invisible. Training for the time hole's anniversaries. We missed the pandemic, we both agreed. Loved it, in fact. It felt nice to admit aloud. Then we came clean:

After Nanno's revelation, our George-half, knowing full well the danger of disturbing the equal-opposite force, never really stopped with the self-deletions. Not as frequently indulging, granted, but not stopping.

"Are you serious?" we asked ourselves then. "Can you please stop?"

After a long silence, we responded.

"It's hard to. None of it will last anyway."

"How do you know you're not hurting us both?"

"I just know."

"How?"

"Because I feel like that thin, dark line anchoring the USO is starting to seek me out every 5:12 A.M. wherever I am, whether I'm looking at the craft or not. Have you been feeling like that? No. Because we're two different fucking people, Anne."

That heart-to-heart a week and a half ago is the last real one we've had.

And we were being serious. Half of us really is just shutting down inch by inch—one slow-motion, years-long suicide of decaying entropy.

Plus, snapping back to the present (hah), this very day's T-Pose run saw George-half omitting the passcode delay to us, and if Gets somehow contorts enough to reach the Glock, George-half is apparently the last to care about dying by our own hand anyway. It's petty but after all this frozen time, that's just our right.

So our male half adjusts the Raider's driver seat, wondering if another heart-to-heart may be back in the cards at Line 9 Diner, unaware that the enby tied to the back is packing.

"We'll talk about the *pow* thing from the Joint Base when we debrief, too, if you want."

We roll our eyes. "Tomorrow, George."

"Tomorrow."

Our little town is now named Pandemonium. The surviving clueless soldiers raid the red-marked houses of those who thought that Arturo Vasquez, and by extension the Christian God, chose them to be spared over all others. People are noticing, and frantically they try to scrub their doors clean.

Our Anne-half waves into a few windows, jogs with good form to a parking garage. Fighting continues in the streets. Hotwiring an old sedan, we roll down the windows and flip through the local airwaves as we take the scenic route to Arturo's trailer park.

"Stay inside, I beg you," urges one station. "Away from windows—if you have a basement—"

"Get the marks off your door!" another station insists.

"Leave town—"

"Shelter in place—"

And in our Raider, we switch the radio off. Gets Lo has been fully conscious for a while now, has given up their vain struggles. "Why are y'all doing this to us?" they say in monotone, not giving us an iota of their emotions.

"We respect the hell outta you," we say. "If we had friends it'd be you folks."

Gets snorts. "Well at least I know you don't have friends."

The exhalation through our nose is heavy.

"Your face hurt?" they continue.

"Although to be real with you, Getty," we pretend we don't hear them, "I think you're hanging onto Arturo a bit too hard. You two seem to be having a bit of a rough one today, huh?"

"How 'bout your hand? I know I broke that."

"Just because you give all of your heart to someone, it don't guarantee yours is the heart they need, ultimately, right? In my ineloquent way, I'm trying to say don't beat yourself up, or him, for doing something as beautiful as giving someone all of yourself."

The town's bedlam finally falls away. The glittering bay opens to our right. We climb for two minutes. Gabriel Vasquez's favorite white bus at the auto cemetery's perimeter, blazing in fitful moonlight, revolves far above our driver's side window. We flit to the rearview: Gets, tangled in the seatbelt, stares blankly at the soft-top roof.

"What would you suggest?" they ask.

"Keep it beautiful. Move on."

Their eyes meet ours in the mirror. "I have a feeling we're talking about you two," they say.

We smile and focus back on the road.

The original owner of the Raider is probably missing it sorely, especially now that we've invoked Uberwall. We treat the SUV better anyways. We nudge it just a little off the road and into the tall grass, point it downward to face the bight in the Bay cliff, then stop.

"I had to cheat to put you back where you end up," we sigh and crank left into neutral. "But Anne didn't. She played Arturo perfectly. I've no doubt he's only a little ways down this hill, right behind us. All this to say don't worry, you're not alone. He's gonna see everything."

# A COLD GLOW

We emerge from our Raider and it immediately rolls downhill.

# 28

# GETS LO

A roaring. Uneven terrain passing faster and faster by.

The cliff's edge fills more of the windshield by the millisecond. I'm headed for the bight.

I try—fail—to clamber to the front. Too constricted. I thrash against gathering momentum. For a wild second I hallucinate my employee Nick Valento behind the wheel, speeding away from the Amazon sortation floor to both our deaths, liquor in hand—laughing? No, just screaming. Screaming so loud.

The old vehicle *clangs* against what must be a rock at the exact moment I thrust as hard as possible toward the front. The far end of the taut seatbelt that binds me dislodges like a missile, its buckle cracking a window before beaming me in the forehead.

My arms can work uncontested; I claw at the door nearest as the belt falls away. Grasp my fingers over the doorlock but the shuddering suspension rocks me away. Flings me back.

The driverless SUV groans past thirty. The entire windshield is the cliff's edge. Hundred meters, no more.

I make again for the lock, throw myself onto it. Pull it up at last.

I tear the pig's Glock from my coat, brace myself, then push it against the craning door, pushing it out wide enough to jump.

But it collides with another low boulder and the door bangs shut, careens the Glock out into the grass—snaps my arm inward, jutting broken bone through muscle out my forearm.

The disembodying agony renders me mute, but Nick Valento is still screaming.

20 meters. 15. The SUV and I are both on autopilot.

The pummeled door at my feet now—still unlocked. I fight the gravity that now pins me to the dirty floor; with one arm flip and lurch forth as the ground levels for a moment just before the drop. Nothing but indigo sky, cold stars, water down below:

I'm going over or I'm not.

# 29

# ARTURO VASQUEZ

I'm telling you, I'm in a time loop! We all are and I've found out! What possible explanation is there for everything I did today?" In Thaxton Pratt's sleek truck, I argue with my phone's reflection of me. The whole burning town has been inexplicably unplugged from the outside world yet there's a lime-green dot shining next to my front-facing lens. Not my doing.

I noticed it running slow when I first stole the vehicle. Not just from all the notifications, either. All online apps are currently useless.

I know I'm the focus of the world anyway. I don't need to see what Kathy in Missouri has to say about it, I need to get it right. Oh, and only after I tested my theory by turning my phone off did the green light appear. They're spying on me.

To live through culture forever I must play to my most important audience, not the biggest. The biggest fans will play catch-up, always do. For example, I know Trump already Tweeted about me, and He's an addict, so it's reasonable to assume He's watching if He's not busy but I'm not even doing it for Him.

No, I'm speaking directly to the 19-year-old cryptographer from Langley—that's where the Pentagon is, right? The wired kid who puts in the grunt work holding my signal to record me, as my good friend Anne described earlier in the afternoon. That comment stuck with me. Said 19-

year-old is the likeliest person to immediately leak all recorded footage of the most famous man in the news cycle.

Whole decade I've seen those Top Secret leaks over Discords and PC games incessantly on my Chat. Shit, I know 19-year-old me'd leak the first juicy thing I got.

"And the thing in the gym where I put that woman on the spot, that..." I grit my teeth and accelerate past a pair of masked men who overturn a flaming trash can. "I take all that back, that was just . . ." Again I feel her wet lips and tongue pull my heart out through my helpless fucking dick, shudder in shame, ". . . nothing, that was some drama from high school."

And statistically it's best for my target audience to assume I'm secretly straight. A 19-year-old boy in an intel job is easily woker than his superiors, but more inclined to publicly agree with heteronormatives. "That, well, maybe it was a little something," I try to look like I haven't momentarily crawled out my own skin while I performatively bite my lower lip for the Nation, "but *everything else*, though . . ."

Enough reprobation. It's time to deliver the undiluted story. No lies. "Don't worry about the gas, it packs a punch but it's *sleeping* gas—" *I'm told*, I almost say, but stop. Anne from the afternoon would not have an issue with killing people. I already knew she was capable of killing people.

The old dead prepper in his unit, I didn't trust Anne's story about him at all. It couldn't have been just a random murder that we *happened* to step by to get her sleeping gas. There are, like, whole-ass laboratories in town. We didn't need to go to some basement. She for sure killed the guy herself (how I do not know) and was trying to jog something in my past: In medical school, we students pranked each other with cadavers more than once.

Or, I retroactively realize, she was sending a knowing message to me. "Liked cadaver pranks as a med student? I'll make some fresh ones if you think about running away again. Including you."

Fuck.

"Look I'm not a monster—even if some of y'all have given me every right," I say.

Approaching the edge of Liltin not currently under military siege, I zoom by dozens of homes with doors painted Passover red. Homeowners, shop owners, and renters try to scrub off my instructions in a frenzy. Must not be the most welcoming visual for our occupiers.

I lean my head out the window, point, and laugh. Some recognize me and go white. My cackling rips through the block and I begin to head uphill, toward my trailer.

"You know what?" I sigh to my captive kid in Langley like an overworked father figure. "Fine, I'll drop the act. It is Divine Intervention. I am a vessel for Christ the King. Shit, maybe I *am* him. Now I for one think that's a bit excessive . . . but it *is* what Jesus would think before understanding he was Jesus, isn't it? Maybe I'm the second coming. Look how I got all my local wicked to fall *so hard* for the simplest ruse. Demon Elite, you're next!"

I laugh myself to tears. Or make it look like I do, at least.

Because inside I fear I've cheated, taken some shortcut that not even I understand. How'd the military even pull up and start unloading on everyone? Did I miss what caused it all to happen?

This is supposed to be my Mischief Night. *Mine.* Things may be going crazy, but it doesn't feel personal enough. I can't see my signature in it. I've not administered the requisite charge needed to flood this time hole, to break free.

I'm done spilling to my surveillants. I've given the wired kid in the SCIF enough content to cut while the oldheads, if I haven't given them a heart attack designer drugs can't fix, no doubt prefer I incriminate myself endlessly. I will leave them wanting. I have outsized opps now, more heat than any one guy can handle—half of me cannot *wait* to reset at sunrise. My luck just needs to hold for . . . I check the dash to see 8:16 P.M.

Almost 12 more hours? This is *stressful.*

*I won't be here, I won't be here,* I outright pray. *I won't be here tomorrow.* Melodic and zippy like all good prayers are. There will be no one here tomorrow to hold accountable. I'm sure Anne will be reset back to normal, too, and remember me. I wish she hadn't glitched out of her higher awareness, just because Gets wanted to butt their alcoholic ass in—

My ears suddenly pound, a *whoop whoop whoop* from my one cracked window, the air beating itself irate like a drum. I raise it.

*Gets.* Now that's someone pretty personal to me.

Like the air at my window, I whip myself up into panicked breaths. The night is young and we might still be sharing phone locations. With a stink-eye to Langley, I power on, open my contacts, tap around, and bingo. GPS is still up, I guess. There they are.

I shout. Gets is less than a quarter mile down the road and heading the same direction: my trailer park.

"No the fuck you don't." I floor it.

I will be so good to them tomorrow, I promise myself.

From a distance my bayside town looks so much lovelier, its pall of smoke lit from below in flickering orange. My hopes for exactly what this place deserves are being fulfilled. It feels great to be right.

Then I realize Gets' traveling pin has come to a standstill on my map. Hugging the curve upward, Liltin disappears from view. Just me and the moon up here. I pass a vacated bus stop and slow—Gets is under 500 feet ahead.

But I can't spot them. Leaving the truck on idle just like Thaxton Pratt, I stroll across the slope, search. Too far from town to hear the screams, I am nonetheless able to taste a subtle sprinkling of sulfur as I gasp in the air. Clouds travel quickly up here. My fitful shadow is dreadfully distinct against dancing grass.

A jostling echoes up to my ears the moment Gets' pin resumes moving quickly downhill. I place the sound as a gleam catches my eye. A car, a bulky one. Maybe it's the drugs but it looks familiar. It's bucking and gathering speed, aimed directly at the edge.

"Huh?" I call Gets' phone. I feel my heart ramp as the vehicle's outline recedes. Three rings, four.

"You have reached Gets Lo—well, no you haven't," comes their voicemail as their vehicle drives directly over, plummeting like a stone.

The splash is barely audible. Gets' pin goes dead. I should look over. I should go to the edge and check, I tell myself. I realize I'm drooling a little bit.

*I should've gone down there and checked*, I think again as I'm speeding the black truck uphill. What did I want to see, anyway? Charred remains? Confirmation that the person who loved me is gone, that they were even in the car to begin with? Would that make it any more my doing, qualify it for my Mischief Night? I press my fingers behind my eyes so hard I see stars. It's all gone too abstract. If Gets just died tonight, I feel nothing. I'm fucking this up; the chaos has gotten away from me, signature nowhere in sight.

And what would that signature even look like, anyway? My inability to answer stresses me further. If I fail, I wake up caught in the same day with no progression, unaware of every opportunity I've lost. Anne will declare me a lost cause and leave me alone. Unrealized. Dead in the water. Stuck to Liltin Yew like a fly to sticky paper.

As if to footstomp this nightmare, there are red and blue lights scorching the heart of my trailer park. Too consumed in my desperation to care—it's not an uncommon sight here and it is, after all, one crazy night—my breathing slows as the lights get more prominent the closer I drive to my own home.

The three trucks look like the one I've jacked. Mine doesn't have the letters DHS on the side, though.

The masked ICE agents haven't been here long: The front door hasn't been taken off its hinges. The agents pound on it, shining flashlights in the windows, calling my name and Gabby's.

Fucking Gabby. Judging by the scene, he's right inside like a trapped animal.

I'm searching the cop's dash in a panic. Some kind of weapon, anything. I find a foldout blade in a stubby multitool. My teeth chatter uncontrollably. I turn out the glove compartment. A Punisher facemask. Nothing else.

A couple agents cast quizzical glances at my lookalike truck but don't approach. In fact, they've stepped down from my front door and seem to huddle next to my expensive birdfeeder. Until Americans start killing these folk, they'll stay this bold. Nobody from neighboring trailers comes out to intimidate. Half the trailers' doors are dripping with fresh bleach.

I give one last glance to the black screen of my phone, its lime green light still engaged. I exhale. On tiptoes, I reach up to the truck's roof and feel around on the suction-cupped siren until some switch clicks.

I hit my best angle one more time for my phone. "Pray for me, buddy." I stand on the gas.

The truck's treads dig hard into dirt as I stop behind theirs. Facemask on, my Class Reunion suit ruffled but regal, I strut with purpose about 10 feet wide of them, nod curtly, close the distance to my front door.

"Is that him?" I hear, and then they're all clamoring.

I only manage to get the screen door unlocked but Gabby flings the front door open and slams it behind as I fall into our living room. "It's you!" he cries in Spanish. "What's going on, Artie? Where've you been?"

"You haven't been watching the news?" I shoot back, also in Spanish. Mask off. He shakes his head then jumps as our front door rattles heavily. I look around—

I spot a suitcase. It's been Gabby's ever since our first vacation to the Vatican as kids.

"This your bugout case now? Sorry, brother, they've got the place surrounded."

"No," he says with his head down. "That was from before they showed."

Furious knocks on the door. "Arturo Vasquez, you are ordered to remove yourself from your domicile immediately!"

"Hold up," I snap over my shoulder, loud enough to be heard.

"We are granted puh—plenary authority by the Department of Homeland Security," the same booming voice recites with the linguistic discipline of a weatherman. "We will enter your domicile and forcibly remove you if you refuse to comply." *Domicile*, like he needs us to remember we own a trailer, not a house. I tilt my head and roll my eyes and Gabby does the same. Our mannerisms have a lot of overlap.

"Hold up," I call back more sternly. After some curses we hear boots trudge away. "So wait, where were you trying to go?"

His voice shakes. "North."

"Seattle?"

He shakes his head, points further up. "Canada."

"Are you serious?"

"I have . . . friends from the old days who just moved up into a big condo together. They're all sober, they said for a few months I can—"

"Gabby, we were born in Puerto Rico! We're citizens!"

"You say that *right now* as if it could matter any less?" Another *thud* and the door buckles all around its deadbolts. Not many hits left in it. "And that's not even why." Fighting tears, he sighs heavy. "I have to leave. You're not—I can't forget the worst of me when I'm around you. And it's not your fault. I've put you through too much."

I don't know what to say. Splintering chunks of the front door fill the silence.

Certainly can't deny it. We both know I barely treat myself with hope, let alone my infamous mess of an older brother. I really have given up on him.

"I'm sorry," I mumble and pull him into a hug.

I have never experienced my older brother shrink in stature as much as he does just now. It's like he expects to either wilt or catch a right hook. After the next *thud* I hear ICE counting through a crack in my door as if already inside.

Something seems to shift on Gabby's gaunt face as he looks into mine. Incredulity, then a sudden, acute fear like I've transformed into something unfathomable. "Arturo, are you high?"

He's the reason I'm still in this small town. The reason our parents condemned us both to squalor. I stuck to his side and after a decade of managing his damage he says *he's* done being around *me*, recoils at my presence like I'm a villain.

I couldn't see my signature before, and now I'm looking at its every sad brushstroke all at once. The door crumples.

Two rifles with rail-mounted lights lock onto us, but I've already put my brittle brother into a headlock, raised the dull blade of Thaxton Pratt's multitool to his throat.

"I dare you!" I'm challenging, pulling us back and out of view of the living room windows. My voice is so high it can't be mine. "Come closer! I dare you!" Gabby, in shock, stutters pleas; I hear him say we'll be fine. I tighten my grips and focus on my voice. "Come on! Give it a try!" That's a better, lower octave now. Dramatic and scary. Their bodycams film me as they inch in.

"Stop!" one of them shouts and they freeze in terror.

My hand's wet.

# 30

# VADA IKEBE

My VR screen datamoshes as I approach the red/black figure. *Reify*'s in-game music is designed to fade the further from camp one travels. Thorns scratch my legs and I stand still, but push my character forward to the opening of the mineshaft. The image crushes and crunches.

"What're you doing, Vay?" Taek-su's voice comes from behind me.

Through churning pixels I fixate on the rogue human asset, keep her in my center. My character makes it all the way up to her. A jpeg smile is slapped onto the white, blonde, blocky face like the legless children from TLI.

A red glow fades in from the end of *Reify*'s world: the belly of the mine. The glow drifts forward, throwing the wooden tunnel into relief. This lighting is baked into our game's climax and cued on arrival of the final barrage of enemy AI. Aside from the frozen woman the shaft remains empty.

Is the figure supposed to be Amy? The hair isn't dissimilar, the face nondescript, but Amy doesn't dress in joggers. However, going off her step-brother Daniel's revelation regarding her planned TLI admittance as soon as she's out of the coma—

"Vada!" Taek-su says, closer now. "You're freaking me out."

"Something's up there in the mine." I lift the goggles from my face.

"What?"

I shove my headset his direction. "In the game, something we didn't put there. Look." I try to give him my hand strap controllers, but: "I'll take the case, just look, Taek-su."

"It's a gun," he says warily.

"I know," I say as patiently as I can, "I'm the one who told you to grab it."

Gripping the case's handle, it's heavy in my hand, a time bomb counting down. He flips on the headset's second pancake lens for both his eyes, and takes the hand straps, fiddling with the joysticks. I see nothing from the direction of the real-life mineshaft. I'm blind in the darkness. But I feel my dream tugging me, calling. My phone has a flashlight and plenty of battery.

"Are we still live?"

Face in headset, Taek-su checks and then nods. "What am I looking at? Who is this?" he whispers. His mouth is agape. "Is that Amy?"

At this point I'm inclined to say yes—before I can a commotion interrupts us.

From the heart of the lit-up COVID camp Kristen is shouting. Daniel/SalishUs chases Rundee between picnic tables. "Stay back, dude! You're a whole-ass adult!"

"Give me the camera!"

"Daniel stop!" Kristen tries, their voice echoing. "100 thousand people are watching."

"That's exactly why they need me!" SalishUs doesn't waiver.

"Come on, let's go," I urge Taek-su and let him run ahead of me toward our friends before I stop, ignite my flash, turn heel, and make a break for the mine. There is no clear path through the thorns, so I tank it, wincing. What a vivid dream I'm having; the pain is authentic.

Taek-su is calling out but he's ensnared in the camp's cacophony now. And the woods are surprisingly noisy around me. Twigs snapping, branches shaking, it's like I bring a gale. It is not how a normal forest behaves.

With an effortful grunt I steady myself on a tree; I've reached the tunnel. It is the ass-end, the mine's uppermost part burrowed somewhere uphill. In '20 and '21 Amy and I were never tall enough to fully explore; a bolted retractable ladder at a leaky L-turn always hung just out of reach, even if we stacked.

My dreaming subconscious comes through for me: moonlight highlights the high wooden threshold at the exact moment there is a kicking of stones, echoing from within.

I squeeze the light from my phone to my palm to smother it. Eyecap itches like hell. The SalishUs gun case whines quietly. I tamp down my ragged breaths and wait, crouched.

The game becomes reality. Out steps a blonde, white woman in black and red joggers splattered with mud. Definitely not my comatose best friend. She must be in her 30s, thick athletic frame; head on a swivel, she emerges directly from the mine's center, not trying to hide.

This explains the mystery woman's shock when Oh Taek-su sneaks behind me and whispers, "Vada, people are here."

Not whispered quietly enough. The woman starts; she raises her hand and it ignites with a whip-crack and we hit the ground immediately after. The woman fires off two more rounds. My breath buffets the dirt and sullies my face. Fifty yards behind me I hear something like a metallic *hiss* and I hear the screaming of Rundee, of Kristen, of Daniel Deadwyler.

Taek-su grabs me and we flatten our backs on the tree, revolve against it as the woman's footsteps approach, but it doesn't work.

"Who—" she starts, gun trained, then lowers. We're just kids.

"You're Bonnie Cossio." Taek-su's eyes are wide. "From the—the article."

The woman backs away. The metallic *hiss* magnifies over our friends' screams and the three of us turn: a gas fire spouts forth from the campground's generator.

The odds of this Bonnie Cossio shooting it from across the valley are cartoonish. It's as if the generator were placed with the foresight to catch her bullet. The fire spreads fast, eats up foliage and wood.

And even I can see in its scorching glow the silhouettes of over a dozen people, some masked, who surround the camp. A giant pickup truck with license plate DEVST8R rolls coal brazenly close to the blaze.

"Cossio!" call a few barely twenty yards away.

"Stay away," she half-sobs through gritted teeth; no doubt we're the only ones who can hear her, and she doesn't linger to confirm. She launches away from us parallel to the hillside.

I'm in the mineshaft before I can think. Taek-su tries to forcibly redirect me towards our friends, but a burst of gunfire assaults the outside from every direction; Taek-su shouts; I was expecting it. This is the part of the dream where I have to fight. This is the turbulence. I want to make it to the end. I want to see where it's leading.

"Come on."

"But Vada, they're out there—"

"Yeah. Everyone's out there," I say simply and the mineshaft lights up.

Literally it lights up. The same red glow from *Reify*'s climax, except this light source is motivated. Bell-sized diodes spaced evenly on the low ceiling fade up all at once. It can't be motion-controlled or Bonnie Cossio—whose battle cries still come muffled—would've discovered them first.

"W-were these on a timer?" Taek-su tries to cover his breakdown.

"Nah." They might be if this weren't all just my dream lighting our way. I stopped critiquing the logic hours ago. Taking this chance to do my latanoprost drop, my hand doesn't shake. I step over a puddle and lead us to the L-turn. The retracted ladder is not so retracted anymore: Bonnie freed it on her way down. I jump right onto it and get moving.

"Vada!" Taek-su runs to catch up, grabs the rung in front of my face. "WHAT ARE YOU DOING?" He's hyperventilating. Getting in the way.

"Well, I'm finding Amy," I say, like he should know.

I about short-circuit his brain. He's grabbing his heart. I squint my eye: He's been helping me all dream long, but now no? What in my subconscious has shifted?

"Rundee! Kristen! They're back there!" He throws his arms toward the raging way we came in, looks at me as if I've lost it.

"Nope. Uh-uh. No time," I say tersely and scale the ladder in seconds.

"The fuck?!" He's screaming it. He keeps screaming while I get the good sense to pull the ladder up behind me, just in case my dream decides to pull any other fast ones.

"Call your dad! Call 911!"

"Dad hates me," I say, laughing. It's another clammy L-turn up here. I shine my phone's flash and spot Bonnie Cossio's fresh shoeprints leading straight to me. I get a feeling that's not the way.

A few paces down the other passage and yup. The beckoning of more soft red lights. "I'mma give you a big ol' kiss tomorrow, Taek-su baby," I call down in response to his screams and run down the passage, a wholly undiscovered country, like I've clipped out *Reify*'s geometry.

I remind myself to ignore the cuts to my legs. The Taek-su betrayal is just AtaVada, my moralizing id. *Don't forget your friends* type shit and message received, staying humble. That's not what the fuck this entire fictional day has been for.

It's not a lesson I'm hunting. I think it's a feeling.


**Weeeeeee**


reads the message on my phone's screen as I run. I'm chasing Amy. Horrifying movie from what I've heard; I'll never watch it.


**good its absolute bullshit.**

*Or it's just a product of its time,* I shrug, gliding through the dripping corridor and casting my mind all the way back to . . . when'd it premiere, late 1990s? *They didn't know what they didn't know.* Switching hands between SalishUs' gun case and my phone, I Google it.

**naahh they knew tf. u think lesbians didnt exist? They didnt kno exactly what they didnt want to kno**

That sounds about right. I sigh. I miss my best friend. There's no way this doesn't end with my best friend. She is who I'm presenting this game for, anyway. I examine the mineshaft. I would be claustrophobic and afraid in real life, especially under these circumstances; I can still hear a few *bangs* from camp all the way in here. There's even a chasm that I just barely jump across.

Even knowing none of it is real, it's not like I want to return to the summer camp horror show. Something best to forget; when lucid dreaming if you let something unsavory stick it'll multiply. My dream of course agrees. The mineshaft comes to another exit, and when I step out to the open, moonlit basin, I can see the Twice Loved Institute a couple miles away.

So it's not just Amy I'm saving, it's all the kids. I haven't felt fatigued in a dream before. I try to fly again, but fail. I pick lingering thorns from my legs and resume my jog.

**r u sure it IS all for me tho?**

"What?" I ask aloud. "Oh, *Reify*?" There is no response, so I think a bit as the compound gets nearer. *Reify*'s story was about Amy's experience and mine. We gave all the enemy designs key features that reflected our MAGAt counselors, none of whom shared a legal qualification between them—all of them the camp attendees' parents. And I'm hoping the money we get from selling it will find Amy better care. But on balance, *Reify* was supposed to be everybody's launchpad. For me, a proof of concept for Ivy League colleges.

"It's for me too, of course." I think I'm halfway to TLI. The ground is marshy in places. I am no fan of the detailed traversal in this dream.

**if something goes wrong and the game doesn't sell, will u blame it on me? rushing to put it on the marketplace etc.**

"Amy." I am breathless, and it's not due to the jogging. "No."

She doesn't message for the rest of the journey. The clouds cover the moon, so I have to go back to using my flash, and with the marshes, it takes more time. There seem to be fireworks going off all the way back in Liltin Yew. That's what it sounds like. Summer solstice is a big deal in my mind, after all.

I reach the rehab. At the front corner of the perimeter I remember we are virtually on the Nisqually border. I dragged my friends to this very spot to protest this place's construction in '23. TLI's displayed totem pole reads as half-assed cultural sensitivity to most, and as a petty trophy of my family's severed heads to me. My real family, not the ones who think "lowest on the totem pole" is an accurate idiom. Dad's family is one degree separated from the people that locked mine up in boarding schools and disappeared them.

The gates are wide open, and a single news van scoots away from the spartan main building—almost running me over actually. The far side of the compound shits black water into the Duwamish River.

The front door is locked; that's okay. Dad taught me how to shoot a gun when I was four. It's a dream, though, so it better not matter. SalishUs' case clatters onto the steps as I slam the full mag into the pistol and shoot around the door's lock. Wow! The kick feels fucking real.

My heart pounds as I step inside. This is the climax, and it's truer enemy territory than anything back at camp. If it's not Amy or another kid TLI is using for labor, I'll shoot anyone I see on sight.

But now I'm scared. Because now it does feel real. Like all vivid dreams do, lucid or not, the conclusion is always where the lines blur the most, and in my dream's case, it's an adrenaline spiker. I wish Amy would text me, give me direction, or hell, just step out at this point. Please.

It doesn't help that every clinical room and hallway is empty. This is more of a haunted house than those tunnels. I'm lost. The smell is unbearable. That has to be the river. It can't always smell like this, it's insane. There is sparse signage on hallway corners but it's like trying to learn a language. These must be intentionally minimal in the event that a child escapes. I lead with the gun.

"Dorms." There it is. Getting warmer. I shoot the glass of another locked door. Taek-su is ringing me—of course my inner AtaVada is revolting. I need to hold it back, hold the dream together. I'm losing control. I don't know if I'm dreaming anymore but *yes I do* and I have to keep it together because I have to get to the end.

Empty dorms, empty dorms. Where the fuck are the kids? The smell is seeping through my skin. I call out to Amy and the painted cinderblock walls insulate my voice. Pass an empty kitchen, an empty lounge.

A light flickers behind a hallway door. The door is unlocked.

I have 6 rounds left. If I'm dreaming I can will that up to infinity. I enter silently and check all the corners: the end furthest seems to have a small, inset office. I don't go there yet, though. I'm fixating on the wall leading to the office. No fewer than six numbered VR headsets dangle from bulky mounts.

There were always six legless child avatars in the YewVerse. I reviewed my old logs just hours ago, and . . . well, was that already my dream? Had Amy texted me by then? I saw them in the morning, live, coming off my all-nighter. That wasn't also the dream, right?

Stop. Poking at the dream's genesis during its climax makes me more unstable. I have to resist. I rip the nearest headset from its charger and boot it up, my pistol lowered to my side.

The ugly salmon-orange YewVerse appears with not even a second of loading. Am I about to see the invisible assets the kids were handling? Looking around, I thumb the joystick from one of the dangling hand strap controllers, but movement is disabled. The YewVerse has to show me something first.

It's a fat, blue logo that fills the whole screen.

## PredictAct

A sudden *slam* from the room I'm in runs a hot bolt through my every nerve and I swear I hang in the air for a full second. Almost shoot into the padded floor. My VR character jerks around too (the logo's faded; movement is allowed).

I drop the headset and bring the gun up, shuddering from the scare, crouch-walking to the inset office. I peer through glass.

A uniformed man's back is turned, expensive over-ear headphones pressed tightly over his hair. A TLI-emblazoned cap is on the desk where he sits with his back to me, tucking into reheated leftovers.

The man, bopping along to his headphones and wholly unaware, sits beside a server as tall as the paneled ceiling. Large cooling tanks, neon double-helix designs. I lean in and scowl: It is freshly installed, probably by this guy, not only powerful but all dressed up, making it some mystical, shiny obelisk for the children it's enslaving.

Yeah, found my villain. I shoot the guy in the fucking head. Oh goddammit I don't like that. That was way too real. I look away from the body collapsed into the shiny server and spot a surveillance camera in the corner where I entered. Its light blinks.

It's on.

Composing myself, I wipe the disgust from my face, stand up straight. I hold my arms out wide, a sardonic little T-pose of myself, dip one arm and bow.

*All right, Amy. Did the thing. What next?* I check my phone.

**just wake up, Vada.**

That's it? *What?* My eye goes hot, tears bending vision of the empty flickering room. *I don't even get to see you?* It's embarrassing, because I know she's watching. Maybe the meaning just hasn't caught up to me yet. It will come on the other side, I'm sure of it. So I try.

**Wake up.**

I'm trying but I don't know how.

# 31

# OUR SYSTEM IS ANY AND ALL

Before the doubts creep in and tangle, Arturo is glad he has done it. It's written on his face. The relief at puncturing so thoughtlessly, the power at ending what he has deemed the nexus of his undignified suffering. He was worried he didn't have the capacity for such cruelty.

The ICE stormtroopers want more than anything to shoot, but this supernatural prophet is to be taken alive; many, many superiors watch the bodycam feeds. So many in fact that the live link is clumsy, unencrypted—not like Liltin Yew can access Internet right now anyway, right? Our she-half has tapped in from the neighboring scrapyard.

They must watch the innocent older brother bleed. And Arturo must hold Gabby in his arms as he spasms, as he drowns and empties at the same time. Shock shoves its way into Arturo. In 4K resolution his face contorts to bug-eyed horror. They bark at him to drop the knife. He does. They order him to hold his arms out at his sides. He does that too. Gabby's body buckles and twitches.

He doesn't put his arms behind his head and interlace his fingers. He keeps them out as if demanding a hail of bullets, while begging forgiveness for those who know not what they've done, as if he is crucified. He's found God. When neither bullets nor forgiveness arrive, he begins to wail.

He falls to his knees and clamps his brother's pooling wound with sputtering sorrys. You'll be here tomorrows. I love yous. Using the last of his strength, Gabby tries to push him off, frightened eyes hollowing.

—

We close our dongled-up laptop and crush it with a rusty drive shaft as the cuffs close on our preacher. At least the big crescendo still came relatively smooth. We close our eyes, sigh. Fuckin' influencers, eating fame from their shifting plates. Anyway.

"TLI and *Reify* are chugging along," we hear ourselves say from around a pointy pile of dead GM vans. "'Course, William's not there to take Vada's bullet, just the guard instead—"

"I've told you I can probably help with that."

"No, no. William's mine. I'll get it to happen one of these days. But otherwise, no complications. Happy anniversary, Anne."

We nod. "Happy anniversary, George." We still can't get over the battered face. "How would you grade it?"

A look of faux contemplation. "About a 4."

"Out of 100?"

"Something like that."

"No," we smile. "More like a 3.5. Out of 5."

George-half thinks it's a joke. "But the passcode. The ripple effect."

We walk upwards from the scrapyard, twirling grass between our fingers. This T-Pose run wasn't quite the petrichor we crave, but, "Sometimes it's meaningful when you have to fight for it. Not always, but tonight it created accidental art, like I told you earlier."

We very much agree with the part about fighting for it. Abreast of Anne-half, we side-eye, try to keep our love at a distance. Try to say that we don't care who said, *pow*, a half-second early this morning, that the overlap is fine with us. Our Anne-half feels our eyes, clears our throat, and redirects attention to the sweeping Liltin Yew vista below.

Against the water and far, far in the distance is a human figure we identify via distinct outline of a tech coat. Gets Lo hobbles up the hill, having evaded their fate at the bottom of the Bay.

Both halves of us notice. "You're fucking kidding."

"On it," growls our male half, eager to correct today's mistake. "You go on. We'll meet at—"

We hold up a hand. "I'll wait up here, change back into my sweats. We'll go together."

We don't feel worthy of this outpouring of grace but, knowing our Anne half, this is the time to double down. It shows effort, receptiveness. "Uhh, okay, it'll just be a second. You know, why wait 'til tomorrow to debrief? It's, what, 9:11? Sundown on the dot. Let's clear out the overnight room at the Mansion." It's our favorite spot in Vancouver. Hopping the border after today's antics could be another welcome challenge.

We get what we really mean: We don't even have to cap this anniversary with a gaze upon our aquatic Unmaker. Fuck that noise, that stupid thing.

We sigh, but smile. As Gets limps upward to the scrapyard, a beady line of red and blue lights breaks from the broken town, the only cars that had time to swap the tires we slashed. They make their way up the cliff toward the Vasquez residence. ETA 10 minutes.

We gave all of ourselves to one another, all our history shared and otherwise. When our histories expired, we gave every inch of our present, often literally. When we were barred from giving what was inside our bodies we gave each other everybody else. Yet there remain things we can't give. Humanity, maybe? Not enough to share between the two of us. Our she-half has long accepted that our natural in-road is to reflect our inarguably hopeless circumstance onto others; our male half would maybe rather it all be over.

With a snarl we relive the talk with Gets in the goth bar, the enby so dismissively labeling us cheats, charlatans, as if we didn't actually *know anyone* in Liltin Yew, as if we were the most horrendous thing they had ever met.

Now Gets climbs into the doorless, empty white bus. We steel ourselves. This is why we queued up T-Pose: pledging our strength to carry on, keep us whole, not waste our time.

But isn't that all this is anyway? That's what we wonder when Gets lets us into the ruined bus. They've stepped back a few rows. A broken arm is slung in their tech coat.

"Say again?" they ask breathlessly.

"We said, 'isn't this all just a waste of—'"

Gets has a Glock.

Well, where did they get that?

Our whole history crashes against us. All those extra suicides we indulged in behind the other half's back; the slow onset of fatigue; the USO's freezing rays eking into the deepest ruts of our brain. The certainty that with the next one we could easily slip away.

"Why is this night different from all other nights?" we ask, and Gets blinks.

To be honest, once our she-half wedded the Mischief Nights over the Trick-or-Treats, that was exactly what we were seeking: the thrill of finally leaving. But the grace we've bestowed upon ourselves today, the 3.5 out of 5, is a mote of hope: maybe a signal of flexibility, or at least a first step to something simpler.

Suddenly we want to put in effort a bit longer.

Gets is no stranger to violence, but they only ever fight to pacify or contain threats. The gun is trembling at their side. "You're no killer," we try. "Not like Arturo. Just because you did nothing to stop that kid at your first job from punching his ticket, that doesn't . . . that doesn't make you who you are." Are we begging?

And is it true they *always* aren't a killer? If anyone can be twisted into anything, is that really them at all, or are they just the vessels we inhabit? A foreign emotion has fully inhabited us, blindsided entirely. We do not know what will happen. Utterly captivated, we don't move.

Gets raises the Glock now. In our mind, this death would be more than self-orchestrated enough to qualify against us. We're afraid. Holy fuck, *we are afraid*. How long has it been? That is some *high* adrenaline! Perhaps we really can give something new to ourselves: the closest thing to freedom for us both.

Our cackle sharply strikes all through the cramped metal tube; feathers ruffle from a family of house finches at the bus's back. We've woken them up. Seven inches to the right of the finch nest is an etched scribble of the almost prehistoric Etruscan word, Φerso. Gabriel Vasquez wrote that himself. It would only be visible if one were to scrub decades of grime.

We try not to forgive Gets. Can't look at them with a single thing apart from respect. "We'll take you to Gabby's body! I bet we can still save Arturo! Stranger things have . . . Don't do this. Please don't—" Despite full knowledge of the direness of our situation we just keep laughing. Wow. Fear. What a bespoke reminder.

I ask them one more time.

*"Mah nishtanah halailah hazeh mikol haleilot?"*

The birds fly out.

Gets Lo, out of necessity, has conditioned themself for years to go for center mass, every time. But with their dominant arm in pieces, and with the hangover finally apexing underneath the waves of tremendous pain, their aim is irreconcilably far off. So their very first shot lands right between our eyes.

We only hear it.

Our she-half plunges from the treeline vantage to the scrapyard, and as the distant police sirens near, we break into a sprint. We forgot about Thaxton Pratt's gun.

No, that's not right. We didn't forget—Gets was supposed to go over the bight, dammit, so we dumped it from our brain.

That's forgetting, we remind ourselves.

With light feet we reach the back of the white bus. Gets stumbles from its doorless entry, steadies themself on its hood and vomits. They discard the gun and head down the knotted hill, waving their one good arm in the direction of the approaching caravan.

We want to look inside and see ourselves, but something shuts us down. A feeling, like a prickly sort of sphere, seems to push itself outward in our chest. The feeling is curious, contradictory. A shifting ratio of positive to negative. All we know is we shouldn't look inside. Give some respect to our male half, for a change. Some privacy. It has been so long without seeing it that we might even be a little disturbed, which could ruin this unexplainable feeling. We'll just debrief tomorrow.

Gets has reached the road. Two vehicles break from the caravan while the rest continue toward Arturo's trailer park. Awash in light, Gets points up to the white bus, and we go prone on the grass.

"Help me," we hear them pant as we crawl to the caravan. "There's . . ." Then they go quiet. We nod to ourselves, our chin bouncing on the dirt, worm-level. Gets is smart; they're going to lie. The unspeakable prickly feeling takes over our whole body, infects our limbs.

"Did someone attack you?"

"Yes."

"Where is the attacker now, um . . .?"

"Over the cliff. In—in his car." Gets stammers as much truth as possible: "It was me or him. I had to do it. You have to believe me, please."

"They're telling the truth!" Unable to contain it, exploding up from the grass, the enby and two police officers recoil. "Saw the whole thing from right here. Car swerving and shit. They barely escaped with their life."

"Who are you?"

Anne Oxendine spouts some babble about there being nowhere to hide and fleeing the town carnage. Gets, mortified, all fight spent, is bracing themselves, but when the badges' heads are turned, we wink. *See you tomorrow*, we mouth.

They know us only at our worst.

The officers—Jake and Millie, they have a workplace romance thing going—load us with assurances into their respective cars. Buzzing, humming, reeling, the prickly elation is identified, and this anniversary solidifies as the most momentous so far.

It's a feeling like gliding over a depthless dread. Gliding, not flying—termination is the point. For the first time, waiting it all out seems doable. All that may be required is to lose track of time.

Stepping over to the backseat, the door is opened. In the precinct there is a holding room which faces the east. It will be an easy request to afford a view to the first ray of dawn before its wild reset. A cold glow. I can hear Gets is shouting from the other vehicle, fixed squarely on this second siren; they give me a blanket, and as I'm wrapping it snugly around my shoulders, I realize that I have never felt more alive.

# 32

# WILLIAM TILLER AND BOUNDARIES

The return drive to Liltin Yew is animated. Twice there are encounters of shared physical intimacy in the rental Focus: one play-push, then later a brief application of pressure to the leg when an errant driver almost brains them. William Tiller of course appreciates both instances, but he feels like he's riding a far older kind of high, a more cerebral intimacy he hasn't allowed himself since after his ex-girlfriend. The sun dips and the sky's darkening glow turns colder as they reach Hunter's ranch outside town.

Old, weather-chewed picket fences. Between lines of thick firs muddy gravel fills his tires. A single light is on behind the front porch.

"Wait for me here? I'll bring coffee."

Not meaning to snoop, he steals only a glimpse when she walks inside. Candles, boxes. Many plants. Her daughter, who Bill knows now is named Anohni, is sprawled on a shag sofa with her girlfriend; filling the far wall is a woven tapestry of a woman whom Hunter, emerging with two wine bottles, identifies as Rachel Aliene Corrie.

"Apparently there's some kind of pop-up event going on in town," she says. "Our mayoral candidate put some huge concert together. That's what Anohni tells me. We're lucky Bull Elk isn't far. Here, quick. Come 'round this way, I'm showing you my favorite gun. Promise it'll be quick."

Her acres-wide backyard reaches the edge of the Puget Sound. Hunter meets him at a shed with a shotgun case and two pairs of over-ear protection. She flips a floodlight; Bill can see the border of grass and marsh. Unsheathing her gun, she says, "This is an A400 Xtreme Plus." It's all coyote brown with black accents.

"Okay," Bill says, trailing off.

She has him pull clay for her and, with a thunderclap, she explodes several airborne clay pigeons. "Those cougars ain't stand a chance this fall," she purrs.

"Impressive." Bill takes off the earphones as Hunter's daughter calls out the back window, "Mom, *go away!*"

"In a second, bunny! Bill, before you make a cougar joke, you want a shot or two?"

Bill shakes his head and she gets to cleaning the shotty's barrel. "Too many firsts today already. Plus, I'm ideologically opposed, sorry."

"You should be. Sorry, I mean." Hunter says without skipping a beat. "Lemme present you a standpoint: we both walk into the wrong place, and they'll tear us apart for separate *and* shared reasons. Cis white folk finally say, 'they're coming for us, they're coming for us.' We know *they've* been here. I'm glad you have a great family but don't pretend that some of these small towns, some of these little cities you gig in, you don't sleep in your car instead of showing yourself to some inbred fetal alcohol abomination on the off-chance they call in a hate crime."

"Mm."

"Look, I'm not saying 'just buy a gun'! You're smart, you'd train on something as dangerous as a gun well enough to understand how to better value and maintain your own safety. At *least* you wouldn't let the dumbest guy in the room get the drop on you as easily."

"And what if that dumbest man in the room has a gun too?"

Hunter tips her head. "Hence the training. A level playing field would be a nice upgrade, wouldn't it, from a standpoint theory or two? Somethin' to think about. Let's go drink, though."

He profoundly disagrees with Hunter Dames yet the prospect of intellectual debate with her seems strangely exciting. Now that's truly rare. Maybe it has something to do with the way she is looking at him. *Everyone is like me in more ways than I expect*, Bill thinks. *And in many I don't, they'll be different.*

Bull Elk Motel is just 2 miles away. The manager/receptionist Susan is MIA; he smells French onion soup. Bill spots the key to Room 203 alone on the corkboard. He ducks under the dreamcatchers to hop the desk and grab it, then smacks his work debit on the table with a scrawled note. He leaves his server build for TLI in the rental's backseat, covers it in blankets just to be safe. "Gonna tell me I should be guarding my livelihood with the 2nd Amendment?"

"I'm actually gonna tell you to shut the fuck up," Hunter leers and the two of them ascend the motel's exterior steps to the second floor at 9:42 P.M..

He edges into 203; it looks normal. Striped wallpaper. Double bed, clean. A bulky screen on the long entertainment stand with its built-in minifridge. "Well, let's get to looking for lenses," Bill barely gets done saying before Hunter is on him, pressing herself into him, their tongues melting into one another. He squeezes her ass and she stifles a little moan while digging in her nails. She bites his lip.

"Why so soon, William? Are we about to put on some kind of show?" Her fingers play over to his ribs, his abs, his waist near the faint scar from his suprapubic tube surgery. His find their way under her camo.

"What a day." His whisper is more of a growl.

"Mm." She slides her hands free of him and addresses Room 203 in general: "Okay, that concludes the free show. Let's do a sweep," she says back to William, beaming her subtly stained teeth.

The two keep their shoes on while surveying the back closet, the boring bathroom. Nothing in the showerhead or electrical outlets, air duct at the ceiling, clock by the bed.

Inwardly stimulated more than sufficiently, now is typically when Bill either gives a few tantalizing pumps to extend his erection or, even better, have his hookup do it for him. However, his head is swimming in uncharted waters. Hunter wants it; he wants to give her everything she wants, and for the very first time in years, more. Is he really thinking about asking to go slow? How does one even go about that? He half-scoffs, nervously.

They check every single one of the lights and hold each other's gazes the closer they get to completing the room. Not the TV nor modem nor any of the circular knobs on drawers.

"Maybe our Mystery Matchmaker left us more beers," Bill says and opens the entertainment stand's fridge.

The two wires protruding from the little camera inside are clipped; their copper spindles at the end are like needles, but still Bill covers the lens with his thumb as he inspects. For good reason. He's installed diodes in devices much smaller than this, and sure enough the camera's housing has a side slot adequately sized for a mini lithium coin battery.

"Check it out. Good going," says Hunter, awed. Then she frowns. "Wait, it was just in the fridge, already ripped out and everything?"

"Mhm." Bill opens the camera's side slot.

A little piece of paper is folded neatly. "Come on," Hunter whispers, as he unfolds it.

**No cameras. But if you like, maybe leave your front door open? :)**

"'Leave it open?' Excuse me?" Hunter sits on Room 203's thinly carpeted floor. "What does that mean, like they're gonna come in? Gonna come have a nice chat?"

"If it even is more than one person," Bill says, frowning as well. "I was named George and you were named Anne, right? What if it's just one person?"

"What if it's an automated system, like a program?" Hunter throws her arms out.

"Tinder piloting some next-level AI?" he laughs.

"Wouldn't really explain why it wants us to open our door . . ."

"Your daughter said there's some event in town tonight." Bill bends to hand Hunter the note as he crosses to the locked door.

"She wasn't sure what kind. Think it's connected?"

With a shrug he first unlocks, then pulls on the door, bringing the outside world into the room.

The covered exterior hall lining the top floor is populated by exactly one collarless orange cat, which patters down the stairs when Bill peers out. Apart from that not even the well-lit parking lot below is inhabited. There is a sound, though. Echoing music from the heart of the town.

"This how Liltin Yew sounds on a Saturday?" he asks.

"I don't live right there," Hunter, behind him now and looking out, says. "Summer solstice concert, baby. Quinn Gershwin's definitely winning the election now." She backs away slowly, sitting on the bed. Bill glances at her, then goes and sits there too.

From the edge of the bed they watch an empty door frame.

A breeze from the parking lot moseys on in and plays across them both.

Hunter's hand closes over his. Bill flushes, flustered, and almost gasps. There is no reason to be surprised at a gesture so small. He squeezes her fingers. No, not surprise. Inexplicably, he is moved.

The more she almost absentmindedly caresses his fingers, the more he tries to puzzle out why he reacts so largely, and he mirrors her motion in what probably comes across as a feverish fashion, an amateur palm reader. What relaxes his grip to ease his hand against hers is just a very, very potent notion that they have known each other a lot longer than one single day.

Which has to be how he feels her decide as he does, turning mutually to face one another. "You know, a thought occurred to me."

"Yeah?"

"Say George and Anne are real matchmakers."

"Okay?"

"They're kind of assholes, aren't they?"

"They are," Hunter nods and she stands, crosses to the motel door, pushing it gently shut as Bill begins to take off his shoes.

He manages to shake the left shoe before I arrive in the doorway.

"Hey-o," I say.

Hunter's arms flinch a bit, but she is not super shocked. They were both half-expecting someone to show up, anyway. "Um, you are . . .?" she says.

"I'm Anne," I finish for her.

Hunter's whole face shifts, then she exclaims loudly, "You were in my high school!"

I nod. "We didn't really talk."

William stands from the bed, smoothing his shirt and pants, all wide-eyed intrigue. Such an unassuming guy. "And, so, uh, how have you—"

"One sec," I interrupt and gesture at the exterior hallway behind. "C'mere."

The distant celebratory music is overtaken by a *booming*, and the motel shakes on its foundations: Fireworks launch from the heart of Liltin Yew. I lean on the rail and Bill and Hunter inch out unsteadily to join.

"So this . . . is what you wanted us to see?" Bill nervously scratches his chin stubble. "The door."

"I mean it'd be a nice perk of leaving it open," I look at him sideways. "But let's face it, y'all were always gonna close it." The lovebirds gawk at me, so I continue. "Think of it as a test. You aced the test."

"Where's George?" asks Hunter. I stare at her for a long moment.

"He thought you two were the sweetest in town. Sweeter than us. I guess he wasn't wrong." Bill leaves a hand on the rail and keeps his face inscrutable as I tell him, "I mean I can't seem to get fully inside your head, for instance. I feel I know enough about you, but to me you're one of those people who're still stuck in third person, if that makes sense. Not judging you or anything. Just stating a fact. George, though." I look back to the fireworks, which have begun to wind down. "I think that was George's biggest mistake, actually. Dude thought he could be everyone."

"Did he pass?" Hunter asks me gently, a logical assumption given her widowed history.

It takes a minute to calibrate my response. "No, no, he's here." I can't look at her. "But since yesterday, he's . . ." I inhale slowly. "He's just visiting. For, um, our class reunion. He doesn't recognize me anymore."

Bill notices how it seems I'm telling a story more to myself than them.

"Oh, girl, that's hard," Hunter tries awkwardly.

"If you don't mind," Bill says delicately, "*how* exactly did you manage to match us and set things up all over—"

"Predictive technology," I handwave. "Brand partnership thing."

"You're the one with the Insta!" Hunter points at me and covers her mouth while Bill, with a million more questions, looks on.

"I'm the one with the Insta."

"Well, will you try talking to this George guy again?" she asks, as genuinely as she can this time, seizing on an opportunity to influence a beauty influencer. Which is not her fault.

"If I do that, he just becomes another piece of furniture," I say simply. William and Hunter try to parse it; I hand them a phone before tears can overtake me. "Anyway, your prize for passing the test is $164,000 each. Your bank accounts are linked to PredictAct, same password as your emails. Just open and initiate deposits. I gotta go see to Getty."

"I—our bank accounts?" William Tiller, hand in his Viking mohawk, blubbers as I walk away.

"Is Getty your dog?" calls Hunter, barely containing her excitement.

I laugh myself down the exterior stairs and the fireworks end. "Yeah!"

# TOMORROW

# 33

# CASPER

I am not allowed to leave town. LYPD lack the bodies to protect every witness, particularly once so many cops go on leave awaiting indictment for their actions in the streets on the night of the 21st; Washington State steps in. The FBI steps in. I was Arturo Vasquez's significant other. I am juggled between them all.

A handful of recordings of the Liltin Yew massacre manage to slip through the admin's firewall. Some kid at the Pentagon leaks the phone tap and bodycams from Arturo's arrest, and the narrative effectively ends. The prophet becomes the only feared influencer on earth. But the localized Internet blackout is wide enough for others to fill with speculation, false flags, AI disinfo discourse, and the rabid desire for it all to be "a Liltin Yew problem." A civil war soft-launches in fits and starts across the nation. It's quashed in 27 days.

Crowds travel to either worship Arturo or attempt bombing his prison or both. He is moved from Liltin Yew to undisclosed federal holding. Locked under a deadly NDA, I am one of the few who knows the holding is not too far from Casper, Wyoming.

Arturo's leaked ramblings from that night are those of a crazy person, but that makes me more than a little crazy too, as well as many others on the Internet—and, crucially, thousands in Liltin Yew. When prompted to speak he only breaks down so they enlist me, his embattled enby ex, to elicit testimony.

The testimony is played at Vasquez's highly publicized criminal trial, which serves as a welcome distraction from the present Middle East ethnic cleansing. At first there'd been a push to make the court proceedings private, or at least held in a larger venue, but Liltin Yew Mayor Bonnie Cossio leads the prevailing wave of public opinion. Shipped over from Casper, he is shackled to a glass box in the center of the court.

On-site and at-home viewers alike hear me asking the prophet the world's questions. One trillion *how*s. A prison jumpsuit's intermittent shuffling is the only indication of his presence. When I exhaust myself, reduced to asking why Arturo murdered his older brother, there comes the prophet's only addressing of the events that will ever publicly surface. The gain on the audio is heavily boosted for this part: everyone's ears fill with static.

"I'm not supposed to be here."

The official tally from the 21st caps at 539.

I spearhead a concurrent civil suit, and it reaches a fever pitch both in the streets and online thanks to Liltin Yew truthers, and there are thousands. The defendants are two alumni of Liltin Yew High who were visiting for the Class of 2010 reunion.

George Wheeler and Anne Oxendine's respective lawyers are quick to criticize the evidence. An angry accusation at the reunion? A handful of LYPD officers insisting they had taken in the visiting woman? Okay: where are the security camera feeds? Matter of fact, where are *any* police recordings from that fateful day? Colossal coincidence, that. And absolutely zero evidence on Wheeler.

I hear Vada Ikebe's court-appointed lawyer wants to ride my coattails. I wish she could. I don't know the girl, but I have sympathy for her and her surviving friends. She was clearly played just like Arturo. I know I need to talk to her but the feds won't dream of it. They definitely want to keep the victims isolated from each other, and they do in so many ways. I hear families are separated. I hear clemency is granted to some, eyes are turned, deals are cut, but I don't know for whom. I need to talk to Ikebe for information on George and Anne.

So I drop a note walking by her lawyer and tell her where to meet me during her next scheduled FaceTime with Vada in detention. When that time arrives, I shake the pigs on the way there.

"There is no George or Anne that I know from this." Vada is resolute and lucid but her voice rasps from sobbing. "There is a lot of Arturo Vasquez, though."

I ground myself, tame my fury for just the moment to glean more information.

"I saw it, your boyfriend's arrest." She says. "He held his arms out at his sides and left them there." When I don't understand why she's bringing it up, she says, "The asset in my game demo that none of us put there, the one I saw live. It was T-Posing." She breaks. "I T-Posed after I murdered the TLI employee."

I assure her that it wasn't truly her; her lawyer's phone suddenly drops all connection, and I am never afforded the lapse in security to speak to her again.

George moves and acts fundamentally different from how he interacted with me that day. His face is not battered; his hand is not broken. There is no hole between his eyes. Down to the smallest microexpressions, he is simply not the same man. He and Oxendine vehemently deny knowing one another.

Halfway through the suit, though, Wheeler is caught confiding he met Anne that night on a neighboring booze cruise and skinny-dipped—but likely at his team's advice, he immediately distances himself from the comment. Footage from that very booze cruise doesn't even contain them. Before long other alumni and total strangers lend their support.

Weeks stretch thinly into one long unbroken nightmare. My sleep wanes along with my community and financial support. The police officers who were set to testify drop out and are reassigned.

Public perception shifts sympathetically to a small town mortally wounded by a senseless, mysterious tragedy, flailing recklessly to piece it all together.

It is hard enough reliving the day over and over and over while testifying in front of my ex's slack-jawed stares. Hunted by conspiracy theorists of all ages, by podcasters, by opportunists, I have nothing real to offer them.

Because the criminal trial is over. Setting aside the supernatural, which we all agree is present yet defies precedent, dozens of deaths are pinned to the prophet beyond reasonable doubt. Clinical psychologists corroborate Vasquez's present condition as religious psychosis, exhibiting severe DID symptoms. And with how the public sees it, he certainly had been an army of one. The verdicts satisfy nobody—surprise nobody, either.

He is guilty, and he acted alone.

—

On the last Friday of the civil trial, I fumble some numbered notecards outside the courthouse steps while confirming the latest GoFundMe shortfall. They scatter in the wind. Gathering them up, a hand reaches out to return a few. George Wheeler, stealing a cigarette from his severe legal team. Our eyes meet. The siren's are searching, concerned. Almost forgiving, like in the gutted white bus.

Not a siren, a real person.

All agreements are reached by the next Tuesday. Whether it is against George and Anne's better judgment to drop everything or not, including the fees, I'll never know.

But I do know how to tail someone.

In the bleak midwinter I watch from across a Chicago street. George's premium RideShare deposits him outside an upscale Italian restaurant and he attempts a hug that Anne Oxendine declines. They sit at a window.

Whatever is said, nervous energy animates him and she is mostly quiet. When she excuses herself to the restroom, George dips a snuff spoon into a little vial and does a quick bump. With an awkward handshake, they part shortly after.

They are strangers.

I don't recognize myself either. It's time to retreat.

Borders are closed, so it's not like I can resume my old career in Europe, and if I protest anything anymore, everyone will know who I am. Not trying to hold this spotlight. So I relocate to Casper, Wyoming. Only once, I request visitation. Arturo of course refuses.

Not many people are claiming property around here at the moment. Save for old high school classmates, whom I avoid. I change my appearance; I don't want to. My ailing dad, with some muted apologies—dry laughs, hesitant hugs, and unpleasant smells—departs the mortal coil shortly after my return. Up a piece of property for the first time in my life, I am hired right into the sortation warehouse's management this time, far too experienced for a trial 90 days. I perform at an acceptable level. Team Lead of the Month at least once a year. I haven't had a drink in five.

Vada Ikebe has become the figurehead of the Liltin Yew Truthers movement after my surreptitious departure. She is barely aware. The third interim admin shops her around federal prisons before she is gladly taken in by Georgia, the first state to sign up for televised firing squads. It's a shame the way her high profile comes to an end, but what can I do.

Certain age-old cans kicked down the proverbial road finally become too heavy. Casper is unaffected by the drone strike in the Dakotas that buried silos, immured sentries. No one wanted to anticipate an infiltration from such a close ally, and using our own weapons no less. That part, at least, isn't new.

The Overton window marches ever rightwards. Christofascists abate but not before taking too many with them; they have conjured their precious hell. From my barren six acres I wish I can join the resistors. I have hypertension and am tired. Mistaking my first heart attack for simple heartache, I spend a whole day in the living room rearranging furniture, trying to ease it before finally driving thirty miles to the hospital. Kendrick is right about grief.

But Arturo reaches out.

Negotiating a compassionate release for the prophet has been too ludicrous to consider, but the sixth "interim" regime consists of people who were young when June 21st happened. They're fans. Not Truthers, but fans of Arturo's fire and brimstone style. Easy political points for the shaky regime's base; the very idea that the prophet once again walks amongst the public will no doubt intimidate a few more into compliance.

Release's many conditions fall in line with the lifestyle I have long ago accepted. Tall fences are erected around my land within a year. Arturo and I install them by hand.

He has a talent for attracting blue jays into the feeder by their creek. The climate has shifted the birds' domain slightly west, and I consider Arturo's successful efforts to attract them a modest achievement.

His characteristically loud conversational tone has disappeared. Most conversation inexorably leads to *coulda, shoulda, wouldas*. Arturo never stops wanting to believe what Anne told him about the loop. "Even if it was all true . . ." he says rarely, "so what." He cannot leave that day.

Whenever I relapse he takes my bottles and pours them out. There are nights we sleep in the same bed and nights we don't. The thirties become the forties and through the addition of a dog and two cats, everybody passes the time together.

On a frigid late night in the loo, bathing amidst guerrilla broadcasts, I feel that now-familiar pang in my heart come more insistent. I labor out of the sunken tub and slowly sink to the linoleum floor, sighing. The clenching tightens like a vise. In a standing mirror that Arturo and I ventured into town to buy from a cozily scented antique store, I watch myself with something akin to bemusement.

The mirror's frame is ugly, unpainted cherry. Offset where the nailed-together molds don't quite match dimensions. I have not seen it from below for years, and only just now rediscover two protruding tickets from the Nirvana tribute concert of '44. The room behind me melts away, but not into blackness. The mirror melts too. I catch a distinct sense this will be the last time I feel sadness. After that, I'm ready.

The space has become much smaller. Weirdly familiar. Arturo's old domicile in Liltin Yew, I realize with relish, from decades back. The trailer's front door is open behind my equally floor-level form. I can't feel anything, but I am certain I've been rendered immobile. A solitary figure stands in the threshold looking out to the break of dawn. A woman. I know that shaggy lob. She is wreathed in smoke and her fingers flex in the flames. Skin drips. Red and blue lights dye the exterior, first faint, then harsh.

"Hey, Anne," I manage.

She glances back at me, shocked. She disappears.

I glimpse something else.

It's as if I have stared into the sun long enough for its rays to dance, to consume. A kaleidoscope. I glimpse it long enough to wonder at its shape from the outside. Or am I outside already? I'm not sure. I can't tell.

# ACKNOWLEDGEMENTS

I first got this idea in January 2022, road-tripping home from the Badlands. I should first thank the other two people in the car with me when I did that along with the Badlands themselves.

Next I thank my incredible developmental editor, Sandra Kasturi. The novel was (if you can imagine) way more unwieldy when she parsed through it, and it wouldn't even scrape what it is today without her invaluable help. My copy editor, Max Zell, happens to be my dear friend and saved me from thousands (upon thousands) of embarrassing gaffes before releasing this. Justin Wested was the very first of my friends to read this all the way through and, years later, I found myself aligning with his critiques more often than not. Also Andrew Herold is a spectacular typesetter.

Finally, I must thank: Lauren Ellett, Meagan Scott, Cielo Bellerose, Emery Laine, Marcos Izaguirre, and Azequay Rice.

# AFTERWORD

What effect has the death of accountability had on those of us who've benefitted? In 2022 this question, along with my own processing of some hella thorny self-lore, provided my book's fuel.

Jeffrey Epstein was still freshly dead, if by dead you mean wearing a fat suit and an articulable mask of Donald Trump.

Black Lives Matter at the height of their exposure was robbed by several opportunists. Virtually every single MAGA Republican also enriched themselves off market-conscious outrage mills and policies that killed people. Meanwhile apolitical crypto rug-pulls brought forth the Metaverse blip, contorted into NFTs, and finally reached systemic capacity with "AI startups." TrumpCoin was pump-n-dump'd the moment he was reelected. Today it's worth approximately $0.002.

Under pervasively unpunished illegality many of us on ground level were kinda forced into opportunism ourselves. Nothing wrong with that in a vacuum, but it's become more linked to survival: life itself has been priced out down here, post-pandemic. Down here we do get punished.

Emerging predictive markets gamble on the outcomes of air strikes in Iran and Israel. Even the exorbitantly wealthy periodically participate, because why not? With insider knowledge it's an effortless extra six or seven figures. I think we all feel our system locking inexorably into a darker place.

If even a handful of those maintaining the system—generations old it may be, but younger and less inevitable than they want us to think—were to meet accountability, the system could shift. Not just incrementally. More of us wouldn't have to try playing along, twisting ourselves to avoid that inexorable locking. Less of us would have to convince ourselves that playing the game makes the game sacred.

# ABOUT THE AUTHOR

Jason Sealy is from Pittsburgh, PA, and loves all kinds of storytelling. He/they recently completed a Bachelor of Multidisciplinary Studies in Library Science and is readying to enter a Master's degree in Public Administration. A very bad little stint in the military dropped them into Omaha, Nebraska, which they hope to leave soon for a classic combo of coastlines and cliffsides. They have two cats.

9 798899 517779 1